APTITUDE, LEARNING, and INSTRUCTION

Volume 1:
Cognitive Process Analyses
of Aptitude

Edited by
RICHARD E. SNOW
Stanford University

PAT-ANTHONY FEDERICO
*Navy Personnel Research and
Development Center*

WILLIAM E. MONTAGUE
*Navy Personnel Research and
Development Center*

 LAWRENCE ERLBAUM ASSOCIATES, PUBLISHERS
1980   Hillsdale, New Jersey

Lawrence Erlbaum Associates, Inc., Publishers
365 Broadway
Hillsdale, New Jersey 07642

Library of Congress Cataloging in Publication Data

Main entry under title:

Cognitive process analyses of aptitude.

  (Aptitude, learning, and instruction; v. 1)
  Proceedings of a conference sponsored by the Office
of Naval Research and the Navy Personnel Research and
Development Center, Held Mar. 6–9, 1978 in San Diego,
Calif.
  Bibliography: p.
  Includes indexes.
  1. Ability—Congresses. 2. Cognition—Congresses.
I. Snow, Richard E. II. Federico, Pat-Anthony.
III. Montague, William Edward. IV. United
States. Office of Naval Research. V. Navy Personnel
Research and Development Center (U.S.) VI. Series.
BF431.A5763   vol. 1   370.15'2s   [370.15'2]
ISBN 0-89859-043-4   80-18040

Printed in the United States of America

These volumes are dedicated to the memory of

JOSEPH W. RIGNEY
Professor of Psychology
University of Southern California

whose career contribution to Navy personnel and training research cannot be overestimated. Still extending that contribution, he lost his life en route to San Diego on September 25, 1978, leaving the chapter found in volume 1 as one of his last works.

Contents

Volume 1:
Cognitive Process Analyses
of Aptitude

Volume 2:
Cognitive Process Analyses
of Learning and Problem Solving

Foreword

Marshall J. Farr
Office of Naval Research

This conference takes on a formidable task, that of trying to relate in a meaningful way the processes underlying human aptitude and intelligence to the cognitive aspects of learning and the real world of instructional practices. Trying to link aptitude in a systematic way to learning and instruction means a number of different things. It means confronting a Pandora's box of individual differences, as one tries to make sense out of human variability. It means having to bring together, as Cronbach pointed out in his 1957 APA Presidential Address, the psychometric approach of correlational psychology with the methodology of experimental psychology. It means a focus not only on both *organismic* and *treatment* variables but an equal concern with their *interaction*.

Aptitude, or even *ability*, is not a typical experimental psychology construct. I looked under the subject index of my 1954 Woodworth and Schlosberg *Experimental Psychology*, the edition to which many of the current crop of cognitive psychologists were exposed, and was not surprised to find no index entry for either *aptitude, ability*, or even *intelligence*. (In all fairness, the authors do acknowledge that organismic variables are of some consequence, with a listing of *individual differences* and a subheading *ability-performance* listed under *learning*.)

Although mainstream experimental psychology in about 1954 was relatively insensitive to the approach of correlational psychology, Kohler, one of the fathers of Gestalt psychology, recognized the issue in his 1947 classic, *Gestalt Psychology*. In discussing Fechner and his psychophysics work, he states:

> Today we can no longer doubt that thousands of quantitative psychophysical experiments were made almost in vain. No one knew precisely what he was measuring.

Nobody had studied the *mental processes* upon which the whole procedure was built. . . . When observing the energy with which able psychologists measure individual intelligences, one is almost reminded of Fechner's time. From a practical point of view, it is true, their work is obviously not without merits. It seems that a crude total ability for certain performances is actually measured by such tests. For, on the whole, the test scores show a satisfactory correlation with achievements both in school and in subsequent life. This very success, however, contains a grave danger. *The tests do not show what specific processes actually participate in the test achievements.* The scores are mere numbers which allow of many different interpretations [pp. 44–45, italics mine].

It is instructive to note how this quote by Kohler foreshadows the following notion expressed by Cronbach and Snow (1977) in the preface to their *Aptitudes and Instructional Methods:*

This state-of-the-art report has been more difficult to assemble than anticipated when we began in 1965. One reason is the breadth of the topic. To study scores on conventional ability tests is not sufficient, for the student's response to instruction is, in principle, conditioned by *all* his characteristics, including personality traits. It is necessary also to consider what Glaser calls "the new aptitudes," the specific intellectual-processing skills that are lost from sight in an aggregate mental measure [p. viii].

The Office of Naval Research (ONR) has long had an abiding interest in trying to link individual ability and aptitude differences with learning. As Federico discusses in some detail in Chapter 1 in this book, ONR sponsored a 1965 symposium at the University of Pittsburgh that focused on the ways in which people differed in their learning and how these ways might be measured as individual differences. (The proceedings were edited by Gagné (1967) and published as *Learning and Individual Differences.*) In this Pittsburgh conference, Melton concludes that there is an impressive consensus to the effect that we must consider individual-differences variables in terms of the *process* constructs of contemporary theories of learning and performance. And Melton concisely pinpoints the then-emerging zeitgeist when he states:

The most significant development in theoretical and experimental psychology in recent years is acceptance of the need for theoretical statements about processes or mechanisms that intervene between stimuli and responses. The argument is no longer about whether such intervening processes occur and have controlling effects on behavior, but about their defining properties, their sequencing, and their interactions [p. 240].

For about the last 6 years, ONR has been conducting a thematically oriented contract research program aimed, in large part, at developing the kind of broad theoretical framework necessary for a workable *process* interpretation of aptitude, learning, and performance. The papers in this collection are generally addressed to three broad areas that are central to these interests of the ONR Personnel and Training Research Programs. One area is concerned with individual differences in information processing, as revealed in simple laboratory or psychometric tasks. Whereas conventional measurement of abilities and aptitudes relies on the actuarial criterion of their success in distinguishing between high- and low-level individuals, the emphasis here is on the direct measurement of the component, basic information-processing operations that undergird the target abilities.

The second area focuses on the structural aspects of learning and performance, using tools and concepts from semantic memory theory to describe what is learned and how it is learned. And the third area is aimed at the management of instruction: It addresses itself to the kinds of research and instructional designs required for effective implementation of adaptive instruction.

ONR primarily supports mission-oriented basic research. The cosponsor of this conference, the Navy Personnel Research and Development Center (NPRDC), generally supports more applied research. That organization's support in this case demonstrates the strong practical implications it sees in this research. ONR and NPRDC are proud to have joined forces in what we believe will become a landmark work in the field.

MARSHALL J. FARR
Director, Personnel and Training
Research Programs
Office of Naval Research

REFERENCES

Cronbach, L. J. The two disciplines of scientific psychology. *American Psychologist,* 1957, *12,* 671–684.

Cronbach, L. J., & Snow, R. E. *Aptitudes and instructional methods.* New York: Irvington, 1977.

Gagné, R. M. (Ed.). *Learning and individual differences.* Columbus, Ohio: Merrill, 1967.

Kohler, W. *Gestalt psychology.* New York: Liveright, 1947.

Melton, A. W. Individual differences and theoretical process variables: General comments on the conference. In R. M. Gagné (Ed.), *Learning and individual differences.* Columbus, Ohio: Merrill, 1967.

Woodworth, R. S., & Schlosberg, H. *Experimental psychology* (rev. ed.). New York: Holt, 1954.

Acknowledgments

This book reports the proceedings of a conference sponsored by the Office of Naval Research, Arlington, Virginia, and the Navy Personnel Research and Development Center, San Diego, California, under Grant No. N0014-78-G-002 to Stanford University. The conference was held March 6–9, 1978, in San Diego. The views and conclusions contained in this document are those of the authors and should not be interpreted as necessarily representing the official policies, either expressed or implied, of the Office of Naval Research, the Navy Personnel Research and Development Center, or the U.S. Government.

The editors wish to thank Marshall J. Farr, Director, Personnel Training and Research Programs, Office of Naval Research; James J. Regan, Technical Director; Earl I. Jones, Program Director for Independent Research; Richard C. Sorenson, Director of Programs; John D. Ford, Jr., Program Director for Instructional Technology, Navy Personnel Research and Development Center; and Gerald J. Lieberman, Vice Provost and Dean of Research, Stanford University, for making the conference possible. Thanks are also due to Patricia Jones, David Landis, Florence Miller, and Walter Spencer for their help with the varied details of conference arrangement and manuscript preparation.

RICHARD E. SNOW
PAT-ANTHONY FEDERICO
WILLIAM E. MONTAGUE

1 Adaptive Instruction: Trends and Issues

Pat-Anthony Federico
*Navy Personnel Research
and Development Center*

SUMMARY OF PRECEDING PERTINENT SYMPOSIA

In the beginning of Book VII of the *Republic,* Plato (ca. 388 B.C. /1950) mentioned a dialogue between Socrates and Glaucon in which the former relates the allegory of the cave. Imagine a subterranean cave dwelling with a long entrance from above that extends the entire width of the cave. In this cavern since their childhood are men whose legs and necks are chained so that they can neither raise themselves and move about nor turn their heads left or right. Consequently, these shackled men can look only in front of them. Behind and above them, some distance away, a fire is burning. On higher ground, between the fire and the prisoners, is a road along which there is a wall. This upright structure serves as a screen somewhat similar to that used by puppeteers, which they set up in front of audiences in order to show their marionettes. Along this wall are other men who are carrying all sorts of objects (e.g., statues of different men and animals). Some of these bearers are silent, whereas the rest are speaking or making other utterances that echo off the wall in front of the prisoners.

Due to their predicament, these confined men see only shadows of themselves and other creatures cast by the fire on the wall of the cave opposite them. These unfortunate individuals consider these shaded images to be real objects and things. Also, these men hear only echoes from the opposite wall of voices and other sounds made by some of the carriers of manufactured articles behind them. The prisoners, however, think that the utterances are real, too, and come from the shadows passing in front of them. That is, for these bonded men, the real world that they know consists of constantly changing, forever fleeting shadows and echoes. They are totally unaware and completely ignorant of any entities or beings existing outside their dim cave in the world of light—the really real world. This is the ideal or Platonic world of immutable, immaterial, transcendent forms in which all real, mutable, material, ordinary things partake in their existence and are made known or intelligible. Education itself should be such that it enlightens us to seek and understand the ultimate, eternal, unchangeable universals of individual, concrete things from which they derive their being and essential nature.

I would like to extend this allegory as follows. Many of these prisoners who were in the darkened cave were psychologists. Some were experimental psychologists, and others were correlational psychologists. These two groups were manacled by their models, methods, and measures. The empiricists were restricted by: (1) their analytical approaches, which grew out of intense objectivism and reductionism; (2) their science of behavior, which manipulated independent variables and measured dependent variables in order to be able to control and predict behavior based only on objectively observable data, thereby discarding introspectionism; (3) their vehement dislike of mentalism and the associated notions of consciousness, mind, and imagery; (4) their emphasis on stimulus–response, acquisition, extinction, reinforcement, discrimination, generalization, transfer, inhibition, habit-family hierarchy, and peripheral responses; and (5) their "black box" framework, which originated classical and operant conditioning research on animals assumed to be directly generalizable to human learning and performance.

The correlationists were restrained by: (1) their mental, performance, and proficiency tests used to identify faculties, traits, abilities, aptitudes, and other complex constructs; (2) their comparison of interindividual behavior derived from a differential approach to intelligence, personality assessment, and related attributes based upon test batteries, measurement profiles, taxonomic categories, and score interpretation; (3) their quantification, selection, classification, prediction, and standardization of behavior employing tests, surveys, questionnaires, sampling distributions, and mathematical procedures; (4) their reliance on multivariate statistical techniques with accompanying intercorrelations, variances, factors, components, dimensions, communalities, rotations, patterns, coefficients, reliabilities, and validities; and (5) their two-factor, multiple-factor structure of the intellect and other theories of intelligence that have some relevance to applied situations in education, industry, and the military.

Because of their constraints, psychologists from these two disciplines, in a sense, saw only shadows and heard only echoes. Neither of these schools of psychology was enlightened enough to transcend its ordinary orientation and analyze the nature of those cognitive processes intrinsic to human learning and aptitude per se.

Correlational psychology concerns itself exclusively with variance among organisms; experimental psychology concerns itself exclusively with variance among treatments. In his presidential address to the American Psychological

Association, Cronbach (1957) declared that it is not sufficient for each of these areas of psychology to adopt primary principles and procedures from the other. A united discipline of psychology not only will be interested in organismic and treatment variables but also will be concerned with the otherwise ignored interactions between organismic and treatment variables. Attempts should be made to anchor concepts created in correlational psychology to variables manipulated in experimental psychology, and vice versa. If this is done, the psychology of aptitude and ability can be joined with the psychology of learning and performance to produce an ultimate conceptual framework. A theory sufficiently inclusive to consider individual differences, past and present environments, and states of organisms will permit the prediction of performance with precision. To do this successfully, the labors of these two distinct disciplines of psychology must be combined and not proceed on independent parallel paths. In this joint effort, these separate schools of psychology will be united with common measures, methods, recommendations, and, most of all, a common theory.

Gagné (1967) organized a conference dealing with learning and individual differences that was convened at the Learning Research and Development Center, University of Pittsburgh, April 1965, and was sponsored by the Office of Naval Research, Personnel and Training Branch. The purpose of this meeting was to define the essential issue of individual differences in learning, and to describe the suppositions and limitations associated with this problem. It was expected that new perspectives of learning as process would produce novel hypotheses concerning the essence, salience, and measures of individual differences in learning. In this respect, this major symposium was an important milestone and turning point in the history of the psychology of learning.

During his general remarks on the meeting, Melton (1967) emphasized what appeared to him to be of fundamental importance for future progress. He considered the theme of the symposium to be "that we frame our hypotheses about individual differences variables in terms of the process constructs of contemporary theories of learning and performance [p. 239]." The most important development in experimental and theoretical psychology then was the general opinion that there was a need for conceptual formulations of processes or mechanisms that intervene between stimuli and responses. Participants of the conference proposed a novel scheme for examining the multifaceted relationships between individual differences and learning and performance. Nevertheless, they neglected to suggest a satisfactory process theory of human behavior. In order to create such a speculative framework, more must be understood concerning the primary processes involved in learning and performance. One means conducive to producing a process theory is to classify mechanisms that are intrinsic to individual differences in the learning process per se. That is, a taxonomy should be established of intersubject variability in processes that are not only inherent in learning but also dependent on learning for their existence.

Melton recommended that investigations of individual differences concentrate upon analytical aspects of process specification as seen in contemporary theories of learning and performance. This is one approach that will increase the likelihood of making important progress in the comprehension of individual differences. However, this alone is not a panacea. Another means of reaching this end is to seek a rapprochement of stimulus–response (S–R) and information-processing (I-P) theories in order to produce an improved process theory of human learning and performance. Both of these conceptual schemes employ process terminology to explain the nature of the internal mediation between stimulus input and response output. S–R theory in essence has emphasized the forming and strengthening of elemental bonds and chains. It typically minimizes attentional, perceptual, and central processes (e.g., rules, strategies, schemata, concept utilization). I-P theory, though, has stressed intellectual mechanisms in performance that involve attentional, perceptual, memorial, decisional, and informational processes. The integration of S–R and I-P approaches would not only be a theoretical tour de force but also an excellent conceptual context within which to investigate individual differences in learning and performance.

Resnick (1976) planned a conference concerning the nature of intelligence that was held at the Learning Research and Development Center, University of Pittsburgh, March 1974, and was supported by the National Institute of Education. Because the diverse interests of developmental, differential, and experimental psychologists were focusing on cognitive processes, it appeared to be appropriate to consider the possibilities for reconceptualizing and resolving the primary processes that are involved in intelligence. This was underscored by the fact that experimental psychologists have made important advancements in their investigations of cognitive processes relevant to intelligence by applying rigorous procedures. The symposium provided a "snapshot" of the notion of intelligence during a time of transition in its definition. The theme of the meeting was to inquire into the nature of the cognitive and adaptive processes inherent in intelligence, and to ascertain how these mechanisms might be connected to measured intelligent performance. Fundamental to the symposium was the attitude that the further comprehension of intelligence was dependent on relating this concept to intrinsic cognitive processes (i.e., those internal mechanisms that are presumed to be essential to intellectual behavior—e.g., sensory recognition processes, short-term and long-term memory, and cultural set). Current advancements in cognitive theory, particularly developments in information-processing concepts, were emphasized throughout the meeting. It was suggested that these psychological mechanisms be utilized in order to comprehend more completely the processes basic to intellectual behavior. Also, it was recommended that performances on tests be considered as the consequences of interactions of individuals with their respective biological, cultural, and intellectual environments—especially, linguistic contexts. It was maintained that mental measurement must be refined and reappraised within the framework of important developments in cognitive processes and cultural concerns. The conference reflected a change in the conceptualization of intelligence as measured performance to mental mechanisms. Voss (1976) commented on the proceedings of the symposium by stating that the time had arrived to construct tests based upon intrinsic psychological processes. He asserted that tests will likely be designed to measure precisely psychologically important processes.

Klahr (1976) arranged a meeting, the subject of which was cognition and instruction. This conference was sponsored by the Office of Naval Research, Personnel and Training Research Programs, and the Advanced Research Projects Agency. The objective of this gathering was to specify some contributions that recent research in cognitive psychology can provide toward the resolution of salient issues in instructional design. Glaser (1976a) commented generally on the proceedings of this symposium. During his discussion, he presented a structure for considering some possible components of a prescriptive linking science of instructional design. This served as a framework for his remarks. He considered the process of instruction to be involved in the production of competence in a student and in the development of those cognitive structures and overt behaviors that distinguish between a novice and an expert in a specific content area. The primary emphasis of his comments on the conference was the comprehension and facilitation of the continual development from ignorance to knowledge, from novice to expert.

Glaser thought that the major theme of the meeting was competence in process as the objective of instruction. While remarking on the meeting, he identified and elucidated the components of a psychology of instruction. The first component involves the description and analysis of competent performance. Task analysis is essential to this constituent of instructional design. Consequently, novel procedures must be produced for describing expert performance and specifying subject-matter content in terms of primary psychological processes (e.g., attention, perception, and short-term storage). By conducting task analysis of competent performance and specifying component processes intrinsic to task performance, attempts can be made to teach these mental mechanisms to individual learners. Also, ascertaining via task analysis the most efficient manner of performance makes possible the design of instruction so that it approaches the most efficient procedure for implementation.

According to Glaser, a minor theme of the symposium involved diagnosis and description of the initial state in which a student commences a course of learning—the second element of instructional design. Teaching treatments need to be planned by taking into consideration an assessment of the beginning condition of the learner; that is, the initial state of the student should be specified in terms of processes intrinsic to competent performance. This would enable the design of alternative instructional treatments that accommodate these processes. Also, this would permit an attempt to improve a student's competence in these mental mechanisms, thus increasing the likelihood of an individual benefiting from typical teaching techniques.

There was some implicit interest in the meeting regarding the transition from the initial performance of a novice to the terminal performance of an expert. With respect to this third component of instructional design—conditions that facilitate the acquisition of competence—Glaser mentioned that our knowledge of the learning process is inadequate. Available information about learning is couched in terms of a descriptive science (e.g., the nature of reinforcement, discrimination, generalization, and attention) and not in terms of a prescriptive science (i.e., the application of knowledge to plan the conditions of instruction). This descriptive knowledge of learning should be used to generate research that will likely lead to prescriptive knowledge for optimizing the outcomes of instruction for distinct students. In order to implement these prescriptive pedagogical paradigms, an adequate conceptual formulation is required of how a student masters increasingly complex performances by arranging the present responses of his or her repertoire, manipulating environmental events and situations, and employing developed knowledge of how one learns.

Glaser remarked that there was some concern at the conference regarding the measurement of the consequences of instruction in the short and longterm (i.e., in terms of immediate feedback and extended effects such as delayed transfer and generalization). In order to assess suitably these instructional results, criterion-referenced tests should be used instead of norm-referenced tests. Measures need to be designed, developed, and interpreted with respect to those cognitive processes considered to be intrinsic components of competent performance. This would allow the assessment relative to objective criteria of a student's progress toward approaching and developing competence—the fourth element of instruction design. That is, criterion-referenced tests should be created to assist instructors in deciding when a student's performance approximates terminal competence. The informative feedback obtained from this measurement can be employed to plan and execute additional instructional treatments.

Anderson, Spiro, and Montague (1977) convened a conference concerning schooling and the learning of knowledge. This symposium concentrated on several important problems dealing with the acquisition, organization, production, restoration, and utilization of knowledge. Gagné (1977) was one of the overall discussants of the proceedings of the conference. The major theme he extracted from the presentations of the meeting was that a schema served as the primary element of the processes of learning and storage. This idea of schema is partly specified by a network of interrelations generally regarded as existing among the constituents of a concept; that is, it is a complex structure that holds together many peripheral or related entities stored in memory. During the symposium, different types of schemata were identified and ascribed distinct purposes—specifically: (1) storage and retrieval of propositional knowledge; (2) initiation and regulation of action; (3) formation and modification of attitudes; and (4) generalization and interpretation of ideas.

In his general comments on the meeting, R. C. Anderson (1977) also asserted that the principal notion evolved was schema. A primary theme pervading the presentations and discussions during the conference was that a student's state of knowledge is the foremost determiner of what can be acquired from an educational experience. This is so because schooling itself provides the student with ineffable knowledge that serves as a structure or context for understanding new situations and experiences. Present knowledge "tunes" an individual to see, comprehend, and interpret objects and events in a particular manner.

R. C. Anderson considered the implication of the meaning of schema for schooling and the necessity for this concept. Recently, many American psychologists have convinced themselves that the presumptions of their conceptual frameworks have been essentially incorrect. Philosophically and methodologically empiricists and behaviorists, they regarded the human organism, like lower organisms, to be controlled by the presence or absence of specific sensory input that elicited or evoked certain response output. Within this speculative scheme, it was supposed that complex higher-order processes, patterns, and structures of responses could be conceived as concatenations or chains of simplistic lower-order reactions, units, and bonds. Nevertheless, the behaviorists did not make important progress in reaching this goal. Much to their dismay, Chomsky (1957) demonstrated that it was theoretically and practically impossible to explain linguistic proficiency in terms of stimulus–response pairs. Also, the advancement of artificial intelligence efforts by programming increasingly sophisticated computers to model fundamental human performance has been frustrated by "bottom-up" analyses, data-driven approaches, and superficial representations. These simulation strategies demonstrated themselves to be ineffective for practically all but the most simple problems and trivial cases. Because of this unsatisfactory situation, it became necessary to simulate inherently human functions by programming computers to store elaborate representational systems and knowledge structures in order to mimic more closely intrinsically personal activities (e.g., the process of recognition). When humans recognize objects, shapes, people, and so forth, they usually produce several alternative hypotheses based upon a scant number of perceptual cues that are considered in reaching a decision. The perceptual suppositions or mental representations that are generated in the recognition process cannot reasonably be isomorphic to incoming stimuli. This is so because the schema that immediately accounts for what is recognized entails expectations or hypotheses about undetected characteristics or unseen features.

The implication of the concept of schema is that in practically all domains of human performance (e.g., perception, recognition, retention, recollection, interpretation, and comprehension), there is an important interaction of sensory input with existing knowledge structures. That is, there is not only the "bottom-up" processing of incoming stimuli but also the "top-down" imposing of mental schemata (Rumelhart & Ortony, 1977). The notion of schema seems necessary to explain the fact that individuals undoubtedly exceed mere sensory input in their assorted acts of cognition by constructing or employing an internal framework that does not exist independently in external stimuli. According to R. C. Anderson, schema usage and change are essential to schooling and the acquisition of knowledge as opposed to only accumulating information. Without schemata into which they can be assimilated, educational experiences as well as sensory stimuli are incomprehensible. Consequently, it is improbable that important subject-matter content can be mastered without the appropriate production and utilization of schemata. This leads to two salient issues—specifically: How can the creation, application, and alteration of schemata be measured to evaluate instruction? How can these cognitive structures be sufficiently represented to teacher and student alike, so that informative feedback will be available to guide instruction (Glaser, 1976a)?

These four preceding conferences suggest the following:

1. We should consider individual differences in processes intrinsic to learning and performance.
2. We should change our conceptualizations of intelligence and other cognitive abilities and aptitudes and contemplate them as processes.
3. We should think about the essential components of instructional design— analysis of competent performance, diagnosis of initial performance, acquisition of competence, and evaluation of instruction—in terms of processes.
4. We should regard schema usage and change as essential aspects of the acquisition of knowledge that determine what a student can learn from instruction.

What can be extracted from these ideas (which are not only indicative, but also formative, of the present zeitgeist) is that we should explore various alternative approaches for adapting instruction to individual differences among learners. Specifically, we should consider the following possibilities.

ALTERNATIVE APPROACHES TO ADAPTIVE INSTRUCTION

Relevant Cognitive Processes

During the last several years, interest in cognitive processes involved in memory and learning has increased dramatically. Many texts recently published emphasize the mental mechanisms mediating human performance (e.g., J. R. Anderson, 1976; Anderson, Spiro, & Montague, 1977; Bobrow & Collins, 1975; Cermak, 1975; Crowder, 1976; Estes, 1975–1976; Kintsch, 1970, 1974; Klahr, 1976; Melton & Martin, 1972; Neisser, 1967; Newell & Simon, 1972; Norman,

1970; Paivio, 1971; Resnick, 1976; Solso, 1973; Sternberg, 1977; Tulving & Donaldson, 1972). At the same time, the previously distinct perspectives of educational and cognitive psychology seem to have converged. Among the several reasons for this phenomenon are the following: (1) Many experimental psychologists have shifted their interests from limited laboratory studies to practical educational considerations; (2) much research and theoretical interest has been generated by Jean Piaget's (1936/1952, 1945/1951) concepts of cognitive development; and (3) numerous studies reflect an increased attention to individual differences, not for discriminating among people, but for prescribing instructional treatments as a function of cognitive characteristics (Kogan, 1971; Rigney & Towne, 1970; Seidel, 1971).

These process perspectives of learning and performance, as opposed to traditional behavioristic theories, stress the use of cognitive operations or mechanisms in the acquisition and retention of knowledge. Within this framework, students are perceived as processors of information input, manipulators of intellectual throughput, and producers of performance output. Some of the operations that learners perform during these intervening stages of cognition include selecting, encoding, organizing, storing, retrieving, decoding, and generating information. These mechanisms may involve conjuring images, memorizing items, analogizing notions, rehearsing performances, and elaborating contents. Other aspects of these internal processes consist of recognizing patterns of incoming stimuli, exercising decision rules for emitting relevant responses, formulating heuristic hypotheses when appropriate judgmental paradigms are not available, and producing algorithms for problem solving. All of these mediating activities are largely under the voluntary and conscious control of the learner (Boutwell & Barton, 1974; Glaser, 1972; Glaser & Resnick, 1972; Melton, 1967; Rigney & Towne, 1970; Rohwer, 1970a, 1970b, 1971; Seidel, 1971; Tobias, 1976).

It is these cognitive processes that should be considered in the design and development of adaptive instructional systems. Customary measures of abilities, aptitudes, and other attributes have been produced primarily for predictive purposes. These selection instruments were not created as tests of cognitive processes that mediate distinct types of learning and performance. Therefore, traditional psychometric measures are not indices that suggest how to support and facilitate the processes of acquiring knowledge or evoking performance (Federico, 1978). It appears that if instruction is to be successfully accommodated to individual differences among learners, then mediation mechanisms or their correlates must be measured and employed to prescribe particular teaching treatments. Intervening processes used by distinct students to learn, retain, and retrieve a specific subject matter must be analyzed before the most appropriate instructional technique can be selected. Ascertaining the nature of this mediating cognitive activity will allow the selection of alternative teaching strategies and tactics that will increase the effectiveness and efficiency of instruction.

Within this conceptual structure it is not necessary or sufficient to speculate or determine which abilities or aptitudes might be related to learning and performance. In the traditional aptitude-treatment-interaction (ATI) orientation (Cronbach & Snow, 1969, 1977), it has been customary to examine variations in abilities and aptitudes among students to select instructional treatments, and to neglect differences in intervening cognitive activities among these same students. The very processes intrinsic to learning should be paramount considerations in adapting instructional techniques to individual differences. Otherwise, as has become evident, the entire effort is futile. To take into account these mental mechanisms, it may be necessary to establish a taxonomy of dissimilar learning tasks and to determine the various cognitive mediators used by different students to master these distinct tasks. Based upon this knowledge, it should then be possible to assign instructional treatments to students to support their mediational mechanisms and, thus, to facilitate the learning of different tasks. Consequently, accommodative instructional systems are designed around relevant cognitive processes, not irrelevant mental abilities and aptitudes. In this context, the psychological processes employed by students in taking these ability and aptitude tests are actually more important than the psychometric results themselves (Di-Vesta, 1973; French, 1965; Glaser, 1972; Rigney & Towne, 1970).

The cognitive processes used by learners in task mastering, problem solving, and decision making should be determined, measured, and monitored. This chore can be facilitated by employing computer-based instructional and informational systems. Once the appropriate measurement procedures are developed, they may be applied in an interactive mode. Then it would be possible to shape or support a student's mediation activity intrinsic to learning or performance. Under these circumstances it is not the subject matter that is primary but rather the internal processes used in acquiring, retrieving, and applying this content; that is, the mental mechanisms employed in learning and performing emerge more importantly than the subject matter itself. Consequently, when learners encounter new tasks to be mastered, new facts to be remembered, and new rules to be acquired, they should be able to cope better with these situations by applying or transferring their mediation skills regardless of the content area.

Cognitive Processes as Individual Differences

Research results (e.g., Coop & Sigel, 1971) suggest that there is a wide range of variability among individuals regarding the psychological processes they use to mediate the acquisition, organization, retention, and generation of knowledge. These differences may be attributed to students' adopting different learning sets they perceive to be pertinent to the task at hand. Therefore, the disparity among students in acquiring, retaining, and retrieving information may not be due to dissimilarities in general abilities and aptitudes, but rather to differences in learning sets, competencies, schemata, knowledges, and rules the students bring into the instructional environment (Glaser, 1976a, 1976b; Rumelhart & Ortony, 1977; Scandura, 1971, 1973, 1977). This implies that to master a primary task, the student should learn the supporting subordinate skills and the proper integration of these secondary competencies. These sustaining learning sets, schemata, skills, and knowledges are cognitive mediators themselves that facilitate the transfer of lower-level competencies to higher-level competencies in the learning hierarchy. It should be noted that the supporting internal processes or mental mechanisms employed in the initial phases of learning will likely be quite distinct from those used in the final phases of learning. This shift in importance in the intervening cognitive processes used in mastering a task should be useful for adapting instruction to individual differences (Boutwell & Barton, 1974; Briggs, 1968; Fleishman & Bartlett, 1969; Gagné & Paradise, 1961; Snow, 1976b).

Traditional psychometric theory, ironically, has not sufficiently considered the variability among individuals. Correlations between psychometric measures of abilities, aptitudes, and other attributes and performance indices do not provide insight into the nature of the mental mechanisms that account for these behavioral differences. However, this does not preclude psychometric instruments from being used for predictive purposes. Although psychological testing has traditionally been employed to type or categorize people according to taxonomies of abilities and aptitudes, it has neglected to identify the internal processes that underlie such classifications. Consequently, to account for individual differences adequately, theoretical constructs are needed that are derived from a cognitive processes frame of reference. (Carroll's, 1976, conceptualization of psychometric tests as cognitive tasks in order to produce a new structure of intellect may be considered as a significant first step in this direction.) Instead of normatively based, psychometric measures of abilities and aptitudes with their static, trait-like properties, what is needed are individually based, idiosyncratic indices of cognitive processes with their dynamic, state-like properties. With them, instruction can be optimized by prescribing treatments to support mediation activity or to modify detrimental, interfering mediation activity (Glaser & Resnick, 1972; Hunt & Lansman, 1975; Seidel, 1971).

Sufficient empirical evidence exists to support the thesis that intervening processes are inherently involved in learning and performance (e.g., Estes, 1975–1976; Melton & Martin, 1972; Paivio, 1971; Solso, 1973; Tulving & Donaldson, 1972). It appears very likely that individual variability in acquiring, retaining, and retrieving knowledge can be analyzed in terms of the processes intrinsic to this cognition. Within this context, cognitive processes themselves are considered as individual-difference variables that are potentially useful for adaptive instructional purposes. Seldom have variations in mediation mechanisms or psychological processes been employed to accommodate pedagogical procedures to differences among pupils. Not to examine the likelihood of using these mediational processes for adaptive instruction is to negate the very essence of the individual differences in learning and performance (Boutwell

& Barton, 1974; Coop & Sigel, 1971; Glaser, 1972, 1976b, 1977; Hunt, 1976; Labouvie-Vief, Levin, & Urberg, 1975; Melton, 1967). It may be worthwhile to identify the types of cognitive processing used by different individuals as they endeavor to learn distinct tasks. This information may be used either to adapt instructional treatments to maintain mediation mechanisms, or to modify the mental elaboration itself so that it is more conducive to task mastery. In appropriate cases, individuals could even be taught the mediating processes or the elaborating techniques contributing to learning or to performing a particular task. Many different instructional treatments specific to cognitive processes are possible (Coop & Sigel, 1971; Glaser, 1972, 1976b; McKeachie, 1974; Rigney, 1976; Rohwer, 1970a, 1970b; Schroder, Driver, & Streufert, 1967; Snow & Salomon, 1968). It appears highly probable that the new aptitudes or cognitive processes can be modified by appropriate training to produce a potentially powerful procedure for adaptive instructional purposes. Research is required to resolve this issue: Is it better to assign instructional treatments to capitalize on potent cognitive processes, or to assign instructional treatments to improve impotent cognitive processes (Berliner & Cahen, 1973)?

Cognitive Styles

Although commonalities must exist, to some extent students use their own modes of information processing to acquire, retain, and retrieve subject-matter content. This implies that acquisition and subsequent performance are dependent on how the learner manipulates and processes material to be learned. The ways in which a student selects, encodes, organizes, stores, retrieves, decodes, and generates information are called ''cognitive styles'' when they affect learning and performance.

> Cognitive styles can be most directly defined as individual variation in *modes* of perceiving, remembering, and thinking, or as distinctive ways of apprehending, storing, transforming, and utilizing information. It may be noted that *abilities* also involve the foregoing properties, but a difference in emphasis should be noted: Abilities concern level of skill—the more and less of performance—whereas cognitive styles give greater weight to the *manner* and form of cognition [Kogan, 1971, p. 244].

These predominant modes of information processing are presumed to be relatively stable and somewhat trait-like. In fact, cognitive styles have been considered the ''new aptitudes.'' Presumably, they are acquired, general tendencies and, as such, involve the transferring of predominant modes of information processing or preferred learning sets to the acquisition, retention, and retrieval of new knowledge (DiVesta, 1973; Glaser, 1972; Kagan, Moss, & Sigel, 1963; Kogan, 1971; Snow & Salomon, 1968).

It should be noted at this point that some dispute has existed regarding the differentiation of cognitive style from general ability. One line of thought proposes that it is improbable for cognitive style (e.g., field independence) to be distinct from general ability (e.g., verbal intelligence). A significant amount of variance seems to be common to the measures of these two psychological constructs. Although there supposedly is this commonality, it does not preclude the existence of some aspects of cognitive style that are separate from general ability. The other line of thought emphasizes that psychometric tests of cognitive style are independent of indices of general ability and aptitude. Consequently, information on cognitive style complements information on general ability and aptitudes. This implies that both sets of data are important with respect to the assignment of alternative instructional treatments to students as a function of differential characteristics (Kogan, 1971; Satterly, 1976; Vernon, 1972).

Messick (1976, pp. 7–9) discussed several distinctions between cognitive styles and mental abilities:

> Cognitive styles differ from intellectual abilities in a number of ways, and contrasting them with abilities serves to illuminate their distinctive features. Ability dimensions essentially refer to the content of cognition or the question of *what*—what kind of information is being processed by what operation in what form? . . . Cognitive styles, in contrast, bear on the questions of *how*—on the manner in which the behavior occurs. The concept of ability implies the measurement of capacities in terms of maximal performance, with the emphasis upon level of accomplishment; the concept of style implies the measurement of characteristic modes of operation in terms of typical performance, with the emphasis upon process.
>
> Abilities, furthermore, are generally thought of as unipolar, while cognitive styles are typically considered to be bipolar in the sense of pitting one syndrome or complex of interacting characteristics . . . against a contrasting complex at the opposite pole of the distribution. Abilities vary, then, from zero or very little to a great deal, with increasing levels implying more and more of the same facility. . . . Cognitive styles, on the other hand, range from one extreme to an opposite extreme, with each end of the dimension having different implications for cognitive functioning.
>
> . . . Conceptualizing cognitive styles has a certain typological flavor, and styles are often described as if they were types, or even stereotypes, when in reality individuals are distributed continuously between the extremes with considerable variation in the cluster and degree of components comprising the style.
>
> . . . Another major way in which cognitive styles differ from abilities is in the values usually conferred upon them. Abilities are value directional: having more of an ability is better than having less. Cognitive styles are value differentiated: each pole has adaptive value in certain circumstances. The high end of ability dimensions is consistently more adaptive, whereas neither end of cognitive style dimensions is uniformly more adaptive; in the latter case adaptiveness depends upon the nature of the situation and upon the cognitive requirements of the task at hand. . . . Cognitive styles also differ from abilities in their breadth of coverage and pervasiveness of application. An ability usually delineates a basic dimension underlying a fairly limited area.

. . . Cognitive styles, in contrast, cut across domains. They appear to serve as high-level heuristics that organize lower-level strategies, operations, and propensities—often including abilities—in such complex sequential processes as problem solving and learning.

Cognitive style itself is a psychological construct that was created to indicate the consistency in the manner of information processing (Messick, 1976). However, there has been some inconsistency among researchers themselves regarding the operational definition of this abstract concept. Many different measures and methodologies have been contrived, designed, and utilized by investigators in order to identify and define an individual's cognitive style (Kogan, 1971). Consequently, this single term has been employed by a number of researchers to refer to distinctly different aspects of psychological processing. It seems, then, that the use of this construct in the literature has become highly investigator-specific, which can distress the reader.

Some important dimensions of cognitive style are field dependence versus field independence, scanning, breadth of categorizing, conceptualizing styles, cognitive complexity versus simplicity, reflectiveness versus impulsivity, leveling versus sharpening, constructed versus flexible control, and tolerance for incongruous or unrealistic experiences (Kogan, 1971; Messick, 1976). These constituents of cognitive style are typical representations of the many modes of mental processing that have been ascribed to account for individual differences in psychological functioning. Although a few of the terms employed to refer to the components of cognitive style may be unfamiliar, most of them relate to familiar, dynamic, state-like variables such as attention, expectancy, concentration, or anxiety (Coop & Sigel, 1971; Kagan & Kogan, 1970; Kahneman, 1973; Kogan, 1971).

Cognitive styles themselves seem to be mutually compatible and relatively permanent. This is to the extent that some components of cognitive style appear to oppose any alteration via experimental manipulation. Consequently, a difficult dilemma arises concerning how to adapt instruction: Is it better to assign instructional treatments to capitalize on potent cognitive processes, or to assign instructional treatments to improve upon impotent cognitive processes? The latter alternative, however, implies that cognitive style is changeable. This could produce a different orientation toward adaptation—rather than accommodate alternative instructional treatments to cognitive style, accommodate cognitive style to alternative instructional treatments. This approach to adaptation is probably precarious, because a certain cognitive style that is compatible to one instructional treatment may not be compatible to another instructional treatment. Therefore, what would be a facilitating learning set in one pedagogical context may be an inhibiting learning set in another pedagogical context (Kogan, 1971).

This unconventional concept of the changeability of cognitive style is undoubtedly different from the conventional concept of the stability of general ability and aptitude. It appears possible to modify cognitive styles more than mental abilities and aptitudes to achieve accommodative instruction. However, this does not preclude the possibility of altering aptitudes themselves as a means of adapting pedagogy. It seems likely that the new aptitudes or cognitive processes can be modified by appropriate training to produce a potentially powerful procedure for adaptive instructional purposes. This implies that these new aptitudes or cognitive styles are changeable and consequently are capable of being learned as well as forgotten. Used adaptively, these new psychological aptitudes or processes can be: (1) employed to prescribe initial instructional strategies; (2) modified to yield sequential cognitive styles; and (3) considered for selecting terminal teaching tactics. It should be noted that a contrary point of view emphasized the stability and generality of cognitive style. From this perspective, the invariability and universality of cognitive style are ascribed to their association ~~personality~~ with generalized intellectual ability. Within this alternative conceptual framework, cognitive style is not changeable; consequently, it is not trainable for adaptive instruction (Boutwell & Barton, 1974; Glaser, 1972; Glaser & Resnick, 1972; Mischel, 1969; Rigney, 1976; Witkin, Goodenough, & Karp, 1967).

Investigations should be conducted that consider appropriate psychological processes and use relevant learning materials before generalizations can be validly and reliably made to the real-world classroom environment. There are many important problems that must be studied and resolved prior to extrapolating and adopting a process approach to adapting instruction for the customary classroom setting based on cognitive styles. Some of these issues are as follows (Coop & Sigel, 1971):

Does the cognitive style of the individual student in a given classroom influence his learning ability? Does style determine how a student might learn best? Does style determine what a student chooses to learn? Does style interact with teaching method to produce different optimum learning situations for students with differing cognitive styles? Does the type of teaching method to which students are exposed effect any change in their cognitive styles? Can we design teaching methods to facilitate particular students with particular cognitive styles? Do different types of materials used in the presentation of stimuli to students interact with the students' cognitive style to influence the learning outcome? . . . One of the most critical tasks for psychological researchers is that of clarifying the existing construct of cognitive style through systematic investigation. [To what degree do different constructs of cognitive style overlap?] What is the factor structure of each existing construct of style? What are the major dependent variables affected by different stylistic preferences or abilities? Such dependent variables as how learners approach various learning tasks, the ease and speed with which they finish these tasks, and the retention and organization of the information gained from these tasks would seem to be germane areas for further research. Further research also may investigate the feasibility of constructing style profiles of individual students similar to current personality profiles. These style profiles, which would incorporate a number of existing measures of cognitive style, may prove to provide more sensitive data for educators as a basis for truly individualized instructional programs [pp. 156–160].

Within-Task Measures

Some researchers (Leherissey, O'Neil, Heinrich, & Hansen, 1973; O'Neil, Spielberger, & Hansen, 1969; Tennyson, 1975; Tennyson & Boutwell, 1973) have attempted to establish ATIs using within-task measures rather than pretask measures. It has been customary to employ pretask measures of abilities, aptitudes, and other attributes to predict a learner's behavior during instruction. This is done before prescribing specific teaching treatments to individuals as a function of their incoming characteristics. It has been suggested that within-task measures of student behavior and performance while actually in the instructional situation itself—such as number of errors, response latencies, and emotive states—can be used for adaptive purposes. Such measures taken during the very course of learning may provide for the manipulation and optimization of instructional treatments and sequences on a much more refined scale, such as varying the amount of prompting, feedback, incentives, and examples (Atkinson, 1976). This micro-treatment approach to adaptive instruction is an alternative to the macro-treatment approach proposed by the traditional ATI formulation, which employs premeasures for selecting teaching treatments (Cronbach, 1967; Cronbach & Gleser, 1965; Cronbach & Snow, 1969, 1977).

The use of micro-treatments based upon within-task measures does not preclude the use of macro-treatments based upon pretask measures. These distinct instructional strategies should be utilized to complement one another; that is, once the optimal macro-instructional treatment has been selected for an individual as a function of pretask measures, micro-instructional treatments can be selected for the same individual as a function of within-task measures. If course content is complex, then it is possible to design an instructional system with multiple modules and entry points. Under such circumstances, pretask measures may be employed to determine the appropriate level of difficulty for commencing instruction for an individual, and within-task measures may be employed to manipulate treatments for a student as a function of his or her continuously monitored learning behavior. The advocated criterion for accommodating instruction, then, is the correct classification of the student's successes and failures that are manifested over the course of learning. This is the suggested sine qua non for optimally prescribing instructional treatments. In addition, the increased reliability of a sequence of within-task state measures as opposed to a single, pretask trait measure should improve the validity of adaptive instructional decisions.

It is necessary not only to evaluate the effectiveness and efficiency of these suggested adaptive instructional strategies but also to conduct cost–benefit analyses of these teaching alternatives. The costs incurred in actually individualizing instruction may preclude its implementation. Also needed is a meaningful conceptual framework that can be used a priori to generate hypothetically oriented and programmatically driven research on adaptive instruction based upon a coherent theory of cognitive processes (Labouvie-Vief et al., 1975; Salomon, 1972). Also, it may be better to modify the single best instructional treatment than to adapt teaching strategies based upon uncertain ATI research. Bunderson and Dunham (1970) mentioned that instead of attempting to establish significant disordinal interactions (Berliner & Cahen, 1973; Cronbach & Snow, 1969, 1977; Snow & Salomon, 1968) as the basis from which to assign alternative macro-teaching treatments to students, those useful results from ATI research should be employed to establish the optimal instructional program for low-aptitude personnel. Subsequently, micro-instructional treatments can be used in an adaptive fashion within this exemplary program.

Learner Control and Dynamic Characteristics

The identification of ATIs may be inadequate and unnecessary for individualizing instruction. Merrill (1975) systematically examined some of the assumptions implicit to the ATI approach for adapting teaching techniques to individual differences advocated by Cronbach and Snow (1977). In contrast to what is inherent in the ATI formulation pertaining to the permanence and pervasiveness of differential individual attributes, Merrill emphasized that it is the momentary mutability of these characteristics that determines the optimal instructional treatment for the learner. That is, student performance is not affected by stable attributes but by their dynamic characteristics. Likewise, it is not fixed, preset instructional strategies that have utility for ATIs but transient teaching tactics. For adapting instruction to individual differences, it may be better to assume that dynamic, state, idiosyncratic variables are more useful for predicting pupil performance than stable, trait, aptitude measures:

> The search for the interaction of stable trait aptitudes and fixed treatments is never likely to be of instructional value. At the very moment one has identified such a relationship the aptitude configuration of the student has changed, never to be repeated. Hence the finding is descriptively interesting but prescriptively of little or no value [Merrill, 1975, p. 221].

Adapting instruction based upon traditional ATI investigations will probably produce pupils who are instructional system dependent. Rather than having teaching techniques selected for them, passive students should be given the opportunity to choose instructional treatments actively. Learners can become system independent by enabling them to manipulate and accommodate treatments to their own, momentary cognitive requirements. This can be accomplished by designing a dynamically adaptable instructional system in which students actively and continuously select the instructional treatments that are most appropriate to their idiosyncratic states. The measurement of stable, trait-like aptitudes is not a prerequisite for the implementation of this actively accommodating individualized instruction. Merrill's learner control approach to adaptive pedagogy is an important departure that goes beyond the ATI formulation supported by Cronbach and Snow.

Learner control may be an alternative procedure for accommodating instruction to the dynamic characteristics of students. However, its effectiveness depends to a large extent on how well each individual student can decide which learning strategy is optimal for him or her at any one moment. Some students may not be as adept as others at selecting appropriate learning strategies for themselves or at managing their own instruction. Also, some students may not even care to control their own learning or may feel that they are being shortchanged because the teacher is not there constantly to guide them. What little evidence there is regarding learner control (Steinberg, 1977) underscores the fact that much remains to be discovered regarding this adaptive pedagogical procedure. This is especially so regarding this salient question: Which individual characteristics of students are indicators of success in this dynamic instructional environment? Not all learners are capable of, or inclined toward, exercising any control over their learning strategies (Beard, Lorton, Searle, & Atkinson, 1973). Some may believe that this is another case of the blind leading the blind. What is urgently needed is research that identifies: (1) which cognitive characteristics of students are salient for learner control; and (2) which students can sufficiently function and benefit in this dynamic instructional environment.

Tests that measure mutable and particular properties of students may be more amenable to ATIs (Goldberg, 1972). Paradoxically, however, it may be feasible to use measures of intelligence in an accommodative manner for instruction. It is not unreasonable to consider intelligence to be as changeable as motivational, emotional, and physiological fluctuations. This is contrary to the traditionally held belief that psychometric indices of intelligence are stable over long as well as short intervals. Within this speculative framework, noted changes in intelligence have typically been attributed to errors of measurement. Data have been obtained, however, that demonstrate that intelligence has state-like characteristics. Short-term changes have been observed in intelligence in the form of consistent fluctuations in convergent and analogic-semantic reasoning and figural reasoning. The implication of this is that these changes may be characteristic of intelligence in general (Horn, 1972). Consequently, if intelligence has state as well as trait attributes, then it may be appropriate for use in a truly adaptive instructional system. Likewise, the distinction made between fluid and crystallized intelligence (Cattell, 1963; Snow, 1976a) may have some utility for producing significant disordinal ATIs (Cronbach & Snow, 1969, 1977).

Other aspects of psychometric measures may be used for individualized instruction. During the administration of a psychometric instrument, the sampled abilities may substantially shift in their importance. This is especially apparent in prolonged practice on psychomotor and printed tests where factor structure and salience change over distinct phases (Fleishman & Hempel, 1954). Alterations in factor pattern and prominence with practice underscore the primacy of establishing which abilities account for the variance at separate stages of performance on a test. Presumably this would maximize the predictive power of psychometric instruments for adapting instruction. Knowing which abilities contribute to individual differences at both earlier and later phases of performance may be useful for prescribing optimal instructional treatments over the course of learning.

Psychophysiological Procedures

Lateral hemispheric specialization of the brain has been employed as a physiological indicator of two different modes of cognitive style (Doyle, Ornstein, & Galin, 1974; Galin, 1975; Galin & Ellis, 1975; Galin & Ornstein, 1972): A verbal, analytic, sequential, syllogistic mode of information processing has been associated with left-hemisphere activity for normal, right-handed individuals; a spatial, synthetic, simultaneous, intuitive mode of information processing has been associated with right-hemisphere activity for such individuals. Cognitive style has been reliably related to patterns of spontaneous electroencephalographic (EEG) lateral asymmetry. For normal people performing verbal-analytic tasks, there is usually an increase in alpha waves or idling rhythm over the right hemisphere; for these people performing spatial-synthetic tasks, there is usually an increase in alpha waves or idling rhythm over the left hemisphere. The presence of the alpha or idling rhythm itself is an index of diminution of information processing within that hemisphere. It has often been noted that some individuals predominantly employ the verbal-analytic cognitive style for learning, problem solving, and decision making, whereas others predominantly employ the spatial-synthetic cognitive style for these tasks. Also, individual differences in cognitive style have been related to reflective eye movements (Galin & Ornstein, 1974). When individuals are asked a question demanding a certain amount of reflection, they avert their eyes briefly before answering. It has been suggested that direction of gaze may be an indicator of the major mode of information processing. Right-eye movements may index a relatively greater activation of the left hemisphere; left-eye movements may index a relatively greater activation of the right hemisphere.

A student's difficulty in mastering a certain subject-matter content or performing a particular task may be due to an inability to adopt the appropriate mode of information processing. Since EEG and reflective-eye-movement data may provide useful procedures for assessing preferred cognitive styles, it should be possible to ascertain which information-processing modes facilitate the learning and performing of a task, and which information-processing modes interfere with the learning and performing of a task. It may be feasible to train students whose predominant cognitive style is verbal-analytic to become more spatial-synthetically oriented when appropriate to the task; and to train students whose predominant cognitive style is spatial-synthetic to become more verbal-analytically oriented when appropriate to the task. Biofeedback training techniques could be used to instruct individuals to adopt the proper information-processing mode to facilitate the learning and performing of a specific task. Instructional strategies themselves could be adapted to conform to a learner's preferred cognitive style. It seems likely that initial learning and subsequent performance may be enhanced by presenting subject-matter content in the medium that is most congruent with a student's major mode of information processing. For verbal-analytically inclined individuals, acquisition, retention, and retrieval may be facilitated by employing a primarily verbal medium; and for spatial-synthetically inclined individuals, acquisition, retention, and retrieval may be facilitated by employing a primarily visual medium.

In contrast to the spontaneous EEG, the evoked potential provides several advantages in the study of human memory. The spontaneous EEG reflects at any given moment a myriad of processes only a few of which may be related to information processing. For example, nonspecific factors such as attention, arousal, emotion, motivation, and background equilibrium changes interfere with the detection of information-retrieval processes. The evoked potential, on the other hand, allows for the synchronization of neural activity by a stimulus bearing task-relevant information. Thus, the "signal-to-noise" ratio can be enhanced, and neural activity time-locked to the momentary presentation of an information-bearing stimulus can be isolated from non-time-locked activity [Thatcher, 1976, p. 65].

By using sophisticated computer-aided techniques, averaged evoked potentials (AEP), which are elicited by the presentation of distinct stimuli in different sensory modalities, have instigated researchers to conceptualize cerebral activity during learning and memory to be more than simply localized to specific topological regions of the brain. Instead of the place analogue of human information processing, which is implied in the lateral hemispheric specialization of the cortex as already mentioned, several investigators (Bartlett & John, 1973; John, 1972, 1975; John, Bartlett, Shimokochi, & Kleinman, 1973; John & Thatcher, 1976; Thatcher, 1976; Thatcher & April, 1976; Thatcher & John, 1975) have proposed that all cortical structures are equipotential for any specific function. However, these sites distinctly vary from one another according to their own signal-to-noise ratios for each specialized action.

In this context *noise* signifies random electrical activity of a cerebral neuron, and *signal* signifies synchronous electrical activity of a cerebral neuron firing in rhythm with other functionally similar neurons. The greater the signal-to-noise ratio of the particular region of the brain, the more this architectonic area is involved in a particular action. Structures traditionally thought to control a specialized function are actually those with the highest signal-to-noise ratio for that unique activity. Practically every region of the brain contributes to many different functions. The amount of involvement, though, varies directly with its signal-to-noise ratio relative to other implicated areas. This speculation regarding brain activity has been referred to as statistical configuration theory. It implies that many cognitive functions are distributed among the numerous structurally distinct regions of the cortex and that certain areas contribute more than others to any particular cerebral activity. Localized regions of the cortex do not participate in an all-or-none fashion in specialized cognitive activity. Each architectonic area of the brain contributes in a graded manner, on the average, to almost every cognitive function. It is not the localization of excitability that matters (e.g., left versus right idling cerebral hemisphere) but rather the rhythm of activity of one area relative to another; that is, various regions of the brain combine statistically to produce cognitive output. The rhythm of their average firing rate determines the nature of the cognitive function. Consequently, within this context, there is no one-to-one correspondence between specialized cognitive activity and a specific cerebral site. All cognitive functions are ascribed to the activity of the total brain itself. Even memory for a certain event or fact is physiologically encoded as frequency-specific activity of the entire brain—it is not mapped onto a particular cerebral region. This equipotential conceptualization of brain activity is in contradistinction to the traditionally promulgated theory of localized cortical function.

It is recommended that research be conducted to determine the feasibility of using this other working model of the brain for suggesting alternative teaching strategies. Possibly, instructional treatments could be accommodated to conform to a learner's preferred mode of information processing as specified by computer-based AEP techniques. The equipotential paradigm of cerebral function, together with the advanced technology necessary to investigate and identify this phenomenon, could be employed to adapt instruction to dynamic state variables of different students. In a computer-based, individualized, interactive instructional environment, physiological indicators could be monitored within task during the course of learning. These psychobiological measures may provide information suitable for adaptive instructional purposes to permit a more refined manipulation of teaching treatments. The addition of within-task physiological indicators may increase the reliability of assessment techniques customarily used for accommodating instruction to student characteristics. Within-task, as well as pretask, psychophysiological parameters should be more objective and unbiased indices of cognitive processing than traditional psychometric tests of abilities and aptitudes. Some evidence already demonstrates the improved validity of psychobiological variables over aptitude measures for predicting subsequent student performance (Lewis, Rimland, & Callaway, 1976, 1977). Consequently, the physiological correlates of human learning and memory mentioned earlier may be more relevant for assigning alternative instructional treatments than are customary psychometric measures.

THE THEME OF THIS MEETING

There has recently been a noticeable increase of research activity dealing with cognitive processes in relation to aptitudes and abilities, learning and performance, and task analysis and instructional design. The advent of a process theory has provided the impetus and common basis for much of this research. A new brand of instructional psychology seems to be emerging from this confluence, which is aimed at the improvement of instruction by understanding the interrelationships that exist among aptitude, learning, and instruction from a cognitive processing perspective.

After several years of work, the time now seems ripe for taking stock. Some basic lines of research have progressed far enough to allow us to sketch at least the beginning of an integrated conceptual framework based upon processing notions, which can be adopted to generate theory, research, and development to produce prescriptive pedagogical procedures. Implementation of various forms of adaptive instruction has outdistanced the reach of traditional concepts and methods of instructional design, development, and evaluation.

The intent of this conference is to bring together outstanding individuals whose research reflects the latest theoretical thinking about cognitive processes in aptitude, learning, and instruction. It is hoped that presentations by participants combined with ample discussion will provide a "state-of-the-art" summary of the field and identify directions for further instructional research, development, and implementation.

REFERENCES

Anderson, J. R. *Language, memory, and thought.* Hillsdale, N.J.: Lawrence Erlbaum Associates, 1976.

Anderson, R. C. The notion of schemata and the educational enterprise: General discussion of the conference. In R. C. Anderson, R. J. Spiro, & W. E. Montague (Eds.), *Schooling and the acquisition of knowledge.* Hillsdale, N.J.: Lawrence Erlbaum Associates, 1977.

Anderson, R. C., Spiro, R. J., & Montague, W. E. (Eds.). *Schooling and the acquisition of knowledge.* Hillsdale, N.J.: Lawrence Erlbaum Associates, 1977.

Atkinson, R. C. Adaptive instructional systems: Some attempts to optimize the learning process. In D. Klahr (Ed.), *Cognition and instruction.* Hillsdale, N.J.: Lawrence Erlbaum Associates, 1976.

Bartlett, F., & John, E. R. The equipotentiality quantified: The anatomical distribution of the engram. *Science,* 1973, *181,* 765–767.

Beard, M. H., Lorton, P. V., Searle, B. W., & Atkinson, R. C. *Comparison of student performance and attitude under three lesson-selection strategies in computer-assisted instruction* (Tech. Rep. No. 222). Stanford, Calif.: Institute for Mathematical Studies in the Social Sciences, Stanford University, 1973.

Berliner, D. C., & Cahen, L. S. Trait-treatment interaction and learning. In F. N. Kerlinger (Ed.), *Review of research in education: 1.* Itasca, Ill.: Peacock, 1973.

Bobrow, D. G., & Collins, A. (Eds.). *Representation and understanding: Studies in cognitive science.* New York: Academic Press, 1975.

Boutwell, R. C., & Barton, G. E. Toward an adaptive learner-controlled model of instruction: A place for the new cognitive aptitudes. *Educational Technology*, 1974, *14*(5), 13-18.

Briggs, L. J. Learner variables and educational media. *Review of Educational Research*, 1968, *38*(2), 160-176.

Bunderson, C. V., & Dunham, J. L. *Research program on cognitive abilities and learning* (Final Rep.). Austin, Tex.: The University of Texas, 1970.

Carroll, J. B. Psychometric tests as cognitive tasks: A new "structure of intellect." In L. B. Resnick (Ed.), *The nature of intelligence*. Hillsdale, N.J.: Lawrence Erlbaum Associates, 1976.

Cattell, R. B. Theory of fluid and crystallized intelligence: A critical experiment. *Journal of Educational Psychology*, 1963, *54*(1), 1-22.

Cermak, L. S. *Psychology of learning: Research and theory*. New York: Ronald Press, 1975.

Chomsky, N. *Syntactic structures*. The Hague: Mouton, 1957.

Coop, R. H., & Sigel, I. E. Cognitive style: Implications for learning and instruction. *Psychology in the Schools*, 1971, *8*(2), 152-161.

Cronbach, L. J. The two disciplines of scientific psychology. *American Psychologist*, 1957, *12*, 671-684.

Cronbach, L. J. How can instruction be adapted to individual differences? In R. M. Gagné (Ed.), *Learning and individual differences*. Columbus, Ohio: Merrill, 1967.

Cronbach, L. J., & Gleser, G. C. *Psychological tests and personnel decisions*. Urbana, Ill.: University of Illinois Press, 1965.

Cronbach, L. J., & Snow, R. E. *Individual differences in learning ability as a function of instructional variables* (Final Rep.). Stanford, Calif.: School of Education, Stanford University, 1969.

Cronbach, L. J., & Snow R. E. *Aptitudes and instructional methods: A handbook for research on interactions*. New York: Irvington Publishers, 1977.

Crowder, R. G. *Principles of learning and memory*. Hillsdale, N.J.: Lawrence Erlbaum Associates, 1976.

DiVesta, F. J. Theories and measures of individual differences in studies of trait by treatment interaction. *Educational Psychologist*, 1973, *10*(2), 67-75.

Doyle, J. C., Ornstein, R., & Galin, D. Lateral specialization of cognitive mode: II. EEG frequency analysis. *Psychophysiology*, 1974, *11*(5), 567-578.

Estes, W. K. (Ed.). *Handbook of learning and cognitive processes* (Vols. 1, 3, & 4). Hillsdale, N.J.: Lawrence Erlbaum Associates, 1975-1976.

Federico, P-A. *Accommodating instruction to student characteristics: Trends and issues* (NPRDC TR 79-1). San Diego, Calif.: Navy Personnel Research and Development Center, October 1978.

Fleishman, E. A., & Bartlett, C. J. Human abilities. *Annual Review of Psychology*, 1969, *20*, 349-380.

Fleishman, E. A., & Hempel, W. E. Changes in factor structure of a complex psychomotor test as a function of practice. *Psychometrika*, 1954, *19*(3), 239-252.

French, J. W. The relationship of problem-solving styles to the factor composition of tests. *Educational and Psychological Measurement*, 1965, *25*, 9-28.

Gagné, R. M. (Ed.). *Learning and individual differences*. Columbus, Ohio: Merrill, 1967.

Gagné, R. M. Schooling and the relevance of research: General discussion of the conference. In R. C. Anderson, R. J. Spiro, & W. E. Montague (Eds.), *Schooling and the acquisition of knowledge*. Hillsdale, N.J.: Lawrence Erlbaum Associates, 1977.

Gagné, R. M., & Paradise, N. E. Abilities and learning sets in knowledge acquisition. *Psychological Monographs*, 1961, *75*(14, Whole No. 518).

Galin, D. Two modes of consciousness and the two halves of the brain. In R. E. Ornstein (Ed.), *Symposium on consciousness*. New York: Viking, 1975.

Galin, D., & Ellis, R. R. Asymmetry in evoked potentials as an index of lateralized cognitive processes: Relation to EEG alpha asymmetry. *Neuropsychologia*, 1975, *13*, 45-50.

Galin, D., & Ornstein, R. Lateral specialization of cognitive mode: An EEG study. *Psychophysiology*, 1972, *9*(4), 412-418.

Galin, D., & Ornstein, R. Individual differences in cognitive style—I. Reflective eye movements. *Neuropsychologia,* 1974, *12,* 367–376.

Glaser, R. Individuals and learning: The new aptitudes. *Educational Researcher,* 1972, *1*(6), 5–13.

Glaser, R. Cognitive psychology and instructional design. In D. Klahr (Ed.), *Cognition and instruction.* Hillsdale, N.J.: Lawrence Erlbaum Associates, 1976. (a)

Glaser, R. Components of a psychology of instruction: Toward a science of design. *Review of Educational Research,* 1976, *46*(1), 1–24. (b)

Glaser, R. *Adaptive education: Individual diversity and learning.* New York: Holt, Rinehart & Winston, 1977.

Glaser, R., & Resnick, L. B. Instructional psychology. In P. H. Mussen & M. R. Rosenweig (Eds.), *Annual review of psychology.* Palo Alto, Calif.: Annual Reviews, 1972.

Goldberg, L. R. Student personality characteristics and optimal college learning conditions: An extensive search for trait-by-treatment interaction effects. *Instructional Science,* 1972, *1*(2), 153–210.

Horn, J. L. State, trait and change dimensions of intelligence. *The British Journal of Educational Psychology,* 1972, *42*(2), 159–185.

Hunt, E. Varieties of cognitive power. In L. B. Resnick (Ed.), *The nature of intelligence.* Hillsdale, N.J.: Lawrence Erlbaum Associates, 1976.

Hunt, E., & Lansman, M. Cognitive theory applied to individual differences. In W. K. Estes (Ed.), *Handbook of learning and cognitive processes. Volume 1: Introduction to concepts and issues.* Hillsdale, N.J.: Lawrence Erlbaum Associates, 1975.

John, E. R. Switchboard vs. statistical theories of learning and memory. *Science,* 1972, *177,* 850–864.

John, E. R. A month of consciousness. In G. E. Schwartz & D. Shapiro (Eds.), *Consciousness and self regulation: Advances in research* (Vol. I). New York: Plenum Press, 1975.

John, E. R., Bartlett, F., Shimokochi, M., & Kleinman, D. Neural readout from memory. *Journal of Neurophysiology,* 1973, *36,* 893–924.

John, E. R., & Thatcher, R. *Functional neuroscience. Vol. I: Foundations of cognitive processes.* New York: Halsted Press, 1976.

Kagan, J., & Kogan, N. Individual variation in cognitive processes. In P. H. Mussen (Ed.), *Carmichael's manual of child psychology* (Vol. I). New York: Wiley, 1970.

Kagan, J., Moss, H. A., & Sigel, I. E. The psychological significance of styles of conceptualization. In J. F. Wright & J. Kagan (Eds.), *Basic cognitive processes in children: Monograph of the Society for Research in Child Development,* 1963, *28,* 73–112.

Kahneman, D. *Attention and effort.* Englewood Cliffs, N.J.: Prentice-Hall, 1973.

Kintsch, W. *Learning, memory, and conceptual processes.* New York: Wiley, 1970.

Kintsch, W. (Ed.). *The representation of meaning in memory.* Hillsdale, N.J.: Lawrence Erlbaum Associates, 1974.

Klahr, D. (Ed.). *Cognition and instruction.* Hillsdale, N.J.: Lawrence Erlbaum Associates, 1976.

Kogan, N. Educational implications of cognitive styles. In G. S. Lesser (Ed.), *Psychology and educational practice.* Glenview, Ill.: Scott, Foresman, 1971.

Labouvie-Vief, G., Levin, J. R., & Urberg, K. A. The relationship between selected cognitive abilities and learning: A second look. *Journal of Educational Psychology,* 1975, *67*(4), 558–569.

Leherissey, B. L., O'Neil, H. F., Jr., Heinrich, D. L., & Hansen, D. N. Effect of anxiety, response mode, subject matter familiarity and program length on achievement in computer-assisted learning. *Journal of Educational Psychology,* 1973, *64,* 310–324.

Lewis, G. W., Rimland, B., & Callaway, E. *Psychobiological predictors of success in a Navy remedial program* (NPRDC-TR-77-13). San Diego, Calif.: Navy Personnel Research and Development Center, December 1976.

Lewis, G. W., Rimland, B., & Callaway, E. *Visual event related potentials: Toward predicting performance.* Paper presented at the Event Related Brain Potentials in Man Conference, Airlee, Virginia, April 1977.

McKeachie, W. J. Instructional psychology. *Annual Review of Psychology,* 1974, *25,* 161–193.

Melton, A. W. Individual differences and theoretical process variables: General comments on the conference. In R. M. Gagné (Ed.), *Learning and individual differences.* Columbus, Ohio: Merrill, 1967.

Melton, A. W., & Martin E. (Eds.). *Coding processes in human memory.* Washington, D.C.: V. H. Winston, 1972.

Merrill, M. D. Learner control: Beyond aptitude-treatment interactions. *AV Communication Review,* 1975, *23*(2), 217–226.

Messick, S. Personality consistencies in cognition and creativity. In S. Messick & Associates, *Individuality in learning: Implications of cognitive styles and creativity for human development.* San Francisco: Jossey-Bass, 1976.

Mischel, W. Continuity and change in personality. *American Psychologist,* 1969, *24,* 1012–1018.

Neisser, U. *Cognitive psychology.* New York: Appleton-Century-Crofts, 1967.

Newell, A., & Simon, H.A. *Human problem solving.* Englewood Cliffs, N.J.: Prentice-Hall, 1972.

Norman, D. A. (Ed.). *Models of human memory.* New York: Academic Press, 1970.

O'Neil, H. F., Jr., Spielberger, C. D., & Hansen, D. N. Effects of state-anxiety and task difficulty on computer-assisted instruction. *Journal of Educational Psychology,* 1969, *60,* 343–350.

Paivio, A. *Imagery and verbal processes.* New York: Holt, Rinehart & Winston, 1971.

Piaget, J. [*The origins of intelligence in children*] (M. Cook, trans.). New York: International Universities Press, 1952. (Originally published, 1936.)

Piaget, J. [*Play, dreams, and imitation in childhood*] (C. Gattegno & F. Hodgson, trans.). New York: Norton, 1951. (Originally published, 1945.)

Plato [*The republic*] (A. Lindsay, trans.). New York: Dutton, 1950. (Originally published, ca. 388 B.C.)

Resnick, L. B. (Ed.). *The nature of intelligence.* Hillsdale, N.J.: Lawrence Erlbaum Associates, 1976.

Rigney, J. W. *On cognitive strategies for facilitating acquisition, retention, and retrieval in training and education* (Tech. Rep. No. 78). Los Angeles: Department of Psychology, University of Southern California, 1976.

Rigney, J. W., & Towne, D. M. Taskteach: A method for computer-assisted performance training. *Human Factors,* 1970, *12*(3), 285–296.

Rohwer, W. D., Jr. Images and pictures in children's learning. *Psychological Bulletin,* 1970, *73,* 393–403. (a)

Rohwer, W. D., Jr. Mental elaboration and proficient learning. In J. P. Hill (Ed.), *Minnesota Symposia on Child Psychology,* 1970, *4,* 220–260. (b)

Rohwer, W. D., Jr. Learning, race and school success. *Review of Educational Research,* 1971, *41,* 191–210.

Rumelhart, D. W., & Ortony, A. The representation of knowledge in memory. In R. C. Anderson, R. J. Spiro, & W. E. Montague (Eds.), *Schooling and the acquisition of knowledge.* Hillsdale, N.J.: Lawrence Erlbaum Associates, 1977.

Salomon, G. Heuristic models for the generation of aptitude-treatment interaction hypotheses. *Review of Educational Research,* 1972, *42*(3), 327–343.

Satterly, D. J. Cognitive style, spatial ability, and school achievement. *Journal of Educational Psychology,* 1976, *68*(1), 36–42.

Scandura, J. M. Deterministic theorizing in structural learning: Three levels of empiricism. *Journal of Structural Learning,* 1971, *3,* 21–53.

Scandura, J. M. *Structural learning I: Theory and research.* London: Gordan & Breach, 1973.

Scandura, J. M. Structural approach to instructional problems. *American Psychologist,* 1977, *32*(1), 333–353.

Schroder, H. M., Driver, M. J., & Streufert, S. *Human information processing: Individuals and groups functioning in complex social situations*. New York: Holt, Rinehart & Winston, 1967.

Seidel, R. J. Theories and strategies related to measurement in individualized instruction. *Educational Technology*, 1971, *11*(8), 40–46.

Snow, R. E. *Research on aptitudes: A progress report* (Tech. Rep. No. 1). Stanford, Calif.: School of Education, Stanford University, 1976. (a)

Snow, R. E. *Theory and method for research on aptitude processes: A prospectus* (Tech. Rep. No. 2). Stanford, Calif.: School of Education, Stanford University, 1976. (b)

Snow, R. E., & Salomon, G. Aptitudes and instructional media. *AV Communication Review*, 1968, *16*, 341–357.

Solso, R. L. *Contemporary issues in cognitive psychology: The Loyola symposium*. Washington, D.C.: V. H. Winston, 1973.

Steinberg, E. R. Review of student control in computer-assisted instruction. *Journal of Computer-Based Instruction*, 1977, *3*(3), 84–90.

Sternberg, R. J. *Intelligence, information processing, and analogical reasoning: The componential analysis of human abilities*. Hillsdale, N.J.: Lawrence Erlbaum Associates, 1977.

Tennyson, R. D. Adaptive instructional models for concept acquisition. *Educational Technology*, 1975, *15*(4), 7–15.

Tennyson, R. D., & Boutwell, R. C. Pre-task versus within-task anxiety measures in predicting performance on a concept acquisition task. *Journal of Educational Psychology*, 1973, *65*, 88–92.

Thatcher, R. W. Electrophysiological correlates of animal and human memory. In R. D. Terry & S. Gershom (Eds.), *Neurobiology of aging*. New York: Raven Press, 1976.

Thatcher, R. W., & April, R. S. Evoked potential correlates of semantic information processing in normals and aphasics. In R. Rieber (Ed.), *The neuropsychology of language—Essays in honor of Eric Lenneberg*. New York: Academic Press, 1976.

Thatcher, R. W., & John, E. R. Information and mathematical quantification of brain state. In N. R. Burch & H. L. Altshuler (Eds.), *Behavior and brain electrical activity*. New York: Plenum Press, 1975.

Tobias, S. Achievement treatment interactions. *Review of Educational Research*, 1976, *46*(1), 61–74.

Tulving, E., & Donaldson, W. (Eds.). *Organization of memory*. New York: Academic Press, 1972.

Vernon, P. E. The distinctiveness of field independence. *Journal of Personality*, 1972, *40*, 366–391.

Voss, J. F. The nature of "the nature of intelligence." In L. Resnick (Ed.), *The nature of intelligence*. Hillsdale, N.J.: Lawrence Erlbaum Associates, 1976.

Witkin, H. A., Goodenough, D. R., & Karp, S. A. Stability of cognitive style from childhood to young adulthood. *Journal of Personality and Social Psychology*, 1967, *7*, 291–300.

2 Aptitude Processes

Richard E. Snow
Stanford University

The terms in my title refer to two concepts in modern psychology that are not usually connected, because they pertain to rather different frames, or perhaps levels, of reference. But a main purpose of this conference, in my view, is to examine ways in which they might be connected, theoretically and empirically, to explain individual differences in complex, cognitive learning and thus to find ways of controlling, or erasing, or adapting to such differences for instructional improvement. Thus it seemed that a good way to start off this conference was to charge into the wilderness between these two terms directly.

This chapter, therefore, comes in the form of a cavalry report from that wilderness, designed to give an initial correlational description of some of the complexities and emergent properties to be found there, and to provide some rough map of the terrain that the advancing process theories must ultimately capture.

It makes a point to pursue this metaphor one step further. Lee and his army could usually count on substantial help from Stuart's cavalry reports, but when they were most needed, the correlational cavalry was off somewhere sharpening its factor analytic swords. Although that endeavor had some useful consequences, it resulted in the neglect for some decades of what, I think, is the most important substantive role for the correlational arm of cognitive psychology. That role is to provide an advance-guard description of real-life cognitive complexity much like a cavalry report. At least, that is the role this chapter is meant to play.

Aptitudes are psychological constructs about individual differences in learning or performance in specified situations. The situations of interest here are those in which human beings learn from instruction. To claim that a measure of some human performance characteristic represents aptitude here, one must show that the measure bears predictive relation to learning under instruction. Aptitude constructs are typically operationalized for this purpose as one or more score continua, the scores having been obtained systematically from some kind of test or task performance. All such operationalizations of aptitude are proxies for underlying or correlated psychological differences. Whatever the measure, the psychological differences portrayed by an aptitude construct are assumed to be, or to have been, process based in part. When some aptitude measure shows relation to learning outcome, and particularly when this relation can be seen to vary under different experimental or instructional conditions, then there is the clear implication that that aptitude is in some way involved in learning processes, at least in that situation. Whether the processes represented by aptitude measures are related to, or are the same as, those represented by learning measures is a question for theory and further research.

This conference reviews, and seeks further to promote, process-oriented research on individual differences in learning and cognition to answer such questions, and to enrich our conception of aptitude, learning, and instruction thereby. Most of the participants probably share Glaser's (1972) optimistic view that such research will identify "new aptitudes" different in kind from the "old aptitudes." Although this is an important possibility, my own expectations are that the new and the old will be found to differ more in form than in kind, and that an improved conception of human learning and cognition will need to be built on their combination. (See Snow, 1977b, 1978, for elaboration of this view.) Because it is the old aptitudes that still consistently predict learning from instruction, that is the place I think it best to start. The object is to convert existing aptitude constructs into more detailed models of individual differences in cognitive processing, and to trace the operation of these through the activities involved in instructional learning.

Having defined *aptitude,* the term *process* also needs some attention at the start; its referent is often taken for granted. We usually take *process* to mean an active change or series of changes showing consistent direction in the ongoing psychological functioning of the organism. But the "changes" can refer to changes in a dynamic functional system as in some learning theories, or to changes in the information being processed by a static system as in some cognition theories, or to changes in both. We need to keep in mind, I think, that in research on instructional learning, we are dealing with phenomena involving changes in both. Further, there are cognitive processes discernible in the second-to-second and minute-to-minute changes that occur during learning or information-processing activities. But there are also processes discernible in the week-to-week and month-to-month adaptation of learning and processing activities to instructional conditions and to the "accretion", "restructuring," and "fine tuning" of organized knowledge and skill (to use Rumelhart & Norman's 1976 terms) seen in the kind of complex learning that occurs over courses of instruction. There seem to be different levels of processing complexity and perhaps also different depths of processing (Craik & Tulving, 1975) implied here. It is not clear that the same terms should be applied throughout. Different theoretical models may be required to account for processes at different levels. And some aptitude constructs may well apply to one level or kind of processing and not another. Clarification of this problem will come, not from the production of new dictionary definitions, but from theory and research that carefully identify what level and kind of processing they are presumably concerned with.

In the meantime, I would propose a broad, provisional definition of aptitude processes that tries to cover all of the foregoing, albeit loosely. Aptitude processes are those predictable, directed changes in psychological functioning by which individual learners:

1. adapt or fail to adapt to the short-term and long-term performance demands of instructional conditions.
2. develop or fail to develop the expected organization of knowledge and skill through learning activities, and
3. differ from one another in the quality or quantity of learning outcome attained thereby.

Aptitude process differences exist before and operate through, but are also produced by, instruction to account for individual differences in learning outcome. To trace through this complex network, one needs analysis and measurement of aptitude processes, learning activities, and instructional task components operating all along the way to criterion performance requirements.

Figure 2.1 is an attempt to sum up this introduction and provide a schematic outline for the terrain to be captured. There are existing aptitude constructs (A) for which there is strong evidence of relation to learning outcome variables (O); hence the solid arrow. However, traditional research on aptitude treated the instructional situation, and individual differences operating within it, as a black box. It also took the outcome variables as given. And it failed to produce process models that could connect the aptitude constructs to outcomes. Research on aptitude-instructional-treatment interaction (or ATI for short—Cronbach & Snow, 1977) took a first step into the black box by showing that A–O relations varied as a function of instructional treatment variables (T). Something important regarding aptitude processes must be happening inside the box if treatment manipulations alter input–output relations. These relations are shown as broken arrows because—though the evidence is clear that ATI exist—the many inconsistencies in A–T–O relations cannot be summed up simply, as can the evidence on A–O relations. The dashed path shows the route that I think must now be taken and is now being taken by thoughtful cognitive psychologists. Aptitudes must be analyzed into process components (p, q, r, s) that can be traced through an analysis of instructional task components and learning activities $(b, c, d, e, \ldots$

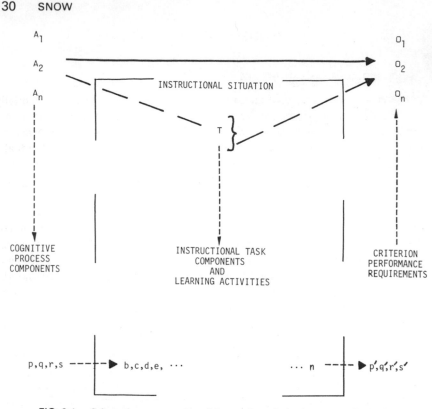

FIG. 2.1.   Schematic representation of the standing relation between aptitude (A) and outcome (O) variables, the interaction of A with instructional treatment (T) variables in this relation, and the analysis of these relations into cognitive process (*p, q, r, s*) and learning process (*b, c, d, e, ..., n*) components.

n) for different treatments, and then mapped onto the details of criterion performance requirements (*p', q', r', s'*) to explain individual differences in learning outcome.[1]

The remainder of this chapter has three main sections: One summarizes the evidence from research with tests concerning the A–A, A–O, and A–T–O relations implied in Fig. 2.1; another reports some attempts to produce A–*pqrs* analyses; and a third suggests how one might trace such analyses through the rest of the instructional learning network back to an account of 0 variables. Some process hypotheses about aptitudes are built up along the way. Also identified along the way are the various alternative approaches available for measurement of aptitude processes.

---

[1]The small-letter designations for cognitive process parameters are simply placeholders for several potentially different kinds of processing constructs. I am reserving capital letters B through N and P through Z for process constructs in the middle range, closer in complexity to A, T, and O.

MODELS OF APTITUDE

Approaches to Measurement

There are at least six types of measurements that can be used, at least potentially, to reflect aptitude processes. Three of these are thought of as "maximum-performance" measures; assuming that individuals are motivated to perform, such measures should show the best performance of which each individual is capable on a given occasion. Some maximum-performance tasks that can represent aptitude have been built on a psychometric (test) model,[2] emanating from designs established by Binet, Thurstone, and others. In contrast to these, two other types of maximum-performance tasks that might reflect aptitude have been built on some kind of learning model, or on what can be called cognition models. Both these forms have their origins in the tradition of Ebbinghaus, Galton, and McKeen Cattell; but more recent tasks, particularly those built on the cognition model, have not been designed to measure individual differences at all but rather to reflect some process aspect of a general cognitive theory. Beyond these, there are two types of "typical-performance" measure, so called because they seek to describe what individuals do in a situation, or typically do in a class of situations, rather than what they are able to do. One is based on some form of direct observation of activities associated with cognitive performance; the other on introspective interview or questionnaire measures of study or work methods, preferences, styles, strategies, motivations, and so forth, before and during cognitive performance. Finally, there are also status or categorical attributes (such as sex, SES, or various occupational or training categories) that may reflect either maximum or typical aptitude differences, because they index underlying aptitude continua with which they are correlated. These may be much more important for future research than they have been in the past, because they can reflect rather directly real-world aptitude and performance differences.

Used in combination, these various measures may prove to be complementary in important ways. They may have different strengths and weaknesses, however, and may appear to suggest somewhat different models of aptitude processes; it will thus be important to understand their similarities and differences.

Test Models

Though Binet, Thurstone, and others had process hypotheses in mind when they constructed many of their tasks, the underlying hypotheses were largely lost in

[2]The term *test* is preferred to the term *psychometric* in distinguishing this form of aptitude measure from those based on other models; *psychometric* applies to all psychological measurement, not just that based on norm-referenced tests. Referring to *tested* aptitudes helps also to distinguish maximum-performance tests from typical-performance questionnaires, both of which are based on psychometric models.

the subsequent development of mental-testing technology. Most such tasks came to be interpreted as reflecting a static trait, indicating the "quantity" of "ability" someone "possesses."

But this need not be so. Tests are simply cognitive tasks with certain characteristics. Usually, they pose a numbered series of discrete problems to be solved during some total time limit. The problems are chosen to reflect a range from easy to difficult and to be either relatively heterogeneous, (as in most tests of prior educational achievement) or distinctly homogeneous (as in ability-factor reference tests). Whereas some tests are designed to reflect the speed with which an individual can solve simple problems, many are designed more to show the power of an individual's ability—that is, the level of problem difficulty the individual can reach successfully; most tests reflect a mixture of speed and power. Time allocation to particular problems in the series and order of solution are usually controlled by the individual. Some practice trials are given to check understanding of instructions, but the tests themselves are not typically long enough to allow extended practice within the test. Although separately timed halves can sometimes show practice effects, performance usually does not become automatic; and strategies adopted early in the task, as well as strategy shifts along the way, may play a large role in determining final score, especially on tests with some degree of speeding.

Process theories do not yet exist for such tasks. There are now some process models for some of the kinds of items found in tests, but a performance model for items is not necessarily a model for a test performance composed of such items. It would be wrong to conclude from this that tests as such do not measure important process differences. Carroll (1976) has already shown how one might begin to construct process hypotheses for the kinds of ability tests found in the ETS kit of cognitive-factor reference tests (French, Ekstrom, & Price, 1963). Also, from just the global description already given, one can form the more general hypothesis that almost any total test score continuum probably reflects some combination of the efficiency of different individuals in organizing processing strategies to face new kinds of mental problems and their control of this organization and its sustained application through an entire test performance, as well as the increasing item-difficulty levels at which they can carry out these performance activities for mental problems of different types. It may be that all aptitude tests reflect differences in the assembly and control functions involved in test processing, as well as in particular functions associated with item processing. Simon (1976) suggested just this in discussing the description of individual differences in intelligence implied by work on computer simulation programs for cognitive tasks. He noted that although the same basic processes may be involved in many different tasks, they not only are used more or less frequently in different tasks but also may be *organized in more than one way for performing a given task, and may differ greatly in effectiveness as a result.* To quote Simon's (1976) summary:

Proficiency in a task may depend on how the basic processes and relevant knowledge have been organized into the program for task performance. . . . It is not certain to what extent [intelligence] is to be attributed to common processes among performance programs, or to what extent it derives from individual differences in the efficacy of the learning programs that assemble the performance programs [p. 96].

We should here be reminded that some very old definitions of intelligence, from Binet on, include such phrases as "adaptation to a goal," "capacity to reorganize behavior patterns for effective action," "maintenance of definite direction and concentration," "autocriticism," and, in sum, "ability to learn." (See Snow, 1978a, for complete quotations and references.) It is reasonable to suppose that such processes operate within, as well as between, tests or tasks.

In short, we can imagine that the cognitive system includes at least three kinds of process functions: assembly processes, control processes, and performance processes. Most research on information processing has concentrated on the third function, so most cognitive theories look like performance programs. More recently, attention has been turning to the executive functions, but these are thought of mainly as control processes. The primary executive function, however, would appear to be assembly; the computer program analogy has for too long left out the programmer. It may be that mental tests, or at least some mental tests, represent assembly or learning functions, as well as control functions, to a significant degree. This is not to deny the importance of individual differences in performance processes; it is rather to place them in a larger context.

The evidence so far accumulated on mental tests supports and elaborates this hypothesis. Many of these tests have been studied for decades by correlating them with one another and with various learning and performance criteria. Enough evidence has now accumulated to establish several facts about tested aptitudes and to suggest some crude theory about aptitude processes.

A–A Relations.   A first fact about ability tests is that they usually intercorrelate, and correlation matrices involving large numbers of such tests typically show a characteristic form. Much intercorrelational research has shown persistent clusters of tasks; those within one cluster correlate more strongly with one another than they do with tasks in other clusters. These persistent patterns of correlations have been subjected to various forms of factor analysis, cluster analysis, and multidimensional scaling. From this work, a fairly consistent structural model has emerged.

The multidimensional scaling in Fig. 2.2 shows each of a large battery of mental tests as a point in two-dimensional space; the closer two points are in this space, the more strongly these two tests are correlated. These data come from a sample of 241 California high-school students participating in our current research project. But similar patterns can be seen in data originally reported by

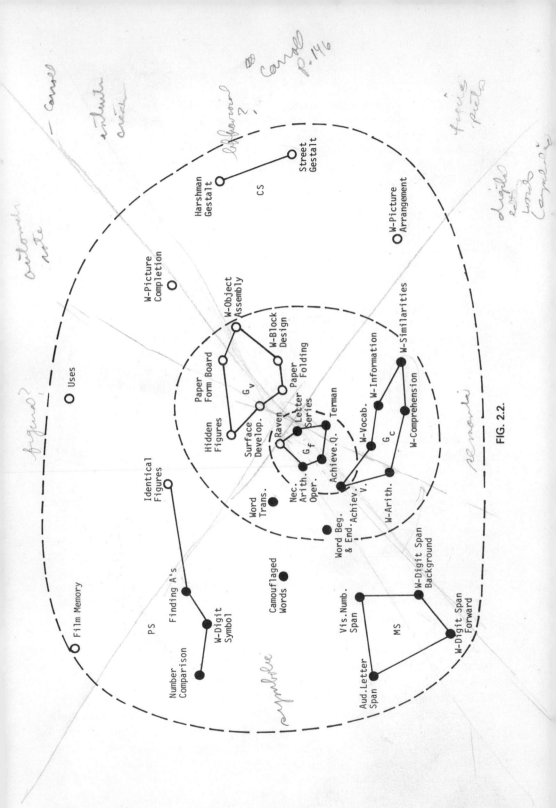

FIG. 2.2.

Thurstone and others (see also Guttman, 1965). Points connected by heavy solid lines come together in the same factor or cluster when these data are factor analyzed or cluster analyzed by various methods. The capital-letter designations identify the factor labels typically attached to these clusters in past work. (See Snow, Lohman, Marshalek, Yalow, & Webb, 1977, for details on these analyses and comparable analyses on a sample of 123 Stanford undergraduates as well as the combined sample.) G_c stands for crystallized ability in Cattell's (1971) terms, including measures of verbal knowledge, reading comprehension, and prior educational achievement. The factor would be thought of as a fairly general dimension including most measures of scholastic ability, or "verbal–educational ability," to follow traditional British parlance (Vernon, 1965). G_f stands for another constellation consisting of abstract and often nonverbal reasoning tests and some spatial and figural tests; it would be called "fluid ability" by Cattell (1971) and "spatial–mechanical ability" by the British factorists. (For short, I opt for Cattell's terms, referring to the two as G_c and G_f, for crystallized and fluid ability, respectively.) G_v identifies "visualization," a constellation of figural and spatial relations tests. The distinction between G_f and G_v is often difficult to make; here G_f and G_v appear separable in the multidimensional scaling but not in the factor analysis. There is other evidence that spatial problems can often be solved by logical analytic processes rather than visual image processes (French, 1965; Lohman, 1978). The more tests allow a mixture of such processes, the more their intercorrelations would force G_f and G_v to combine in factor analyses. G_{fv} is occasionally used to denote this. *MS, PS,* and *CS* label Memory Span, Perceptual Speed, and Closure Speed factors, respectively.

Contour lines have been added to the scaling to distinguish central, intermediate, and peripheral regions, following Guttman's (1965) approach. The interpretation usually is that tasks falling in the more central regions involve abilities that are somehow more general, central, or complex than tasks falling in the more peripheral regions. Jensen (1970) interprets the peripheral-to-central dimension as representing the increasing complexity of mental processing required by the tests and perhaps also the increasing abstractness of test content. Were Fig. 2.2 a dart board, the bull's-eye would locate Spearman's *g,* or general intelligence (see also Marshalek, 1977).

Why should different tests consistently intercorrelate? The more central tests correlate with a wider range of other tests (hence the term *general*), and G_f tests appear to be the most central. Perhaps they represent to a greater degree the kinds of assembly and control processes needed to organize on a short-term basis adaptive strategies for solving novel problems. The more complex and varied the sequence of novel problems, the more adaptive the processing system needs to

---

FIG. 2.2. *(Opposite page)* Multidimensional scaling of between-test correlations in a battery administered to high-school students ($N = 241$). *W* identifies subtests of the Wechsler Adult Intelligence Scale.

be. The Raven Progressive Matrices Test is perhaps the archetypical example of such a task, and one usually finds it in the center, as in Fig. 2.2. The central tests may also share particular performance processes, and/or similar organizations of such processes, with other tests. But as one moves out to the periphery of Fig. 2.2, one encounters increasingly "specific" tests—that is, tests that appear to require fewer, simpler processes applied over and over again in a sequence of highly similar items. Memory Span tests, Perceptual Speed tests such as Identical Pictures or Number Comparison, and the Closure Speed tests are all good examples of this. The items are simple and similar to one another; the tests are either highly speeded as in perceptual speed tests or closely time regulated as in memory span tests; and thus perhaps the assembly, control, and performance processes involved in them are simpler and more automatic. Much less adaptation of processing is required over the sequence of items in such tests.

Note also that a diagonal line drawn from upper left to lower right in Fig. 2.2 contrasts fairly neatly those tests based on digits, letters, or words (solid points) with those based on pictures or figures (open points). This makes Guttman's point again that different pie-shaped cuts in the space identify different test contents. Here, though, is the added implication that the main content distinction may be between digital and analogic processing. It is not reasonable to pass off content distinctions among ability factors as trivial, as some have done in the past; different contents may require different processes.

A–O Relations.   A second fact about aptitude tests leads to some further hypotheses about aptitude processes. One constellation of aptitude tests identified in Fig. 2.2, namely G_c, consistently provides strong predictions of learning outcomes across a large sample of conventional instructional environments. An example of this is found in Table 2.1, which shows a distribution of predictive validity coefficients obtained using the American College Testing Program's high-school test battery as a predictor of later college performance, with and without the inclusion of high-school grades as an additional predictor (data are from Lenning, 1975). Each coefficient is based on the freshman class of 120 participating institutions and represents a pre–post correlation computed across 1 year of instructional learning. The correlations range from 0.15 to over 0.65, with a median of 0.48. The two kinds of predictors together yield many correlations over 0.65, and the combined predictor median is 0.60.

Measures such as ACT or high-school rank are assumed to reflect individual differences in prior scholastic learning effectiveness. They would correlate with SAT-Verbal, and to some extent with SAT-Quantitative, as well as with the various vocabulary, reading comprehension, information, and mathematics achievement tests that go into the definition of G_c; and all these tests usually serve as good general predictors of conventional educational achievement. Note that information-processing experiments that include SAT-V and SAT-Q or the like in their correlational analyses are essentially representing G_c.

TABLE 2.1
Distribution of Multiple Correlations of ACT Test Scores
With Freshman Grade-Point Average
in 120 Colleges and Universities, With and Without
High-School Grades in the Multiple[a]

Levels of Multiple Correlation Obtained	ACT as Predictors	ACT and High-School Grades as Predictors
over .65	5	30
.60–.64	5	22
.55–.59	13	30
.50–.54	20	19
.45–.49	34	3
.40–.44	20	10
.35–.39	9	3
.30–.34	8	2
.25–.29	5	1
.15–.24	1	0
	120	120
Median co-efficient	.48	.60

[a] Data from Lenning (1975).

We know nothing of the differences among the college environments involved in Table 2.1, and no one would argue that those data say anything much about processes. But why are G_c measures often better predictors of learning outcome than G_f measures?[3] One reason may be that G_c represents the long-term accumulation of knowledge and skills, organized into functional cognitive systems by prior learning, that are in some sense crystallized as units for use in future learning. Because these are products of past education, and because education is in large part accumulative, transfer relations between past and future learning are assured. The transfer need not be primarily of specific knowledge but rather of organized academic learning skills. Thus G_c may represent prior assemblies of performance processes retrieved as a system and applied anew in instructional situations not unlike those experienced in the past, whereas G_f may represent new assemblies of performance processes needed in more extreme adaptations to novel situations. The distinction, then, is between *long-term* assembly for transfer to *familiar* new situations versus *short-term* assembly for transfer to *unfamiliar* new situations.

[3]It is true, unfortunately, that most studies use tests that mix G_c and G_f in some degree, so the distinction often cannot be checked in prediction studies; the interpretation then rests on an undifferentiated G.

A–T–O Relations.　The data of Table 2.1 suggest rather good predictive validity for G_c measures across a broad range of college learning environments. But the range of coefficients is also broad, and this implies that G_c aptitude interacts with college environmental variables. That is, instructional treatment variables may influence the aptitude–outcome relations across learning situations. A large number of aptitude–treatment interactions have been reported involving all sorts of instructional treatment variables and aptitude measures (Cronbach & Snow, 1977; Snow, 1977b), so it is a fact that ATI exist.

An example may help bring such gross trends down to where process hypotheses can be formulated to account for why G_c aptitude relates to learning outcome differently under different instructional conditions. One study that showed such effects also attempted to distinguish G_c and G_f. Sharps (1973) conducted a field study of Individually Prescribed Instruction (IPI) using fifth-grade classes in four schools. There were 134 students who had experienced IPI programs throughout their school years and 139 students who had experienced only "conventional" classroom instruction. The treatments spanned the year. Six aptitude tests yielded two composites: one for G_c, the other for G_f. Outcome measures at the end of the year included vocabulary, reading comprehension, arithmetic concepts, and arithmetic problem solving.

ATI was clear for G_c, not for G_f, on all outcome measures. Figure 2.3 shows the regression results for the reading comprehension outcome; a similar pattern was observed on other outcome measures. IPI reduced the relation of G_c to outcome. In so doing, it became a superior treatment for low-G_c students but inferior for high-G_c students. Treatment main effects were slight. G_f gave some correlation with outcome but little or no interaction.

The results replicate those of another study (Crist-Whitzel & Hawley-Winne, 1976) that obtained the same ATI with G_c in another yearlong evaluation of IPI in sixth-grade mathematics.

IPI is a system of individually paced instruction relying on specific pretests, geared to carefully specified objectives and sequenced content, with frequent checkpoints as guides and feedback on learner progress, plus mastery tests for each unit. As such it combines many features of the kinds of treatments found in past research to help lower-ability learners. The ATI interpretation seems to be that IPI structures learning activities in some detail, doing for lower-ability students what they may not be able to do for themselves (i.e., compensating for an inaptitude by removing much of the organizational and strategic burden, and providing careful control over learning activities, attention, persistence, and encouragement). It is "directed" learning to a far greater extent than is typical of conventional teaching and thus may remove the assembly and control burdens that the latter situation demands of each learner. In doing this, however, IPI may be dysfunctional for the more able students, who can organize their own learning; they already possess efficient assembly programs for the cognitive activities required by conventional instruction, so they seem better off with the conven-

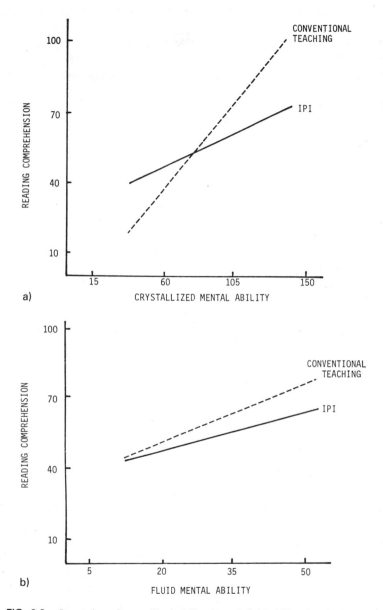

FIG. 2.3. Interaction of crystallized ability (a) and fluid ability (b) with two instructional treatments using reading comprehension as outcome measure. (After Sharps, 1973.)

tional situations in which they can easily keep up and perhaps move ahead. In effect, they are exercising and capitalizing upon prior assemblies with which they are already comfortable. Whether the apparent dysfunction for them should be attributed to cognitive interference, to motivational "turnoff," to both, or to other factors is unclear. In any event, ATI analysis demonstrates once again that no one instructional treatment is best for everyone, even one that is to some extent individualized. It also moves our process hypotheses one step further along.

To understand such ATI further, however, we need more analytic understanding of these aptitude processes in learning and how they manifest themselves in different kinds of instruction. For this, we need to turn to the more detailed component relations pictured back in Fig. 2.1 and thus to a section on learning and cognition models of aptitude.

Learning and Cognition Models

Models of aptitude based on learning tasks or on cognitive processing tasks are also possible. In the case of learning models for aptitude measurement, not much developed from the early work of Woodrow and Gulliksen and their students in the 1940s and 1950s. In the case of cognition models, on the other hand, very much has developed in recent years, as later chapters in this book demonstrate.

Rose's battery of information-processing measures provides a base to which new and more complicated conceptions of aptitude processes can be related. The work of Hunt, Frederiksen, and Carroll bears in on the processes that help to make up what we call G_c aptitude; Cooper is elaborating a process conception of G_v aptitude; and Sternberg and Pellegrino and Glaser are moving toward a process theory of G_f. At some point in the future, these special theories will need to be pieced together into a more complete fabric; they must, because test measures of these abilities correlate. We will then be closer to a process representation of general intelligence; whether or not it is ultimately called that does not really matter.

A-pqrs Relations.   Attempts to measure individual differences in learning using simple laboratory learning tasks were beset with methodological as well as conceptual problems from the start, and they generally failed for reasons detailed elsewhere (Cronbach & Snow, 1977; Glaser, 1967). The initial idea was that if simple gain across trials in a learning task correlated with mental ability tests, this would justify defining intelligence as learning ability; otherwise, not. The correlations were near zero; so the conclusion was that intelligence is not learning ability (Woodrow, 1946). But given the strong A–O relations noted earlier, the more reasonable conclusion should have been that simple rote and practice tasks in the laboratory do not measure learning as it takes place in instruction. Because the laboratory learning scores did not correlate with anything, they also did not measure aptitude processes.

In later work, the learning model usually specified several parameter scores to capture key features of each individual's acquisition curve over trials, again on simple learning tasks; intercept, slope, curvature, asymptote, and learning rate or trials-to-criterion are examples of the parameters used. Again, correlations with tests were not high except where ability tests and learning tasks were essentially identical, as in rote memory span, for example. The learning measures did not correlate with one another between tasks; these correlations were actually lower than those between some ability and learning measures. Those ability–learning correlations that seemed notable do not strongly support the view that different special abilities are involved in different kinds of learning (see, e.g., Allison, 1960; Gulliksen, 1961; Stake, 1960) but can be interpreted to suggest that a general ability construct is associated with learning across different tasks that involve conceptual content (Cronbach & Snow, 1977). G_f and G_c were not distinguished in these data, unfortunately, but a reanalysis is currently underway in our project to check this possibility.

Unlike the earlier learning models, the cognition models define parameters to capture process distinctions directly. The measurement model is designed to fit a theory of the task. If parameters of these models were to correlate with aptitude tests or proxies for them, they would carry with them specific hypotheses about aptitude processes. Even in the absence of such correlations, the same basic approach might be used to produce process theories of the aptitude tests directly. Sternberg (1977) in particular has shown how this might be done.

An experiment by Loftus and Loftus (1974) demonstrates how cognitive process models can provide a richer base than the earlier laboratory learning tasks for understanding individual differences in learning. The study concerned retrieval of information from semantic memory. It also shows, at least by analogy, something further about the processes that may be represented by G_c aptitude. Subjects were graduate students in psychology who differed in degree of learning experience in graduate school. They were asked to recall the name of a psychologist, given one of six areas of psychology and the first letter of the psychologist's last name. Reaction time was measured for each student under two conditions: letter first, followed by area designation; area first, followed by letter. It was expected that advanced graduate students would show a pattern of results like that often obtained previously with any well-learned categories: Reaction time should be faster when the letter follows the area designation, rather than vice versa, because the learner can find the location in his or her semantic memory structure where the area designation is stored while the restrictive letter is being presented, thereby saving overall time in the two-step retrieval process. Retrieving the name *Piaget,* for example, should be faster in response to the stimulus order ''Developmental-P'' than with the order ''P-Developmental.''

Figure 2.4 is redrawn from that given by Loftus and Loftus because by convention, aptitude variables are always assigned to the abscissa. The results show a clear ATI pattern. With advanced graduate students, the area–letter order of presentation requires less retrieval time than does the letter–area presentation order. With beginning students, the difference between conditions is small and actually reversed! Relatively inexperienced students—lower in crystallized knowledge of psychology—seem not to possess the kind of organized memory structure held by advanced students. To quote from Loftus and Loftus (1976):

> The implication is that when a student "learns about" psychology, this learning consists of changing the semantic organization of his knowledge about psychology and/or the process of retrieving information about psychology.
>
> [This] suggests a substantial departure from traditional notions about "what is learned" and "what should be tested". In typical educational settings, the student is viewed as learning *facts*. . . . It seems reasonable, however, on intuitive, theoretical, and empirical grounds that "what is learned" goes considerably beyond fact acquisition. Indeed, it is the case that the process of learning involves a reorganization of semantic information and implementation of new retrieval schemes [p. 152].

The reversal for novice graduate students may also make sense. One might speculate that such students learn names first before gaining a well-organized

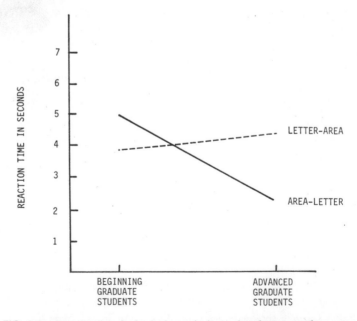

FIG. 2.4.   Reaction time for beginning and advanced students to produce a psychologist's name under two orders of stimulus presentation (letter–area; area–letter). (Data from Loftus & Loftus, 1974, 1976.)

conception of disciplinary subdivisions. Thus, the letter-first condition allows them to start running through their list of associations early; the area designation then helps them to reduce the list or select from it.

The levels-of-training variable used by Loftus and Loftus, incidentally, is a status index of aptitude differences that is at least analogous to what is meant by G_c. It is also analogous to a learning outcome variable. As learners progress through years of instruction, they differ progressively in knowledge and skill organization and in the retrieval and application of these assemblies in the service of new learning. What is important here, then, is the possibility that the sort of semantic structure and retrieval differences obtainable in experiments such as the Loftus–Loftus study may be similar to those to be discerned over years of educational development and reflected by general scholastic ability and achievement tests (i.e., by G_c).[4] Other measures of speed of symbolic encoding and matching, temporal order preservation, and speed of retrieval seem also to yield correlations with G_c aptitude measures under certain conditions (Carroll, 1976; Chiang & Atkinson, 1976; Hunt, Frost, & Lunneborg, 1973) and may also be seen as processes relevant to the construction and application of learned assemblies.

The work to date on cognition models of aptitude shows promise. But it has a long way to go before adequate analyses of aptitude or of learning in real instructional settings will be in hand. And there are pitfalls to be avoided if this research is to go beyond the point where work on the earlier laboratory learning models foundered. Some of these are discussed in a later section of this book (pp. 283–292). A particular concern here is that existing cognition models provide too narrow a set of specific processing concepts and measures. We turn, then, to some other more exploratory approaches to the study of relations between aptitudes and cognition and learning process components.

Typical Styles and Strategies

There are many individual-difference constructs that are, or might be, couched not in ability terms but in terms of cognitive styles, problem-solving strategies, study habits, personal preferences, etc.; these are intended to be descriptive of typical rather than maximum performance. Because individual differences in learning from instruction might well rest to a significant degree on such differences, style and strategy constructs become candidates for research on aptitude. Such constructs have often been interpreted in process terms, and the methods of measurement used to represent them might be uniquely useful in obtaining more detailed descriptions of aptitude processes.

---

[4]In discussion, Donald Norman has pointed out that the Loftus–Loftus finding may reflect more of an immediate strategy difference rather than a more fundamental difference in semantic organization or retrieval.

Among the methods that have been or might be used for this purpose are: general self-report questionnaires, such as the *Survey of Study Habits and Attitudes* (Brown & Holtzman, 1966); task-specific introspective reports by subjects, such as are used in building computer simulations of cognitive performances (Newell & Simon, 1972); direct observations of cognitive or learning task performances, such as those used by the competent teacher, counselor, or intelligence test administrator (Cronbach, 1970); mediated observations of cognitive or learning performances, such as those obtainable through eye-movement records (Just & Carpenter, 1976) or the protocol printouts of computer-aided instruction; and, finally, performance tasks that elicit stylistic or strategic behavior directly (Hunt & Sullivan, 1974; Kogan, 1976; Witkin, 1976).

The last method has perhaps been most used to measure individual differences in cognitive styles. The first method has seen some use in educational research, and there is evidence that general questionnaire variables of this sort correlate both with G_c aptitude and with college achievement outcomes, as well as with various personality factors (Brown & Holtzman, 1966; Rutkowski & Domino, 1975; Snow, 1977b). The next section gives an example of how introspective reports and eye-movement records can be used in coordination to help develop process descriptions of ability test performances. In a later section, an example is given of the use of computerized instructional records to measure individual differences in learning activities.

Other A–pqrs Relations

Exploratory work in our current research project sought to describe individual differences in cognitive performance on different types of mental-test items using eye-movement records taken during performance and/or introspective reports collected after performance, as well as the usual latency and error scores. Details of these studies are presented elsewhere (Lohman, 1977; Snow; 1977a; Snow, Lohman, Marshalek, Yalow, & Webb, in preparation; Yalow & Webb, 1977).

One set of data comes from 48 high-school students who were presented with six items from each of seven ability tests, representing ability factors referred to earlier as G_c, G_f, G_v, and CS. Items were administered in a rear-screen projection box arranged so that eye-movements could be filmed during performance. After this, introspective reports were collected by an interviewer using standardized checklists for each task. For this purpose, subjects were allowed to review several paper versions of the items they had seen in the projection box. The subjects had been chosen from the pool of 241 (used in the analysis of Fig. 2.2) to represent extreme groups on G_c and G_f; but many other aptitude reference scores were available on them.

Devising adequate scoring systems for such data is no easy matter, and we are still not satisfied, or finished, with the analysis. But it is now clear that a combination of these kinds of data is of significant help in producing process descriptions of aptitude test performances. Aptitude process hypotheses arising from this work can then be checked in more focused experiments.

The approach can be illustrated for two tasks—the paper-folding and vocabulary tests. One can think of these tasks as representing G_c (vocabulary) and a combination of G_f and G_v (paper folding).

Figure 2.5 gives sample eye-movement tracks for several subjects on several paper-folding items. Time flow is from the top of each figure down. Numbers indicate the length of each gaze in seconds. The balloons attached to each track indicate the location of each subject's oral response and the response alternative (A thru E) chosen; the response is correct in each case except in Fig. 2.5f. In actual presentation, the stimulus portion of the item appeared above the row of response alternatives. The subject's task for each item was to understand the pictured series of folds in a piece of paper and the location of the punched hole after the last fold, and then to identify which of the response alternatives would represent the punched paper when unfolded.

Figure 2.6 provides a flowchart representing several of the individual differences in processing that seem to be apparent from the eye tracks and introspective reports. Subjects differ not only from one another but also within themselves across items, as expected. The first step for virtually all subjects is some form of stimulus analysis. But individuals differ widely in the degree to which they show systematic and sustained stimulus comparison processes here and in the time they devote to this step. Compare the subjects pictured in Fig. 2.5a and b with those pictured in e and f, for example. Subjects in Fig. 2.5a and b show a systematic progression through the folding process, with no backtracking. Introspective reports from such subjects suggest that they are mentally constructing either an iconic or a symbolic representation of what the unfolded paper should look like and then scanning the response alternatives to find a match. An introspected strategy index reflecting the amount of such reports for each individual over all items answered correctly correlated significantly with 20 of 35 reference ability scores. The correlation of this index with a G_c ability factor score was .65; with Wechsler Verbal IQ, it was .69, and with a reading achievement test, it was .66. The index correlated only .38 with the G_f factor score and .42 with Wechsler Performance IQ.

Subjects in Fig. 2.5e and f do not report using such a strategy. Their stimulus processing appears to be haphazard, without systematic comparison of stimulus folds. Instead, they show many searching eye-movements back and forth between stimuli and response alternatives, and they tend to report use of an elimination strategy, attempting to narrow down to correct alternatives by comparison of specific stimulus and response features or cues.

The flowchart in Fig. 2.6 shows these two basic patterns of processing. High-ability subjects tend to show more of the constructive matching strategy, whereas low-ability subjects show more of the response elimination strategy. It is significant to note, however, that many subjects show both patterns across items;

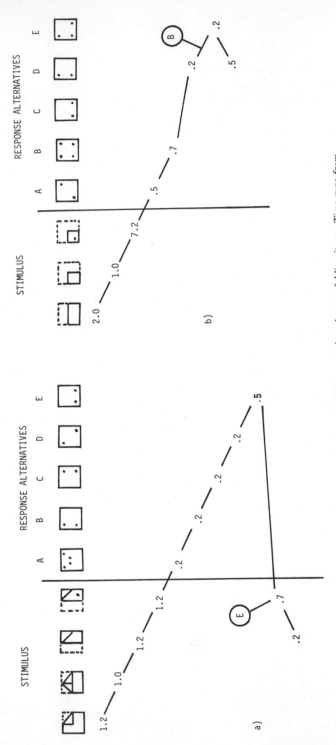

FIG. 2.5. Eye-movement tracks for six subjects on selected paper-folding items. Time runs from top down in each track. Numbers indicate pauses in seconds. Letter balloons indicate point of oral response and alternative chosen.

46

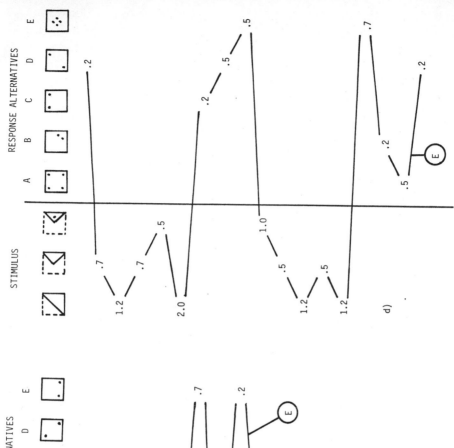

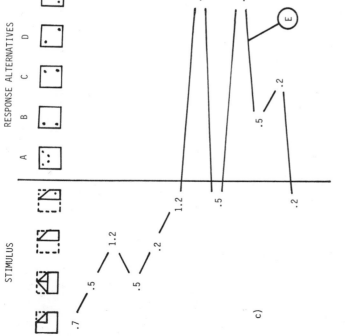

FIG. 2.5. *continued*

48

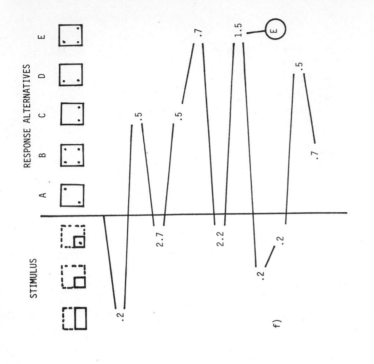

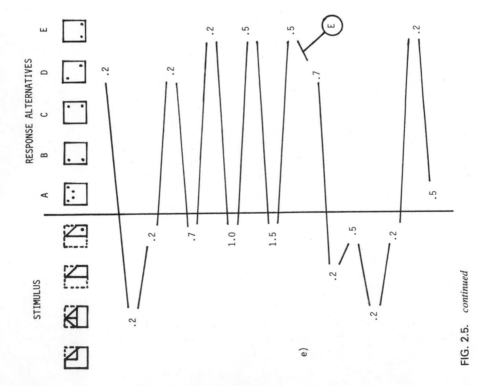

FIG. 2.5. *continued*

the response elimination strategy appears to be one of several fallback approaches used when an item proves difficult to solve by constructive matching.

Several other aspects of the eye-track differences are also pictured in Fig. 2.5. Some subjects start with an orientation glance at the response alternatives (Fig. 2.5d and e); most do not. Some subjects, while showing similar forms of eye tracks, differ in time taken for different steps (Fig. 2.5a and b). Some subjects interrupt their stimulus processing with quick checking glances back to a stimulus during response scanning. There are also patterns showing multiple cycles of stimulus analysis and/or response scanning (Fig. 2.5d). Finally, the pattern in Fig. 2.5a shows a double checking step in which the subject looks back at the punched stimulus figure at the end of his or her solution before responding. Some subjects show this double checking often; some rarely if ever.

The important point, however, is that high-ability subjects, even though they may show patterns like Fig. 2.5a and b on some items, will shift through patterns like c and d to show response elimination patterns like e and f on some difficult items. Low-ability subjects show more of the d, e, and f patterns throughout their performances. Thus, Fig. 2.6 has been constructed as a general flow diagram through which different individuals take different routes. Constructive matching is the main route for high-ability subjects. Response elimination is a fallback strategy for them, whereas it appears to be the principal strategy for low-ability subjects. Further, in many of the eye tracks for low-ability subjects, one gets the impression that they cannot help looking quickly at the response alternatives; they seem to lack some inhibitory or control mechanism that the high-ability subjects use to sustain their stimulus analysis. Low-ability subjects also report more subvocal verbalization during performance and more guessing than do high-ability subjects.

Thus it appears that high-and low-ability subjects differ in their efficiency in assembling a systematic strategy for the task, their control of its application, and their flexibility in changing strategies as item characteristics demand. A theory of individual differences on this task will need to include these assembly and control functions along with performance process hypotheses.

The Fig. 2.6 flowchart can also serve as a summary of the data for the vocabulary task if one dropped the double-checking loop and substituted somewhat different subprograms into the stimulus and response analysis blocks to represent encoding and retrieval of semantic features. Again, the main ability correlate seems to be the contrast between constructive matching and response elimination, as well as time spent in both stimulus and response processing. Figure 2.7 shows three subjects on some vocabulary items. The subject in Fig. 2.7a reports knowing the meaning of the stimulus as a direct associate and rapidly scanning alternatives to match one with the correct meaning. This is the same subject whose paper-folding eye tracks are presented in Fig. 2.5a and who claimed to use a similar strategy to solve those problems.

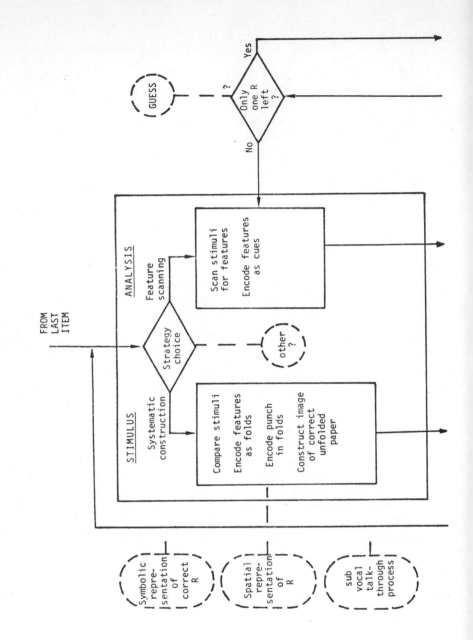

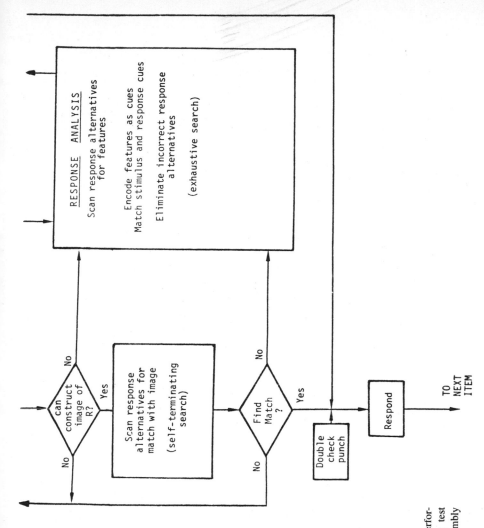

FIG. 2.6. Flowchart model of a performance program for the paper-folding test
showing individual differences in assembly
and control strategies.

51

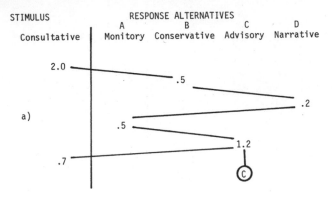

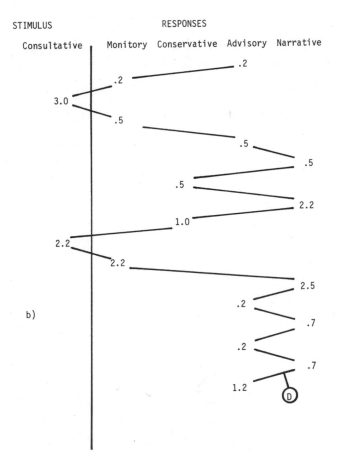

FIG. 2.7.   Eye-movement tracks for three subjects on selected vocabulary items. Time runs from top down in each track. Numbers indicate pauses in seconds. Letter balloons indicate point of oral response and alternative chosen.

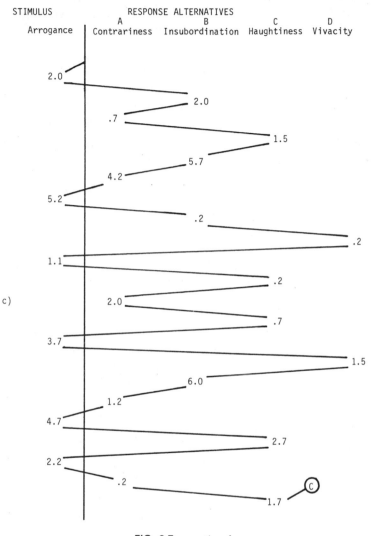

FIG. 2.7.   *continued*

The subject in Fig. 2.7b claims not to be sure of the meaning of both the stimulus word and the first alternative. He therefore eliminated the two alternatives he thought were wrong and randomly chose from the other two. The rapid switching behavior at the end of that figure is probably indicative of that process. The subject in Fig. 2.7c claims not to know the meaning of the stimulus word or of any of the alternatives. She reported having made her selection by analyzing all the words to the best of her ability. The extended duration on each alternative during the time the subject is likely to be analyzing the words can be contrasted with the rapid switching in Fig. 2.7b when the subject reports making a random guess with no attempt at analysis.

Through all these data, the general ability distinctions seem easy to make. That is, subjects scoring high and low on general mental tests are clearly distinguishable in ways that suggest process differences. The data do not, at least not yet, clearly distinguish G_c and G_f as separate kinds of ability in process terms. They do show, however, that it is primarily G_f that accounts for differences in response latency on tasks like paper folding, whereas G_c correlates with response latency on tests like vocabulary.

It does seem that combining eye movement and introspective data with reaction time and error data may be a useful way of gaining some process description of mental test performance. The data so far collected show that for many subjects, processing strategies shift from item to item, as well as from test to test, as a function of difficulty level. This suggests the existence of executive processes of some sort and argues that task theories that assume consistent processing throughout a test will be insufficient.

We turn next to an analysis of individual differences in the complex of processing activities involved in learning from real instruction.

Analyses of Learning Activities.   This part of our research was a study conducted in collaboration with Keith Wescourt. It sought to trace aptitude differences through the individual differences in learning activities observable during 15 hours of instruction in a course on computer programming. The course of instruction chosen for use in this investigation was the BASIC Instructional Program (BIP), a computerized short course available at Stanford University (see Barr, Beard, & Atkinson, 1975; Wescourt, Beard, Gould, & Barr, 1977). Computerized instruction provides a unique setting in which to study such issues, because it permits detailed multivariate measurement of accumulative learning activities over an extended period.

Subjects were 28 Stanford undergraduates on whom reference aptitude test scores were available. The posttest provided an ultimate measure of learning outcome, but there were several intermediate measures that could be used to summarize learning differences. Since BIP teaches a large collection of specific programming skills, one can obtain acquisition curves for each learner across the sequence of programming tasks BIP presents. Thus total number of skills acquired in 15 hours on BIP is an outcome measure, and one can also obtain learning parameter scores from several kinds of skill acquisition curves. Figure 2.8 shows one type of curve (skills acquired as a function of number of tasks seen) for each of four subjects and indicates three curve parameters that were extracted as summary learning scores for each subject; these were slope, intercept, and standard error (to reflect gross deviation from linearity). Finally, BIP accumulates a record of each learner's activities in interaction with the program. Because BIP attempts to adapt to each student, it selects new tasks to present to

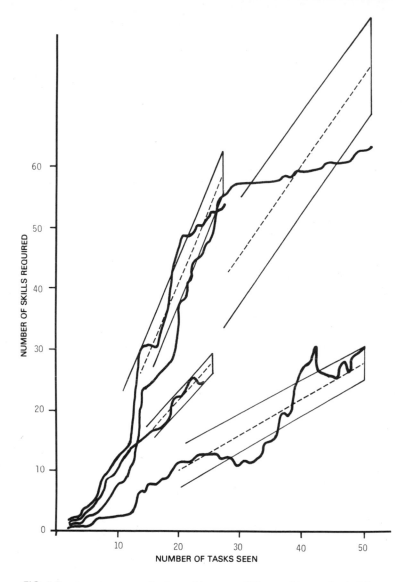

FIG. 2.8.   Learning curves for four subjects over 15 hours of instruction in BIP.
Regression slope and standard error serve as parameter measures for each subject.

each learner based on his or her learning history. It also offers various aids that
can be called upon by the learner. Variables showing the proportion of tasks
completed successfully, the amount of difficulty or lack of understanding each
learner reports, frequencies of asking for hints, asking for a model or other
representation of the program the learner is trying to write, or of quitting the task

under various conditions are all available from the BIP protocols after instruction is completed.

Figure 2.9 is a first attempt at a path diagram showing some of the relations of aptitude measures to learning activities, learning curve summary, and learning outcome variables. It is a selection from a more complicated network. Three aptitude factors are shown on the left. In addition to those defined earlier, G_f and G_c, included here also is a personality factor defined from the California Psychological Inventory: Independence-Flexibility (*I-F*). There is also a specific aptitude test for computer programming that is called diagraming (*D*). Arrows indicate correlations that are noteworthy ($r_{.05} = .37$). Several significant findings deserve mention.

First, learning curve and outcome measures are strongly predicted by two aptitude factors and these two only. One is G_f (or G_{fv}), the factor score reflecting fluid analytic reasoning and visualization, defined by tests such as Raven and paper folding. The diagraming test also seems to reflect this kind of ability. Note that crystallized ability G_c appears not to relate importantly to learning in this situation. BIP is a novel instructional situation in which general prior scholastic ability may not be so relevant as the short-term adaptive facility represented by G_f. Restriction of range on G_c in this college sample seems not to explain its low correlations.

The other factor offering prediction is a personality questionnaire variable reflecting self-reported flexibility and independence in academic work. This suggests that aptitude for learning, at least in this situation, combines aspects of ability and personal style differences.

These general factors, and some more specific factors not in Fig. 2.9, show correlation not only with learning summary and outcome variables but also with variables reflecting individual differences in learning activities during program performance. We have not yet completed our analysis of these activity variables; there are other more detailed process variables yet to be pulled from the BIP protocols. And the correlation and regression analyses that relate aptitude, learning summary, and activity variables will need to be sharpened. But it is notable at this stage that aptitude test scores obtained in February 1976 can predict how much help learners will ask for or how many times they will quit a task during instruction a year and a half later, in June 1977.

Status Categories

Categorical variables of the sort used by Loftus and Loftus are proxies for aptitude differences, and comparison of aptitude measures among status groups of this sort is an age-old method of construct validation. A good modern example of the value of such work for theoretical purposes is the summary by Witkin, Moore, Goodenough, and Cox (1977) of differences on field independence-dependence measures among various occupational and vocational choice groups.

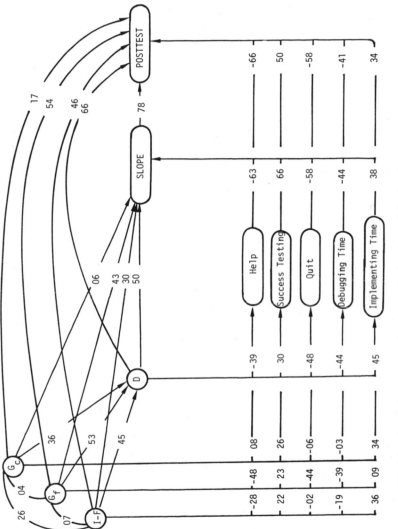

FIG 2.9. Correlations among selected aptitude, learning activity, learning summary, and outcome measures for the **BIP** course. $N = 28$. Decimals omitted.

Only one point need be added here. In educational and military training settings, naturally occurring aptitude and performance outcome differences are regularly indexed by such categorical variables. Yet little use is made of these in cognitive psychological research in these settings. Task analyses aimed at performance process differences and conducted to allow within- and between-categorical-group comparisons should provide a powerful means of connecting cognitive process models of individual differences directly to real-world criteria.

TOWARD A THEORY OF APTITUDE

It is far too early to talk seriously about a theory of aptitude. But it seems not premature to combine hypotheses arising from the present research together with some old theorizing by Ferguson (1954, 1956) and Cattell (1963, 1971) to provide a framework for theory-oriented research. This can be only briefly summarized here but is elaborated further elsewhere (Snow, 1978b).

Ferguson argued that abilities develop through experience as transfer functions. The more an ability is exercised, the more it develops; this exercise benefits related abilities by transfer processes, so that the more similar two abilities are, the stronger the transfer relation between them. Conversely, the more similar two tasks are, the stronger their transfer relation and the more highly correlated the resulting abilities. Thus, to refer back to Fig. 2.2, when the abilities involved in performance on the Terman analogies test are exercised, abilities required by the Raven matrices are benefited more than are the abilities involved in digit span, etc. There is some evidence to support this notion, though it comes from research on psychomotor abilities (Heinonen, 1962). Over long learning experience, Ferguson expected that constellations of ability would appear as a result of these transfer functions, and we can think of G_f, G_c, and G_v (and the strong central relations between them represented by G, or Spearman's g) as resulting from such transfer functions.

Now take the major cognitive aptitude factors in turn. G_c, crystallized ability, would be interpreted by Cattell (and by Horn, 1976) as representing a coalescence or organization of prior knowledge and educational experience into functional cognitive systems for retrieval and skilled application to aid further learning in future educational situations. Because this kind of ability is thought to be accumulated and structured across years of experience in conventional schooling, it is likely to be a stable individual difference, relatively unmodifiable by short-term training interventions and applicable as aptitude in future educational settings similar in instructional demand to those in which these crystallized assemblies have been useful in the past.

Thus, G_c measures are often better predictors of learning outcome in conventional educational settings than are G_f measures, because the crystallized assemblies represented by G_c are products of past educational settings similar in processing demands to future educational settings. Olson (1974) has argued that "intelligence is skill in a medium." My variation on that theme would be that G_c aptitude is skill in the conventional school medium.

As in the IPI study reported earlier and in many other studies, the relation of G_c to learning outcome is strongest in the conventional instructional treatments. This is consistent with much ATI research (Snow, 1977b). When such an instructional treatment is modified to reduce the need for conventional assembly and control processes, as IPI attempts to do, then the relation of G_c to learning outcome goes down, and ATI appears. The effect is to help those learners whose prior educational experience has not resulted in strong development of conventional learning skills while creating a situation in which those who *have* developed strong conventional learning abilities are less able to apply them. IPI does not change the medium of instruction qualitatively, but it structures and segments the presentation to avoid some of the medium-related skills.

What then is G_f? Cattell and Horn see it as facility in reasoning, particularly where adaptation to new situations is required and where, therefore, G_c skills are of no particular advantage. If this view is correct, we should expect G_f to relate to learning outcome under instructional conditions that are in some sense new, unlike those that the individual learner has faced in the past. Ability to apply previously crystallized learning skills (G_c) would not be relevant here, but ability to adapt to new kinds of learning or performance requirements (G_f) would be relevant.

What constitutes a "new" learning situation is not really clear. But one can predict that as an instructional situation involves combinations of new technology (e.g., computerized instruction, or television), new symbol systems (e.g., computer graphics or artistic expressions), new content (e.g., topological mathematics or astrophysics), and/or new contexts (e.g., independent learning, collaborative teamwork in simulation games), G_f should become more important and G_c less important. Thus, the BIP course was a novel experience for students, and adapting to it seems to have required G_f.

G_f and G_v are separable at times, with some measures, in some populations. Often, however, the close correlation between measures from each constellation suggests that some individuals, or all individuals sometimes, use G_f processes to perform G_v tasks. Again, it may be individual differences in the novel assembly and control of spatial processing that underlie this correlation, rather than a basic relation between fluid-analytic and spatial performance processes.

Process theories of these aptitudes, the distinctions between them, their development through formal and informal learning experience, and their respective relations to new learning in different instructional situations are a basic need in cognitive and instructional psychology. These theories will need to account not only for individual differences in performance processes but also for the assembly and control processes that organize and maintain the performance: It may be these aspects of aptitude that account for relations among aptitude tests and their persistent relation to learning outcomes.

TOWARD ADAPTIVE INSTRUCTION

The need for adaptation to individual differences among learners is a problem now at center stage in instructional psychology (Glaser, 1977). There are proposals that broadly different types of instruction should be designed to fit students with differing aptitude patterns. This form of adaptation relies on aptitude measures taken prior to instruction and seeks to capitalize on ATI; it has been termed *macroadaptation* (Cronbach & Snow, 1977). Another form, termed *microadaptation* by contrast, arises from research on the continuing development of interactive computer-based instruction.

The data maintenance capability and flexibility of the computer allows new generations of computer-based instruction increasingly to use "response-sensitive" instructional strategies (Atkinson, 1972). Potentially, the computer can be made to monitor the sequence and pattern of learner responses, adjust subsequent instruction accordingly, and thus optimize each individual student's trajectory over an entire course (Suppes, 1977).

The two forms of adaptation can be made complementary. One can imagine several broad streams of instruction geared to major differences in student aptitudes, with response-sensitive decisions made along the way in each. Further, information on prior aptitudes might be used to extra advantage in the minute-to-minute decisions of the response-sensitive computer, and the detailed learning history accumulated by the computer on one instructional topic might be joined with other sources of aptitude process information in planning the molar instructional units to come. To date, however, research concentrating on broad aptitude dimensions has not included detailed analyses of individual differences in learning progress occurring in the interim between aptitude and outcome measures. Conversely, research on computerized instruction has been content to base adaptive decisions only on the individualized learning histories built up during the specific instructional exercise at hand.

If the research approach suggested here can succeed in connecting aptitudes understood as process differences to learning activities in instruction, and then to learning outcome, it will also provide a data base for effective combination of macroadaptive and microadaptive instructional design.

ACKNOWLEDGMENTS

The research reported herein was sponsored by the Personnel and Training Research Program, Office of Naval Research, and Advanced Research Projects Agency under Contract No. N00014-75-C-0882. The views and conclusions contained in this document are those of the author and should not be interpreted as necessarily representing the official policies, either expressed or implied, of the Office of Naval Research, the Advanced Research Projects Office, or the U.S. Government.

Much of the work described in this chapter was conducted with the assistance of David Coffing, Janet Freitas, Randi Kutnewski, Andrea Lash, David Lohman, Brachia Marshalek, Dan Webb, Noreen Webb, and Elanna Yalow.

REFERENCES

Allison, R. B. *Learning parameters and human abilities* (NR 151-113). Unpublished report, Educational Testing Service, 1960.

Atkinson, R. C. Ingredients for a theory of instruction. *American Psychologist,* 1972, *27,* 921-931.

Barr, A., Beard, M., & Atkinson, R. *The computer as a tutorial laboratory: The Stanford BIP project* (Tech. Rep. No. 260). Stanford, Calif.: Stanford University, Institute for Mathematical Studies in the Social Sciences, 1975.

Brown, W. F., & Holtzman, W. H. *Survey of study habits and attitudes, Form C.* New York: The Psychological Corporation, 1966.

Carroll, J. B. Psychometric tests as cognitive tasks: A new "structure of intellect." In L. Resnick (Ed.), *The nature of intelligence.* Hillsdale, N.J.: Lawrence Erlbaum Associates, 1976.

Cattell, R. B. Theory of fluid and crystallized intelligence: A critical experiment. *Journal of Educational Psychology,* 1963, *54,* 1-22.

Cattell, R. B. *Abilities: Their structure, growth, and action.* Boston: Houghton Mifflin, 1971.

Chiang, A., & Atkinson, R. C. Individual differences and interrelationships among a select set of cognitive skills. *Memory & Cognition,* 1976, *4,* 661-672.

Craik, F. I. M., & Tulving, E. Depth of processing and the retention of words in episodic memory. *Journal of Experimental Psychology: General,* 1975, *104,* 268-294.

Crist-Whitzel, J. L, & Hawley-Winne, B. J. *Individual differences and mathematics achievement: An investigation of aptitude-treatment interactions in an evaluation of three instructional approaches.* Paper presented at the meeting of the American Educational Research Association, San Francisco, April 1976.

Cronbach, L. J. *Essentials of psychological testing* (3rd ed.). New York: Harper, 1970.

Cronbach, L. J., & Snow, R. E. *Aptitudes and instructional methods: A handbook for research on interactions.* New York: Irvington, 1977.

Ferguson, G. A. On learning and human ability. *Canadian Journal of Psychology,* 1954, *8,* 95-112.

Ferguson, G. A. On transfer and the abilities of man. *Canadian Journal of Psychology,* 1956, *10,* 121-131.

French, J. W. The relationship of problem-solving styles to the factor composition of tests. *Educational and Psychological Measurement,* 1965, *25,* 9-28.

French, J. W., Ekstrom, R., & Price, L. Kit of reference tests for cognitive factors. Princeton, N.J.: Educational Testing Service, 1963.

Glaser, R. Some implications of previous work on learning and individual differences. In R. M. Gagné (Ed.), *Learning and individual differences.* Columbus, Ohio: Merrill, 1967.

Glaser, R. Individuals and learning: The new aptitudes. *Educational Researcher,* 1972, *1,* 5-12.

Glaser, R. *Adaptive education: Individual diversity and learning.* New York: Holt, Rinehart & Winston. 1977.

Gulliksen, H. Measurement of learning and mental abilities. *Psychometrika,* 1961, *26,* 93-107.

Guttman, L. The structure of relations among intelligence tests. *Proceedings, 1964 Invitational Conference on Testing Problems.* Princeton, N.J.; Educational Testing Service, 1965.

Heinonen, V. A. A factor analytic study of transfer of training. *Scandinavian Journal of Psychology,* 1962, *3,* 177-188.

Horn, J. L. Human abilities: A review of research and theory in the early 1970s. *Annual Review of Psychology,* 1976, *27,* 437-485.

Hunt, D. E., & Sullivan, E. V. *Between psychology and education.* Hinsdale, Ill.: Dryden, 1974.

Hunt, E., Frost, N., & Lunneborg, C. Individual differences in cognition: A new approach to intelligence. In G. H. Bower (Ed.), *Psychology of learning and motivation* (Vol. VII). New York: Academic Press, 1973.

Jensen, A. R. Hierarchical theories of mental ability. In W. B. Dockrell (Ed.), *On intelligence.* Toronto, Canada: The Ontario Institute for Studies in Education, 1970.

Just, M. A., & Carpenter, P. A. Eye fixations and cognitive processes. *Cognitive Psychology,* 1976, *8,* 441–480.

Kogan, N. *Cognitive styles in infancy and early childhood.* Hillsdale, N.J.: Lawrence Erlbaum Associates, 1976.

Lenning, O. T. *Predictive validity of the ACT tests at selective colleges* (ACT Research Rep. No. 69). Iowa City: American College Testing Program, Research and Development Division, 1975.

Loftus, E. F., & Loftus, G. R. Changes in memory structure and retrieval over the course of instruction. *Journal of Educational Psychology,* 1974, *66,* 315–318.

Loftus, G. R., & Loftus, E. F. *Human memory: The processing of information.* Hillsdale, N.J.: Lawrence Erlbaum Associates, 1976.

Lohman, D. *Eye movement differences reflecting aptitude processes.* Paper presented at a symposium entitled "Research on Aptitude Processes," American Psychological Association Convention, San Francisco, August 1977.

Lohman, D. Spatial abilities: Individual differences and information processing. (Tech. Rep. No. 8). Stanford Calif.: Stanford University, School of Education, Aptitude Research Project, September 1978.

Marshalek, B. *The complexity dimension in the Radex and Hierarchical models of intelligence.* Paper presented at a symposium entitled "Research on Aptitude Processes," American Psychological Association Convention, San Francisco, August 1977.

Newell, A., & Simon, H. A. *Human problem solving.* Englewood Cliffs, N.J.: Prentice-Hall, 1972.

Olson, D. R. (Ed.) Media and symbols: The forms of expression, communication, and education. *The Seventy-third Yearbook of the National Society for the Study of Education.* Chicago: University of Chicago Press, 1974.

Rumelhart, D. E., & Norman, D. A. *Accretion, tuning, and restructuring: Three modes of learning* (Rep. No. 7602). San Diego: University of California, Center for Human Information Processing, August 1976.

Rutkowski, K., & Domino, G. Interrelationship of study skills and personality variables in college students. *Journal of Educational Psychology,* 1975, *67,* 784–789.

Sharps, R. *A study of interactions between fluid and crystallized abilities and two methods of teaching reading and arithmetic.* Unpublished doctoral dissertation, The Pennsylvania State University, 1973.

Simon, H. A. Identifying basic abilities underlying intelligent performance of complex tasks. In L. B. Resnick (Ed.), *The nature of human intelligence.* Hillsdale, N.J.: Lawrence Erlbaum Associates, 1976.

Snow, R. E. *An overview of current research on aptitude processes.* Paper presented at a symposium entitled "Research on Aptitude Processes," American Psychological Association Convention, San Francisco, August 1977. (a)

Snow, R. E. Research on aptitudes: A progress report. In L. S. Shulman (Ed.), *Review of research in education,* (Vol. 4). Itasca, Ill.: Peacock, 1977. (b)

Snow, R. E. Theory and method for research on aptitude processes: A prospectus. *Intelligence: A Multidisciplinary Journal,* 1978, *2,* 225–278. (a)

Snow, R. E. *Toward a theory of aptitude.* Invited address, Division C, American Educational Research Association, Toronto, March 1978. (b)

Snow, R. E., Lohman, D. F., Marshalek, B., Yalow, E., & Webb, N. *Correlational analyses of reference aptitude constructs* (Tech. Rep. No. 5). Stanford, Calif.: Stanford University, School of Education, Aptitude Research Project, September 1977.

Snow, R. E., Lohman, D. F., Marshalek, B., Yalow, E., & Webb, N. *Aptitude-process relations: Analyses of individual differences in eyemovement records and instrospective reports* (Tech. Rep. No. 11). Stanford, Calif.: Stanford University, School of Education, Aptitude Research Project, in preparation.

Stake, R. E. Learning parameters, aptitudes, and achievements. *Psychometric Monographs,* 1960, No. 9.

Sternberg, R. J. *Intelligence, information processing, and analogical reasoning: The componential analysis of human abilities.* Hillsdale, N.J.: Lawrence Erlbaum Associates, 1977.

Suppes, P. *Some global models of learning and performance.* Paper presented at the annual meeting of the American Psychological Association, San Francisco, August 1977.

Vernon, P. E. Ability factors and environmental influences. *American Psychologist,* 1965, *20,* 723–733.

Wescourt, K. T., Beard, M., Gould, L., & Barr, A. *Knowledge-based CAI: CINs for individualized curriculum sequencing* (Tech. Rep. No. 290) (Psychology and Education Series). Stanford, Calif.: Institute for Mathematical Studies in the Social Sciences, October 3, 1977.

Witkin, H. A. Cognitive style in academic performance and in teacher–student relations. In S. Messick (Ed.), *Individuality in learning.* San Francisco: Jossey-Bass, 1976.

Witkin, H. A., Moore, C. A., Goodenough, D. R., & Cox, P. W. Field-dependent and field-independent cognitive styles and their educational implications. *Review of Educational Research,* 1977, *47,* 1–64.

Woodrow, H. The ability to learn. *Psychological Review,* 1946, *53,* 147–158.

Yalow, E., & Webb, N. *Introspective strategy differences reflecting aptitude processes.* Paper presented at a symposium entitled "Research on Aptitude Processes," American Psychological Association Convention, San Francisco, August 1977.

3 Information-Processing Abilities

Andrew M. Rose
American Institutes for Research

INTRODUCTION

In essence, the "information-processing approach" is a general theoretic framework within which it is possible to study cognitive performance. The central assumption of this approach is that a number of operations or processing stages occur between a stimulus and a response. The stimulus presentation initiates a sequence of processing stages. Each stage operates on the information available to it. These operations transform the information in some manner; furthermore, these operations take a measurable amount of time. The output of each processing stage is in the form of transformed information, and this new information is the input to the succeeding stage. Typically, two theoretical components are postulated in information-processing analyses: a structural component, which describes or defines the nature of the information at a particular processing stage; and a functional component, which describes the operations of a stage.

These components are usually described as analogues to computer system structures. For example, structural concepts such as short-term sensory storage, short-term and long-term memory, and rehearsal buffers are common in the literature, as are information-processing functions such as encoding, translating, decoding, and so on. These concepts are used to formulate information-processing models of tasks. Typically, tasks are represented by sequential flow diagrams, in which blocks represent component structures and processes. The major concerns of research are to identify these components and to determine how they operate.

The range of tasks that have been modeled by researchers varies from fairly simple cognitive skills like deciding whether or not two visually presented letters are the same or different, to such complex activities as reading text and solving algebra word problems. As one might expect, the component processes employed by these models likewise span a wide range. My discussion focuses on a description of these various processes, the tasks that they are purported to explain, and other practical or applied functions that an analysis of component processes might serve.

Approximately ten years ago (at the first conference on this topic), Melton (1967) made the following comments with respect to theoretical process variables and individual differences:

> We have at this time no general theory of human learning and performance. Therefore, we have no necessary and sufficient list of process constructs or variables that can serve as the foci of individual-differences research. . . . The process concepts to be examined will depend on the level of analysis that our theoretical-experimental approach has achieved and on the level of analysis and range of task variables that the theoretical model attempts to encompass [p. 242].

During the past decade, there have been major analytical and methodological advances in approaches to the study of component processes. We are all familiar with most of these developments: the rediscovery of Donders and the subtraction method logic, the additive-factor method, mathematical modeling, computer simulation, and so on. We are currently experiencing the development of what might be called second-generation methodologies—techniques that increase the power of previous methods as well as expand the scope of potential applications. Included in this group are such things as Sternberg's (1978) componential analysis, Calfee's (1976) generalization of the additive-factor method, and Frederiksen's (1978) extension of confirmatory maximum-likelihood factor analysis. Fortunately, this conference includes discussion of these advances firsthand, so I do not need to summarize them. My purpose in mentioning these techniques is to indicate that although substantial methodological work remains to be done, these developments have greatly extended our capabilities for the discovery and analysis of component processes. Previous restrictions, such as the limitation of applications of the additive-factor method to single-variable designs, have been lifted. We now possess the tools to improve greatly the quality and testability of our theories and models.

In his summary remarks, Melton also commented on the notion of a taxonomy of processes. Other researchers, especially those interested in individual differences, have commented on the need for deriving a relatively small collection of information-processing abilities that could account for performance on a wide variety of tasks. Such a taxonomy or catalog could serve many important functions, both for theory and for practical applications. It should be possible, for example, to reconcile theoretical differences among various "schools of

thought'' through the use of a common set of constructs. Carroll's (1976) characterization of a set of factor analytically derived abilities in terms of cognitive
processes is a case in point. Other examples are Melton's process models of
''classic'' S–R association learning paradigms and Hunt's (1978; Lansman,
1978) work on individual differences and memory. On an applied level, a small
set of theory-based information-processing abilities would be particularly useful
for assessment purposes.

My own current ONR-funded research program deals with the development
and validation of a test battery of information-processing tasks. This chapter
describes the contents of the battery as it presently stands. The battery is designed
to be used as an assessment device for performance evaluation in the context of
personnel management. Another application of this type of test battery includes
assessing the effects of unusual environments on cognitive performance. For
example, we used some of the tasks in a study of the effects of hypoxia and of the
impact of a drug designed to preadapt subjects to high altitudes. We are also
using some of these tasks to evaluate the effects of shipboard motion. Although
the literature is not particularly large, there are a few other research programs
involved specifically with the analyses of individual differences in information
processing, including Hunt's (1978) program at Washington and Keele and
Hawkins' (Hawkins, Church, & de Lemos, 1978; Keele, Neill, & de Lemos,
1978) work at Oregon, among others. Probably the heaviest concentration of
research on component processes is in the areas of reading and instruction.

Given that a compendium of component processes would be useful, what
should this list look like, and how should it be constructed? There are several
properties that each candidate process should possess: Each should be reliably
and independently measurable; each should be generalizable to a wide variety of
tasks; and the list should be parsimonious, limited to the fewest number of
independent components that could meaningfully describe performance in the
widest variety of tasks. Most importantly, these components must have construct
validity; the processes and operations represented are theorized to be ''real'' in
the sense that they are discrete and take measurable amounts of time. Each
construct must have a history of empirical and theoretical support, and there must
be a well-specified rationale for the measurement technique employed. The idea
of construct validity is stressed here because the integrity of an information-
processing approach rests on its underlying theories and models. Furthermore,
the techniques used to identify and isolate component processes are principal
exemplars of the important notion of converging operations.

There are several ways by which a list of information-processing structures
and functions can be constructed. One method is by popular acclaim. Recently,
in an extensive review of the information-processing literature, I kept an informal
tally of the most popular concepts—the ones that were most frequently cited,
discussed, and experimentally explored. I found good structural agreement with
Bower's (1975) ''modal'' summary of processing stages. Most general models of

the human cognitive system include a short-term sensory storage or buffer component; a memory component consisting of two or three subsystems distinguished by relative time duration of information storage—short-term, intermediate-term or working memory, and long-term storage; a response selection or generation component; and a central or executive processor. On the other hand, there is much less unanimity in the literature with regard to component functions, other than those functions whose identity is derived from the corresponding structural component (for example, storage and retrieval operations).

Another approach that has been taken to compiling a list of component processes is to define arbitrarily a domain of tasks and to determine analytically or empirically the necessary and sufficient operations for modeling all the tasks in that domain. An excellent example of this approach is provided by Carroll's (1976) work on the characterization of a set of factor analytically derived abilities in terms of cognitive processes. His domain included psychometric tests from the French, Ekstrom, and Price (1963) Kit of Reference Tests for Cognitive Factors. This set was presumed to contain good marker tests for 24 different factors. Carroll used as his structural components Hunt's distributive memory model, which contains short-term sensory stores; a short-term, an intermediate-term, and a long-term memory; and a conscious memory processor or executive. This system was extended by incorporating a production system that controls the information flow. The information-processing functions are, in Carroll's (1976) terminology, *operations,* which are defined as "control processes that are explicitly specified, or implied, in the task instructions . . . and that must be performed if the task is to be successfully completed [p. 42]." These operations are of three types: attentional, memorial, and executive. Of particular interest are the latter two, which he further subdivided as follows: There are three kinds of memorial operations—storing, searching, and retrieving. Executive operations are exemplified by such things as simple judgments of stimulus attributes such as to reveal identity, similarity, or comparison between two stimuli; manipulations of memorial contents, such as "mentally rotating" a visuospatial configuration; and information transformations that produce "new" elements from combinations, reductions, etc., of old elements. In all, 20 different operations and strategies were derived iteratively.

Another domain of tasks that have been analyzed is that involved in reading text—for example, in the types of operations hypothesized in Frederiksen's component skills model of reading. His model consists of four major processes: visual feature extraction, perceptual encoding, decoding, and lexical access. The latter three have subcomponents. One very attractive feature of this model is that each component fits Calfee's experimental design requirements for an independently isolable process; that is, each component has associated with it a factor set and a measure set.

A factor set consists of one or more independent variables, variation in which is presumed to influence the corresponding process and that process only. A measure set consists of one or more dependent variables, each of which reflects the operation of the corresponding process and that process only. Calfee (1976) points out that:

> For a process model to serve any useful purpose theoretically or practically, we ought to be able to specify the input–output features of each processing state—what sorts of variables affect the operation of each stage, and how can the operation of each stage be measured? If every factor interacts with every other factor, and if we have no clear-cut way of measuring the underlying processes, so that every measure correlates with every other measure, we have gained little understanding no matter how elaborate our flow charts [p. 26].

Given this property of his reading model, Frederiksen has been able to conduct empirical investigations of his hypotheses. Another domain of tasks that have been analyzed and evaluated in terms of component processes is the set of complex skills studied by Simon (1978). He determined the components necessary for a computer program to perform six tasks: the extrapolation of sequential matters such as numbers or letter sequences, the translation and solution of algebra word problems, the Tower of Hanoi puzzle, perception in chess, understanding task instructions, and spelling English words. As Simon points out, the use of computer modeling has a built-in empirical test—namely, a running program.

The last domain that I discuss is a set of tasks I have investigated as part of my current test battery development project. This set of tasks was gleaned from the information-processing literature as representatives of well-understood and empirically studied experimental paradigms. These tasks were selected with several criteria in mind:

1. The information-processing construct or concept had to have a history of empirical and/or theoretical support. The interest here was in constructs that had been developed over a period of time and in research paradigms that had been replicated under a variety of conditions. This criterion was relaxed only in instances where a paradigm was considered to be a "classic" measure of a particular construct but where no evidence of replication could be found in the literature.

2. There had to be an adequate theoretical rationale for the paradigm actually measuring the particular information-processing construct that it was intended to measure. The focus was on construct validity rather than theoretical sophistication. Studies concerned primarily with the development of mathematical models for certain operations, with the task itself of only ancillary relevance, were excluded from further consideration.

3. The experimental task itself had to be one that was adaptable to a paper-and-pencil format, to a small digital computer, or to some other form that could easily be administered in a group setting.

4. Enough performance data had to be available so that preliminary estimates could be made regarding the extent of individual variation expected for the task.

OPERATIONS

In general, all tasks included in the battery can be described as a series of operations, where an operation is defined following Carroll (1976). Each task can be specified by some combination of eight operations. These operations are now described:

Encoding: the operation by which information is input into the system, including the initial set of processes that converts the physical stimulus to a form that is "appropriate" for the task. Different task demands may require different levels of analysis of the stimulus. Posner (1969) has called this dimension "abstraction"—the process by which different types of information about the stimulus are extracted—in other words, the level of stimulus analysis demanded by the task. For example, a visual search task might require only that the subject extract physical or structural information about the stimulus; a memory search task might require the extraction of name information; and a semantic search task might necessitate semantic or "meaning" information.

Constructing: the operation by which new information structures are generated from information already in the system. This is what Neisser (1967) and others have called "synthesis"; in the present context, we can limit the use to situations where additional features of the stimuli, beyond those initially encoded, must be abstracted.

Transforming: the operation by which a given information structure is converted into an equivalent structure necessary for task performance. In contrast to constructing, transformations do not involve any new information abstraction; rather, this operation requires the application of some stored rules to the information structure already present.

Storing: the operation by which new information is incorporated into existing information structures while its entire content is retained.

Retrieving: the operation by which previously stored information is made available to the processing system.

Searching: the operation by which an information structure is examined for the presence or absence of one or more properties. The information structure examined may be one already in the processing system or one external to it (e.g., a visual array).

Comparing: the operation by which two information structures (again, either internal or external to the processing system) are judged to be the same or different. The information structures need not both be physical entities (as in the comparison of two objects); likewise, a physical entity can be compared to a stored representation or description in order to determine identity.

Responding: the operation by which the appropriate (motor) action is selected and executed. In many information-processing investigations, the response operation is itself the object of study. Various microprocesses have been uncovered; however, the current study was designed to minimize performance variability due to differential response demands of the tasks.

Each of the eight tasks included in the present battery is described next, first in terminology employed by the particular investigators, and second as a function of some of the operations just elucidated. These latter descriptions do not, of course, represent the original authors' conceptions of the paradigms.

TASK DESCRIPTIONS[1]

Letter Classification (Posner Task)

The process of matching or recognition at various levels of stimulus complexity is basic to most cognitive tasks. Posner and Mitchell (1967) developed an experimental paradigm that "provides an opportunity to observe processing at different levels within the experiment [p. 393]." In their task, the subject was shown pairs of letters and had to decide whether the letters were the same or different. The independent variable was the instruction upon which the subject was told to make the classification. The instructions used to define "same" were:

1. Physical identity (e.g., the pair AA is to be classified as "same" whereas AB is "different"); or
2. Name identity (e.g., Aa is "same," Ab is "different"); or
3. Category or rule identity (e.g., if the rule is one of letter category, a stimulus pair is "same" if both members are vowels or if both members are consonants, such as AE or BD).

The typical findings were that the classification reaction times (RTs) increased as the instructions varied in the foregoing order. The ordinal relationships among these processing "nodes" (and the time differences between them) were quite reliable and have been demonstrated to generalize to other stimuli (e.g., numbers, Gibson figures). It also has been shown that these types of classifications

---

[1]For ease of discussion, a shortened label for each of these tasks is used—namely, the principal author's name. Thus, the letter classification task is addressed as the Posner task, etc.

are serial (i.e., subjects derive the names of the letters before proceeding to analyze whether they are both vowels or both consonants).

The procedure in the current project used the three Posner and Mitchell experimental conditions. The category identity condition was modified slightly in that the vowel category and the consonant category were tested conjointly. In the Posner and Mitchell study, the two categories were tested in separate blocks of trials.

In terms of our operations, the three conditions all involve an initial encoding of letters. In the physical match case, the subject then compares the representations of the letter patterns and finally selects and executes the appropriate response. The name case requires an additional operation of retrieval of "name" information from long-term memory (LTM). Subjects then compare the letter names. In the rule condition, experimental evidence indicates that subjects retrieve name information prior to retrieving categorical information (i.e., subjects categorize *names* of letters as vowels or consonants rather than the physical patterns). They then compare the representations of the letter categories.

Lexical Decision Making (Meyer Task)

Rubenstein, Garfield, and Millikan (1970) developed a procedure designed to investigate the processes by which humans can recognize written words. On each trial in their paradigm, a string of letters was presented, and the subject had to judge whether it was an English word or nonword. Performance on this lexical decision task depended on operations that mediated the recognition of printed words in various contexts—that is, graphemic and/or phonemic encoding, followed by accessing of lexical memory. Various investigators have argued that printed words are recognized directly from visual representations (graphemes), whereas others have claimed that recognition is mediated by a phonological (phonemic) representation.

The Rubenstein et al. procedure has been modified by Meyer (e.g., Meyer, Schvaneveldt, & Ruddy, 1974) in order to separate the effects of graphemic and phonemic factors on recognition. As in the Rubenstein et al. experiments, subjects were presented with two strings of letters, displayed successively, on each trial. Reaction time (RT) was measured for each string separately. The critical variables were the graphemic and phonemic relations within the pairs of words. For example, the words could be both graphemically and phonemically similar (e.g., *bribe–tribe*), graphemically similar but phonemically dissimilar because they do not rhyme (e.g., *couch–touch*), and so on. Meyer et al. formulated and tested various hypotheses concerning the relative speed of recognition for word pairs; for example, it was found that graphemic similarity alone inhibited performance (e.g., in the pair *couch–touch*, RT to *touch* was slower than predicted from baseline control conditions). In contrast, phonemic as well as graphemic similarity facilitated recognition (e.g., in the pair *bribe–tribe,* RT to *tribe* was faster than to the second word of graphemically and phonemically dissimilar word pairs).

The Meyer et al. paradigm was modified in the present study to include a category of phonemically similar but graphemically dissimilar word pairs (e.g., *laugh–half*).

In terms of operations, both the "word" and "nonword" stimulus presentations require the subject to encode a letter string; the "mediation" hypothesis can be formulated as the (optional) construction of a phonemic or graphemic representation. Presumably, this paradigm will identify those subjects who have a propensity for one construction or the other. Following this construction, both conditions require the search of LTM for a match. When a match is found (in the word case), subjects select and execute the appropriate response. If a match is not found (in the nonword case), it is hypothesized that subjects conduct a further search—this time, of the lexical rules in LTM in order to decide whether or not a letter string is an acceptable construction. Following this search, subjects select and execute the appropriate response.

Graphemic and Phonemic Analysis (Baron Task)

Baron (1973; Baron & McKillop, 1975) has developed a procedure for the study of individual differences in the speed of phonemic (acoustical) and graphemic (visual) analysis of printed information (e.g., sentences or phrases). He argued that lexical memory can be accessed through both visual and phonological representations of a printed word; also, he argued that a visual analysis is the faster of the two for normal readers. The basic paradigm used in his studies was to "force" subjects to analyze phrases visually and phonologically. More specifically, he had subjects decide whether various printed phrases made sense or were nonsense. Three conditions were required. In the first condition, two kinds of phrases were used: sense (S) phrases, and those that *sounded* sensible because of a homophone (e.g., *it's knot so*) but *looked* like nonsense (called H phrases). In this first condition (SH), subjects were instructed to classify a phrase as making sense or nonsense on the basis of its *appearance* (so that H phrases were judged as nonsense). The second condition used H phrases and true nonsense (N) phrases (e.g., *new I can't*). In this second condition (HN), subjects were instructed to classify the phrases on the basis of how they *sounded,* so that H phrases were judged as making sense. The third condition used S and N phrases. In this third condition (SN), subjects were free to choose whatever basis they preferred for making S and N judgments. The basic analysis was to determine which of the first two conditions better predicted the third condition. For example, if a particular subject was a "visual" encoder, he should have had "problems" with the HN condition, and his SH performance should have been a good predictor of SN performance. The results (as reported in Baron & McKillop, 1975) indicated the existence of reliable and predictable individual differences: Some subjects were "visual," others "phonemic" encoders.

The procedure in the current study used Baron's three conditions. However, we obtained RTs on a trial-by-trial basis rather than after a trial block.

In terms of operations, all three conditions (SH, HN, and SN) require the subjects to encode semantic phrases. Following this encoding, the different conditions force subjects to construct either visual or acoustic representations of each phrase: The SH condition needs a visual representation, the HN condition needs an acoustic representation, and the SN requires either an acoustic or a visual representation. Following this construction, subjects must search LTM for what we call "phrase rules"—that set of information or rules that enables them to decide whether or not a phrase meets acceptable language structure rules. In all conditions, subjects then select and execute the appropriate response.

Short-Term Memory Scanning (Sternberg Task)

Sternberg (1967, 1969) developed an experimental paradigm to "study the ways in which information is retrieved from memory when learning and retention are essentially perfect [1969, p. 423]." The general procedure was to present a list of items for memorization that was short enough to be within the immediate memory span (typically, this "memory set" contained one to four items). Next, the subject was asked a question about the memorized list (again, typically, the question concerned the presence or absence of a stimulus from the memorized set), and his or her delay in responding to the question was measured. The particular manifestation of this general procedure used in the current work was the "item-recognition task." The stimulus ensemble consisted of the digits 1 through 9. On each trial, a set of digits was selected arbitrarily and was defined as the positive or memory set. After a short pause, a test stimulus (a single digit) was presented. The subject had to decide whether the test digit was a member of the positive set. Performance was measured in terms of RT from test-stimulus onset to response.

The typical findings were that the functions relating RT to memory set size are approximately linear and with roughly equal slopes for positive and negative responses. This outcome has been observed in many different situations, including differences in stimulus ensemble, subject group differences, and memory set sizes. The paradigm also resulted in reliable individual differences with respect to the slope and intercept parameters of the RT by memory-set-size function. The procedure in the current study was essentially a replication of Sternberg's "varied set" procedure, wherein the memory set was changed from trial to trial.

In terms of operations, we consider those events that take place starting from the presentation of the target number, because it is assumed that this paradigm does not measure any aspect of storing or retrieving information. Thus, when the target stimulus is presented, subjects must encode the number. Following this encoding (which may be visual or acoustic, depending on the nature of the representation of the memory set), subjects compare the target with the memory set. This comparison is (generally) accomplished in a serial, exhaustive manner; all items in the memory set are compared prior to the selection and execution of the appropriate response.

Memory Scanning for Words and Categories (Juola Task)

Memory search processes for word names and for categorical information about words were investigated in an experiment by Juola and Atkinson (1971). They used a short-term memory search paradigm similar to that used by Sternberg (1967) in which a short list of items was presented, followed by a single probe item that might or might not be a member of the memorized list. Two major conditions were run in the Juola and Atkinson study: a "word scan" condition and a "category scan" condition. In the first condition, the memory set consisted of from one to four different words. A positive probe stimulus was one of the words in the memorized list, whereas a negative probe was a word that did not match any of the memory set words. Thus, this condition was essentially a replication of the Sternberg paradigm, using words rather than numbers. The second condition in the Juola and Atkinson study also involved a memory set of from one to four words; however, these words were semantic category labels (e.g., *color, relative,* etc.). Positive probe stimuli were instances of one of the memory set categories (e.g., if the memory set was *color, relative,* a positive probe might be *blue*).

The results of this experiment (and a replication by Juola & McDermott, 1976) showed an increase in response time with the number of memory set items in both conditions. Furthermore, when linear functions were fit to the data, the functions had equivalent intercepts for the two conditions, but the slope was much greater for the categorization condition. The authors argued that the comparability of intercepts indicated that categorization and comparison involve many similar processes that do not depend on the size of the memory set (e.g., probe word encoding, response decision and execution), whereas a difference in slope indicated that fundamentally different types of search or comparison processes are involved in the two conditions.

The procedure used in the present research was a modification of the Juola and Atkinson task in that: (1) the same category labels were used in both conditions; (2) a relatively small set of categories was employed; (3) several exemplars of each category were used in the categorization condition; and (4) negative probes were members of other categories used as memory set items.

In terms of operations, the "word scan" condition is essentially equivalent to the Sternberg task in that it requires the encoding of the target stimulus (in this case, a word rather than a number), followed by a serial comparison of that representation with the items in the memory set, and the selection and execution of the appropriate response. The "category scan" condition requires an additional operation—the retrieval of categorical information from LTM. The pattern of their results indicates that this retrieval operation is performed each time the target word is compared to a member of the memory set, rather than just once. The results also suggest that the comparison operation is serial and self-terminating in this condition, rather than exhaustive.

Linguistic Verification (Clark Task)

Clark and Chase (1972) developed and tested a model to account for how people compare information from linguistic and pictorial sources. Their model applied to a particular type of sentence verification task in which the subject was presented with a display containing a sentence and a picture. The sentence was of the form: "star (plus) is (is not) above (below) plus (star)" and the picture was either ⚹ or ⚹. The subject had to decide whether the sentence was a true or false description of the picture. The model accounted for the latencies of the subject's judgments in terms of four operations or stages (sentence encoding, picture encoding, comparing, and responding) that were serially ordered, with component latencies that were additive. The subject formed internal representations of the sentence and the picture in terms of their underlying propositions and then performed a series of comparison operations to check the overall congruence of the representations. Clark and Chase found that verification time consisted of the addition of one or more of four parameters that accounted for 99.8% of the variance in response latencies.

The procedure in the current study was a replication of the sentence verification task as used by Clark and Chase.

The foregoing description is compatible with the operations terminology used here in that each type of sentence requires an encoding of a sentence and a picture, a comparison of those representations, and a response selection and execution. In addition, our terminology requires that two additional operations be included: constructing of what has been called a "kernel" representation, and transforming of the representation based on the particular modifiers in the various sentence types. For example, Clark and Chase argue that "below" is transformed into "not above"; similarly, they argue that negations and "truth indices" are likewise transformed, depending on the given sentence configuration.

Semantic Memory Retrieval (Collins & Quillian Task)

A topic of considerable concern to psychologists is how semantic information is stored, organized, and retrieved. Of the many paradigms used to investigate these issues, one of particular interest requires subjects to make true–false decisions about propositions (Collins & Quillian, 1969). Subjects were presented with sentences such as "A canary can fly" or "A canary is an animal" and were asked to ascertain the truth of the statement. The results of the Collins and Quillian (1969) studies using this paradigm supported a theory that semantic information is hierarchically organized in memory. Names of semantic categories are stored at the nodes of a network, along with "pointers" that indicate the relationship between that category and others (e.g., subset or superset relationships are represented as a direction to a different, lower- or higher-order node) and "pointers" to other words indicating properties of that category. Given this structural model and a number of assumptions, the authors were able to make predictions about retrieval time. These assumptions are: first, that both retrieving a property from a node and moving up a level in a hierarchy take a measurable amount of time; second, that the times for these two processes are additive wherever one step is dependent on the completion of another step; and third, that the time to retrieve a property from a node is independent of the level of the node.

Collins and Quillian (1969) reported results consistent with hypotheses generated from their model. For example, they found that subjects could confirm sentences such as "A canary is a bird" more rapidly than "A canary is an animal"; furthermore, "property" sentences such as "A canary can sing" were more quickly confirmed than "A canary has skin." The former comparison was predicted from the hypothesis that "canaries" are a subset of "birds," which are a subset of "animals"; in order to judge that canaries are animals, the subject must first access the "bird" node, then the "animal" node. Similar reasoning applies to the second example: "Singing" is a property of canaries, whereas "having skin" is a property of animals.

Subsequent research has generated other storage and retrieval models that could account for these data. However, it was felt that this paradigm was still useful as a means of generating reliable data on how subjects access a particular (restricted) information structure, especially a structure that could conceivably be organized hierarchically. Hence, the Collins and Quillian paradigm was adapted for the purposes of the current project but interpreted only in terms of the information structures contained in the stimuli. The adaptation involved creating additional sets of positive sentences and generating companion sets of negative sentences according to the property and set rules used with the positive sentences.

In terms of operations, both "superset" and "property" sentences require the subject to encode the sentences and construct kernel representations. Both sentences also require the retrieval of superset information from LTM; property sentences also require retrieval of property information. Finally, both sentence types require the selection and execution of the appropriate response.

TABLE 3.1
Operational Overview of Tasks

Task Condition	OPERATIONS							
	Encode	Construct	Transform	Store	Retrieve	Search	Compare	Respond
POSNER PHYSICAL	Encode letters						Compare representations of letter patterns	Select and execute response
POSNER NAME	Encode letters				Retrieve name from LTM		Compare representations of letter names	Select and execute response
POSNER CATEGORY	Encode letters				Retrieve name from LTM; Retrieve category from LTM		Compare representations of letter categories	Select and execute response
MEYER WORD	Encode letter string	Construct phonemic or graphemic representation				Search in LTM for "word"		Select and execute response
MEYER NONWORD	Encode letter string	Construct phonemic or graphemic representation				Search in LTM for "word"; Search in LTM for "word" rules		Select and execute response
BARON SH (Visual)	Encode semantic phrases	Construct visual representation				Search LTM for "phrase" rules		Select and execute response
BARON HN (Acoustic)	Encode semantic phrases	Construct acoustic representation				Search LTM for "phrase" rules		Select and execute response

BARON SN	Encode semantic phrases	Construct visual or acoustic representation				Search LTM for "phrase" rules		Select and execute response
STERNBERG	Encode target number						Compare numbers (serial)	Select and execute response
JUOLA WORD	Encode target number						Compare words (serial)	Select and execute response
JUOLA CATEGORY	Encode target word				Retrieve category from LTM		Compare categories (serial)	Select and execute response
CLARK AND CHASE	Encode sentence / Encode picture	Construct kernel representations	Transform "below" representation / Transform "negation" representation / Transform truth indices				Compare sentence and picture representations	Select and execute response
COLLINS AND QUILLIAN SUPERSET	Encode sentence	Construct kernel representation			Retrieve superset information from LTM			Select and execute response
COLLINS AND QUILLIAN PROPERTY	Encode sentence	Construct kernel representation			Retrieve superset information from LTM / Retrieve property information from LTM			Select and execute response
SHEPARD AND TEGHTSOONIAN	Encode numbers			Store items in LTM	Retrieve numbers from LTM		Judge strength of activation	Select and execute response

Recognition Memory (Shepard & Teghtsoonian Task)

Shepard and Teghtsoonian (1961) developed a procedure for measuring the capacity of human memory under "conditions approaching a steady state"—where the possibility of rehearsal is minimized and the interference of preceding material is maximized. They argued that situations that confront people with a continuing sequence of items and require them to retain as much as possible of the most recently presented information (e.g., continuous monitoring of complex displays) involve memory processes differing from those tested by most other paradigms. The procedure they employed was a recognition task: Subjects were presented with a lengthy list of items and were asked to identify each item as "old" (i.e., previously presented) or "new." The lists were constructed so that the interlist intervals between the original and test presentations of items varied. The authors were able to infer a retention function for a single item by plotting probability of recognition as a function of test lag.

In addition to standard parameter estimates, this paradigm is ideal for estimating parameters derived from signal detection theory. Using the observed proportions of the two types of errors (i.e., calling an old item "new" and calling a new item "old"), it is possible to generate, for each subject, an estimate of d' and beta (respectively, an estimate of "true" discriminability, and the location of the subject's subjective decision bias criterion).

The present task used the Shepard and Teghtsoonian procedure; however, the stimuli were reconstructed so that exactly the same number of intervals occurred in a list of items.

In terms of operations, this task requires the encoding and storing (in LTM) of numbers and the retrieval of these numbers from LTM. In addition, the most convenient way to describe the recognition judgment is to consider it as a comparison operation: Subjects compare each number with their LTM set and judge the "strength of activation"; this judgment determines which response will be selected and executed.

Summary

Table 3.1 presents all the tasks included in the present battery and the hypothesized operations included in each task condition. Detailed results of our preliminary research with the battery are reported in Rose and Fernandes (1977). Instructions for administering each task are also included in that source. Here we can present only an overview discussion of results to date.

OVERVIEW OF RESULTS

As noted previously, the key to the approach taken in this study is an analysis of construct validity. The approach adopted to validity warrants elaboration. The concept of construct validity is relatively new in experimental psychology. At its current stage of development and mathematical analysis, construct validity is primarily a question of belief, dependent on the researcher's judgments of support or nonsupport stemming from empirical results. Nunnally (1978) has suggested general procedures for the generation of relevant data. These procedures involve: (1) specification of observables relevant to the construct; (2) determination of the relationship between observables of the same construct; and (3) determination of the extent to which measures of the construct produce results predicted from accepted theories about the construct.

Thus, construct validity depends on a chain of inferences, each link of which relies primarily upon interpretation and judgment. The first link is essentially a series of theoretical hypotheses about the underlying constructs. As such, these hypotheses reflect the author's particular theoretical biases, vocabulary, and task analyses. The next judgment concerns the interpretation of the individual task's group effects as more or less supportive of the underlying operational descriptions. For the most part, we have considered "phenomenon replicability" as presumptive evidence for these interpretations; confidence has been increased not only from the present results but also from the results of other investigators who have performed empirically based converging operations. The next judgment is the designation of measures as reflecting one or more operations. For the many measures that adequately represent task performance, the judgment was made as to the relevance of each to the operational construct. The final step in the chain of inferences is the correlational hypothesis that two measures sharing the same operation will be statistically related. If each parameter was hypothesized to measure only one operation, the evidence could be interpreted straightforwardly. However, the evidence becomes shakier when both parameters measure more than one operation. Without assumptions concerning relative weights or correlations among the operations, the interpretations of the evidence become indirect.

Given the foregoing considerations, the approach implies that each task would be evaluated in three areas. First, where relevant, a primary question would be the replicability of previously obtained phenomena using the same or similar paradigm. Second would be a more "traditional" test evaluation, concerned with such issues as ease of administration and scoring, equipment demands, efficiency (in terms of time to administer and task length), reliability of task performance, and the character of the response distributions in the population as an indicator of the ability of each measure to uncover individual-difference parameters. The third area would be the issues previously mentioned with regard to construct validity and theoretical interpretations of individual and group performance.

Results bearing on the first two areas (replicability and "traditional test" evaluation) are presented at length in Rose and Fernandes (1977). The results indicate that for the most part, the major group effects were replicated in each paradigm. Thus, there is demonstrated empirical and theoretical support for the information-processing constructs contained in the tasks. However, the value of the paradigms for an assessment battery depends primarily on the measures derived from them and the properties of these measures when considered as potential individual-difference variables. This distinction between task effects and measurement properties is particularly important in the present context because most of the paradigms were not originally generated for the study of individual differences; the scientists were primarily concerned with uncovering different aspects of the human information-processing system. Similarly, these paradigms have not previously been considered as test per se; no thought has been given to typical test development issues. Finally, the distinction between group effects and individual measures is critical in that several theoretically independent measures can be obtained from each task. For example, the Shepard and Teghtsoonian task results can be described by a number of different parameters: the "standard" measure of proportion of correct items (or, more finely, proportion of "hits" and "false alarms"), the two parameters of the exponential equation that is the best fit to the probability-correct-by-lag function, and the signal detection theory parameters d' and β.

Given these considerations, a set of 40 variables were selected for detailed examination. These variables are shown in Table 3.2. Also shown in this table are the theoretical operations that these variables are hypothesized to measure. The operations were derived primarily from Table 3.1, which described the operations involved in each task condition. As can be seen in Table 3.2, there are several "redundancies" in the operations measured across the set of variables; many operations are sampled more than once. Also, most variables measure more than one operation.

Thus, the principal data used as inputs to the various construct validity analyses are the observed intra- and intertask correlations, the observed mean RTs for each of the variables, and a variable-by-operation matrix derived from Table 3.2. This matrix consists of the variables listed along one axis, the operations listed along the other, and the entries of "1" or "0" depending on the presence or absence of each operation in the composition of each variable. Using these inputs, two major analyses were conducted. The first was a general "model-fitting" procedure using the correlations and the variable-by-operation matrix; the second was a regression analysis where the operations were used to predict the observed RTs where estimates were obtained for the durations of the variables.

Model Fitting

The notion of converging operations can be stated roughly in terms of experimental design—the idea is to include in the same experiment some tasks that are hypothesized to involve a particular process and some tasks that do not. The pattern of empirical correlations among the tasks is then evaluated and inferences made about the validity of the particular process. In the present case, however, it

TABLE 3.2
Operations for Each Task Measure

Measure	Operations	Measure	Operations
POSNER PHYSICAL	• Encode letters • Compare representations of letter patterns • Select and execute response	JUOLA WORD SLOPE POSITIVE, NEGATIVE RESPONSES	• Compare words (serial)
POSNER NAME	• Encode letters • Retrieve name from LTM • Compare representations of letter names • Select and execute response	JUOLA CATEGORY INTERCEPT POSITIVE, NEGATIVE RESPONSES	• Encode target word • Select and execute response
POSNER CATEGORY	• Encode letters • Retrieve name from LTM • Retrieve category from LTM • Compare representations of letter categories	JUOLA CATEGORY SLOPE POSITIVE, NEGATIVE RESPONSES	• Retrieve category from LTM • Compare categories (serial)
POSNER NAME MINUS PHYSICAL	• Retrieve name from LTM	CLARK AND CHASE "BASE" TIME	• Encode sentence • Encode picture • Construct kernel representations • Select and execute response
POSNER RULE MINUS NAME	• Retrieve category from LTM	CLARK AND CHASE "BELOW" TIME	• Transform "below" representation
MEYER WORD	• Encode letter string • Construct phonemic or graphemic representation • Search LTM for "word" • Select and execute response	CLARK AND CHASE "NEGATION" TIME	• Transform "negation" representation
		CLARK AND CHASE "COMPARISONS" TIME	• Transform truth indices
MEYER NONWORD	• Encode letter string • Construct phonemic or graphemic representation • Search LTM for "word" • Search LTM for "word" rules • Select and execute response	COLLINS AND QUILLIAN SUPERSET INTERCEPT	• Encode sentence • Construct kernel representation • Select and execute response
BARON SH	• Encode semantic phrases • Construct visual representation • Search LTM for "phrase" rules • Select and execute response	COLLINS AND QUILLIAN SUPERSET SLOPE	• Retrieve superset information from LTM
		COLLINS AND QUILLIAN PROPERTY INTERCEPT	• Encode sentence • Construct kernel representation • Retrieve property information from LTM
BARON HN	• Encode semantic phrases • Construct acoustic representation • Search LTM for "phrase" rules • Select and execute response	COLLINS AND QUILLIAN PROPERTY SLOPE	• Retrieve superset information from LTM
BARON SN	• Encode semantic phrases • Construct visual or acoustic representation • Search LTM for "phrase" rules • Select and execute response	SHEPARD AND TEGHTSOONIAN LAG FUNCTION EXPONENT, INTERCEPT	• Encode numbers • Store items in LTM
		SHEPARD AND TEGHTSOONIAN p ("hits"), PROPORTION CORRECT	• Retrieve numbers from LTM
STERNBERG INTERCEPT POSITIVE, NEGATIVE RESPONSES	• Encode target number • Select and execute response		
STERNBERG SLOPE POSITIVE, NEGATIVE RESPONSES	• Compare numbers (serial)	SHEPARD AND TEGHTSOONIAN d'	• Judge strength of activation
JUOLA WORD INTERCEPT POSITIVE, NEGATIVE RESPONSES	• Encode target word • Select and execute response	SHEPARD AND TEGHTSOONIAN p ("false alarms"), β	• Select and execute response

NOTE: The following three measures are presented in the results section but are not included here:

1. Posner "different" which is based on calculations across the three conditions,
2. Meyer "phonemic facilitation" which indicates an individual subject's propensity towards phonemic or graphemic encoding, and
3. Baron SH/HN which indicates an individual subject's propensity towards acoustic or visual encoding.

is in practice impossible to interpret the empirical correlation matrices for several reasons. First, in the 40-by-40 matrix, there are 780 correlations; although it is conceptually possible to generate 780 hypotheses concerning the magnitude and direction of these correlations, it is simply not an efficient strategy to evaluate each hypothesis. Second, most of the variables measure more than one operation; it is far from apparent what the correlations between any two variables should be if, for example, they have one operation in common and a second operation not in common. Third, there is no assumed independence of operations among tasks; that is, it is entirely possible that all measures are positively intercorrelated or that the correlations are mediated by higher-level "strategies." Therefore, an alternate procedure was adopted.

This alternate procedure involved the calculation of the theoretical "distance" between each pair of variables in terms of the component operations. The variable-by-operation matrix was examined, and pairwise distances were calculated via the simple procedure of counting all operations present in both variables and dividing that sum by the total number of operations present in either task. From these calculations, a theoretical intervariable distance matrix was constructed. Finally, the correlation between the two matrices—the empirical intercorrelations and the theoretical distances—was calculated. These correlations (obtained from various configurations of the variable-by-operation matrix) ranged from $r = .22$ to $r = .37$.

It is difficult to say whether or not these correlations represent "good" or "bad" model fits. Certainly, the fact that nonzero correlations were obtained can be interpreted positively, especially given the somewhat arbitrary original selection of operations. Moreover, it is clear that "improvements" of the fits could be accomplished if the variable-by-operation matrix were modified iteratively. Nevertheless, we believe that this fairly simple model-fitting procedure is a potentially valuable tool; in addition, we are encouraged by the positive relationship between the theoretical and empirical matrices.

Regression Analyses

Another procedure that was used to "evaluate" the validity of the hypothetical operations was to consider the operations as predictors of the empirical measures in a regression paradigm. Basically, each obtained measure was considered as being composed of one or more operations that could be added together linearly to produce an observed response time. In the general linear models procedure, the model fit could be evaluated directly in terms of the obtained multiple R (the proportion of variance accounted for by the entire set of predictors); in addition, this procedure generates parameter estimates as beta weights (since the predictor matrix contained only 1s and 0s) for each of the predictor variables.

Several such regression analyses were performed. The obtained R^2s ranged from $R^2 = .66$ to $R^2 = .72$. All these values were statistically significant.

The pattern of parameter estimates for the general linear models procedure also supports the construct validity of the operations, in that the magnitudes of these estimates are intuitively in line with expectations. For example, constructing was estimated to have a duration of approximately 750 msec; transforming, of approximately 224 msec; and searching, of approximately 150 msec.

The results from several other analyses (as well as a more extensive presentation of the foregoing analyses) could be provided; however, the general pattern of results is consistent. The theoretical operations hypothesized to determine task performance do, both empirically and inductively, account satisfactorily for significant aspects of performance. Naturally, the definitions of information-processing constructs and the assignment of these constructs to variables should both be iterative activities. Likewise, the analysis procedures should be examined carefully and hopefully improved upon; it should be possible to develop some standard construct validation procedures. However, to the extent that the present experiment has shed light on some of these issues, further research in the information-processing analysis of performance will benefit.

REFERENCES

Baron, J. Phonemic stage not necessary for reading. *Quarterly Journal of Experimental Psychology,* 1973, *25,* 241–246.

Baron, J., & McKillop, B. J. Individual differences in speed of phonemic analysis, visual analysis, and reading. *Acta Psychologica,* 1975, *39,* 91–96.

Bower, G. H. Cognitive psychology: An introduction. In W. K. Estes (Ed.), *Handbook of learning and cognitive processes* (Vol. 1). Hillsdale, N.J.: Lawrence Erlbaum Associates, 1975.

Calfee, R. C. Sources of dependency in cognitive processes. In D. Klahr (Ed.), *Cognition and instruction.* Hillsdale, N.J.: Lawrence Erlbaum Associates, 1976.

Carroll, J. B. Psychometric tests as cognitive tasks: A new "structure of intellect." In L. Resnick (Ed.), *The nature of intelligence.* Hillsdale, N.J.: Lawrence Erlbaum Associates, 1976.

Clark, H. H., & Chase, W. G. On the process of comparing sentences against pictures. *Cognitive Psychology,* 1972, *3,* 472–517.

Collins, A. M., & Quillian, M. R. Retrieval time from semantic memory. *Journal of Verbal Learning and Verbal Behavior,* 1969, *8,* 240–247.

Frederiksen, J. R. *A chronometric study of component skills in reading.* (Tech. Rep. No. 2). Bolt Beranek & Newman, January 1978.

French, J. W., Ekstrom, R., & Price, L. *Kit of reference tests for cognitive factors.* Princeton, N.J.: Educational Testing Service, 1963.

Hawkins, H. L., Church, M., & de Lemos, S. M. *Time-sharing is not a unitary ability* (Tech. Rep. No. 2). University of Oregon, June 1978.

Hunt, E. *The foundations of verbal comprehension* (Tech. Rep. No. 1). University of Washington, March 1978.

Juola, J. F., & Atkinson, R. C. Memory scanning for words versus categories. *Journal of Verbal Learning and Verbal Behavior,* 1971, *10,* 522–527.

Juola, J. F., & McDermott, D. A. Memory search for lexical and semantic information. *Journal of Verbal Learning and Verbal Behavior,* 1976, *15,* 567–575.

Keele, S. W., Neill, W. T., & de Lemos, S. M. *Individual differences in attentional flexibility* (Tech. Rep. No. 1). University of Oregon, May 1978.

Lansman, M. *An attentional approach to individual differences in immediate memory* (Tech. Rep. No. 2). University of Washington, June 1978.

Melton, A. W. Individual differences and theoretical process variables: General comments on the conference. In R. M. Gagné (Ed.), *Learning and individual differences*. Columbus, Ohio: Merrill, 1967.

Meyer, D. E., Schvaneveldt, R. W., & Ruddy, M. G. Functions of graphemic and phonemic codes in visual word-recognition. *Memory & Cognition,* 1974, *2,* 309–321.

Neisser, U. *Cognitive psychology*. New York: Appleton-Century-Crofts, 1967.

Nunnally, J. C. *Psychometric theory*. New York: McGraw-Hill, 1978.

Posner, M. I. Abstraction and the process of recognition. In G. H. Bower & J. T. Spence (Eds.), *The psychology of learning and motivation: Advances in research and theory*. New York: Academic Press, 1969.

Posner, M. I., & Mitchell, R. F. Chronometric analysis of classification. *Psychological Review,* 1967, *74,* 392–409.

Rose, A. M., & Fernandes, K. *An information processing approach to performance assessment: I. Experimental investigation of an information processing performance battery* (Tech. Rep. No. 1). American Institutes for Research, November 1977.

Rubenstein, H., Garfield, L., & Millikan, J. A. Homographic entries in the internal lexicon. *Journal of Verbal Learning and Verbal Behavior,* 1970, *9,* 487–494.

Shepard, R. N., & Teghtsoonian, M. Retention of information under conditions approaching a steady state. *Journal of Experimental Psychology,* 1961, *62.* 302–309.

Simon, H. A. On the nature of understanding. In A. K. Jones (Ed.), *Perspectives in computer science*. New York: Academic Press, 1978.

Sternberg, R. J. *Isolating the components of intelligence* (Tech. Rep. No. 2-78). Yale University, January 1978.

Sternberg, S. Two operations in character recognition: Some evidence from reaction-time measurements. *Perception & Psychophysics,* 1967, *2,* 45–53.

Sternberg, S. The discovery of processing stages: Extensions of Donder's method. *Acta Psychologica,* 1969, *30,* 276–315.

4 The Foundations of Verbal Comprehension

Earl Hunt
The University of Washington

It is currently fashionable to extoll the intuitive, holistic, nonverbal process of the right hemisphere at the expense of the picky, verbal, serial processing of the left (Fincher, 1976). The tyranny of language is deplored by those who profess to be humanists. This is amazing. Language is what makes us human; few of us have the spatial orientation of a hawk. The predominant mode of our thought is verbal, and if we are going to understand human cognition, we must understand verbal thinking.

It is easy to measure verbal aptitude. By asking a few basic questions about vocabulary, grammar, and simple paragraph comprehension, one can predict performance in a wide variety of situations. To illustrate, Table 4.1 shows the correlations between verbal aptitude scores, as measured by a conventional scholastic aptitude test, and grade point averages for a variety of majors at the University of Washington. Outside academia, similar relationships have been found. Table 4.2 shows the verbal aptitude scores achieved by a group of World War II aviation cadets as a function of their subsequent civilian occupations. There are real, easily measured differences in verbal competence, and these differences have importance in our lives. Why these differences exist is very much an open question.

Differential psychologists search for the genesis of verbal competence by searching for a set of basic traits from which observed differences in behavior can be generated. Their methods of investigation are designed to reveal how many "basic" traits must be postulated and to determine how these traits are related to other talents, such as spatial reasoning. My colleagues and I have taken a rather different approach, based upon our view of thinking as a problem in information handling. We have examined tasks that, on theoretical grounds, ought to be

TABLE 4.1
Correlations Between Verbal Aptitude Scores (Washington Precollege
Test—Verbal Composite) and Game-Point Average in Selected Major

Anthropology	.34	English	.30	Scandinavian Lang.	.34
Astronomy	.35	History	.35	Nursing	.41
Chemistry	.19	Psychology	.27	Forestry	.34
Economics	.30	Sociology	.31	Mathematics	.14

Source: University of Washington records.

TABLE 4.2
Mean Standard Scores of Cadets on Air Force Test Battery
(General Intelligence) as a Function of Later Occupation

Accountant	.28	Lawyer	.39
Chemical Engineer	1.06	Physician	.59
Engine Mechanic	− .28	Social Worker	− .08
Insurance Salesman	− .05	Vehicular Mechanic	− .72

Data from Thorndike and Hagen (1959).

important in handling linguistic information-processing problems, and we have asked how behavior on these tasks is related to performance on verbal aptitude tests. An important point is that we are not trying to "explain the test scores." Rather, we view the tests as convenient measures to assure that we obtain a range of verbal competencies in the populations we study. As is shown later, we are quite willing to use other measures of general intellectual competence. Our goal is to understand how information processing varies over individuals, not to predict the variance on a specific test.

It would be nice to believe that our approach will coalesce with more traditional research on aptitudes. After all, we are studying the same phenomena. There is no guarantee that this will happen. Indeed, my colleagues and I have begun to suspect that there are fundamental conceptual incompatibilities between the ways that differential psychologists and information-processing psychologists view the problem of explaining individual differences (Hunt & MacLeod, 1978). The explanations I propose for our findings complement, rather than replace or amplify, the explanations generated by conventional psychometric studies.

THEORETICAL CONSIDERATIONS

A basic assumption of information-processing psychology is that language messages are handled in stages. The first is a decoding stage, in which arbitrary physical patterns are recognized as representations of concepts in the lexicon.

The second stage is an active memory stage, in which the recognized lexical items are rearranged in memory until they form a coherent linguistic structure. The third is the sentence-processing stage, in which the semantic meaning of the linguistic structure is extracted and incorporated into our knowledge of the current situation. In the fourth stage, the current situation itself is analyzed with respect to information held in long-term memory, and if appropriate, a response is chosen and emitted.

If people were literally computers, and if human languages could be analyzed by the techniques used to deal with computer languages such as FORTRAN or ALGOL, these stages would be executed in a strict sequence. People are not computers, and language analysis is not sequential. Nevertheless, the concept of stages is a useful one even when allowance is made for plentiful feedback between stages. I shall argue that individual differences appear at each of the stages of information processing and that they are important in determining verbal competence. My concrete evidence, though, is confined to an analysis through the sentence-processing level.

A listing of stages does not constitute a model. We must also consider the kind of control involved in analyzing language data. A substantial amount of information processing in the earlier stages of linguistic thought appears to take place in what Posner and Snyder (1975) have referred to as the automatic mode. This mode is, simply defined, an automatic process that takes place whether we wish it to or not, and it does not interfere with other ongoing processes. Recognition of the meaning of very familiar printed words is a good example. This process cannot be suppressed even when it is advantageous to do so (Stroop, 1935). Once past the lexical stage, we begin to see more use of what Shiffrin and Schneider (1977) refer to as ''veiled control processes''—processes that are not subject to conscious inspection but that can be shown to draw upon attentional resources. The search processes that psychologists have postulated to explain memory-scanning experiments are frequently cited examples. Similar veiled processes occur when we are required to understand the meaning of very simple sentences, such as ''The plus is above the star'' (an example to which I return). We are not aware of how we analyze these sentences, but it can be shown that the analysis requires attentional resources.

A third level of attention allocation is represented by the conscious strategies people adopt to make sense out of language stimuli. An example of such a process is the strategy one might adopt for solving multiple-choice test items. One could look at the question, select the best answer given the question, and then search for that answer among the alternatives provided. Another strategy is to read all the alternatives and then examine the question to see which one fits best. Each strategy has different implications about attention allocation, and people are consciously aware of the strategies that they use.

More complex verbal problem-solving situations require still more complex skills for representing and attacking problems. To solve the mystery in a detective novel, for example, one must discover who had the motive, who had the means, and who had the opportunity. Some people may do this by constructing scenarios that they examine for plausibility, perhaps through the use of visual or verbal imagery. Others may prefer the abstract logic of Sherlock Holmes. We know very little about individual differences at this level. Our lack of knowledge is a serious problem, for it biases our theorizing. There is no reason to believe that verbal performance is the result of a linear combination of component abilities, or that the same linear combination of components is applicable throughout the entire range of human verbal competence. Letter-naming speed may be a good discriminator of the difference between the lower and average ranges of verbal ability, whereas the difference between the average newspaper reporter and a Pulitzer prize winner may be more subtle. This must be kept in mind when we draw conclusions from the results of studies of "common garden variety" problem solvers.

In spite of this warning, we must concentrate on what we know. We have found that there are reliable individual differences in mechanistic processes of information handling within the population represented by university students and within populations of somewhat lower ability. These differences appear to account for a substantial portion of the individual variation in verbal competence observed within these populations. The differences we have found do not appear to be associated with differential possession of knowledge about the language but rather with differential ability to manipulate the symbols that comprise it.

STRUCTURAL PROCESSES

Decoding

Lexical analysis requires the decoding of arbitrary physical signals to connect them to conceptual units in a language. The sound /cat/ must be recognized as a referent for the animal. Posner and Mitchell's (1967) *stimulus identification* paradigm has proven to be useful in studying this process. In a stimulus identification study, the subject is presented with a pair of highly overlearned stimuli, usually letters. The task is to state whether the two stimuli have the same name. First, consider the pair A–A. This is a physically identical (PI) pair; it would be possible to determine that these symbols had the same name even if you did not know what that name was. Next, consider the name-identical (NI) pair A–a. In order to complete the identification task, the names of these symbols must be retrieved from memory. A third possibility is that the pair is different (D), as in the case of A–B. If D and NI pairs are mixed, it is necessary to retrieve the names of all letters in order to make the correct response.

Posner and Mitchell, and since them many others, found that it takes longer to make an NI than a PI response. A strictly serial model, in which physical identification is attempted first and name identification attempted only if physical identification fails, justifies subtracting PI reaction time from NI reaction time in order to arrive at an estimate of the time required to retrieve the name of a symbol, surely an important part of verbal comprehension. For brevity, I shall refer to the NI–PI measure. A number of investigators have found that the NI–PI measure discriminates between persons whom one would think to have more or less verbal thinking ability. These data are summarized in Fig. 4.1. The range of the measure is striking. A typical difference between NI and PI reaction times for a college student scoring in the upper quartile of a verbal aptitude test (a ''high verbal'' in subsequent remarks) is 65 msec, whereas educable mental retardates show an NI–PI difference score of over 300 msec (Hunt, 1978).

In spite of the regular and interpretable picture presented by Fig. 4.1, work with the stimulus identification paradigm in other settings has raised serious question about the accuracy of the serial model itself (Posner & Snyder, 1975). It appears more correct to assume that both the NI and PI tasks involve identification at the name level, followed by a binary choice and a motor response. The name retrieval process is more important in the NI task, because the names of two symbols must be retrieved, but the subtraction operation no longer has a simple theoretical interpretation. The resulting analysis becomes quite detailed, because the data analysis technique one uses to derive a measure of name re-

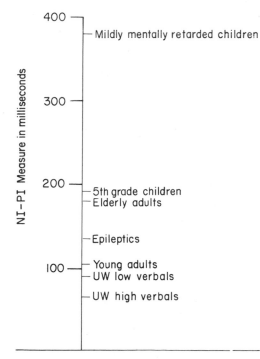

FIG. 4.1. NI-PI Measure for selected groups.

TABLE 4.3
NI and PI Reaction Times in Seconds
for Children at Various Ages

Age	NI	PI	Difference
13	1.91	1.74	.17
10	2.07	1.85	.21
7	2.50	2.21	.29

trieval depends on the precise model one espouses for the task. (See Hunt et al., 1978, for comments on the general problem.) Fortunately for those who wish merely to determine whether or not the name retrieval process is important in individual differences, the fact is that almost any reasonable choice of a response measure is satisfactory. The ratio of NI to PI reaction times increases as verbal competence decreases,[1] and the correlation between measures of verbal competence and NI reaction time alone is generally in the .35 to .45 range (Jackson & McClelland, 1978; Lansman, 1977).

If decoding is an important part of verbal competence, one would expect to show a developmental trend for decoding, as verbal competence clearly grows with age. Table 4.3 presents some data gathered by Judith Warren as part of a doctoral dissertation now in progress. As can be seen, there is a strong developmental trend. Warren also found significant correlations between the NI–PI measure and WISC verbal IQ scores. Furthermore, there were significant sex differences in favor of girls, which is consistent with the general finding that girls outperform boys in verbal tasks (Maccoby & Jacklin, 1974).

Finally, if name retrieval is an important part of verbal comprehension, one would expect it to have its maximum effect upon tests of reading. Jackson and McClelland (1978), using an extreme groups design, reported a correlation of .45 between NI alone and skill in reading in a college population—surely a group with a restricted range of reading comprehension. Our own results in studies of reading comprehension in a more general population confirms Jackson and McClelland's findings and further suggests that the relation found may depend on the level of verbal ability.

We can sum up these results by saying that there clearly is an association between verbal competence and the simple act of identifying the name of a symbol. This observation is of interest for two reasons: It provides (1) a link between an important stage of verbal cognition as identified by cognitive theorists, and (2) individual differences as measured by conventional aptitude tests. Furthermore, the process does not seem to be an operation that would be influenced by differential knowledge possession. Most university students know the alphabet fairly well.

---

[1]This measure cannot be compared across experiments, as motor reaction time will be markedly influenced by apparatus variables.

Holding Information in Active Memory

In principle, one's memory should be involved in such simple cognitive acts as determining that a sentence is grammatical. There clearly are differences in short-term memory capacity that are associated with language capacity, as shown by the many experiments that have related IQ to digit span. The correlation found, however, is often due to a radical drop in digit span in persons with very low general mental competence (Matarazzo, 1972). In order to consider the relation between primary memory and general mental competence in depth, we need to consider in more detail the components of the act of retaining information for a brief period of time.

Hunt, Lunneborg, and Lewis (1975) examined the active memory capacities of "high-verbal" and "low-verbal" college students (i.e., students with low verbal scores for college students). We used a version of the Brown–Peterson short-term memory paradigm, in which the subject was first shown four letters, then repeated aloud a string of digits presented visually one at a time, and finally recalled the letters. Figure 4.2 shows recall performance as a function of the number of digits shadowed. The high-verbal students appear to establish an initial advantage (perhaps due to rapid decoding) and then retain it in the face of the interfering material. This can be explained by the assumption that the high-verbal students code information into recognized items more rapidly than do the

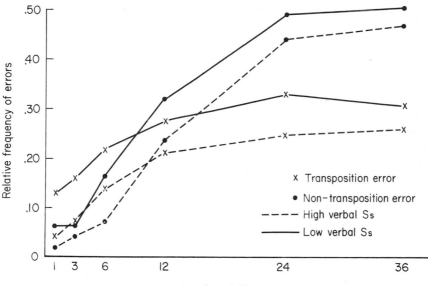

FIG. 4.2.   Frequency of different types of errors in a short-term memory task as a function of type of subjects and number of items in an intervening task (digit shadowing).

low-verbal students, but that they do not have an advantage in resisting interfering material.

In Hunt et al.'s study, very short lists of items were used. What would happen if longer lists were used? Cohen and Sandberg (1977) report a large study of the relation between intelligence and the recall of supraspan lists by Swedish school children. Their subjects had to memorize lists of nine digits, which is well beyond the memory span for most grade-school children. Using a probe recall procedure, Cohen and Sandberg estimated separately the children's ability to recall the first three digits presented (primacy), the middle three, or the last three (recency). They found that the correlations observed between recall and scholastic aptitude were due to the more competent children performing better on the recency portion of the curve. This is shown in Fig. 4.3. Note that this is consistent with Hunt et al.'s results, since the shorter lists that we used would be within the recency portion of the recall curve had we used the Cohen and Sandberg procedure.

The ability to recall strings of digits and letters is not particularly useful in most situations. We need to consider what advantages might be gained by having a good "recency" short-term memory in intellectual tasks in general. We have found evidence for two types of advantage. Larger short-term memories may increase the strategies that a person can use in a problem-solving task, and performance on a short-term memory task may indicate the attentional effort required to hold information in active memory. The less effort required to do this, the more capacity there is available for other tasks.

Suppose a person is asked to recall a list of some 30 or more words. Obviously, errors will be made. Recall will be more accurate if the list is made up of items drawn from relatively few semantic categories—say, animals, vegetables, and minerals. In this case, free recall displays the clustering phenomenon; the

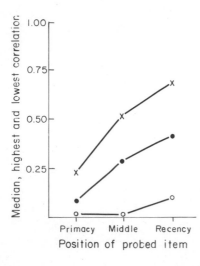

FIG. 4.3.   Representative results for correlation between STM recall and aptitude. (From Cohen & Sandberg, 1977.)

TABLE 4.4
Clustering Index by Recall Order and Verbal Aptitude

	Hunt et al. Full List	Schwartz: Data by Order of Recall		
		1st 1/3	2nd 1/3	3rd 1/3
High verbal	.68	.29	.81	.79
Low verbal	.84	.71	.82	.84

Note: Items are presented in random order.

typical subject will recall items from one semantic category and then items from another (Bousfield, 1953). Hunt, Frost, and Lunneborg (1973) found, somewhat to our surprise, that high-verbal students cluster less than low-verbal students. The relevant portion of our data is shown in Table 4.4. This result was something of a puzzle to us until Schwartz (1976) combined it with the results on short-term memory. Schwartz reasoned that high verbals could affort not to cluster part of a supraspan list because they could simply read out the last few items from active memory. If this were the case, then high verbals should show less clustering than low verbals on the first few items recalled but progressively more clustering as recall progressed, because the later-recalled items would be retrieved from long-term, rather than from active, memory. Table 4.4 also shows Schwartz's data; it is clear that his hypothesis was borne out. Because of their greater short-term memory capacity, the high verbals had a strategy available that the low verbals could not use.

The fact that students with high verbal aptitude scores have larger active memories need not imply that they have larger skulls. An alternative formulation of active memory capacity focuses upon the allocation of attention. Lansman (1978) combined the Atkinson and Shiffrin (1968) continuous paired-associates procedure with the secondary task methodology (Norman & Bobrow, 1975) to measure the effort devoted to memorizing information. Her subjects had to respond to a light by pressing a button while keeping track of the changing state of zero variables (no memory load), two variables (light memory load), or six variables (heavy memory load). There was a substantial increase in reaction times to the light signal from the no-memory load to the light-load condition, even though subjects made virtually no errors under the light load. Furthermore, the amount of increase in the light-load condition was a predictor of the number of errors that would be made in the high-load condition. This demonstrates the fact that active memory maintenance is an attention-demanding act, and that there are individual differences in the ability to bring attentional resources to bear on it. Because memory load is a component—but only one component—of tasks such as sentence parsing or solving simple arithmetic problems (Hitch, 1978), and because these tasks are also attention demanding, it is clear that it would be advantageous to be able to devote less capacity to memory and more to problem solving in many situations. But is it the case that the verbally competent simply have a greater attentional capacity, or are they more able to focus their resources?

ATTENTION ALLOCATION

Posner and Boies (1971) distinguished three separate aspects of attention—general arousal, the capacity to restrict attention to task-relevant cues, and the ability to switch attention from one task to another. All, one, or two of these components might vary with general verbal aptitude. An unpublished experiment by Steven Poltrock (1977) provided some relevant data. Sixty high-school students participated in a series of tasks designed to measure different aspects of the ability to control attention.

In order to measure general attention level, we used a simple, two-choice reaction-time task in which the subject faced a screen on which a light appeared. The light could appear at either of two locations, and the subject's task was to press a switch immediately under the light location. Thus this task provides a measure of general alertness, plus a component due to choice reaction time under conditions of high stimulus–response compatibility.[2] Measuring selective attention presented a more difficult problem, as one could imagine different forms of selective attention, depending on the nature of the stimulus to be attended to and the nature of the interfering stimuli. We decided to average performance on three separate tasks thought to require selective attention. These were as follows:

1. The Stroop (1935) effect—measured by the time required to name the ink in which color names were printed minus the time required to name the color of the ink in which asterisks were printed.

2. The time required to read aloud a randomly ordered sequence of words minus the time required to read the same words in a coherent text. The reading of random words requires that the subjects suppress the normal tendency to scan ahead when reading aloud in order to pick up cues concerning voice and intonation.

3. Shadowing in the presence of dichotic interference. Mixed lists of words and digits were presented to each ear. The task was to report the digits presented to one of the ears; the measure of interference was the number of intrusions, defined as the report of a digit presented to the wrong ear.

In order to obtain an overall measure of sensitivity to selective attention, the scores in these three tasks were standardized and added.

[2]A warning signal always preceded the choice signal in this experiment. In retrospect, we ought to have compared conditions with and without the warning signal in order to measure the speed with which subjects could alert themselves to the stimulus situation.

TABLE 4.5
Correlations Between Verbal Aptitude and Attention Measures

	Attention Switching	*Verbal Aptitude*
Selective attention	.30	.40
Attention switching	—	.48

Finally, we required a measure of attention switching. Here, fortunately, we could benefit from previous work (Gopher & Kahneman, 1971; Kahneman, Ben-Ishai, & Lotan, 1973) that had shown substantial individual differences in a variant of the dichotic listening paradigm. As subjects shadowed one ear, they were signaled to switch to the other ear. On control trials, they simply received a signal indicating that they should continue to monitor the ear they were then shadowing. Our measure of speed of attention reallocation was the number of digits correctly reported immediately following a switch.

There was no correlation ($r = -.06$) between the simple reaction-time task and verbal aptitude. On the other hand, there were significant correlations between verbal aptitude and measures of both selective attention and attention switching. These correlations are shown in Table 4.5. In addition to the significant first-order correlations, both selective attention and attention switching have significant partial correlations with verbal aptitude when the other attention measure is controlled.

This experiment is, at best, a start toward the study of attentional factors in intellectual competence. Although a great deal of work needs to be done, the result is consistent with the idea that the control of attention is important. This becomes of interest when we consider an explicitly verbal task that requires attention allocation—the comprehension of sentences.

SENTENCE COMPREHENSION

The experiments considered in this section deal with verification of simple linguistic descriptions of a simple world. The task was developed by Clark and Chase (1972), who used sentences of the form "Plus is above star" or "Plus is not below star" and pictures of the form ($^+_*$) or ($^*_+$). In the sentence-first version of the paradigm, the subject is first shown a sentence, then a picture, and must indicate whether or not the sentence accurately described the picture. The dependent variable is verification reaction time—the time between display of the picture and the subject's response. An alternative procedure involves presenting a large number of pictures and sentences in paper-and-pencil form and asking how many the subject can verify in a fixed time. There is a correlation of .70 between the two procedures (Lansman, 1977).

The sentence verification task has a number of features that recommend it as a measure of verbal information processing. On the face of it, the task is impossible unless one knows the meaning of words; on the other hand, the words used are so common that they can be presumed to be in the vocabulary of every junior-high-school graduate. We are confident that any variations in verification time due to individual differences in word identification will be due to decoding differences rather than differences in vocabulary. It is an attention-demanding task, as can be shown by an analysis using the secondary task methodology (Hunt & MacLeod, 1978), and the attention demands are closely tied to the complexity of the comparison process. Verification reaction times increase for negative as compared to affirmative sentences, and false sentences generally take longer to be rejected than true sentences do to be confirmed (Clark & Chase, 1972). Given these facts, it is not surprising to find that people with high verbal aptitude scores are more rapid at sentence verification (Baddeley, 1968; Hunt, Lunneborg, & Lewis, 1975; Lansman, 1977). The correlation between sentence verification reaction time and verbal aptitude measures is generally in the .35 to .55 range. Lansman (1978) found that this correlation can be substantially improved by introducing choice reaction time as a covariate. Note that this is a reasonable thing to do because the final motor response is a choice of making the "true" or "false" response. When simple choice reaction time (measured by a procedure similar to that used by Poltrock and Hunt) was "held constant," the partial correlation between sentence verification time and a vocabulary test was .73. A similar correlation was found with a reading comprehension test. As the vocabulary and comprehension measures in Lansman's study referred to tests taken as long as three years before the experiment itself, this correlation approaches the test–retest reliability of the psychometric measure. Furthermore, on the face of things, there is no reason why someone who knows many words should also be quick at verifying sentences consisting of simple words.

These results are encouraging to those who seek a rapid measure of verbal competence that is not bound to knowledge. I now report some studies that show how much strategies can influence information processing. A slight change in procedure—from the simultaneous presentation condition used by Baddeley and by Lansman to the sentence-first procedure used by Clark and Chase—introduces a new and significant source of variance. In the sentence-first procedure, the subject can choose different strategies, and this choice can play havoc with an analysis of the traits that underlie performance.

To recall the task briefly, in the sentence-first procedure, the subject is shown the sentence, given a chance to read and comprehend it, and then shown the picture. MacLeod, Hunt, and Mathews (1978) found that when this was done, some people read the sentence, memorized it, described the picture to themselves when it was shown, and then compared the descriptions. Let us call these people "verbal problem solvers." Another group of subjects, whom I shall call "visual problem solvers," used the sentence as a cue to visualize the expected picture and then compared the actual picture to an image of its expectation. Individual performance of the verbal problem solvers was well predicted by a test of verbal aptitude, whereas performance of the visual problem solvers was well predicted by a test of spatial aptitude. This statement, however, does not really capture the contrast between the data of the two groups who, it will be remembered, were exposed to the same stimuli. To bring the distinction out more clearly, Fig. 4.4 plots the mean verification reaction time for each group of subjects as a function of the linguistic complexity of the verification task, calculated by applying Carpenter and Just's (1975) linguistic comparison model to the task.

The close fit of this group to the Carpenter and Just model is not surprising. MacLeod et al.'s method of definition of groups ensured that there would be one

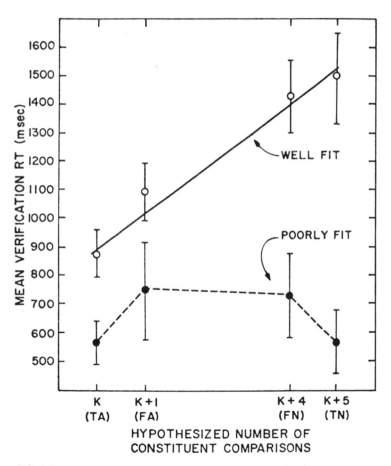

FIG. 4.4.   Reaction time for two groups of subjects as a function of the number of hypothesized components in a sentence verification task. (After MacLeod et al., 1978.)

such group. What is interesting is the complete lack of fit of the second group—a result that was not dictated by the analytical procedures. Further, the visual group's data could not be fit by *any* reasonable linguistic model, as these data show no effect of negation, which many studies have shown to be a powerful psycholinguistic variable.

For one who seeks stable predictors of performance, this result is a minor disaster. We have shown that choice of strategy may determine correlational patterns, a situation that is anathema to orderly psychometric models. In theory, predictive power might be restored by using a person's choice of strategy itself as a marker in making predictions. Unfortunately, this will not work, either, for one

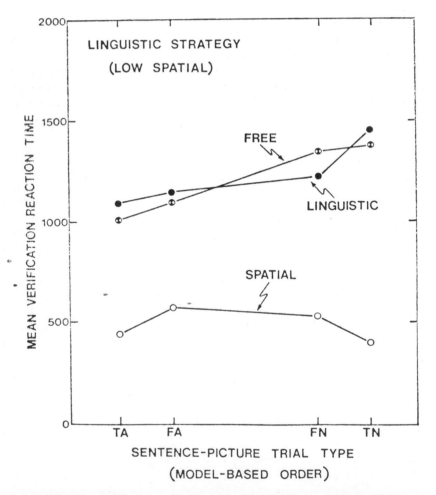

FIG. 4.5. Verification reaction time of a selected subject as a function of the instructions given for use of a strategy of sentence processing.

can change an individual's pattern of data simply by requesting that the subject use an alternative strategy. Figure 4.5 shows some data from one of the subjects in a second study by Mathews, MacLeod, and myself (in press). This subject was first allowed to choose a strategy and evidently chose a verbal one. Subsequently, he was asked to use a visual strategy and then a verbal one. Similar switches can be produced in the behavior of subjects who initially begin with visual strategies. If qualitative changes of behavior can so easily be produced in this straightforward task, how many strategies are there for understanding *War and Peace?*

CONCLUDING COMMENTS

It seems clear that there are strictly mechanical components to individual differences in verbal competence. I have argued that these differences lie in three major areas—automatic, structural processes such as decoding and short-term memory capacity; the ability to control attention; and the use of strategies. Whereas the automatic processes are reasonably stable over time and situation, it is clear that the attentional processes and strategy choices are labile. Are these processes reasonably considered part of intelligence?

They certainly are components of individual mental competence. Given that, who needs the concept of intelligence? I believe that we ought to drop the notion of intelligence as a trait, or even as a space of traits, when we are trying to understand intellectual performance. Traits are statistical abstractions and do not refer to any physical processes inside the head. If our theories of cognition are correct (admitting a big "if"), parameter estimates of information-processing stages and structures may be closer to measuring real things than are the psychometric procedures for trait estimation. When mental competence is to be studied as a phenomenon to be explained, information-processing measures provide more useful dependent measures. For example, it seems to me that studying the genetic correlates of performance on an omnibus "IQ" measure has little point, but that studying the genetic correlates of symbol decoding or short-term memory capacity is reasonable. It seems equally reasonable to speak of two individuals as being comparable in their normal mental competence and then to add that one is more prone than the other to deterioration in attentional control mechanisms due to some pathological condition, such as alcohol intoxication. Is one "less intelligent" than the other? The question does not make sense.

The question changes somewhat when mental measurement is to be used as an independent variable in a predictive situation. At times we legitimately make predictions about abstract concepts on a mass basis—for example, predictions about occupational success as a function of mental competence. In such cases we are predicting from one statistical abstraction to another, and the traditional psychometric methods are quite appropriate. In other cases, though, we may desire absolute, rather than relative, prediction. This is particularly likely to occur when we are interested in the performance of identifiable individuals on specific tasks. To be pragmatic, will Astronaut Smith be able to land the Mars probe within x meters of the target point? In such situations, the absolute information-processing approach to mental capacity may be made more useful than the relativistic approach of psychometrics.

In spite of the fact that this chapter presents a number of correlation coefficients, I stress again that we are not interested in explaining the intelligence test; we simply use these tests as rough-and-ready measures of general competence. We have shown that the measures one would expect to be important in information processing are roughly associated with general competence. If the correlations are not higher, this may be at least as much the fault of the aptitude tests as it is of the information-processing measures. In our future work, my colleagues and I plan to go beyond these correlational studies—to examine how the information-processing measures covary with each other and how they change as individuals and as ecologically valid variables in individuals' lives change. We will be looking at changes in individuals over age, time of day, relationship, and drug state. Although we may never compute another correlation coefficient between an information-processing measure and a psychometric trait (although I suspect we will), we will still be developing a theory of individual differences. This theory is intended to provide a complement to trait theories. It certainly will neither expand nor replace them.

ACKNOWLEDGMENTS

The preparation of this paper was supported by the Office of Naval Research through a contract to the University of Washington (Contract No. N 00014-77-C-0225), on which Earl Hunt is the principal investigator. The research reported here was supported by that contract and by a grant from the National Institute of Mental Health, MH-21795 "Individual Differences in Cognition," to the University of Washington. This paper is the text of a talk given at the Conference on Aptitude, Learning, and Instruction: Cognitive Process Analyses, sponsored by the Office of Naval Research, in San Diego, California, March 1978.

I am happy to acknowledge the considerable advice and assistance I have received from Marcy Lansman, Clifford Lunneborg, Colin MacLeod, and Steven Poltrock over the period during which this research was conducted. Naturally I must shoulder the blame for writing and for any mistakes, misstatements, or erroneous conclusions in this paper, no matter how much I should like to share it!

REFERENCES

Atkinson, R. C., & Shiffrin, R. M. Human memory: A proposed system and its control processes. In K. Spence & J. Spence (Eds.), *The psychology of learning and motivation* (Vol. II). New York: Academic Press, 1968.

Baddeley, A. D. A 3-minute reasoning test based on grammatical transformations. *Psychonomic Science*, 1968, *10*, 341–342.

Bousfield, W. A. The occurrence of clustering in the recall of randomly arranged associates. *Journal of General Psychology*, 1953, *49*, 229–240.

Carpenter, P. A., & Just, M. A. Sentence comprehension: A psycholinguistic processing model of verification. *Psychological Review*, 1975, *82*, 45–73.

Clark, H., & Chase, W. On the process of comparing sentences against pictures. *Cognitive Psychology*, 1972, *3*, 472–517.

Cohen, R. L., & Sandberg, T. Relation between intelligence and short-term memory. *Cognitive Psychology*, 1977, *9*, 534–554.

Fincher, J. *Intelligence*. New York: Putnams, 1976.

Gopher, D., & Kahneman, D. Individual differences in attention and the prediction of flight criteria. *Perceptual and Motor Skills*, 1971, *33*, 1335–1342.

Hitch, G. The role of short-term working memory in mental arithmetic. *Cognitive Psychology*, 1978, *10*, 302–323.

Hunt, E. The mechanics of verbal ability. *Psychological Review*, 1978, *85*, 109–130.

Hunt, E., Frost, N., & Lunneborg, C. Individual differences in cognition: A new approach to intelligence. In G. Bower (Ed.), *Advances in learning and motivation* (Vol. VII). New York: Academic Press, 1973.

Hunt, E., Lunneborg, C., & Lewis, J. What does it mean to be high verbal? *Cognitive Psychology*, 1975, *7*, 194–227.

Hunt, E., & MacLeod, C. M. *The sentence verification paradigm: A case study of two conflicting approaches to individual differences*. *Intelligence*, 1978, *2*, 129–144.

Jackson, M. D., & McClelland, J. L. Processing determinants of reading speed. *Journal of Experimental Psychology: General*, 1978, *108*, 133–150.

Kahneman, D., Ben-Ishai, R., & Lotan, M. Relation of a test of attention to road accidents. *Journal of Applied Psychology*, 1973, *58*, 113–115.

Lansman, M. *Paper and pencil tests for measuring information processing variables* (University of Washington Psychology Department, 1977). Text of report given at the 1977 Western Psychological Association meetings.

Lansman, M. *An attentional approach to individual differences in immediate memory*. University of Washington, Ph.D. dissertation, 1978.

Maccoby, E., & Jacklin, C. *The psychology of sex differences*. Stanford, Calif.: Stanford University Press, 1974.

MacLeod, C. M., Hunt, E., & Mathews, N. N. Individual differences in the verification of sentence–picture relationships. *Journal of Verbal Learning and Verbal Behavior*, 1978, *2*, 129–144.

Matarazzo, J. D. *Wechsler's measurement and appraisal of adult intelligence* (5th ed.). Baltimore, Md.: Williams & Wilkins, 1972.

Mathews, N. N., Hunt, E. B., & MacLeod, C. M. Strategy choice and strategy training in sentence–picture verification. *Journal of Verbal Learning and Verbal Behavior*, in press.

Norman, D. A., & Bobrow, D. G. On data-limited and resource-limited processes. *Cognitive Psychology*, 1975, *7*, 44–64.

Poltrock, S. E. *Individual differences in attentional processes*. Paper presented at the Western Psychological Association meeting, Seattle, Wash., April 1977.

Posner, M. I., & Boies, S. Components of attention. *Psychological Review*, 1971, *78*, 391–408.

Posner, M. I., & Mitchell, R. F. Chronometric analysis of classification. *Psychological Review*, 1967, *74*, 392–409.

Posner, M. I. & Snyder, C. Attention and cognitive control. In R. Solso (Ed.), *Information processing and cognition*. Hillsdale, N.J.: Lawrence Erlbaum Associates, 1975.

Schwartz, S. *Individual differences in information processing: Verbal ability and memory encoding processes*. Text of address given to Midwestern Psychological Association 1976 meeting. (Paper available from author, University of Texas, Medical Branch.)

Shiffrin, R. M., & Schneider, W. Controlled and automated human information processing: II. Perceptual learning, automatic attending, and a general theory. *Psychological Review*, 1977, *84*, 127–190.

Stroop, J. R. Studies of interference in serial verbal reactions. *Journal of Experimental Psychology*, 1935, *18*, 643–662.

Thorndike, R. L., & Hagen, E. *10,000 careers*. New York: Wiley, 1959.

Component Skills in Reading: Measurement of Individual Differences Through Chronometric Analysis

5

John R. Frederiksen
Bolt Beranek and Newman Inc.

Psychometricians have long sought to develop skill measures covering the repertoire of human cognitive abilities (cf. Carroll, 1976; French, 1951; French, Ekstrom, & Price, 1963; Guilford, 1967; Thurstone, 1938; Thurstone & Thurstone, 1941). The goal has been to build tests of information-handling skills that represent particular methods for processing information but that at the same time have applicability across a variety of task environments. Although this early work on cognitive and perceptual abilities is in many ways compatible with modern cognitive psychology in its effort to distinguish component processes in human skilled performance, the historical emphasis upon cross-situational information-processing abilities has limited the utility of such measures in the analysis of the particular component skills that are acquired in becoming proficient within a single task domain, such as reading.

In an effort to develop measures that are diagnostic of the sources of reading disability among naval recruits, we have been engaged in a series of studies of individual differences in the component skills involved in reading. The general goal of this work has been to develop a set of component skill measures that represent the particular information-handling processes used in reading, as they are conceptualized in current theories of the reading process. These include skills involved in the translation of orthographic patterns into "sound" patterns and the accessing of lexical information, as well as perceptual skills of pattern recognition and encoding.

A second goal has been to explore the potential offered by a chronometric approach to the measurement of component skills in reading. There are a number of reasons why the measurement of processing times may provide an important tool for the assessment of skills in young adults. First, it is difficult to generate errors in such basic skills as letter identification, phonic analysis, and the like in mature subjects. Yet individual differences in skill may still be apparent in their processing efficiencies. Second, studies of reaction times in human information processing have served experimental psychologists well in their efforts to build precise models for reading. In particular, the subtractive method for analyzing reaction times (RTs) has proven its value as a technique for deriving measurements that reflect a single locus of information processing. In the subtractive method, the difference in RTs is calculated for experimental conditions that vary in the processing load they place on some single processing subsystem. RT differences (or contrasts) then provide a measure of the relative difficulty in processing under the contrasted conditions. With a careful choice of contrasts among experimental conditions, it has been our hope that measurements of component processing skills can be derived.

VALIDATION IN A COMPONENT SKILLS ANALYSIS

The assertion that a particular RT contrast represents a designated component skill must, in the first case, be backed up by experiments designed to establish the construct validity of the particular contrasts. Thus, the first source of information concerning the validity of component skill measures comes from an analysis of the individual experimental tasks from which the RT contrasts are derived. In this analysis, variations in experimental conditions must be shown to yield the expected changes in response times as required by theory. Moreover, it is expected that there will be differences in the values of RT contrasts for subjects who vary with respect to overall reading proficiency.

The second source of information leading to construct validation results from a comparison of measures derived from different experimental contexts. From a set of experimental tasks, several measures are derived for each hypothesized component process, each one based upon a separate contrast among RTs for a different set of experimental conditions. A theoretical prediction can then be made about the relationships among these skill measures: Alternative measures of a designated component skill are hypothesized to form a common factor that is distinct from the factors formed by other component skills. Note that it is the high degree of specificity about the component skills measured by the chosen RT contrasts that will allow us to generate and test a specific hypothesis about the factor structure underlying our set of component skill measurements. And verification of this hypothesis will permit us to conclude with confidence that the component skills derived from our model of reading do, in fact, represent the postulated sources of individual differences among readers.

Finally, the role of component skills in establishing an individual's general level of reading ability can be investigated by using the component skill factors to predict other, more general measures of reading performance. This provides us with a third source of validating information—the evidence that particular component skills contribute to skilled reading as measured by conventional tests of reading ability and comprehension.

In summary, the methods I am advocating represent, in Cronbach's (1957) words, "a true federation of the [two] disciplines [p. 673]" of scientific psychology. First, I am suggesting that individual-differences variables (such as general reading proficiency) be included systematically in each of a series of experimental studies. This allows us to investigate in each study interactions between aptitude variables (reading ability) and experimental treatments, and to determine which contrasts among treatments are best able to describe differences among individual readers. Second, I am suggesting that the deductive, theory-based methods of experimental psychology be adopted as the primary basis for establishing the basic measures (contrasts) that are to be used in later analyses of covariances among skill measures. The goal is to develop measures of individual differences that represent single, component processes. Third, I am recommending that the methods of confirmatory, maximum-likelihood factor analysis be adopted as the basis for testing hypotheses about component skills underlying the battery of experimental measurements. The pattern of covariances among such measures must be regarded as an important source of information needed for constraining and validating a general component skills theory of reading. A theory that encompasses such data will be capable of accounting for individual differences in the use of component skills in reading, as well as providing for an assessment of individuals' skill levels for each component.

COMPONENT SKILL MEASURES

The theoretical model guiding the selection of component skill measures is illustrated in Fig. 5.1. The model distinguishes four main processing levels: (1) *Visual feature extraction;* (2) *Perceptual encoding;* (3) *Decoding;* and (4) *Lexical access.* Perceptual encoding is further subdivided into a component representing the *encoding of individual graphemes* and a component representing the *encoding of visually familiar, multigrapheme units* (e.g., SH, ING). Finally, decoding is divided into processes of *parsing* (Spoehr & Smith, 1973), *phonemic translation,* and *articulatory programming.*

A general feature of the model is the notion that although these processes are hierarchically arranged, the initiation of higher-level operations does not necessarily await completion of prior operations in the hierarchy. Thus, lexical access can be initiated on the basis of any of the following input representations: (1) a spatial distribution of visual features; (2) an array of independently encoded graphemes (e.g., T R A I N I N G); (3) encoded, overlapping, multiletter perceptual units, as in ((TR) ((AI) N)) (I (NG)) (see also Fig. 5.2.); (4) a parsed

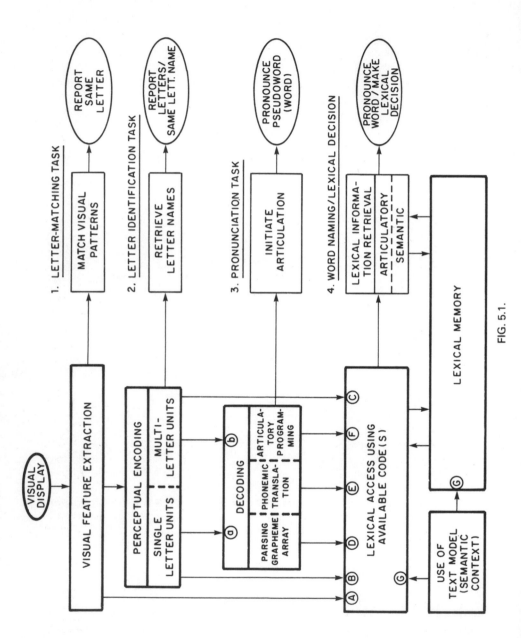

FIG. 5.1.

FIG. 5.2. An illustration of the structural organization that is implicit in the perceptual encoding of multiletter units.

grapheme array (having a form that may be similar to that illustrated in Fig. 5.2.); (5) a phonemic translation of the orthographic pattern, as in t r eI n I η; or (6) a speech contour, having assigned stress and intonation. Input representations 1–6 represent differing depths or degrees of processing prior to lexical access.[1] In a similar fashion, decoding can take place on the basis of (1) a set of independently encoded graphemes, or (2) encoded, multiletter perceptual units. Note that according to the model, the demands placed upon the decoding component are greatly lessened when the grapheme representation is made up of multiletter units having functional utility for decoding, such as affixes, double vowels, consonant clusters, and the like, as illustrated in Table 5.1.

Experimental Tasks

Component skill measures that are referenced to particular stages of processing have been derived from four experimental tasks.

1. Letter Matching.   In the letter-matching task (Posner & Mitchell, 1967), the subject is shown a brief (50 - msec) display containing a pair of letters that: (1) have the same name and form (AA, aa); (2) have the same name but differ in

---

[1]To handle readers' use of context in lexical retrieval, an additional input code (*g*) represents semantic/syntactic constraints based upon a contextually derived model of discourse. However, skills involved in the use of context are not included in the present set of experimental measures and are not considered until later.

FIG. 5.1.   (Opposite page) A schematic rendering of the processing model representing component skills in reading. Four processing levels are visual feature extraction, perceptual encoding, decoding, and lexical access. Initiation of higher-level operations does not await completion of prior operations. Decoding can be initiated on the basis of (a) independently encoded graphemes, or (b) multigrapheme units. Lexical access can be based upon (A) visual features, (B) independently encoded graphemes, (C) multigrapheme units, (D) a parsed grapheme array, (E) a phonological/phonemic translation, (F) a speech code, or (G) semantic/syntactic constraints on word identity. Experimental tasks 1 through 4 require different characteristic depths of processing.

TABLE 5.1
Decoding Under Two Levels of Perceptual Encoding

	Perceptual Encoding	
Process	Single-Letter Units	Multiletter Units
Stimulus	SHOOTING ↓	SHOOTING ↓
Encoded visual units	S/H/O/O/T/I/N/G ↓	SH/OO/T/ING
Decoding: Parsing grapheme array	SH/OO/T/ING ↓	
Decoding: Phonemic translation	ʃutɪη	ʃutɪη ↓
Assignment of stress and intonation	ʃut'ɪη	ʃut'ɪη

form (Aa); or (3) are totally different letters (Ad, ad, AD). The subject's task is to indicate whether the letter names are the same or different by pressing an appropriate response key.

Twenty subjects were tested in this and in the subsequently described experiments. The subjects were high-school students chosen to represent four reading levels on the basis of total scores on the Nelson–Denny Reading Test (the four groups represented percentile ranges of 16–39, 55–80, 88–98, and 99+, respectively). As shown in Fig. 5.3., we found that these four groups of readers differed from one another in speed of letter encoding (measured by the difference in RT for nominally similar and physically similar letter pairs) and, to a lesser extent, in the degree of savings in processing time when nominally similar letters were used instead of unrelated letters.

Given the wide differences among readers in letter-matching performance, two RT contrasts were derived from this task: 1. *speed in letter encoding* (Variable 1 in Table 5.2.) is measured by subtracting the mean RT for physically similar letters (AA, aa) from the mean RT for letters differing only in case (Aa, aA); and 2. *facilitation in encoding jointly occurring letters* (Variable 3) is measured by subtracting the RT for letters differing only in case (Aa, Dd) from the RT for letters that are completely different (Ad, aD). This RT comparision measures what might be termed category facilitation (cf. Posner & Snyder, 1975). These two measures are thought to refer respectively to the two subdivisions of perceptual encoding—encoding of individual graphemes and encoding of multigrapheme units.

2. Bigram Identification. In this task, described by Frederiksen (1978), the subject is shown a four-letter array, preceded and followed by a 300-msec pattern

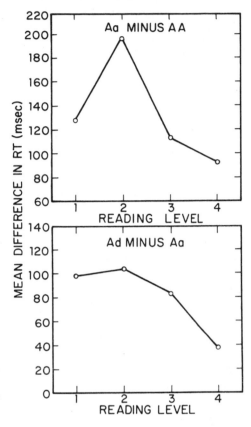

FIG. 5.3.   Differences in mean reaction times in letter matching for nominally similar and physically similar letters (at the top) and for dissimilar and nominally similar letters (at the bottom). Data are presented for four groups of readers.

mask (e.g., ####, followed by SHOT, and that followed by ####).[2] The actual stimulus array varies from trial to trial: On a third of the trials, the stimulus items are familiar English words, whereas on the remaining trials, the items are presented with two letters masked so that only a single pair of adjacent letters (a bigram) is visible (e.g., SH##, #AB#, ##TH). Further, the bigrams are chosen so as to differ in location within the item (positions 1–2, 2–3, or 3–4), frequency of occurrence in English [e.g., TH (high), GA (middle), and LK (low)], and likelihood of occurring in their presented position within a four-letter word [e.g., TH## (high) versus #TH# (low)] (cf. Mayzner & Tresselt, 1965). In all cases, the subject's task is to report all the letters that he or she can see, as quickly and accurately as possible. The response measure is the RT measured from the onset of the stimulus item to the onset of the subject's vocal report of letters.

[2]The pattern mask is, in reality, a figure formed by randomly sampling line segments from all the letters of the alphabet. The stimulus duration is set for each subject so that 90% to 95% of the letters would be correctly reported. It was generally around 90 to 100 msec.

TABLE 5.2

Variables Used in the Component Skills Analysis of Covariance Structures[a]

Variable	Code	Task	Results of ANOVA[+]
1. Speed in letter encoding: RT for dissimilar cases (Aa) minus RT for similar cases (AA, aa).	Letter encoding	Letter matching	$p < .05$
2. Scanning speed: Increment in RT per letter position.	Scanning speed	Bigram identification	$p < .05$
3. Facilitation in encoding jointly occurring letters: RT for dissimilar letters (Ad) minus RT for similar letters (Aa).	Percept. facilitation	Letter matching	—
4. Bigram probability contrast: RT (Low-Prob. Bigram) minus RT (High- & Middle-Prob. Bigrams).	Bigram probability	Bigram identification	$p < .05$
5. Array length contrast: Increase in RT for each added letter.	Length: Pseud.	Pseudoword decoding	$p < .06$
6. Syllable contrast: RT for two-syllable minus RT for one-syll.	Syllable: Pseud.	Pseudoword decoding	—
7. Vowel complexity contrast: RT for -vv- minus RT for -v-.	Vowel: Pseud.	Pseudoword decoding	—
8. Syllable contrast (as above, but for vocalization durations).	Syllable: Pseud. (dur.)	Pseudoword decoding	$p < .01$
9. Vowel complexity contrast (as above, but for vocalization durations).	Vowel: Pseud. (dur.)	Pseudoword decoding	$p < .10$
10. Percent drop in decoding indicators for HFW and Pseudo.: (Sum 5-9 for Pseud. − Sum 5-9 for HFW)/(Sum 5-9 for Pseudowords).	Δ% Decoding Pseud.–HFW	Word naming	—
11. Percent drop in decoding indicators for HFW and LFW: (Sum 5-9 for LFW − Sum 5-9 for HFW)/(Sum 5-9 for LFW).	Δ% Decoding LFW–HFW	Word naming	—

[a] All comparisons are for mean response times unless otherwise noted.
[+] Values of the variable differ for subjects at four reading levels at the indicated significance level.

The results show that subjects who vary in reading ability differ reliably both in their rate of scanning a perceptual array and in their sensitivity to redundancy built into the stimulus. In Fig. 5.4 we have plotted the increment in reaction time required for each shift in the position of the unmasked bigram, from the left to the right. As can be seen, this measure of scanning time (the slope) decreases as reading ability increases. Put another way, the high rate of scanning obtained with high-ability readers (250 letters per second) is five times that obtained with the poorest group of readers (48 letters per second) and suggests that the strongest readers may in effect be processing letters in parallel.

The interaction between bigram frequency and reading ability is also illustrated in Fig. 5.4. The bigram effect is defined as the difference in RT between the higher-frequency bigrams and the low-frequency bigrams. The magnitude of this RT difference can be seen to decrease as reading ability increases. Whereas high-ability readers are capable of efficiently processing letters that occur together in English over a broad frequency band, low-ability readers' efficiency in processing is limited to letter pairs that typically occur together with high regularity.

Based upon these findings, two measures have been derived from this experiment. A subject's *scanning speed* (Variable 2) is measured by subtracting the mean RT for bigrams presented in positions 3 and 4 from the mean for bigrams presented in positions 1 and 2 and then dividing by 2. This gives the increment in RT for each shift to the right in letter position. The *bigram probability contrast* (Variable 4) is measured by subtracting the RT for high- and middle-probability bigrams from that for low-probability bigrams. This variable gives the penalty in processing time brought by reducing the linguistic frequency of a bigram unit by the given amount. Variable 4 provides a second measure of a subject's ability to

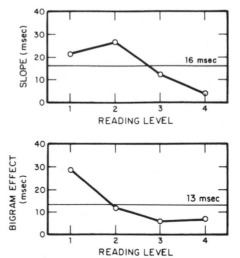

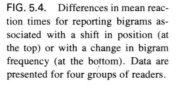

FIG. 5.4.   Differences in mean reaction times for reporting bigrams associated with a shift in position (at the top) or with a change in bigram frequency (at the bottom). Data are presented for four groups of readers.

encode orthographically regular, multigrapheme units. Variable 2 (*scanning speed*) is thought to provide a more general measure of perceptual encoding and to reflect both the single-grapheme and multigrapheme subprocesses.

3. Pseudoword Decoding.   In the pseudoword-decoding task (Frederiksen, 1976, 1978), subjects are asked to pronounce pseudoword tiems that have been derived from actual English words by changing a single vowel (e.g., *brench*, derived from *branch*). The set of pseudowords covers a number of orthographic forms, including variations in length, number of syllables, and type of vowel. We measure the RT from the presentation of the display to the onset of the subject's vocalization and the duration of his or her vocal response.

Differences in vocalization latencies for pseudowords varying in length, vowel complexity, and syllabic structure are shown in Fig. 5.5, plotted separately for our two best and two worst groups of readers. (Results for high- and low-frequency words are also presented for comparison.) These groups of readers appear to differ in the amount of additional processing time they require to handle each added letter. The low-ability readers also pay a greater price in processing time when a simple vowel is replaced by a digraph vowel, and when a one-syllable item is replaced by a two-syllable item. Finally, the good and poor readers differ in their vocalization durations, as shown in Fig. 5.6. Increases in vocalization durations are found for digraph vowels and two-syllable items compared with simple vowels and single-syllable items, and these increments are greatest for the poorer group of readers.

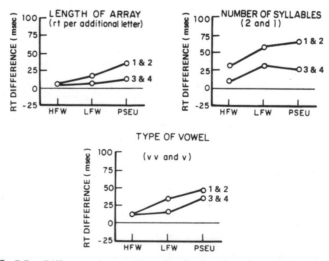

FIG. 5.5.   Differences in onset latencies for the planned comparisons among orthographic forms as a function of stimulus type (high-frequency words, low-frequency words, and pseudowords). Separate plots are given for readers at the top two and bottom two levels.

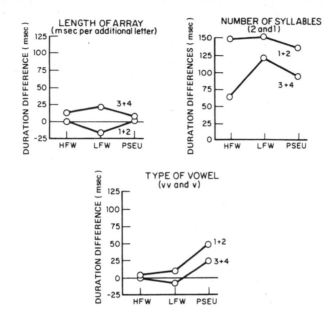

FIG. 5.6.   Differences in vocalization durations for the planned comparisons among orthographic forms as a function of stimulus type (high-frequency words, low-frequency words, and pseudowords). Separate plots are given for readers at the top two and bottom two levels.

These findings led us to derive a set of five measures of decoding: The *array length contrast* (Variable 5) is the increase in mean RT for each added letter for forms that are matched on initial phoneme and orthographic form (e.g., CCVC, CCVCC, CCVCCC). The *syllable contrast* (Variable 6) is measured by subtracting the mean onset RT for two-syllable items from that for one-syllable items that are matched on initial phoneme and orthographic form (e.g., CVC-CV and CVCCV). The *vowel complexity contrast* (Variable 7) is measured by subtracting the mean onset RT for pseudowords having sequences of two vowels (e.g., CVVCC) from that for pseudowords having single vowels (e.g., CVCCC). In addition, the syllable and vowel complexity contrasts were calculated using vocalization *durations,* forming Variables 8 and 9. These contrasts in all cases reflect the increase in processing difficulty occasioned by increasing the orthographic complexity of a stimulus item in a designated manner and are regarded as measures of decoding. It is thought that measures based upon RT to onset of vocalization tap earlier decoding processes of parsing and phonemic translation, whereas measures based upon vocalization durations tap later processes of articulatory programming, stress assignment, and the establishment of prosodic features.

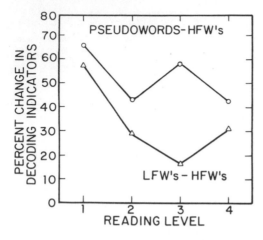

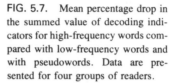

FIG. 5.7.   Mean percentage drop in the summed value of decoding indicators for high-frequency words compared with low-frequency words and with pseudowords. Data are presented for four groups of readers.

4. Word Naming.   This task (Frederiksen, 1976, 1978) is in every respect similar to the pseudoword-decoding task except for the use of English words in place of pseudowords. In addition to variations in orthographic form, the stimulus words have been chosen to represent two linguistic frequencies of occurrence—low-frequency words (having a mean SFI index[3] of 27.0) and high-frequency words (having a mean SFI index of 56.4). Each of the five contrasts already described for the pseudoword-decoding task can also be calculated for the word-naming task, for both high-frequency words (HFWs) and low-frequency words (LFWs). The results of these analyses are also displayed in Figs. 5.5 and 5.6. In general, what we find is a *drop* in the magnitude of these five indicators of decoding efficiency when words are substituted for pseudowords, and this drop is greater for high-frequency than for low-frequency words. With these observations in mind, we have constructed two measures for comparing the extent of use of decoding in processing high-frequency words with that for low-frequency words and pseudowords. The *percent drop in decoding indicators for HFWs and pseudowords* (Variable 10) is measured by summing the values of the five decoding contrasts for both HFWs and pseudowords and calculating the percent drop using the following formula:

$$\% \text{ Drop} = [\text{Sum (Pseudowords)} - \text{Sum (HFWs)}] / \text{Sum (Pseudowords)}$$

The *percent drop in decoding indicators for HFWs and LFWs* is measured in a similar manner, by substituting LFWs for pseudowords in the foregoing comparison. These variables were developed to measure a fundamental characteristic

[3]The SFI or Standard Frequency Index is a logarithmically transformed word-frequency scale (Carroll, Davies, & Richman, 1971). High values represent English words that occur commonly in text; low values represent uncommon words.

of lexical access: the depth of processing of orthographic information that characteristically takes place prior to lexical retrieval. Large values for either of these contrasts indicate a decrease in depth of processing when the stimuli are familiar English words, whereas small values indicate that there is a continued use of word analysis skills in the recognition of common words.

The mean values for each of these measures are given in Fig. 5.7 for each group of readers. There is a trend suggesting that poor readers rely less on word analysis procedures than do more proficient readers when they are reading common English words. However, individual differences in the use of decoding are even greater than differences attributable to overall reading level, and in neither case is the trend statistically significant.

Relation to Hypothesized Component Skills

It has been our belief that the set of measures derived from the four experiments we have described will permit us to distinguish the five component processes already alluded to and listed in Table 5.3. The first two components (or factors) we have refer to the two subprocesses of perceptual encoding. They deal respectively with the encoding of individual graphemes and with multigrapheme units. The third and fourth components refer to hierarchically organized levels of decoding: Phonemic translation includes the parsing of a grapheme array and the application of orthographic rules to derive a phonemic representation. Automaticity of articulation refers to operations performed on an initial phonemic representation in deriving an articulatory or speech representation, including the as-

TABLE 5.3
Definition of Component Processes
Hypothesized in the Analysis of Covariance Structures

Factor	Name	Description
I.	Grapheme Encoding	Efficiency in letter identification.
II.	Perceptual Facilitation in Encoding Multiletter Units	Efficiency in encoding orthographically regular or redundant letter sequences.
III.	Phonemic Translation	Efficiency in applying spelling rules to derive a phonological/ phonemic representation.
IV.	Automaticity of Articulation	Efficiency in articulation; syllabication, assignment of stress, prosodics.
V.	Depth of Processing in Word Recognition	Use of visual or whole-word recognition strategy in recognizing common words.

signment of stress pattern and other prosodic features. The last component process refers to what is probably the most fundamental characteristic of lexical access—namely, the depth of processing of the orthographic code prior to lexical retrieval.

The relations we have described between component skill measures and component processes can be summarized compactly in a factor matrix, shown in Table 5.4. The hypothesized factor structure is represented by the positions of zeros and pluses in the table. A value (or loading) of zero for a variable indicates that that variable is, by hypothesis, not considered a measure of the particular component process and is not expected to be related to that component except through possible correlations *between* component processes. A positive loading (+) indicates that the variable in question is hypothesized to be a measure of the particular component process, although the exact value of the loading remains to be estimated on the basis of data. By reading down a column of Table 5.4, one can see which RT contrasts have been hypothesized to be markers of a given factor. By reading across rows, one can see the hypothesized factorial composition for each variable.

TABLE 5.4
Hypothesized Factor Structure for the Set of Chronometric
Measures of Component Reading Skills

	Factor				
	I	*II*	*III*	*IV*	*V*
Variable	*Grapheme Encoding*	*Perceptual Facilitation*	*Phonemic Translation*	*Automaticity of Articulation*	*Depth of Processing in Word Recognition*
1. Letter encoding	+	0	0	0	0
2. Scanning speed	+	+	0	0	0
3. Percep. facilitation	0	+	0	0	0
4. Bigram probability	0	+	0	0	0
5. Length: Pseud.	+	0	+	0	0
6. Syll.: Pseud.	0	0	+	0	0
7. Vowel: Pseud.	0	0	+	0	0
8. Syll.: Pseud. (dur.)	0	0	0	+	0
9. Vowel: Pseud. (dur.)	0	0	0	+	0
10. Δ% Decod.: Pseu.–HFW	0	0	0	0	+
11. Δ% Decod.: LFW–HFW	0	0	0	0	+

EVALUATION OF THE COMPONENT SKILLS MODEL

Method

So far, this discussion has focused on the nature of component processes in reading and the types of chronometric measures used in their measurement. Our ability to validate the component skills analysis is based upon an important development in the application of statistical theory to the problem of factor analysis, worked out a few years ago by Karl Jöreskog (1970). Jöreskog's technique allows us to estimate directly the parameters of a factor model using the method of maximum likelihood, provided that the number of parameters to be estimated does not exceed the degrees of freedom in the covariance or correlation matrix being factored and that the hypothesized factor matrix is unique in that it precludes rotation of axes. The investigator reduces the number of parameters in the analysis by constraining the parameters of the model (values in the factor matrix, intercorrelations among the factors, or uniquenesses) to have specified values or to be equal to other parameters in the set to be estimated. Jöreskog's (Jöreskog, Van Thillo, & Gruvaeus, 1971) program provides a test of the fit of the hypothesized factor structure represented by the choice of constraints on the values of the parameters. Finally, comparisons among alternative structural models can be made using a likelihood ratio test.

Subjects

Data available for testing the structural model in Table 5.4 are the scores of 20 subjects who were tested on each of the tasks we have described. The subjects were high-school sophomores, juniors, and seniors and represented a wide range of reading ability levels. Their reading scores on the Nelson–Denny Reading Test ranged from the 16th to the 99th percentile. Approximately equal numbers of subjects were drawn from a city and a suburban high school.

Results

The goodness of fit of the hypothesized factor structure is given in Table 5.5, along with estimated values for the factor loadings. The obtained chi square of 38.4 (with 32 degrees of freedom) has a probability of .2, indicating that the sample correlation matrix would be obtained with high likelihood given that the hypothesized structure is the true factor structure. Moreover, the values of the loadings in the factor matrix support in detail the hypothesized component processes model. Factor I, Grapheme Encoding, is clearly marked by the letter-encoding and scanning-speed measures. Factor II, Encoding Multiletter Units, is marked by the perceptual facilitation contrast derived from the letter-matching

TABLE 5.5
Maximum-Likelihood Estimates of Factor Loadings
and Uniquenesses for the Experimental Variables[a]

	Factor					
Variable	I	II	III	IV	V	Uniqueness
1. Letter encoding	1.00	0.	0.	0.	0.	.00
2. Scanning speed	.64	.53	0.	0.	0.	.53
3. Percep. facilitation	0.	.62	0.	0.	0.	.62
4. Bigram probability	0.	.54	0.	0.	0.	.71
5. Length: Pseud.	.16	0.	.77	0.	0.	.36
6. Syll.: Pseud.	0.	0.	.80	0.	0.	.37
7. Vowel: Pseud.	0.	0.	.55	0.	0.	.70
8. Syll.: Pseud. (dur.)	0.	0.	0.	.96	0.	.08
9. Vowel: Pseud. (dur.)	0.	0.	0.	.36	0.	.87
10. $\Delta\%$ Decod.: Pseu.–HFW	0.	0.	0.	0.	.24	.94
11. $\Delta\%$ Decod.: LFW–HFW	0.	0.	0.	0.	1.00	.00

[a] Zero loadings were fixed by hypothesis; the goodness of fit of the hypothesized structure is measured by $\chi^2(32) = 38.4, p = .20$.

task and the bigram probability contrast derived from the bigram identification task. The three decoding indicators calculated from onset RTs in the pseudoword pronunciation task load on the Phonemic Translation factor (III), and the two decoding contrasts based upon vocalization durations load on the Articulation factor (IV). Finally, the measures of processing depth in reading words both load on the last factor (V), Depth of Processing in Word Recognition.

Estimates of the intercorrelations among the factors are presented in Table 5.6. A likelihood ratio test of the hypothesis that the factors are mutually ortho-

TABLE 5.6
Maximum-Likelihood Estimates of Intercorrelations Among the Factors[a]

Factor	I	II	III	IV	V
I. Grapheme Encoding	1.00				
II. Perceptual Facilitation	−.32	1.00			
III. Phonemic Translation	.09	.41	1.00		
IV. Automaticity of Articulation	.58	.24	−.17	1.00	
V. Depth of Processing in Word Recognition	−.11	.52	.08	.01	1.00

[a] A likelihood ratio test of the hypothesis of orthogonality of the factors yielded $\chi^2(10) = 20.29$, with $p < .05$.

gonal yielded $\chi^2(10) = 20.29$, with $p < .05$. The factors can therefore be assumed to be correlated with one another. Several patterns among these correlations are of interest:

1. Factors III–V appear to be mutually orthogonal, suggesting that each is tapping an independent aspect of the reading process. Facility in parsing/ phonemic translation appears to be uncorrelated with processes related to articulation, and the extent of decoding in reading common words is not related to a subject's level of skill at the decoding level.

2. The two aspects of perceptual encoding, on the contrary, do appear to be related to skill in decoding and lexical access. Subjects who are highly efficient in encoding multiletter graphemic units are faster in phonemic translation ($r = .41$) and in articulation ($r = .24$), and tend to use their decoding skills in accessing common English words in their lexicon ($r = .52$). It is subjects who are less proficient in identifying multiletter units who decrease their depth of processing when reading high-frequency words. Interestingly, there appears to be a small, reciprocal relationship between efficiency in single-letter encoding and in encoding multiletter units ($r = -.32$).

3. Finally, it appears that subjects who are rapid in encoding individual graphemes are also more rapid in articulatory processes ($r = .58$).

Evaluation of Alternative Structural Models

Three alternative hypotheses about the factor structure were developed in order to see if the finer distinctions made between subprocesses of perceptual encoding and decoding are necessary. The results of these investigations are presented in Table 5.7. In the first alternative model, we were interested in the distinction between perceptual encoding of individual graphemes and multigrapheme units, represented by factors I and II. These two factors were, accordingly, combined into a single perceptual encoding factor; in all other respects, the model was similar to the general model in Table 5.4. The test of fit yielded $\chi^2(37) = 54.16$ with $p = .034$, leading us to reject the first alternative model and to conclude that a distinction must be maintained between the two aspects of perceptual encoding as originally hypothesized.

In the second alternative model, the distinction between early (parsing, phonemic translation) and late (articulatory programming) decoding processes was dropped. Accordingly, factors III and IV were combined into a single Decoding factor, although in all other respects the model was similar to our original model. The test of fit yielded $\chi^2(36) = 54.0$ with $p = .027$. We were thus again led to reject the alternative model and to conclude that the distinction between levels of analysis within the decoding process must be maintained.

In the third alternative model, we were interested in testing the importance of the distinction between the perceptual parsing of a grapheme array (represented

TABLE 5.7

Test of Fit for Three Alternative Hypotheses
About the Covariance Structure

Alternative Model	Effects on Hypothesized Factor Structure	Number of Factors	Chi Square	d.f.	p
1. No distinctions are made between subclasses of perceptual skills.	Factors I and II are combined into a single Perceptual Encoding factor.	4	54.16	37	.034
2. No distinctions are made between subclasses of decoding skills.	Factors III and IV are combined into a single Phonemic Translation factor.	4	54.00	36	.027
3. No distinction is made between the perceptual encoding of multiletter units and the parsing of a grapheme array as a component of decoding.	Factors II and III are combined into a single Parsing and Phonemic Translation factor.	4	51.12	36	.049

by factor II) and parsing conceived as a component of decoding (factor III). Accordingly, in this model factors II and III were combined into a single factor. The likelihood ratio test yielded $\chi^2(36) = 51.12$ with $p = .049$, and again we were led to reject the alternative model. Evidently the perceptual grouping of graphemes into overlapping, multigrapheme units is distinct from rule-based processes involved in the translation of an orthographically regular array.

Testing the External Validity of the Component Skills Model

A final source of information concerning the validity of the component skill measures lies in their relationship to other, more general measures of reading proficiency. We are interested here in establishing what role the component processes play in setting levels of reading skill, as measured by conventional tests of reading ability and comprehension. Two sets of criterion variables were used: (1) *chronometric measures* representing overall levels of performance in reading individually presented words and pseudowords; and (2) *reading test scores,* including the Nelson–Denny total score (the sum of vocabulary and reading comprehension subtests), Nelson–Denny reading rate, and the Gray Oral Reading Test, total passage score (which includes number of pronunciation errors and reading rate). The loadings of each of these criterion variables on the component skill factors were calculated using a factor extension procedure and are presented in Table 5.8.

Chronometric Measures.   Mean onset latencies for pronouncing pseudowords and low- or high-frequency words (criterion variables 1 to 3) are highly predictable from the component skill factors, with multiple correlations[4] of .85, .75, and .82, respectively. There is a high degree of consistency in the pattern of loadings for each of these criterion variables: Although Grapheme Encoding is postively—but not strongly—related to efficiency in reading words and pseudowords, the ability to encode multiletter units is the strongest predictor of oral reading latencies. Phonemic Translation is related to pseudoword-decoding latencies but not to latencies for pronouncing English words. However, Automaticity of Articulation does turn out to be a strong predictor of reading latencies. Finally, the loadings on the Word Recognition factor support our earlier contention (Frederiksen, 1976) that it is the poorer readers who use a visual or whole-word basis for recognizing familiar words.

The difference in reading latencies for low- and high-frequency words was entered as the fourth criterion variable. The items contributing to the high- and low-frequency scores were balanced in number of letters, so we find that the

---

[4]The multiple correlations are subject to shrinkage and should be regarded only as indices of the degree of shared variance between the component skill factors and the criteria.

TABLE 5.8
Loadings of Criterion Variables on the Component Skill Factors

Criterion Variable	Factor					Squared Mult. Correlation
	I Grapheme Encoding	II Perceptual Facilitation	III Phonemic Translation	IV Automaticity of Articulation	V Word Recognition	
Chronometric Measures						
1. Mean onset latency:Pseudo.	.14	.70	.35	.59	.29	.73
2. Mean onset latency:LFW	.33	.43	.01	.49	.36	.56
3. Mean onset latency:HFW	.27	.55	.12	.46	.35	.68
4. Word-frequency effect (onset RT)	.08	.72	.33	.27	.22	.99
Reading Test Measures						
5. Nelson–Denny: Total score	−.42	−.59	−.02	−.69	−.35	1.00
6. Nelson–Denny: Speed	−.12	−.52	−.23	−.62	−.25	.73
7. Gray Oral	−.39	−.24	.09	−.43	−.37	.53

grapheme-encoding component does not predict this criterion. On the other hand, high- and low-frequency words do differ in the populations of graphemes they contain, and we are thus not surprised to find that the multiletter-encoding factor is a strong predictor of differences in latencies for reading low- and high-frequency words. Finally, the positive loadings on factors III through V suggest again that high- and low-frequency words are analyzed in different ways prior to lexical retrieval.

Reading Test Measures.[5]   The scores for the three reading test measures are highly predictable from the component skill factors, with multiple correlations of 1.00, .85, and .73 for the Nelson–Denny total, reading rate, and Gray Oral Reading Test scores, respectively. Again, the strongest predictors appear to be encoding mutliletter units and Automaticity of Articulation. Subjects scoring highly on the reading tests also tend to be efficient in Grapheme Encoding and to use their decoding skills in recognizing familiar English words as well as less familiar items. Low-scoring subjects again are found to be less efficient in encoding individual graphemes, in perceiving multigrapheme units, and in their degree of automaticity in the final stages of decoding; and they tend to recognize familiar words on the basis of their visual characteristics.

SUMMARY AND CONCLUSIONS

The evidence we have collected supports a component process model for reading that distinguishes at least five component skills:

1. Efficiency in perceptual encoding of individual graphemes.
2. Efficiency in encoding orthographically regular, multigrapheme units.
3. Efficiency in parsing an encoded grapheme array and in applying letter–sound correspondence rules to derive a phonological/phonemic representation.
4. Automaticity in deriving a speech representation, in the assignment of stress and other prosodic features.
5. The process of lexical retrieval, characterized by the depth of processing (perceptual encoding and decoding) that takes place prior to lexical access.

The picture we have gained of the patterns of intercorrelation among component skills and their relatedness to measures of reading proficiency permit us to draw two more general conclusions:

---

[5]The loadings are negative, indicating that efficiency in processing within the domain of each component skill is related to high scores on the reading tests.

1. *Although component processes can be regarded as hierarchically or-dered, the initiation of high-order processes* (e.g., lexical retrieval) *does not necessarily await the completion of earlier processing operations.* Thus, the depth of processing prior to lexical retrieval is seen to vary with the familiarity of a word. High-frequency words may be recognized on the basis of their visual characteristics, without the completion of the grapheme-encoding and decoding processes required for recognizing unfamiliar words.

2. *There are interactions (trade-offs) between the use of skills at one level of processing and the mode of processing and processing efficiency at higher levels of processing.* Thus, an ability to encode perceptually multiletter units reduces the demands placed on the decoding component, with a consequent increase in efficiency of decoding. Readers who have high scores on factor II (Encoding Multiletter Units) are also the fastest decoders, and they are likely to apply their efficient word analysis skills in recognizing common as well as rare words. On the other hand, readers who have a low level of skill in perceptually encoding multiletter units have the greatest difficulty in decoding grapheme arrays into "sound," and they are the ones who are most likely to reduce the depth of processing when visually familiar words are encountered. This processing in-teraction illustrates how the mode of processing at a high level (here, the type of evidence used as a basis for performing lexical access) is influenced by the level of skill in processing at a lower level. The modification in procedures for high-level processing (lexical access) serves to compensate for low efficiencies in lower-level component processes. Thus, the system adapts to its own deficien-cies and is able to improve its overall performance when the stimulus materials permit such an adjustment of processing characteristics to take place. In general, we believe that models for human information processing within a complex domain such as reading will have to account for individual differences in the procedures used by the system in allocating its components for the solution of a problem, as well as for skill differences among subjects in processing efficiencies within the component processes themselves.

EXTENSIONS OF COMPONENT SKILLS ANALYSIS TO READING OF TEXT

Our ideas for extending the general reading model to the processing of text are illustrated in Fig. 5.8. In addition to input from parallel/contingent systems for feature extraction, perceptual encoding, and phonemic and articulatory analysis, the lexical access process has available information derived from the analysis of previous text encountered by the reader. This information is encoded in the reader's discourse model and furnishes the basis for generation of hypotheses about subsequent text that may occur. Accordingly, we distinguish a process of *hypothesis generation,* which is characterized by the quality of inferential

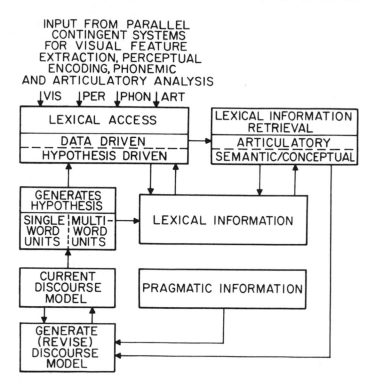

FIG. 5.8. A schematic rendering of processes involved when reading in context. (See text for explanation.)

analysis it performs and by the nature of the hypothesized units that are generated (e.g., single words or words in likely occurring, meaningful sequences). The *lexical access* process is then further characterized by the extent to which it is driven by perceptual data ("bottom-up" processing) or by hypotheses derived from text ("top-down" processing).

As a result of lexical access, semantic/conceptual information about the lexical category becomes available that, along with pragmatic information and information contained in the discourse model, furnishes the basis for generation of a revised discourse model. The information processing involved in building and revising a discourse model (see Kintsch & Vipond, 1977) will determine the rate at which perceptual hypotheses can be generated and, therefore, the degree to which a subject can profit from context in accessing lexical information.

Our current experimental efforts center on the use a subject makes of prior context in generating perceptual hypotheses, and on the extent to which skilled readers are capable of integrating information from perceptual and contextual sources in gaining access to the lexicon. The purpose of the experiment we report (Frederiksen, 1977) was to investigate the influence of semantic and linguistic context on the amount and quality of textual information that can be encoded within a single fixation. Studies of eye–voice span and density of eye fixations per line of text have shown that good and poor readers differ in the amount of text they take in within a fixation (Levin, Grossman, Yang, Kaplan, 1972; Levin & Kaplan, 1970). Marcel (1974) has shown that differences among readers in effective visual field width are greater when the textual material to be encoded is of high redundancy than when it is of low redundancy. Thus, it appears that the ability to utilize contextual information to increase the amount of information encoded in a single fixation may be an important characteristic of proficient readers.

We were interested in distinguishing three processes by which contextual redundancy might influence the *visual span,* or the effective width of the visual field. The first component process deals with the capacity of a reader to profit from sequential redundancies among the words occurring within a single fixation in encoding information within the fixation. The second component deals with the ability of a reader to use a prior semantic or linguistic context to increase the accessibility of the individual words employed in the test phrase. What we have in mind here is the influence of context on the thresholds for semantically relevant items within the subject's internal lexicon, as in Morton's (1969) "logo-gen" system. The third component is concerned with a subject's ability to generate semantically and syntactically appropriate word sequences or phrases based upon the analysis of a prior paragraph context, and that individual's capacity to utilize such hypotheses to guide lexical retrieval. The issue here is the extent to which a reader engages in processes of hypothesis generation and perceptual evaluation/confirmation that can bring the higher-order conceptual analysis of context to bear on the encoding of segments of text.

Design of the Experiment

We have developed a reading task that allows us to distinguish these three aspects of reading in context. Our subjects view a series of displays on the screen of a CRT display. Each series is made up of three frames, as shown in Fig. 5.9. Frame 1 contains a context paragraph. Subjects read the paragraph at their own rate. When they reach the end, they are asked to fixate the spot appearing in the final line of the display and to press a response key. Frame 2 is then presented for 200 msec,[6] followed by the test phrase in frame 3, also for 200 msec. The subject's task is to report as many words or word fragments as can be seen in the test line. In one session, subjects were presented 80 segments of text *with the context passage presented* in each case prior to the test phrase. In a second

[6]In order to ensure that subjects are keeping their eyes on the fixation point, they are asked to report any changes that may have occurred in the fixation spot. These changes are introduced during frame 2 on a quarter of the trials, as illustrated.

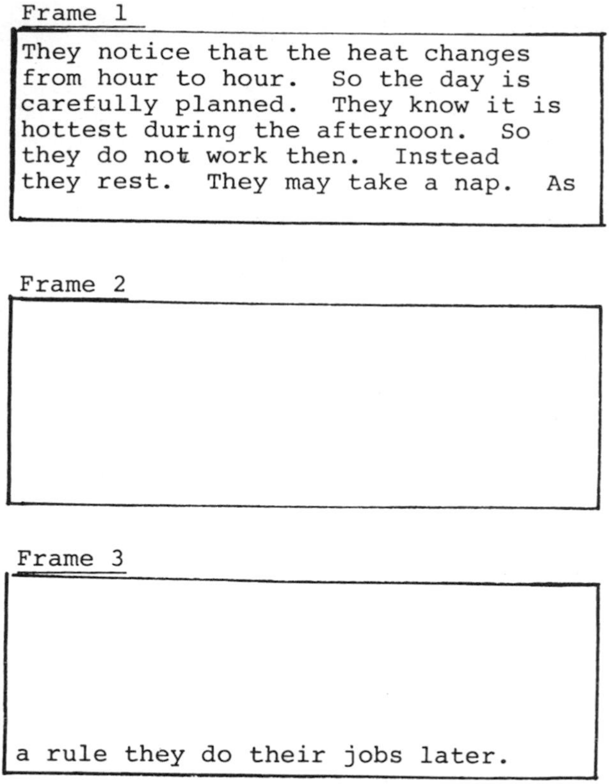

Frame 1

```
They notice that the heat changes
from hour to hour.  So the day is
carefully planned.  They know it is
hottest during the afternoon.  So
they do not work then.  Instead
they rest.  They may take a nap.  As
```

Frame 2

Frame 3

```
a rule they do their jobs later.
```

FIG. 5.9. The sequence of displays used in the context condition. Frame 1 contains the context and is subject terminated. Frame 2, presented for 200 msec, contains the fixation point, here slightly altered in form. Frame 3 contains the test phrase and is also presented for 200 msec.

session, the subjects were presented 80 new test phrases, this time with the *context passages omitted*. Within each session, half the test phrases were presented with their words in *normal sentence order* (as in the illustration), and half the lines were presented with their words in a *scrambled order* (as in ''a later do rule their they jobs''). The occurrence of normal and scrambled test lines was randomized within a session for each subject. The response measures were (1) the effective visual span, defined as the number of letter spaces from the leftmost correct letter to the rightmost correct letter, and (2) response latency in reporting the contents of the test display.

Subjects. The subjects were 16 high-school students in the 10th through 12th grades, who were divided as before into four reading-level groups on the basis of their scores on the Nelson–Denny Reading Test.

Reading Materials. The passages used in the experimental task were taken from the Degrees of Reading Power Test (State of New York, Board of Regents, 1976). The test passages represent 10 levels of text readability, chosen to fall at approximately equal steps on the Bormuth scale. For each readability level, there were eight consecutive test passages that together made up a mini-essay on some topic of general interest. At the bottom of the scale, the passages were made up of shorter, higher-frequency words, and the sentences were shorter and less complex.

To summarize our design, over two sessions each subject was tested: (1) in the presence and absence of semantically constraining context; (2) with the test words either scrambled or in normal sentence order; and (3) at each of 10 levels of text readability. Response measures included: (1) the *visual span,* or distance in letter spaces from the leftmost to the rightmost correct letter; and (2) response time (RT) measured from the onset of the test line to the initiation of the subject's vocal report.

Results of the Context Experiment

The overall effects of variations in context and test line conditions are shown in Fig. 5.10.

A measure of the subject's *ability to process redundant word sequences within a fixation* was obtained by comparing performance for test lines presented in the normal and scrambled word orders when there was no prior context. On the average, there was an increase in visual span of .53 degrees of visual angle (one letter space = .67 degrees) when the test words were presented in normal sentence order. Thus, readers do appear to have the capacity to exploit sequential redundancies among words, even within the time constraints of processing within a single fixation. Moreover, this increase in visual span was accomplished at the same time that there was a reduction in processing time of 169 msec, suggesting that there was an accompanying reduction in processing load. In this case, however, there were no significant differences among the good and less good readers, who appeared to be equally able to profit from sequential redundancy within a fixation.

A measure of the *effects of prior context on word recognition thresholds* was obtained by comparing performance in encoding scrambled word sequence when a prior context was provided with that when the context was omitted. When the test words were presented in scrambled order, the addition of a prior context brought an increase in average visual span of .64 degrees. However, there was essentially no change in response time under these two conditions, implying that the increase in width of the effective visual field was achieved with an actual reduction in the processing time per unit encoded (e.g., per letter) within the field. This suggests that the availability of contextually relevant lexical items is enhanced when there is a semantically constraining context.

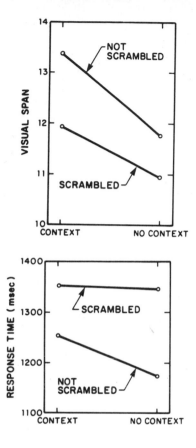

FIG. 5.10. Average performance for all subjects on two dependent variables, for two conditions of text presentation (normal and scrambled order) and context (present and absent).

A measure sensitive to the subjects' use of context in *generating and testing hypothesized word sequences* was obtained by evaluating their performance in encoding sequences of words that were presented in normal sentence order. When the words of the test phrase are presented in sentence order, it is possible to test hypotheses about word sequences or phrases that have been generated on the basis of a discourse model built by the reader. We anticipated that increases in visual span brought about by the presentation of a prior context would be greater when the words in the test line were in normal sentence order than when they were in a scrambled order. The effects of context on visual span were actually nearly twice as great when the test word sequence was normal (an increase in span of 1.10 degrees) as when the words were scrambled (producing an increase of .64 degrees). Interestingly enough, the effect of context on response time was to increase the average processing time by 79 msec. Here, the effect of context is to increase the processing load, rather than to reduce it. This finding is consistent with our interpretation that the sequence of words is, in this case, actively evaluated in the light of contextually derived hypotheses.

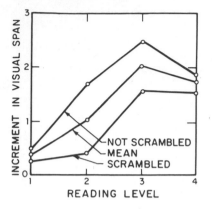

FIG. 5.11. The increment in performance brought about by the addition of a prior paragraph context, plotted separately for readers of varying ability and for the two presentation conditions of the test line (normal and scrambled).

Interactions With Reading Ability

There were differences among readers of high and low ability in their use of context in encoding segments of text. In Fig. 5.11 we have plotted the magnitude of context effects for scrambled and unscrambled test line conditions and for subjects at each of the four reading-ability levels. In general, high-ability readers show greater increments in visual span in the presence of context than do low-ability readers. The poorest readers show little increase in visual span under any circumstances of testing. However, readers in the second group show a sizable increase in span when the test line is presented in normal sentence order but show no increase when the test line is presented in scrambled order. And readers in the top two ability groups show large increases in span for both conditions. There were, however, no differences among groups of readers in their response times for any of the test conditions.

In summary, there appear to be differences among readers of high and low ability in the use of prior context in encoding text. The predictive processes involved in generating hypothesized sequences of words appear to be more broadly distributed in the population of readers than do the processes involved in setting thresholds of lexical availability.

Effects of Text Readability

The texts we employed varied in readability from grade level 4 to grade level 18. Texts of high difficulty tended to have fewer words per line, and the words tended to be longer and were composed of many syllables. On the other hand, texts of low difficulty had more words per line, and the words were shorter and were often of one syllable. We found that despite increases in comprehension difficulty, the visual span increased by a total of .67 degrees as the difficulty

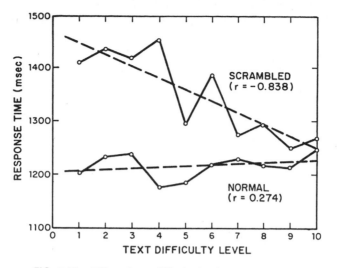

FIG. 5.12.   Effect of text difficulty level on response time.

level of the text was increased from the lowest to the highest level.[7] Thus, within the temporal limitations imposed by the restriction of processing to information gained in a single fixation, subjects are able to encode a larger number of letters when the display contains a small number of long words than when it contains a larger number of shorter words. This finding is consistent with Fry's (1970) observation that in understanding speech, subjects take longer to process items containing a word boundary (e.g., *tempor rizing*) than to process items lacking such a boundary (e.g., *temporizing*).

The effects of text readability on response times depended on whether the test words were presented in a normal or scrambled order. These results are shown in Fig. 5.12. When the test line was presented in normal sentence order, there was no effect of text readability on RT. However, the effect of text readability on RT in reporting scrambled word sequences was pronounced: The RT was greatest when the test line contained many short words and was smallest when the test line was composed of a lesser number of longer words. These results suggest that for scrambled word sequences, the encoding demands are primarily determined by the number of words to be encoded rather than by their length. The fact that this relation does not hold when the test words are presented in normal sentence order suggests that the units of perceptual analysis in that case are most likely larger than a single word.

Aside from the already mentioned effects of text readability, there was no interaction between text difficulty and subjects' reading ability in any of our

[7]Visual span increased linearly with text difficulty; the correlation between these two variables was .78.

analyses. The magnitude of context effects was the same for passages at all points on the readability scale. Because these texts differ greatly in the demands they place on processes of comprehension, we believe that the differences in context effects for good and poor readers are less a reflection of differences in ability to construct appropriate semantic representations than they are measures of our subjects' ability to *apply* such conceptual models in top-down fashion in the encoding of additional text as it subsequently becomes available.

External Validity of Sensitivity-to-Context Measures

Data bearing on the external validity of our measures of sensitivity to context are presented in Table 5.9. These are the correlations of selected contrasts among performance measures obtained in the context experiment with three subtests of the Nelson–Denny Reading Test: vocabulary, reading comprehension, and reading speed. (Correlations with total scores are also given.) Three pairs of contrasts were considered:

1. *Sensitivity to sequential redundancy in encoding words within a fixation.* These two measures are the differences in performance (visual span and

TABLE 5.9
Correlations of Selected Contrasts Obtained in the Context Experiment
With Nelson—Denny Reading Test Scores

| | Test Score | | | |
Contrast	Vocabulary	Comprehension	Speed	Total (Vocab. & Compr.)
Sequential redundancy effect (no context)				
Span	.27	.43*	.13	.34
RT	− .06	.10	− .09	− .00
Context effect with scrambled test phrase				
Span	.38	.49*	.15	.44
RT	.13	.19	.20	.16
Context effect with normal test phrase				
Span	.36	.47*	.40	.41
RT	− .20	− .36	−.11	− .27
Multiple correlation for all three contrasts				
Span	.45	.62*	.45	.53
RT	.44	.57	.42	.50

*$p < .05$.

RT) obtained for normal and scrambled test phrases that are, in each case, presented without an accompanying context paragraph.

2. *Use of context in word recognition.* These two measures are performance differences in encoding scrambled sequences of words, presented in the presence or absence of a prior paragraph context.

3. *Use of context in encoding phrases.* These two measures are differences in performance in reporting normal English phrases that are, or are not, presented as the continuation of a prior context paragraph.

Values for each of these contrasts were calculated for individual subjects on the basis of their performance under the indicated conditions of the context experiment.

The most notable feature of the correlational data presented in Table 5.9 is the fact that for each contrast calculated among measures of visual span, the largest correlation is with scores on the comprehension subtest. Moreover, the lowest correlations are generally with the measures of reading speed.

There is an exception to this pattern, and it is the positive correlation of .40 between use of context in encoding phrases and Nelson–Denny reading speed. This is the only contrast that is appreciably correlated with the speed measure. Thus, it would appear that subjects who show sizable increments in visual span when reading phrases in context are the ones who show the highest reading rates when reading a text for speed and comprehension. These are the readers who are able to utilize prior context and the information encoded in their current discourse model to generate hypotheses about the propositional and syntactic forms that are to follow. An active reading strategy, one that makes use of prior context in the encoding of incoming segments of text, appears to contribute both to reading fluency and to reading with comprehension.

The multiple regression of comprehension scores on the three contrast measures yielded a significant multiple correlation ($R = .62$). The standardized regression weights for the three contrasts were, respectively, .36, .09, and .41. Thus, the independent contributions of contrasts 1 and 3 were sizable, whereas the contribution of contrast 2 was insubstantial given that the other two contrasts were included in the prediction equation. It would appear that sensitivity to sequential redundancy and use of context in encoding phrases[8] are related to a subject's general skill in drawing inferences and identifying the key ideas in text. There is, we might say, a perceptual ramification of skill in understanding prose, and that is the ability to utilize hypotheses generated on the basis of contextual discourse as a guide for lexical search and retrieval.

We note, finally, that measures of speed of responding corresponding to each of the contrasts did not correlate highly with reading test subscores. The major exception to this rule is the correlation of $-.36$ between the third contrast and the

---

[8]Interestingly, these two contrasts are essentially uncorrelated with one another ($r = .048$).

comprehension subtest. There was, as we have seen in Fig. 5.10, an increase in mean RT for reporting normal English phrases that were presented as a continuation of a prior text. The correlation already referred to indicates, therefore, that the most skilled comprehenders were the readers who showed the smallest increases in processing time when reading phrases in context. Incidentally, there was also a negative correlation of $-.38$ between increments in visual span associated with the addition of context and the corresponding changes in RT.[9] Thus, it was readers who showed the largest increments in visual span who showed the smallest increments in processing time. In other words, the readers who could most profit from context were also the ones who were most efficient in perceptually assimilating semantically and syntactically predictable phrases as they were presented.

CONCLUSIONS

I have described an initial experimental attack on the problem of identifying component skills in the reading of text. The results have supported our notion that there are separable component processes related to the use of context in encoding segments of text available within a fixation. Two of these, sensitivity to sequential redundancy and use of context in encoding phrases, are clearly related to a subject's general ability in drawing inferences and identifying key ideas in text—abilities that appear to be tapped in the measure of reading comprehension. Finally, we noted that our measure of subjects' use of context in generating and evaluating hypotheses was also associated with high reading speed in the comprehension subtest of the Nelson–Denny test. The picture we gain is that of a proficient reader who constructs a discourse model while reading and utilizes the model to generate hypotheses about likely occurring propositional and syntactic forms that are to follow. The processes of lexical retrieval in such a reader are to a large extent guided by hypotheses derived from context. However, when recourse is made to data-driven processes for lexical analysis, our proficient reader has a complement of efficient word analysis skills that he or she can utilize. We speculate that at any moment, the lexical retrieval system is not exclusively operating in either data-driven or hypothesis-driven modes but, rather, that it is simultaneously engaged in word analysis processing while attempting to confirm contextually derived hypotheses on the basis of the evidence that is available. It may be that it is the high degree of automaticity developed by proficient readers in the analysis of orthographic forms that makes the integrated processing of perceptual and contextual data a real possibility.

[9]This was the only nonzero correlation we found, for any of our contrasts, between span increments and RT changes.

ACKNOWLEDGMENT

This research was sponsored by the Personnel and Training Research Programs, Psychological Sciences Division, Office of Naval Research, under Contract No. N 0014-76-0461, Contract Authority Identification Number NR 154-386.

REFERENCES

Carroll, J. B. Psychometric tests as cognitive tasks: A new "structure of intellect." In L. B. Resnick (Ed.), *The nature of intelligence.* Hillsdale, N.J.: Lawrence Erlbaum Associates, 1976.

Carroll, J. B., Davies, P., & Richman, B. *The American Heritage word frequency book.* Boston: Houghton Mifflin, 1971.

Cronbach, L. J. The two disciplines of scientific psychology. *American Psychologist,* 1957, *12,* 671-684.

Frederiksen, J. R. *Decoding skills and lexical retrieval.* Paper delivered at the annual meetings of the Psychonomic Society, November 1976.

Frederiksen, J. R. *Text comprehension and the effective visual field.* Paper delivered at the annual meetings of the Psychonomic Society, St. Louis, Mo., November 1977.

Frederiksen, J. R. Assessment of perceptual, decoding, and lexical skills and their relation to reading proficiency. In A. M. Lesgold, J. W. Pellegrino, S. Fokkema, & R. Glaser (Eds.), *Cognitive psychology and instruction.* New York: Plenum, 1978.

French, J. W. The description of aptitude and achievement tests in terms of rotated factors. *Psychometric Monograph,* Number 5. Chicago: University of Chicago Press, 1951.

French, J. W., Ekstrom, R. B., & Price, L. A. *Manual for kit of reference tests for cognitive factors* (rev. ed.). Princeton, N.J.: Educational Testing Service, 1963.

Fry, D. B. Reaction time experiments in the study of speech processing. In B. Malmberg, D. B. Fry, R. Lancia, R. Carré, M. Rossi, J. Paille, & H. L. Lane, *Novelles perspectives en phonetique* (Vol. I). Brussels: Université Libre de Bruxelles, 1970.

Guilford, J. P. *The nature of human intelligence.* New York: McGraw-Hill, 1967.

Jöreskog, K. G. A general method for analysis of covariance structures. *Biometrika,* 1970, *57*(2), 239-251.

Jöreskog, K. G., Van Thillo, M., & Gruvaeus, G. T. *ACOVSM: A general computer program for analysis of covariance structures including generalized MANOVA* (RB-71-1). Princeton, N.J.: Educational Testing Service, 1971.

Kintsch, W., & Vipond, D. *Reading comprehension and readability in educational practice and psychological theory.* Paper presented at the conference on Memory, University of Uppsala, Uppsala, Sweden, June 1977.

Levin, H., Grossman, J., Yang, R., & Kaplan, E. Constraints and the eye-voice span in right and left embedded sentences. *Language and Speech,* 1972, *15,* 30-39.

Levin, H., & Kaplan, E. L. Grammatical structure and reading. In H. Levin & J. P. Williams (Eds.), *Basic studies on reading.* New York: Basic Books, 1970.

Marcel, T. The effective visual field and the use of context in fast and slow readers of two ages. *British Journal of Psychology,* 1974, *65,* 479-492.

Mayzner, M. S., & Tresselt, M. E. Tables of single-letter and digram frequency counts for various word length and letter position combinations. *Psychonomic Monograph Supplement,* 1965, *1,* 13-22.

Morton, J. Interaction of information in word recognition. *Psychological Review,* 1969, *76,* 165-178.

Posner, M. I., & Mitchell, R. F. Chronometric analysis of classification. *Psychological Review,* 1967, *74,* 392–409.

Posner, M. I., & Snyder, C. R. R. Attention and cognitive control. In R. Solso (Ed.), *Information processing and cognition: The Loyola symposium.* Hillsdale, N.J.: Lawrence Erlbaum Associates, 1975.

Spoehr, K. T., & Smith, E. E. The role of syllables in perceptual processing. *Cognitive Psychology,* 1973, *5,* 71–89.

State of New York, The Board of Regents. *Degrees of reading power test.* Albany, N.Y.: State Education Department, 1976.

Thurstone, L. L. Primary mental abilities. *Psychometric Monographs,* No. 1. Chicago: University of Chicago Press, 1938.

Thurstone, L. L., & Thurstone, T. G. Factorial studies of intelligence. *Psychometric Monographs,* No. 2. Chicago: University of Chicago Press, 1941.

6 Discussion: Aptitude Processes, Theory, and the Real World

John B. Carroll
University of North Carolina at Chapel Hill

Rather than discussing the papers in any great detail, I aim to give a rather general theoretical orientation to the theme of the conference—a theme that directs our attention to the possibility of applying cognitive process analysis, whatever that may be, to the design and conduct of instruction, taking into account knowledge about aptitudes and about learning.

At a recent conference that concentrated on the aptitude or individual-difference term of this function, I read part of a paper—now published in its entirety (Carroll, 1978)—that tried to do two things: raise questions about some of the statistical methodology that has been employed in the cognitive process analysis of aptitudes, and pose problems in the theoretical interpretation of the findings in this area. My general worry was over the possible circularity and theoretical futility of defining processes in terms of individual differences, and at the same time searching for individual differences by making assumptions about processes. These problems may well continue to plague researchers, but I do not attempt to consider them again here.

The focus of the present conference is on instruction. But we can't focus on instruction without some consideration of what that instruction is designed to accomplish—not only in terms of relatively immediate changes in knowledge, skill, and behavior but also in terms of more lasting changes that will carry over into long-term achievement and success. This means that we need to consider the mix of requirements on the job. Perhaps Snow's distinction between assembly and control processes, on the one hand, and performance processes, on the other, will be useful here. Jobs must differ considerably in which of these kinds of processes they require. Those of a relatively routine character may be concerned mainly with performance processes. But there are other jobs that put more

139

emphasis on assembly and control processes—jobs in which people have to figure out new ways of solving problems that may come up on the job. Snow's report that a certain kind of computerized instruction (in his Basic Instructional Program) tended to help some people and not others suggests that some kinds of instruction might be counterproductive with respect to the kinds of assembly and control processes that might be required after instruction is terminated. That is, it seems that although some people may show success in a training situation, they are not helped to develop the kinds of assembly and control processes that might be required in actual job performance.

Relevant here also is a point that I emphasize later on—namely, that one must consider the long-term changes in aptitude that may occur over time as a result of instruction and job experience. I remind you of the claims being made by Bloom (1976) about what he calls "mastery learning"—that under a kind of instruction where the individual is given specific help on the problems he or she is encountering, the individual differences appear to decrease on later tasks and learning situations, because individuals have been brought to a point where they can address themselves to these tasks more effectively.

APTITUDES AND APTITUDE PROCESSES

I have some uneasy feelings about the theoretical underpinnings of some of our work on aptitudes and aptitude processes. We address ourselves to what we call "processes" without knowing where these processes sit in a more general behavior theory. Exactly what are these "processes"?

Let me quote Snow's definition of aptitude processes

> Aptitude processes are those predictable, directed changes in psychological functioning by which individual learners
> 1. adapt or fail to adapt to the short-term and long-term performance demands of instructional conditions,
> 2. develop or fail to develop the expected organization of knowledge and skill through learning activities, and
> 3. differ from one another in the quality or quantity of learning outcome attained thereby.

This may be accepted as a definition of aptitude processes, but it does not tell us what aptitude processes really are. I would urge that we can arrive at a basic conception and understanding of aptitude processes only through considering them in the perspective of a more general behavior theory.

Table 6.1 may suggest the levels of theory that would be needed to delineate aptitude processes and their role in instruction. As you see, we need a series of

TABLE 6.1
Levels of Theory Required for Adapting Instruction to
Individual Differences Through Cognitive Process Analysis

Theory Level	Subject Matter
General psychological theory	Genetics, development, maturation, perception, learning, cognition, affect, performance, etc.
Theory of individual differences	Attributes, traits, dimensions of ability, skill, knowledge, personality, etc., and their sources; analysis of individual differences in terms of cognitive process and knowledge requirements.
Theory of the external validity of individual-difference traits	Analysis of real-world tasks, jobs, and courses of instruction in terms of individual-difference requirements; decisions concerning selection and assignment of individuals to tasks, jobs, and courses of instruction and training.
Theory of instruction	Selection and development of instructional modes and events in the light of all the foregoing theories.

theories, one corresponding to each level of the table. At the highest level is general psychological theory, which should tell us something about the role of genetics, maturation, and development; about mechanisms of perception, learning, cognition, affect, and motivation; and about the kinds of performances of which individuals are capable.

Somewhat lower down is a general theory of individual differences, which describes human attributes, traits, measurable levels of skill, knowledge, motives, attitudes, and so forth. But mere description and measurement are not enough. We would need to know to what extent all these dimensions of individual differences are the results of genetic and maturational forces and, particularly, to what extent they are the results of learning, practice, and experience. We would need to know, further, to what extent individual-difference traits can be modified through instruction or other forms of "treatment" and the limits to which, in an individual case, we can expect to modify the trait. We would want to know to what extent levels of skill are related through the kinds of prerequisiteness relations that have been postulated by Gagné (1968), whereby learning task A makes possible learning task B; learning task B makes possible learning task C; and so on. Finally, we would want to ascertain what perceptual, cognitive, affective, and psychomotor processes are involved in the display of skill and knowledge. We might even want to consider the relations of these skills to the constitution and physique of the individual. All these aspects of a theory of individual differences must be considered in reference to a more general behavior theory.[1]

Still lower down in the table is another kind of theory—perhaps not a big theory, but certainly important in considering how individual differences may interact with instruction. I call it a theory of external validity—a theory that is concerned with the relevance of individual-difference traits, skills, knowledges, and the like to real-world tasks. In other words, we should ask to what extent the individual differences we have identified in our research manifest themselves in performance on real-world tasks, courses of instruction, and jobs. What levels of ability, motivation, and so on are required for given levels of performance on these real-world tasks? Answering such questions requires thorough analysis of these real-world tasks, courses, and jobs in terms of individual-difference dimensions.

It's when we get to a theory of instruction, the last level of theory I have represented in the table, that things get even more complicated. To develop a completely adequate theory of instruction, to design instruction that is appropriate for the individual student, and even to decide how much a given trainee will profit from instruction (with the possibility of deciding that assigning the candidate to instruction is not worthwhile), we would need as much knowledge as possible from the other levels of theory represented in the table. For example, to decide whether a job candidate with low ability on a certain dimension should be given instruction at all, we would need to know to what extent that ability is relevant to performance on the job, what kinds of cognitive and other processes are involved in the ability, and to what extent that ability can be modified through instruction or other treatment.

This is only a brief sketch of the levels of theory required to develop a complete theory of instruction that takes into account individual differences in processes. Obviously, I haven't attempted to fill in details; actually, the details are only partially available in our present state of knowledge.

ARE PROCESSES THE ONLY KINDS OF CONSIDERATIONS?

Process is an "in" word. Snow has given us not only a definition of *aptitude process* but of the term *process* itself; I quote from his paper again (see Chapter 2, this volume):

[1]Note that I tend to be eclectic about psychological theory. We can certainly use some principles stemming from radical behaviorism, but at the same time we can't hesitate to apply whatever is valuable from cognitive theory. Skinner (1977) has written an essay on why he is not a "cognitive psychologist"; it would be engaging to counter with some thoughts on why one *should* be a cognitive psychologist.

Having defined *aptitude*, the term *process* also needs some attention at the start; its referent is often taken for granted. We usually take *process* to mean an active change or series of changes showing consistent direction in the ongoing psychological functioning of the organism. But the "changes" can refer to changes in a dynamic functional system as in some learning theories, or to changes in the information being processed by a static system as in some cognition theories, or to changes in both. We need to keep in mind, I think, that in research on instructional learning, we are dealing with phenomena involving changes in both.

Certainly a process involves *change,* but what I like most about Snow's description is the implication that change often involves a change in *information*. Although we talk much about information processing, we tend to concentrate on the processing and overlook the information that is being processed. Often, the problem is that the information is not there to be processed, let alone to be changed! As I tried to demonstrate in "Psychometric tests as cognitive tasks" (Carroll, 1976), a great many of the individual differences revealed by psychological tests are not differences in process but differences in the contents of memory stores. To be sure, these tests may tap differences in processes of storing and retrieving information, but they can properly tap such process differences only if the information is present to be stored, accessed, and retrieved.

A point related to this is that some of the "processes" we have been studying are *produced* by individual differences in memory stores. A good example of this is in the section of Snow's paper that deals with the behavior of individuals responding to vocabulary items that are "difficult" for them. The items are difficult for them simply because they do not have the lexical knowledge required to answer them. I don't really know how useful it is to study the kind of "process" they indulge in when confronted with these items—a kind of random, almost irrational behavior in searching among the alternatives.

A case of process differences caused by the lack of ability in assembly and control processes is the behavior of some individuals in attempting to solve "mental paper-folding" tasks. This behavior is apparently a response to their lack of ability to form images or to trace through, mentally, the steps required to solve the task; the rather unsystematic approaches they took were a response to ability deficits.

I have been tempted to think that the study of processes that arise through lack of ability is somewhat trivial and uninteresting. On the other hand, perhaps such study is not trivial, in the sense that the understanding of processes that arise through ability deficits might be relevant for what has traditionally been called the "diagnosis of learning difficulties," which seems to be one of the key elements in any system of individualized instruction—CAI, mastery learning, or whatever. In such systems, feedback loops must be devised to remedy learners' difficulties that arise either through lack of knowledge and skill or lack of appropriate assembly and control processes.

This distinction between processes, on the one hand, and specific knowledges and skills, on the other, is important in many ways. As yet, we know very little about processes, which have mainly to do with certain aspects of performance. Knowledge and skills are somewhat more tangible, and we know something about how to measure them. Even so, we may fail to recognize the role of knowledges and skills in individual-difference measurements of various sorts. Their role is obvious enough in measurements of, say, the verbal knowledge factor (V); I suspect, however, that analysis would show that they also play a role in measures of perceptual and spatial abilities, insofar as those measures involve learned perceptions of objects, geometric forms and shapes, and the like. Tests of reasoning and mathematical ability can also tap various kinds of knowledges— not only knowledge of number facts, for example, but also knowledge of algorithms and procedures for solving problems. Algorithms and other kinds of strategies for solving problems or achieving task performance can constitute pieces or chunks of stored knowledge that individuals may possess in different amounts. We find many examples in mathematical behavior—algorithms for doing long division or finding the square root, for example (even if it's the algorithm for doing the computation with a hand-held computer)—but there are also algorithms for solving nonmathematical problems, like verbal analogies. Perhaps *algorithm* is too strong a word here; rather than *algorithm* in its formal sense, I have in mind the knowledge of whatever procedures an individual may find useful in solving problems.

To be sure, algorithms and other kinds of procedures can be looked at as sequences of processes, for they often constitute, in essence, ordered series of procedures for handling information. But some of the current work in individual differences in information processing may have lost sight of the fact that individuals may differ in the degree to which they possess knowledge of the total procedure for responding to a task efficiently. Instead, this work has concentrated on the study of the individual processes that make up the total procedure. Much as the work of Robert Sternberg (1977) is to be admired, I wonder whether he has taken adequate account of the possibility that the individual differences he observes in solving analogies may be, in part, due to knowledge of what an analogy is and of the total set of procedures for solving analogies. He has been working, of course, with individuals in Western culture who may in general be expected to know what an analogy is. Consider, however, the reports of Luria (1976) about the behavior of Siberian peasants when confronted with certain reasoning tasks. For example, one of the subjects he studied on a field trip to Siberia in the early 1930s, a 37-year-old illiterate male from a remote village, was given the following problem:

"Cotton can grow only where it is hot and dry. In England it is cold and damp. Can cotton grow there [p. 108]?"

This problem, although not exactly an analogy, requires a kind of formal deduction similar to that required in analogy problems. The subject's first response was simply, "I don't know." Even when pressed to "think about it," he replied: "I've only been in the Kashgar country; I don't know beyond that . . . " When pressed further with the question, "But on the basis of what I said to you, can cotton grow there?" his response was: "If the land is good, cotton will grow there, but if it is damp and poor, it won't grow. If it's like the Kashgar country, it will grow there too. If the soil is loose, it can grow there too, of course."

This subject obviously had no idea of starting from given premises and reasoning from them; he was only trying to answer on the basis of immediate concrete experience. He had never been schooled in anything like formal reasoning. It would be meaningless to try to analyze his behavior in terms of the detailed processes of inference, mapping, and application that Sternberg postulates and observes in Yale undergraduates.

The lesson I draw from all this is that in the study of individual differences in cognitive processes, it is important to consider the kinds of knowledges and skills that individuals may have acquired, and these knowledges and skills may pertain not only to specific pieces of information but also to procedures and algorithms for handling problems. Studies of cognitive information processing must therefore consider not only the individual's processes in handling information but also his or her grasp of the information to be processed and of procedures for working through problems involving information handling. Perhaps it is these latter processes that Snow means by "assembly and control processes," but somehow that phrase suggests to me something much more general and abstract than the kinds of procedural knowledge that I have had in mind in the foregoing discussion.

ACQUIRED KNOWLEDGE AND THE STRUCTURE OF ABILITIES

I would like to apply these thoughts to the interpretation of theories of the structure of abilities. In his paper, Snow presented a figure (Fig. 2.2) that showed a distance scaling of the between-test correlations in a battery administered to high-school students. The mode of analysis used here is interesting; it is rather different from the usual kind of display. In effect, it represents a new "structure-of-intellect" theory whereby tests and abilities can be described in a two-dimensional framework. Snow has already suggested what one of the dimensions may be. Pointing out that "a diagonal line drawn from upper left to lower right . . . contrasts fairly neatly those tests based on digits, letters, or words . . . with those based on pictures or figures," he suggests that "the main content distinction may be between digital and analogic processing." He further implies that these "content distinctions" should not necessarily be passed off as "trivial," because "different contents may require different processes."

This is an interesting conjecture, but the findings are not inconsistent with the notion that the differences are solely of content. But because the display is two-dimensional, we can ask what the other dimension of the circumplex might be. I note that if you draw a line from upper right to lower left, the division may be into a set of more or less "automatic," rote performance factors in the "northwest" corner and, in contrast, a set of more creative, intuitive performances in the "southeast" corner. There may be a genuine process difference here, somewhat reminiscent of Jensen's (1969) distinction between "Level I (associative)" and "Level II (conceptual)" types of abilities.

Of interest also is the fact, pointed out by Snow, that Spearman's g—general intelligence—is in the very center of the display, as represented by tests of G_f, fluid intelligence; whereas tests of G_c, crystallized intelligence, are not far from the center. Snow is probably correct in believing that these general factors are close to the center because they involve assembly and control processes that are used in a great variety of mental operations, even those tested by measures that appear far from the center. Nevertheless, the tests of G_c must also measure accumulated effects of learning. I suspect that there is some rather complex relation between G_f and G_c abilities—possibly this relation is curvilinear and thus not well accounted for by the usual linear factor analysis procedures. Perhaps a model of the relation, with account taken of cumulative environmental effects, could be developed along lines proposed by Baltes, Nesselroade, and Cornelius (1978). Presumably there are some genetic determinants of fluid intelligence, with differences in crystallized intelligence arising also from the degree to which the individual is able to "invest" his or her fluid intelligence in taking advantage of whatever environmental opportunities are available.

These possible relations between G_f, G_c, and environmental opportunities for learning may account for the relationships between verbal intelligence and cognitive process differences that are being found in the research of Hunt and his colleagues (Hunt, Lunneborg, & Lewis, 1975). Verbal intelligence tests and other measures of G_c obviously reflect differences in people's memory stores for language and other types of verbal information. But to account for how those memory stores were built up, we may want to appeal to the notion that people who have good assembly and control processes are the ones who are better able to profit from the environmental opportunities that are available to them. Of course, people do not have anything like equal environmental opportunities, but let's imagine that we are considering a group of individuals who all have approximately equivalent environmental opportunities. Within that group, it would be the ones who have better fluid intelligence—better assembly and control processes, if you like—who would be more likely to build up large memory stores of linguistic and verbal information as reflected by high scores in verbal intelligence tests.

It seems to me that we can think of a third dimension in Snow's chart of abilities—one rising from the paper, so to speak, that represents the level of complexity of mental processes that the individual can attain. As they stand, tests shown near the center of the chart possess wide ranges of item difficulty, such that they can well differentiate among individuals who are able to handle different degrees of mental task complexity. Possibly tests failing more toward the periphery of the chart could also be constructed in such a way as to do a better job of measuring complexity of mental process. We could, for example, make highly complex tests of memory span, or of closure, by presenting more complex kinds of stimuli for the examinee to operate on. With respect to all types of tests, it would be useful to specify—in terms of task parameters—the levels of complexity that correspond to different points on the raw-score scales. Such "quasi-absolute scaling," as I like to call it, should help in specifying the levels of task complexity that an individual should be able to handle in order to attain a given degree of probability of success in any given job or task performance in which a particular ability is implicated.

A consideration of the respective contributions of fluid and of crystallized intelligence in an ability, and of the degree to which the ability reflects accumulated learnings, should help in predicting the degree to which the ability can be modified through training or other forms of treatment. Abilities that are highly dependent on both fluid and crystallized intelligence—and that reflect large differences in memory stores, like verbal ability—are probably less modifiable than, say, perceptual speed. But even in making this assertion, I must be somewhat hesitant, for I am not aware that we know very much of anything about the assembly and control processes that underlie perceptual speed; we do not know whether they are trainable or otherwise modifiable. There is a large realm of research that needs to be done to ascertain the interactions of different kinds of abilities with different kinds of training, practice, and environmental experience. In addition, with respect to an ability like perceptual speed, we would need to know more about its external validity in order to determine whether it would be worthwhile trying to modify or train the aptitude processes underlying it, if indeed such changes are possible.

SUMMARY

The thorough explication of the notion of "aptitude process" and its application in adaptive instruction will require not only a considerable amount of research in the nature of cognitive processes but also an exploration of the long-term development of such processes and their modifiability and educability. Such research must be informed, on the one hand, by an adequate theory of the external validity of these aptitude processes—that is, their relevance to real-world tasks, jobs, and learning situations—and, on the other, by an adequate theory of individual differences that places these individual differences in the perspective of general behavior theory. At the present time we seem still to be a long way from arriving at the knowledge required to take account of aptitude processes in adaptive instruction.

REFERENCES

Baltes, P. B., Nesselroade, J. R., & Cornelius, S. W. Multivariate antecedents of structural change in development: A simulation of cumulative environmental patterns. *Multivariate Behavioral Research,* 1978, *13,* 127–152.

Bloom, B. *Human characteristics and school learning.* New York: McGraw-Hill, 1976.

Carroll, J. B. Psychometric tests as cognitive tasks: A new "structure of intellect." In L. Resnick (Ed.), *The nature of intelligence.* Hillsdale, N.J.: Lawrence Erlbaum Associates, 1976.

Carroll, J. B. How shall we study individual differences in cognitive abilities?—Methodological and theoretical perspectives. *Intelligence,* 1978, *2,* 87–115.

Gagné, R. M. Learning hierarchies. *Educational Psychologist,* 1968, *6,* 1–9.

Hunt, E. B., Lunneborg, C. E., & Lewis, J. What does it mean to be high verbal? *Cognitive Psychology,* 1975, *7,* 194–227.

Jensen, A. R. How much can we boost IQ and scholastic achievement? *Harvard Educational Review,* 1969, *39,* 1–123.

Luria, A. R. *Cognitive development: Its cultural and social foundations.* Cambridge, Mass.: Harvard University Press, 1976.

Skinner, B. F. Why I am not a cognitive psychologist. *Behaviorism,* 1977, *5,* 1–10.

Sternberg, R. J. *Intelligence, information processing, and analogical reasoning: The componential analysis of human abilities.* Hillsdale, N.J.: Lawrence Erlbaum Associates, 1977.

7 Spatial Information Processing: Strategies for Research

Lynn A. Cooper
Cornell University

It is evident that the ability to represent and use information about space and objects in space plays an important functional role in human behavior. Activities as seemingly diverse as planning routes by reading maps, anticipating the course of an approaching object, and solving problems in fields such as architecture, physics, and stereochemistry all involve some degree of spatial skill. Perhaps because of the obvious contribution of spatial abilities and processes to everyday behavior and intellectual accomplishments, such skills have been a focus of vigorous investigation since the development of systematic tests of mental abilities (e.g., Thurstone, 1938).

In this paper, I outline several strategies for studying spatial skills and processes. All of these research strategies reflect my own theoretical orientation toward analyzing spatial performance—an orientation shared by many cognitive psychologists. This orientation, often identified with the "information-processing" approach to cognition, analyses performance on spatial tasks in terms of underlying operations or processes and attempts to understand the sequence and nature of these processes. Thus, I provide no systematic consideration of much of the psychometric work on spatial abilities; nor do I emphasize studies of the relationship between scores on tests of spatial ability and other types of abilities and processes. I should note, however, that psychometric and process-oriented approaches to the study of spatial skills are hardly incompatible. Recently, several investigators have pointed out the fruitfulness of viewing psychometric tests of abilities as cognitive tasks, and they have provided process analyses of the component operations underlying performance on psychometric tests (see, in particular, Carroll, 1976). The experimental work of Hunt and his colleagues (Hunt, Frost, & Lunneborg, 1973; Hunt, Lunneborg, & Lewis, 1975) provides an excellent example of advances that can be made by combining psychometric and information-processing approaches to the study of verbal abilities and processes. A recent study by MacLeod, Hunt, and Mathews (1978) suggests that this research strategy can be profitably extended to spatial abilities. In this experiment, choice of strategy for performing a sentence–picture verification task was found to be predictable from a psychometric measure of spatial ability. So, the relationship between psychometric tests of spatial ability and spatial information-processing tasks appears to be a fruitful direction for research, although as yet little work has been done along this line.

In the next three sections of this paper, I consider three sorts of process-oriented approaches to the study of performance on spatial tasks. I also present ''case studies'' of research using each of the three approaches. The first approach provides an analysis of the mental operations underlying performance on a single spatial task. This approach is typical of much work in the area of visual information processing. Research in this tradition has concentrated on understanding the nature of spatial operations and the implications of these processes for general models in cognitive psychology. The other approaches place more of an emphasis on the diversity and flexibility of spatial information processing. The second approach uses individual differences as a tool for providing a process analysis of performance on spatial tasks. The research strategy here has been to isolate individual differences in performance in a simple visual processing situation. Hypotheses about the nature of the processing differences that underlie the performance differences are developed. Then, the experimental situation is changed in ways that naturally draw upon a particular type of spatial processing strategy. Resulting variations in performance permit inferences about the nature and flexibility of the processing strategies. In the third approach, a direct analysis is made of changes in spatial information-processing strategies resulting from changes in task demands.

ANALYSIS OF PROCESSES UNDERLYING
PERFORMANCE ON A SINGLE SPATIAL TASK

This research strategy is typical of much work in cognitive psychology in the information-processing tradition. In this approach, performance on a single task or on variations of a basic task is examined. The goals are to isolate the set of processes underlying performance and to understand the nature of those internal processes. Generally, inferences about processes are made from chronometric measures. Often, quantitative models or qualitative process descriptions of single tasks are developed. The hope is that knowing how people perform individual tasks will reveal something more general about the nature of cognitive processes. Investigators who use this approach often implicitly assume that individual differences in performance are quantitative but not qualitative. That is, all subjects are assumed to carry out the same basic set of operations in performing the task, but the duration of these internal processes may vary from individual to individual. In the domain of spatial information processing, this approach is equivalent to asking just what processes any one person uses to complete any one item on a standard test of spatial ability. Again, the emphasis is on understanding the nature of basic spatial processes, rather than on determining how groups of individuals score on a large number of items or isolating correlates of measures of overall spatial ability.

A spatial task that has received much recent attention is the "mental rotation" task, and I use this as my example of the "single-task, basic processes" research approach. In the original experiment of this type (Shepard & Metzler, 1971), subjects viewed two perspective drawings of three-dimensional objects. On each trial, subjects had to determine whether the two objects were the same in shape or were mirror images. In addition to a possible difference in shape, the objects could also differ in orientation either in the two-dimensional picture plane or in depth. Shepard and Metzler's now-classic finding was that the time taken to determine that the two objects were the same in shape increased linearly with the angular difference between the two objects. The linear increase in reaction time with angular difference led Shepard and Metzler to suggest that subjects performed the task by "mentally rotating" an internal representation of one object into congruence with the other object and then comparing the two objects for a match or mismatch in shape.

This basic linear relationship between difference in orientation and reaction time has been obtained with a variety of stimulus materials and task modifications. For example, linear reaction-time functions have been found using various type of perspective drawings of three-dimensional objects (Cooper & Farrell, in preparation; Shepard & Metzler, 1971), random two-dimensional polygons (Cooper, 1975), and patterns of dots (Corballis & Roldan, 1975). They have been obtained when a single rotated pattern must be compared with a pattern in memory (Cooper, 1975), when rotations must be carried out before a test shape is displayed (Cooper, 1975; Cooper & Podgorny, 1976; Cooper & Shepard, 1973), and when the discrimination is changed to include subtly different distractors as well as mirror images (Cooper & Podgorny, 1976). Figure 7.1 shows data from a typical mental rotation experiment (Cooper, 1975) in which subjects had to compare a rotated test shape with a memory representation of a standard version of the shape learned in a particular orientation.

Linear reaction-time functions, suggesting mental rotation, have also shown up when special populations have been tested—most notably, children (Marmor, 1975) and the blind, using tactually presented stimuli (Carpenter & Eisenberg, 1978; Marmor & Zaback, 1976). Of considerable interest is the fact that linear relations between time and orientation are found in the data of individual subjects, though the slope of this function varies considerably from person to person (see Cooper, 1975; Metzler & Shepard, 1974). What this means is that although

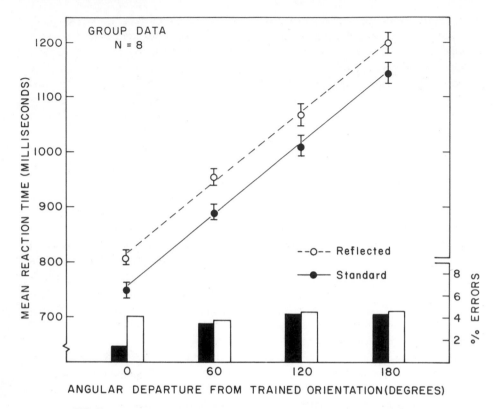

FIG. 7.1.   Mean reaction time plotted as a function of angular difference between the orientation of test shapes and the orientation in which a discrimination between "standard" and "reflected" versions of the shapes was initially learned. Separate functions are plotted for "standard" and "reflected" responses, and best-fitting straight lines are shown for both functions. Error rates for "standard" and "reflected" responses are shown. (From Cooper, 1975.)

a number of strategies are available for performing the task (e.g., comparing the direction in which a single feature points on two visual shapes), people generally choose the strategy that produces the linear function, although they vary in the rate at which they can execute the "rotation" process.

Because the linear relation between orientation difference and judgment time is quite general—holding up over materials, task modifications, and particularly individual subjects—it has been thought to reflect a basic and unitary type of cognitive activity. Thus, it has seemed important to provide a thorough analysis of the processes underlying performance in the rotation task. This analysis has taken two directions. The first has been to isolate the set of processes used in the rotation task. The second has been to characterize the nature of the process of mental rotation itself.

Determining the sequence of processes in the rotation task has been a relatively straightforward undertaking, and various models of the set of processes have been proposed by investigators using different experimental techniques. Cooper and Shepard (1973) have presented a process model of the operations that occur when a subject is presented with a rotated alphanumeric character and must decide whether that character is a normal or a reflected version. The data on which this model is based come from an experiment in which subjects were given advance information about an upcoming character in certain conditions. Specifically, the experiment contained conditions in which no advance information, information only about identity of the character, information only about orientation of the character, and information about both identity and orientation were provided. In the information-processing model of Cooper and Shepard, when a subject is presented with a rotated character, he or she first determines what character has appeared (its identity) and where the character has appeared (its orientation). These two initial operations are assumed to take a constant amount of time regardless of the orientation of the character. The next processing stage is the mental rotation, and the time taken for this increases as the character departs by larger angles from the upright position. Following the rotational transformation, the mentally rotated representation of the character is compared with a stored representation of its normal, upright version. The appropriate response following a match or a mismatch is then executed.

Just and Carpenter (1976) have provided a somewhat different model of the sequence of operations in the rotation task, based on an analysis of subjects' patterns of eye fixations when two visual objects are simultaneously displayed. These investigators break processing down into three component stages. In the first stage, search, corresponding features of the two visual objects are found. In the second stage, transformation, these corresponding features are rotated into congruence in a stepwise fashion. In the final stage, confirmation, a determination is made of whether or not the features of the objects that were not transformed are congruent. For displays like those used by Shepard and Metzler (1971), the time for each stage increases with the angular difference between the two visual objects. For similar two-dimensional displays, however, only the transformation/rotation process shows such an increase in duration (see Carpenter & Just, 1978). Although the models of the rotation task proposed by Cooper and Shepard (1973) and by Just and Carpenter (1976) differ in certain respects, each provides an example of the sort of process analysis that can be applied to a single spatial task.

The second issue that has arisen from investigation of the rotation task—how to characterize the nature of the process of mental rotation—has been difficult to resolve. Controversy has centered on whether "mental rotation" is most appropriately viewed as an analog internal process or whether it can adequately be characterized as a series of discrete, symbolic operations. My own view is that it is not possible to distinguish empirically between all versions of these two alternatives. However, it is possible to rule out certain accounts of the nature of the process of mental rotation on the basis of experimental evidence. For example, the central finding of a linear increase in decision time with increasing angular disparity rules out processes such as a simple comparison of the features of two visual objects in different orientations. Also, Cooper and Podgorny's (1976) finding that rotation rate does not depend on the complexity of the object being rotated suggests that the process is applied integrally rather than in a stepwise or piece-by-piece fashion.

A recent set of experiments (Cooper, 1976a; Cooper & Shepard, 1973; Metzler & Shepard, 1974) suggests quite strongly that the process of mental rotation is, in a certain sense, an analog of an external spatial rotation. The process is viewed as analog in the sense that during a mental rotation, the process passes through an ordered series of states that correspond to the series of stages in the rotation of an external object. These internal states are best thought of as "structured anticipations"—or readinesses for perceiving and responding to a particular object in a particular orientation. In one experiment in this set (Cooper, 1976a), subjects were asked to imagine a shape rotating around a circle at a fixed rate. At some unpredictable moment during the rotation, a test shape was presented, and subjects had to discriminate which of two versions of the shape had been presented. Reaction times were shortest when the test shape was presented in the position that corresponded to the orientation of the rotating internal representation. Times increased as the test shape departed by greater and greater angles from this "expected" orientation. This result is consistent with the idea that mental rotation is analogous to an external spatial rotation, in that the process of mental rotation involves passing through a trajectory of "readinesses" for perceiving a specific object in a specific spatial location.

In summary, in the foregoing section I have used research on mental rotation as an example of an approach to studying spatial information processing. In this approach, a fairly detailed analysis is made of the processes underlying performance of a typical subject on a single spatial task. Results from studies of mental rotation have been quite orderly, and they have told us something about the nature of a basic cognitive process that people are capable of using when faced with a certain kind of spatial problem. Because this research approach seeks to understand the nature of basic spatial processes, little effort is directed toward finding possible *qualitative* patterns of individual differences or determing the range of task modifications that will naturally evoke use of the same basic process. Recently, however, several investigators have used *quantitative* differences among individuals on mental rotation tasks in correlational studies with other tasks and individual-difference parameters. For example, Snyder (1972) and Bahrick and Neisser (personal communication) have studied the relationship between rate of mental rotation and performance on various tests of mental imagery. And Wilson, DeFries, McClearn, Vandenberg, Johnson, and Rashad (1975) have examined sex differences in scores on a mental rotation task as part of their studies of genetic factors in cognitive abilities.

INDIVIDUAL-DIFFERENCE ANALYSIS
OF SPATIAL INFORMATION PROCESSING

This second approach to studying spatial information processing shares many goals in common with the first, "basic-processes" approach in which the operations underlying performance on a single spatial task are analyzed. Unlike the first approach, however, this second approach uses systematic differences between individuals as a tool for understanding the nature of basic spatial processes. The individual differences under consideration are differences in entire patterns of performance on a simple spatial task, rather than quantitative differences between people on an overall test score or differences in the time required to execute a process like mental rotation. The idea is that individual differences in patterns of performance reflect differences in the kinds of processing strategies that different people use to do a particular spatial task. Once hypotheses about the nature of the processing differences are formulated, the task can be changed in ways that seem naturally to encourage one of the hypothesized underlying processing strategies. By observing how individual subjects' patterns of performance change as the processing requirements of a simple task change, a more direct analysis of the underlying processing differences can be made. This approach can also be used to analyze how flexible preferred modes of spatial information processing are in the face of stimulus and judgmental manipulations. Perhaps a concrete example will make the logic behind this sort of research strategy clearer.

As the "case study" illustrating the individual-difference research approach, I present part of a series of recent experiments I have conducted on spatial comparison processes. In most of the experiments, the subject's task is to determine whether two sequentially presented visual patterns are identical or somehow different in shape. Presumably, this task requires the subject to compare a visual memory representation of the first pattern with the second pattern, which is externally available. Of particular interest is the nature of the visual/spatial comparison process. When I began studying this problem, I implicitly assumed that all subjects would perform this relatively simple comparison task in basically the same way. I rapidly realized, though, that performance in even this simple situation could be affected by the natural strategies with which different individual subjects approached the task. At first I regarded the individual differences as a bothersome curiosity that nonetheless deserved explanation. Only later did the individual differences become an interesting research tool.

Two distinct and reliable patterns of performance in individual subjects have been found in what I will call the "basic" visual or spatial comparison task. About 40 subjects have so far been tested on minor variations of the basic task, and I present data from just one illustrative experiment (see Cooper, 1976b, Experiment II, for details). In this experiment, subjects were shown one of five "standard" patterns, each of which was a randomly generated, irregular polygon. The standards varied in complexity, defined as the number of points in the

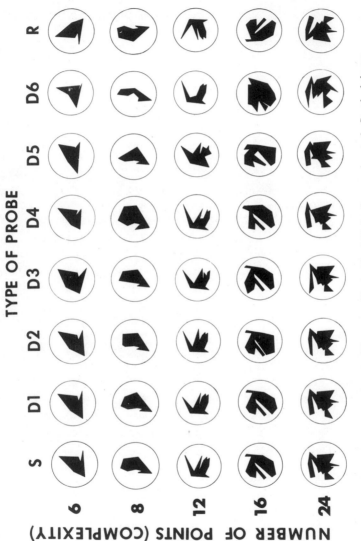

FIG. 7.2. The complete set of shapes used in the "basic" visual comparison task. Standard shapes are shown in the leftmost column. Reflected versions are shown in the rightmost column. Perturbations of the standard shapes, varying in their similarity to the standards, are shown in the middle six columns. (From Cooper & Podgorny, 1976.)

shape. On each experimental trial, one of the five standards was first displayed for 3 seconds. There was a blank interval of either 0 or 3 seconds following the offset of the standard, and immediately following the interval a test shape was presented. The subject's task was to determine as rapidly and accurately as possible whether the test shape was identical to the standard or different in any respect. On half of the trials, the test shape was in fact identical to the standard; and on the other half of the trials, it differed from the standard by an overall reflection or by a perturbation in shape. The five standards and the set of "different" probes for each are shown in Fig. 7.2. As can be seen, the "different" perturbations varied in their similarity to the standards, with D1 perturbations being extremely similar to the standard shapes and D6 perturbations being extremely dissimilar.

Reaction time for making the "same–different" discrimination is plotted in Fig. 7.3 as a function of type of test probe. Only correct reaction times are shown, but an even more revealing analysis of performance can be made by considering both correct and incorrect responses (see Cooper, 1976b). The 10 subjects in this experiment have been divided into two groups, and these groups are plotted separately. Though not shown individually, the pattern of perfor-

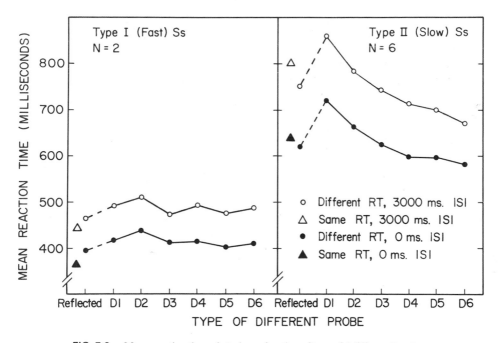

FIG. 7.3.   Mean reaction time plotted as a function of type of "different" probe. Mean "same" responses are also shown. Average data for the Type I subjects are shown in the left-hand panel, and average data for the Type II subjects are shown in the right-hand panel. (From Cooper, 1976b.)

mance for each individual subject in each of the groups follows quite closely the pattern of the average data. The data of the subjects shown in the right-hand panel, called Type II subjects, are typical of results found in many "same–different" comparison experiments when the performance of all the subjects is averaged. Three features of the performance of the Type II subjects are important:

1. Reaction time to "different" test shapes decreases monotonically with increasing dissimilarity between the standard and the test shape.
2. "Same" reaction time is intermediate in speed—slower than the shortest "different" response (to D6 probes), but faster than the longest "different" response (to D1 probes).
3. Overall response speed is slow relative to the subjects shown in the left-hand panel.

Note that these same patterns in performance occur with short (0-second) and with long (3-second) intervals between presentation of the standard and test shapes, but overall response time is slower with the long interval. Because the patterns in performance remain constant over length of interval, I do not consider this variable further.

The data of the other group of subjects, called Type I subjects, are shown in the left-hand panel of Fig. 7.3. These subjects show a considerably different pattern of performance from that of the Type II subjects. The important features of the data of the Type I subjects are:

1. Reaction time to "different" test shapes is virtually constant regardless of the similarity between the standard and the test shape.
2. "Same" reaction time is faster than "different" reaction time to any type of test probe.
3. Overall response time is quite rapid compared to the times of the Type II subjects.

As with the Type II subjects, the Type I subjects show this same pattern for both short and long interstimulus intervals. It is important to note that despite the considerable difference in the patterns of reaction-time performance for these two kinds of subjects, there is very little difference in either the magnitude or the pattern of their errors. The overall error rate is about the same for the two types of subjects (10.3% for Type I subjects and 9.9% for Type II subjects, averaged over the short and long interstimulus intervals). Also, for both groups, error rate decreases monotonically with increasing dissimilarity between the standard and the test shape. So, for Type II subjects, reaction time and error rate are positively correlated, and for Type I subjects these measures are uncorrelated.

These two patterns of performance have been obtained in a number of experiments using slight modifications of the comparison task already described (for data from some of these experiments, see Cooper, 1976b; and Cooper & Podgorny, 1976). The differences between subjects have been intriguing because they involve entire patterns of performance, rather than just a quantitative difference between individuals. That is, the two groups of subjects do not differ merely in their overall response speed or merely in the slope of the "different" reaction-time function. A constellation of performances—involving response speed, sensitivity to similarity of "different" probes, relative speed of the "same" response, and the relationship between reaction time and error rate— covaries systematically within an individual subject and differs between subjects. Because the individual differences are qualitative, in this sense, they may reflect quite different processing strategies that different subjects opt to use in comparing a visual memory representation with an external visual shape. Indeed, certain simple explanations for the performance differences—such as speed–accuracy trade-offs or floor effects on response times—seem unlikely on the basis of the results from just the initial comparison experiment. (See Cooper, 1976b, for a more detailed discussion of these explanations.)

A possible and more interesting explanation places the difference between subjects in the nature of the spatial comparison processes that they naturally use. The Type I subjects could be comparing a visual memory representation with a test shape in a holistic, parallel fashion, seeking to verify that the two representations are the same. This sort of comparison process would not be searching for differences—features that distinguish the memory representation from the external visual shape. Rather, this comparison process would be attempting to find a match between the memory representation and the test shape. If a match were produced by the comparison process, then the response of "same" could be executed. If a match were not found, then the "different" response could be made by default. A unitary comparison process like this could produce the reaction-time data of the Type I subject. Under this account, the "same" response should be the fastest one made. All "different" responses should be of equivalent speed regardless of similarity between the standard and the test shape, because these responses are made by default rather than on the basis of finding the location of a difference between the standard and the test shape. Note, also, that errors could be produced by this comparison process. One need only assume that the memory representation of the standard does not contain all of the information available in the actual shape.

The Type II subjects could be using a more analytic comparison process, and possibly two different and independent processes could produce the "same" and the "different" responses. A process specialized for detecting differences could compare the visual features of the memory representation and the test shape. As soon as this process finds a feature that distinguishes the two representations, the "different" response could be executed. Such a self-terminating difference comparison could produce the monotonic decrease in reaction time with increasing dissimilarity between the standard and the test shape. For the greater the dissimilarity between the two visual representations, the earlier a difference will be found, and the faster the response will be. A second process—perhaps like the single holistic comparison process of the Type I subjects—could operate simultaneously with the difference-detection process. This process might be viewed as being under a time deadline. If a match is found before the deadline has been exceeded, the "same" response is made. However, this process cannot lead to the initiation of a "different" response if a match is not found. This analysis of the comparison strategy used by the Type II subjects has been proposed by others (see, especially, Bamber, 1969) as a general model of "same–different" visual comparison. It is generally referred to as a "dual-process" model. Note that this strategy seems less efficient than the single process presumed to be used by the Type I subjects, for a single process is all that is logically required to perform the comparison task. Nonetheless, there is considerable evidence supporting the dual-process analysis of the performance of some subjects (Cooper, 1976b).

How might one gain more direct evidence concerning the nature of these hypothesized spatial comparison processes? It is at this point that the individual-differences analysis becomes important, because changes in individual subjects' patterns of performance can be used both to test ideas about the nature of the comparison strategies and to determine the range of conditions that will evoke one type of comparison strategy or another. The general research approach, which is somewhat different from much individual-differences research, is as follows. Stable patterns of Type I and Type II performance are identified in individual subjects on the basic spatial comparison task. Then these same subjects are tested on a variety of new but related tasks. It is important to note that the new tasks are constructed with particular purposes in mind. First, the processing demands of the new tasks are rather explicit. Second, these processing demands naturally draw upon one or the other of the hypothesized comparison strategies used by the two types of subjects. The hope is that the new task demands will differentially alter the performance of one type of subject but not the other, or will alter the performance of both types of subjects in identifiably different ways. That is, the new tasks are not intended to make overall performance just better or worse. Rather, the demands of the new tasks should make performance change only if the subject has adopted a particular processing strategy. If new task demands cause an interpretable change in the performance of one type of subject but not the other, then we can draw two conclusions. First, the task demands reflect certain features of the natural comparison strategy of the subjects whose performance remained the same. Second, the processing strategy of the subjects whose performance did change may be natural and preferred, but these subjects can use multiple and optional comparison strategies, depending on the particulars of the situation. Thus, research using an individual-differences analysis of spatial information processing has two central goals—to use individual differences as a tool for understanding the nature of basic spatial comparison processes, and to discover how flexible and optional different comparison processes are both across subjects and within an individual subject.

A series of experiments using this general approach have recently been completed, and I discuss one of these experiments in detail. (For a complete description of the entire series of experiments, see Cooper, in preparation–a.) Eight subjects were tested in these experiments, and their reaction-time and error data from the basic spatial comparison task are shown in Figs. 7.4 and 7.5. Subjects 1, 2, 3, and 4 are classified as Type I subjects. Subjects 5, 6, 7, and 8 are Type II

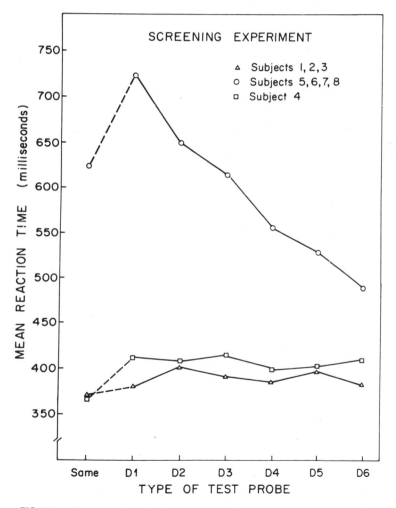

FIG. 7.4.   Mean reaction time plotted as a function of type of test probe. Subjects 1, 2, 3, and 4 are classified as Type I subjects, and Subjects 5, 6, 7, and 8 are classified as Type II subjects.

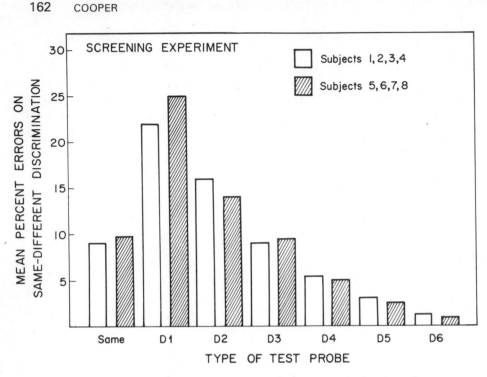

FIG. 7.5.   Mean percent errors on "same–different" discrimination shown for different types of test probes. Subjects 1, 2, 3, and 4 are classified as Type I subjects, 5, 6, 7, and 8 are classified as Type II subjects.

subjects. Subject 4's reaction-time data are plotted separately, as variations in the performance of this subject are important in later experiments.

The first experiment was an attempt to modify the comparison process of the Type I subjects by changing the basic task to require explicitly the detection of difference. The new task again required "same–different" comparison of a memory representation of a standard shape with a test form. The novel feature of the procedure was that the subjects were required, additionally, to indicate in what respect the test shape differed from the standard if they judged the pair of shapes to be different. This was accomplished in the following manner: Random, angular standard shapes were generated, and "different" test shapes were constructed by applying local perturbations of varying magnitude to points within each of four quadrants of the shape. For each quadrant of each standard shape, three "different" probes were selected that varied in their rated similarity to the standard. On each experimental trial, a standard shape was shown for 3 seconds, followed by a 1-second blank interval. The test shape was then presented, and the subject determined as rapidly and accurately as possible whether the test shape and the standard were the same or different. Immediately following the "same–

different'' response, a field of visual noise was presented. If the response was ''different,'' lines depicting the four quadrants of the shape were presented, and the subject had to indicate in which of the four quadrants the test shape and the standard differed by pressing one of four buttons. One of the standard shapes, divided into quadrants, and each of the associated ''different'' probes are shown in Fig. 7.6. In Fig. 7.7, the sequence of events on a typical trial is displayed.

The idea behind this experiment was that adding the new requirement of the detection and report of difference might differentially affect the performance of the two kinds of subjects, given the hypotheses concerning their spatial comparison strategies. For the Type II subjects, performance on the ''same–different'' task should be similar to their performance on the basic comparison task. Also, accuracy on quadrant identification should be relatively high. This is because the natural comparison process of the Type II subject presumably involves checking for differences between the memory representation of the standard shape and the test shape. If this is an appropriate description of the Type II comparison process,

6-POINT SHAPE

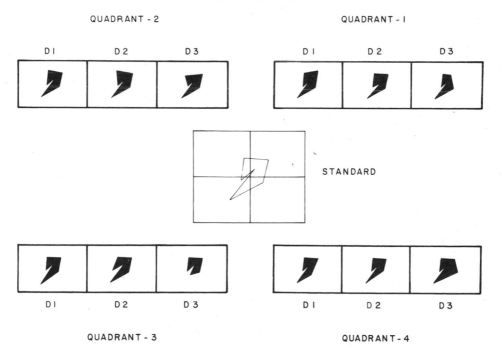

QUADRANT - 2   QUADRANT - 1

D 1   D 2   D 3   D 1   D 2   D 3

STANDARD

D 1   D 2   D 3   D 1   D 2   D 3

QUADRANT - 3   QUADRANT - 4

FIG. 7.6.   One of the five standard shapes and the associated ''different'' probes used in the quadrant experiment. The standard shape is shown divided into quadrants. For each quadrant of the shape, ''different'' probes varying in their similarity to the standard are illustrated.

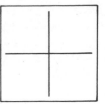

STANDARD SHAPE   TEST SHAPE   NOISE (Masking)   QUADRANT LINES
FIELD

1- Second memory   Same-Different response   Quadrant identification
interval   (Different)   (Quadrant—I, upper right)

SEQUENCE OF EVENTS ON AN EXPERIMENTAL TRIAL

(Quadrant lines appeared only when the response "different" was made)

FIG. 7.7.   Sequence of events on an experimental trial in the quadrant experiment. On this trial, the correct response was "different."

then some information about the nature of the difference actually found should be available for report immediately after the "different" response is made. So because the new processing requirement in this task was designed to evoke the Type II comparison process naturally, no qualitative change in the performance of these subjects should be expected.

The performance of the Type I subjects, however, should be affected by the addition of the quadrant identification. There are two possible ways these subjects could respond to the additional processing requirement. First, it may be that the new requirement is not sufficient to induce these subjects to modify their spatial comparison strategy. If they continue to use the hypothesized holistic comparison process, instead of searching for differences, then the pattern of "same–different" reaction time and error performance should be similar to performance on the basic visual comparison task. This strategy should create problems on the quadrant identification, however. This is because the quadrant task explicitly requires the detection and report of difference. Presumably, the single holistic comparison process will not search for information concerning the location of a difference between the standard and test shapes. So quadrant identification for Type I subjects who do not modify their spatial comparison strategy should be substantially poorer than for Type II subjects.

The second possibility is that the additional processing requirement of the quadrant identification is sufficient to induce the Type I subjects to adopt a more analytic mode of comparison. If their natural, preferred comparison process is nonetheless flexible and optional, then these subjects may be able to switch strategies and become like the Type II subjects in this situation that requires the detection of difference. If so, then their reaction-time performance should change dramatically from performance on the basic spatial comparison task, and their accuracy on quadrant identification should be comparable to that of the Type II subjects.

The reaction-time data from this experiment are shown in Fig. 7.8, and errors on the "same–different" discrimination are shown in Fig. 7.9. For all subjects, error rates decrease with increasing dissimilarity between the standard and test shape, and this pattern is typical of both Type I and Type II performance. It is

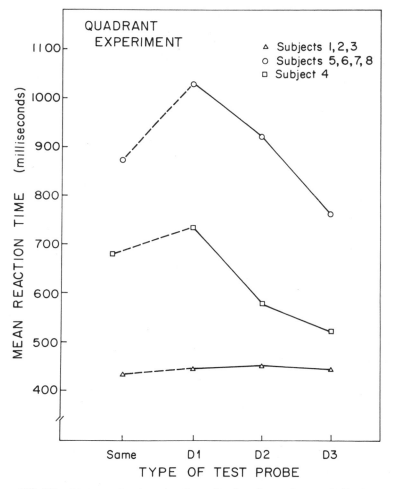

FIG. 7.8.   Mean reaction time plotted as a function of type of test probe for the quadrant experiment.

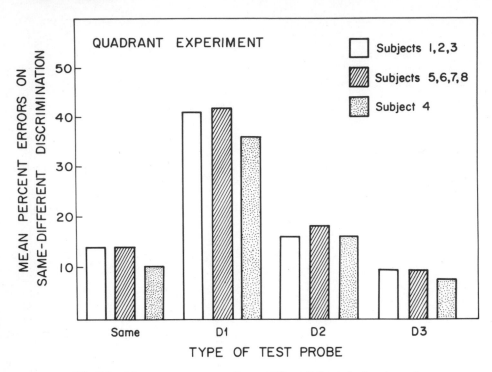

FIG. 7.9.   Mean percent errors on "same–different" discrimination shown for different types of test probes for the quadrant experiment.

clear from the reaction-time data that as predicted, the four Type II subjects show their typical monotonic decrease in "different" reaction time with increasing dissimilarity between the standard and test shape. It is also clear that three of the Type I subjects continue to show a flat reaction-time function over type of "different" probe, as in the basic comparison task. Of particular interest is the marked change in subject 4's reaction-time performance. In the basic comparison experiment, this subject's "different" reaction times showed the typical Type I pattern, but now reaction-time performance is heavily influenced by the similarity between the standard and the test shape—presumably as a result of the added processing demand. Also in line with this subject's change from Type I to Type II performance, overall response time has increased considerably, and the "same" response is now intermediate in speed, rather than fastest as in the basic comparison task.

These reaction-time results suggest that the addition of the quadrant identification was not sufficient to induce subjects 1, 2, and 3 to change their processing strategy but was sufficient to force subject 4 to adopt a more analytic or "difference-detecting" mode of processing. Results from the quadrant identification itself, shown in Fig. 7.10, give further support for this suggestion. For all

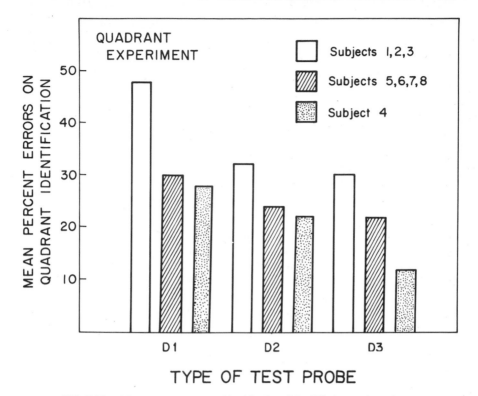

FIG. 7.10.   Mean percent errors on identification of the differing quadrant shown for different types of test probes for the quadrant experiment.

subjects, errors on quadrant identification decrease as the test probe and the standard shape become more dissimilar. Of primary importance is the finding that the subjects who show little effect of similarity on reaction time (subjects 1, 2. and 3) make considerably more errors on quadrant detection than subjects whose reaction times are sensitive to similarity (subjects 4, 5, 6, 7, and 8). This is precisely what should be expected on the basis of the initial hypotheses concerning the processing strategies underlying Type I and Type II performance.

What, then, do the results of this experiment tell us about the nature of spatial comparison processes? First, the data for subjects 1, 2, and 3 lend support to the idea that their natural comparison strategy involves a single holistic process. This type of process was predicted to produce rapid "same" responses, "different" responses of constant speed, and relatively poor quadrant identification. Exactly this pattern was obtained in this experiment. The failure of these subjects to adopt a more analytic comparison strategy suggests that their natural holistic comparison process is not terribly flexible, even when the task calls for an analysis of information concerning differences. Second, the change in subject 4's performance from the Type I to the Type II pattern—presumably as a result of the new processing demand—provides some insight into the nature of the Type II comparison process. This subject's reaction-time performance has been selectively altered in a task specifically requiring the detection and report of differences. What this suggests is that the natural comparison strategy of the Type II subjects (who were not affected by the new processing demand) does indeed involve an analytic search for and detection of difference. So persistence and change in individual subjects' patterns of performance in the face of a particular type of task demand have provided evidence about both the nature of basic spatial comparison processes and the flexibility of these processing strategies.

A question that naturally arises concerns the boundary conditions for obtaining the individual differences in performance. That is, can situations be constructed in which the processing demands are so clear that all subjects will perform in the same way? The answer so far is yes for the Type II mode of processing, but no for the Type I mode. The Type II comparison strategy can be reliably evoked when the visual patterns being compared are so obviously discrete and dimensional that it is virtually impossible to treat them holistically. In the experiment that unequivocally produced Type II performance in all of the subjects—regardless of their performance on the basic spatial comparison task—the stimuli were visual displays that varied on the three dimensions of size, shape, and color. Two levels of size (large, small), two different shapes (square, circle), and two different colors (blue, red) were used. On a typical trial a subject might be asked to make a ''same–different'' comparison of a small red circle followed by a large red square.

For all subjects, ''different'' reaction time decreased monotonically with the number of dimensions on which a standard and a test shape differed. (For stimuli like those used in this experiment, other investigators have reported similar group results. See, for example, Egeth, 1966; Hawkins, 1969; Nickerson, 1967.) If number of differing dimensions is taken as analogous to similarity in the earlier experiments, then all subjects showed the Type II pattern. Presumably, the structure of the stimuli forced both types of subjects to use a comparison strategy based on comparing dimensions or features. Attempts to find a situation that will produce Type I performance in all subjects have so far failed. In one experiment, subjects compared two sequentially presented lines and determined whether they were the same or different in length. The idea was that the length judgment was basically unidimensional and that no obvious feature structure was present in the stimuli. Nonetheless, individual differences similar to those in the basic visual comparison task were found. Experiments using other sorts of visual materials are currently in progress, but it may be that only some subjects are capable of using a holistic comparison strategy.

In summary, this second strategy for research on spatial information processing is based on identifying and manipulating qualitative differences in patterns of performance of individual subjects. In the experiments I presented to illustrate this approach, the individual differences were used as a tool for understanding the nature of spatial comparison processes. Another goal of this approach is to examine the conditions under which a given individual will show flexibility in spatial information processing—that is, will use a comparison process different from the natural, preferred strategy. In the experiments already discussed, the relationship of the individual differences in visual comparison processes to other types of differences between individuals has not been a central focus. One reason for this is that the number of subjects who have been tested and classified is too small to attempt a meaningful correlational study with other quantitative measures of individual differences, such as overall scores on tests of spatial abilities. In other laboratory experiments, though, it has been possible to assess whether the Type I–Type II differences are related to other sources of processing difference. For example, these differences do not seem to be related to alleged differences in the way the two hemispheres of the brain process visual information (Cooper, in preparation b). However, these spatial comparison process differences do seem to be related to individual differences in sensitivity to structure in visual patterns (Cooper & Feuer, in preparation).

ANALYSIS OF THE TASK-DEPENDENT NATURE OF SPATIAL INFORMATION PROCESSING

In the final approach to studying spatial information processing that I discuss, emphasis is placed on the diversity of strategies available for performing spatial tasks. Like the individual-differences analysis, this approach asks how flexible and sensitive processing strategies are to changes in task demands. The concern here is not so much with individual differences in natural processing modes for performing a single type of task. Rather, the concern is with finding how changes in task structure cause changes in processing strategies for a typical subject. This approach challenges to some extent the idea that there are basic processes for performing certain types of spatial tasks and emphasizes the task-dependent nature of processing strategies. One general conclusion emerging from research of this type is that models of basic cognitive processes may reflect little more than the constraints imposed on subjects' performance by the particulars of the processing situation.

As a "case study" of this type of research strategy, I discuss briefly some experiments done by Robert Glushko and myself (see Glushko & Cooper, 1978, for a more detailed discussion). These experiments began as an investigation of how people comprehend descriptions of visual figures and then compare the spatial information in a description with the information in a visual pattern. The experimental situation was similar to the "sentence–picture verification task" studied by Clark and Chase (1972) and Carpenter and Just (1975), but there were important differences. Subjects in our experiment were presented with a visual figure or a verbal description of a figure, and they were allowed to take as much time as they needed to comprehend or construct an internal representation of the figure or visually displayed description. As soon as the subjects indicated that they had comprehended the description or figure, a test figure was presented. Subjects then had to determine as rapidly and accurately as possible whether the test figure did or did not match the originally presented figure or description. On each trial, both comprehension or preparation time (RT_1) and comparison or verification time (RT_2) were recorded.

Both the figures and the descriptions varied in complexity. The figures were composed of two, three, or four component parts, and the descriptions of these figures were one, two, or three propositions (lines) long. Figure 7.11 illustrates typical figures and their corresponding descriptions. Alternative descriptions for each figure were constructed that differed in the lexical items used to describe the spatial arrangement of parts in the figure. The pairs *left/right* and *above/below* were used in different descriptions of a given figure. We included this variation because other investigators have found significant linguistic effects on comparison time in the sentence–picture verification task (e.g., Clark & Chase, 1972; Olson & Laxar, 1973). In these earlier experiments, the marked term in each relational pair (the terms *left* and *below*) required more processing than the unmarked term (the terms *right* and *above*).

The main results of this experiment were as follows:

1. Preparation or comprehension time for descriptions of figures increased
   linearly with the number of propositions in the description, but there

    SQUARE ABOVE TRIANGLE

    TRIANGLE BELOW SQUARE I
SQUARE 2 RIGHT SQUARE I

    TRIANGLE I ABOVE SQUARE I   FIG. 7.11. Typical figures and
SQUARE 2 RIGHT SQUARE I   their descriptions used in Glushko
TRIANGLE 2 BELOW SQUARE 2   and Cooper (1978), Experiment I,
shown for three levels of complexity.
(From Glushko & Cooper, 1978.)

was little effect of complexity on comprehension time for visual figures.

2. Comparison times for both description–figure and figure–figure
   matches were affected very little by the complexity (number of components) of the test figure.
3. None of the description–figure comparison times at any level of complexity showed effects of the markedness of the lexical items used in the
   originally presented descriptions.

The absence of both complexity effects and effects of lexical markedness
suggests that subjects construct a spatial representation of a figure in the
description–figure matching condition. This representation could then be compared against the test figure in a holistic fashion when the test figure is presented.
Under this analysis, figure–figure comparison and description–figure comparison
processes are functionally similar. At the time of comparison, internal representations constructed from descriptions of figures preserve information concerning the spatial structure of the figures described rather than information concerning the surface form of the descriptions of the figures.

This interpretation of the data from our experiment seems straightforward
enough, but it flies in the face of results from and interpretations of earlier
sentence–picture verification studies. In these earlier studies, subjects were typically presented with a one-line description of a visual display either simultaneously with the display or for a fixed period of time before the display was
presented (cf. Clark & Chase, 1972). Under these conditions, only one measure
of total processing time can be obtained. This total processing time generally has
been found to increase with linguistic factors such as the markedness of the
relational terms used in the descriptions of the visual displays. Models of the
processes underlying performance on the sentence–picture verification task
generally hold that both descriptions and visual displays are represented in a
linguistically based (or, more generally, propositional) fashion. These discrete
representations of descriptions (sentences) and figures (visual displays) are then
compared sequentially in order to determine whether or not the description is
appropriate to the visual display. (For models of this general sort, see Carpenter
& Just, 1975; Clark & Chase, 1972.)

Glushko and I reasoned that the differences between the processes we supposed to underlie performance on our task and the processes proposed for the
standard version of the sentence–picture verification task derived from differences in the demands of the two types of experimental situations. In our
version of the description–figure matching task, the subject-controlled preparation interval ensures that enough time is available for subjects to construct a
spatial representation of the described figure that will be adequate for comparison
against that same figure and an entire class of distractor figures. This situation,
then, is optimal for the use of a spatial processing strategy. In the standard

version of the sentence–picture verification task, subjects may not have enough time to generate a spatial representation of the visual display described in the initially or simultaneously presented sentence. A more appropriate strategy in this case may involve comparing a semiprocessed linguistic representation of the sentence with elements in the visual display. Thus, the temporal constraints in the standard sentence–picture task may induce linguistically based processing, even though spatial processing may be more natural and efficient in the absence of those constraints.

A second experiment was done to test systematically this idea that the nature of processing strategies in description–figure comparison is dependent on seemingly minor particulars of the task. Each subject was tested in four experimental conditions. In one condition, a subject-controlled preparation interval was used, as in the earlier experiment. In a second condition, a visual figure and a spatial description were presented simultaneously. In the remaining two conditions, a description was presented for a fixed amount of time (2 or 6 seconds). If the subject felt prepared for the presentation of a test figure before the fixed interval or deadline was up, he or she initiated the presentation of that figure. If preparation was not signaled by the end of the interval, the test figure appeared below the description. In all conditions, the descriptions were either one or two propositions (lines) in length, and the figures contained either two or three component parts. As in the previous experiment, the markedness of the terms used to describe the spatial relations among parts of the figures was varied.

The aspects of the results of particular interest are differences across conditions in: (1) the effects of description complexity (number of propositions) on preparation time (in the conditions in which it could be measured); (2) the effects of figure complexity (number of parts) on comparison time; and (3) the effects of markedness of the relational terms used in the descriptions on comparison time. The effects of description and figure complexity for the four experimental conditions are shown in Fig. 7.12. Inspection of the preparation-time (RT_1) results reveals that, as in the earlier experiment, subject-controlled RT_1 increases with the complexity of the description being comprehended. This is also true for the 6- and 2-second deadline conditions, but the amount of time taken to encode the descriptions is smaller. This decrease in preparation time in the deadline conditions undoubtedly reflects the fact that less time was available for constructing a representation of the description.

The comparison-time data (RT_2) shown in Fig. 7.12 are most revealing. When subjects are given as much time as they need to construct an appropriate representation of the initially presented description, comparison time is rapid and is not dependent on the complexity of the test figure. As the time available for processing the description becomes shorter and shorter, overall comparison time increases, and the effect of figure complexity on comparison time becomes more and more pronounced. This pattern of results is just what we should expect if subjects are using a spatial representation and processing strategy in the subject-

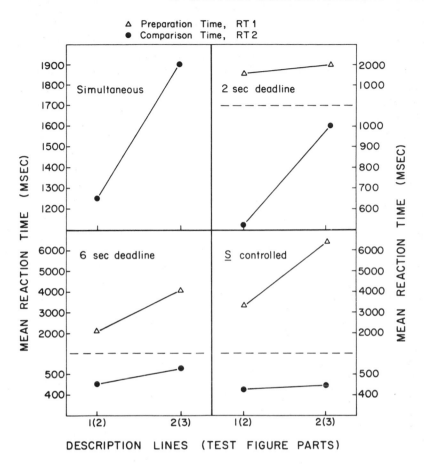

FIG. 7.12.   Mean reaction time plotted as a function of description (and figure) complexity for Glushko and Cooper (1978), Experiment II. The four experimental conditions are shown in separate panels of the figure. Preparation times are illustrated with open triangles, and comparison times are illustrated with closed circles.

controlled condition, but are adopting a different sort of strategy when their preparation time is constrained. When given sufficient time, subjects can construct a spatial representation of the figure described and then efficiently compare this representation with the test figure. When insufficient time is provided to ensure the adequate construction of such a representation on every trial, subjects may adopt one of several strategies, each of which would result in longer comparison times for more complex figures and descriptions. For example, subjects could continue constructing a representation of the description even after the test figure has appeared, and this additional construction time would show up as increased time for processing a more complex figure. Or subjects could encode the description in a fashion that preserved information about its surface form and then compare each element of the description with the spatial relationships present in the visual test figure. The idea of a change from a spatial processing strategy to a more linguistically oriented comparison strategy is supported by the fact that markedness effects on comparison time are absent in the subject-controlled condition. However, these effects are quite pronounced in the simultaneous condition.

In summary, the results of these experiments argue strongly against the idea that a uniform type of processing strategy is used for dealing with spatial information. The results of the initial Glushko and Cooper (1978) experiment question the generality of models of the processes underlying description–picture comparison that have been proposed by other investigators. The results of our second experiment demonstrate that systematic changes in the processing demands of a general type of task can lead to dramatic changes in the pattern of data obtained. These changes in the pattern of data suggest, in turn, that subjects tend to use quite different processing strategies, depending on the particular temporal constraints imposed by the task. The data from this set of experiments are not rich or conclusive enough to indicate in any detailed fashion the nature of the processing changes that occur with variations in parameters of the task. The changing pattern of results does, however, demonstrate the basic point of this approach to research on the processing of spatial information. The basic point is this: People can use diverse and flexible strategies for processing spatial information. An analysis of spatial information processing should consider not only the nature of basic processing mechanisms used to perform individual spatial tasks but also the conditions under which various types of processing strategies are most efficient and appropriate.

CONCLUDING REMARKS

In this paper, I have outlined three related but distinguishable approaches to research on spatial information processing, and I have provided examples of experimental work using each of the approaches. The common goal underlying all of the research strategies is to provide an information-processing analysis of how spatial tasks are performed. The approaches differ, though, in their emphases—ranging from an emphasis on describing in detail the processes used to perform a particular spatial task to an emphasis on analyzing how processing strategies differ from individual to individual and how the nature of processing depends on the particulars of the task.

It seems that process-oriented research could make a valuable contribution to work on the nature of spatial abilities. For if we could discover the nature of the processes used to perform items on tests of spatial abilities, we could then go on to consider just what aspects of these processes might be producing good or poor performance. Research on the task-dependent nature of spatial information processing might help us to understand better which aspects of items on tests of spatial abilities are critical to eliciting one type of processing strategy or another. Still another potential contribution of research on spatial information processing might be in providing additional ways of discovering the relationship between the processes used to perform tests of spatial ability and the processes used in everyday spatial behavior. The approach here would involve designing laboratory experiments that could reveal something about the spatial processes used, say, to navigate through an environment with the aid of a map. A similar analysis could be made of the processes used to perform a single type of item on a test of spatial ability. A comparison of the processes used in the two situations could tell us to what extent ability tests measure the same sorts of processes that are used in everyday, skilled spatial behavior. These are only tentative suggestions about how research on spatial information processing might be used in understanding human abilities. I do, however, find the prospect of this sort of research direction to be a very exciting possibility.

ACKNOWLEDGMENTS

Much of the research reported in this chapter was supported by National Science Foundation Grant BNS 76-22079 to the author. I wish to thank James P. Cunningham for useful comments on this manuscript and for many helpful discussions of the research reported here.

REFERENCES

Bahrick, L. E., & Neisser, U. Personal communication.

Bamber, D. Reaction times and error rates for "same"–"different" judgments of multidimensional stimuli. *Perception & Psychophysics,* 1969, *6,* 169–174.

Carpenter, P. A., & Eisenberg, P. Mental rotation and frame of reference in blind and sighted individuals. *Perception & Psychophysics,* 1978, *23,* 117–124.

Carpenter, P. A., & Just, M. A. Sentence comprehension: A psycholinguistic processing model of verification. *Psychological Review,* 1975, *82,* 45–73.

Carpenter, P. A., & Just, M. A. Eye fixations during mental rotation. In J. Senders, R. Monty, D. Fisher (Eds.), *Eye movements and psychological processes II.* Hillsdale, N.J.: Lawrence Erlbaum Associates, 1978.

Carroll, J. B. Psychometric tests as cognitive tasks: A new structure of intellect. In L. Resnick (Ed.), *The nature of intelligence.* Hillsdale, N.J.: Lawrence Erlbaum Associates, 1976.

Clark, H. H., & Chase, W. G. On the process of comparing sentences against pictures. *Cognitive Psychology,* 1972, *3,* 472–517.

Cooper, L. A. Mental transformation of random two-dimensional shapes. *Cognitive Psychology,* 1975, *7,* 20–43.

Cooper, L. A. Demonstration of a mental analog of an external rotation. *Perception & Psychophysics,* 1976, *19,* 296–304. (a)

Cooper, L. A. Individual differences in visual comparison processes. *Perception & Psychophysics,* 1976, *19,* 433–444. (b)

Cooper, L. A. *Individual differences in visual processing I: Comparison strategies and processing flexibility.* Manuscript in preparation. (a)

Cooper, L. A. *Individual differences in visual processing II: Exploring relationships among sets of processing dichotomies.* Manuscript in preparation. (b)

Cooper, L. A., & Farrell, J. E. *Stimulus structure and rate of rotational transformation.* Manuscript in preparation.

Cooper, L. A., & Feuer, D. *Individual differences in visual processing III: Sensitivity to visual structure.* Manuscript in preparation.

Cooper, L. A., & Podgorny, P. Mental transformations and visual comparison processes: Effects of complexity and similarity. *Journal of Experimental Psychology: Human Perception and Performance,* 1976, *2,* 503–514.

Cooper, L. A., & Shepard, R. N. Chronometric studies of the rotation of mental images. In W. G. Chase (Ed.), *Visual information processing.* New York: Academic Press, 1973.

Corballis, M. C., & Roldan, C. E. Detection of symmetry as a function of angular orientation. *Journal of Experimental Psychology: Human Perception and Performance,* 1975, *1,* 221–230.

Egeth, H. Parallel versus serial processes in multidimensional stimulus discrimination. *Perception & Psychophysics,* 1966, *1,* 245–252.

Glushko, R. J., & Cooper, L. A. Spatial comprehension and comparison processes in verification tasks. *Cognitive Psychology,* 1978, *10,* 391–421.

Hawkins, H. L. Parallel processing in complex visual discrimination. *Perception & Psychophysics,* 1969, *5,* 56–64.

Hunt, E., Frost, N., & Lunneborg, C. Individual differences in cognition: A new approach to intelligence. In G. Bower (Ed.), *The psychology of learning and motivation* Vol. 7. New York: Academic Press, 1973.

Hunt, E., Lunneborg, C., & Lewis, J. What does it mean to be high verbal? *Cognitive Psychology,* 1975, *7,* 194–227.

Just, M. A., & Carpenter, P. A. Eye fixations and cognitive processes. *Cognitive Psychology,* 1976, *8,* 441–480.

MacLeod, C. M., Hunt, E., & Mathews, N. N. Individual differences in the verification of sentence–picture relationships. *Journal of Verbal Learning and Verbal Behavior,* 1978, *17,* 493–507.

Marmor, G. S. Development of kinetic images: When does the child first represent movement in mental images? *Cognitive Psychology,* 1975, *7,* 548–559.

Marmor, G. S., & Zaback, L. A. Mental rotation by the blind: Does mental rotation depend on visual imagery? *Journal of Experimental Psychology: Human Perception and Performance,* 1976, *2,* 515–521.

Metzler, J., & Shepard, R. N. Transformational studies of the internal representation of three-dimensional objects. In R. Solso (Ed.), *Theories in cognitive psychology: The Loyola symposium.* Hillsdale, N.J.: Lawrence Erlbaum Associates, 1974.

Nickerson, R. S. "Same"–"different" response times with multi-attribute stimulus differences. *Perceptual and Motor Skills,* 1967, *24,* 543–554.

Olson, G., & Laxar, K. Asymmetries in processing the terms "right" and "left." *Journal of Experimental Psychology,* 1973, *100,* 284–290.

Shepard, R. N., & Metzler, J. Mental rotation of three-dimensional objects. *Science,* 1971, *171,* 701–703.

Snyder, C. R. R. *Individual differences in imagery and thought.* Unpublished doctoral dissertation, University of Oregon, 1972.

Thurstone, L. L. Primary mental abilities. *Psychometric Monograph,* No. 1. Chicago: University of Chicago Press, 1938.

Wilson, J. R., DeFries, J. C., McClearn, G. E., Vandenberg, S. G., Johnson, R. C., & Rashad, M. N. Cognitive abilities: Use of family data as a control to assess sex and age differences in two ethnic groups. *International Journal of Aging and Human Development,* 1975, *6,* 261–276.

8 Components of Inductive Reasoning

James W. Pellegrino

Robert Glaser
University of Pittsburgh

THE ANALYSIS OF APTITUDE: OVERVIEW

A now-recognized serious shortcoming of research on aptitude and intelligence is the lack of strong theoretical foundations based upon knowledge of human cognition. The theoretical deficit in this field was pointed out by McNemar in 1964 when he emphasized the failure of individual-difference research to "come to grips with the *process,* or operation, by which a given organism achieves an intellectual response [p. 881]." More recent critiques of psychometric research have underscored the necessity for understanding the cognitive processes that are assessed in aptitude measurement (e.g., Estes, 1974; Glaser, 1972; Tyler, 1976).

Psychometrics has been primarily a technological, engineering endeavor, and with the possible exception of work in factor analysis, little theory related to the processes of human cognition has been involved. In contrast to the technological orientation of psychometrics, the experimental psychology of learning and cognition has been largely theory oriented, with little concern for individual differences and practical application (e.g., Glaser, Pellegrino, & Lesgold, 1978; Underwood, 1975). The history of science makes it clear, however, that tests of application are intimately related to scientific growth. Many of the theoretical advances in the physical and biological sciences have been forced by practical questions, and applications have been a strong test of available theory. At the present time, the psychometric assessment of individual differences appears to have reached certain limits due to the lack of a theoretical framework explicitly dealing with cognitive processes. Concurrently, the rapidly developing theories of human cognitive processes are looking to the discipline that comes from application—particularly with regard to the measurement of individual differences—for substantial growth and evolution (e.g., Anderson, 1976; Neisser, 1976).

Beyond scientific concerns, there is an urgent social reason for reexamining psychometric technique and theory. The mental-testing movement has become the major and most sustained attempt to adjust to individual differences in educational settings. Whereas concepts of instruction adaptive to individual differences have had considerable appeal, the form of adaptation that requires the use of aptitude and intelligence test scores has been substantially criticized. Using these tests, individual differences have been assessed for the purposes of selecting and placing individuals into existing settings for education, training, and work. Used in this way, test scores show that one individual is worse or better than another on some performance that is related to a criterion performance such as academic achievement. This differentiation in terms of predictive success provides a very gross basis for adapting to individual requirements (see Glaser, 1977). Little emphasis is given to understanding the relationship between individual differences in intellectual processes and the different instructional environments that individuals require in order to maximize their attainments.

Today this situation is changing, and competent performance is viewed as something not just to be predicted. Current emphasis is on understanding the processes involved in intellectual competence and how these processes can be influenced and utilized to benefit learning. This change in emphasis reflects recognition of the fact that aptitudes are related to learning outcomes and that there are instructional treatments that interact with these aptitudes to enhance or retard achievement (e.g., Cronbach & Snow, 1977). The presence of such aptitude–treatment interactions emphasizes the possibility for more effective adaptation to individual differences. However, the understanding of such interactions has suffered from the lack of explicit process analyses of measured aptitudes. As noted by Snow (1976): "If practical and theoretical use is to be made of aptitude information in instructional work, then individual differences in aptitude for learning will need to be understood, at a more analytic level, as individual differences in psychological processes [p. 1]."

The trend that is encouraged by current psychological knowledge and theory is a reconceptualization of individual differences in aptitudes in terms of processes that positively or negatively influence learning, development, and performance. Based on this knowledge, conditions designed for learning could be adjusted to these individual characteristics; or instruction could be designed so that it directly or indirectly teaches the processes that facilitate learning (Glaser, 1972, 1973). These are some rather lofty and distant goals, but there is strong evidence that psychologists have begun to lay a foundation necessary for their attainment.

Over the course of the past few years, cognitive psychologists and psychometricians have described some initial attempts to characterize individual differences, as measured on aptitude tests, in terms of the structures and processes utilized in the study of human cognition and cognitive development. Within this developing area of aptitude research, there appear to be two general research approaches. The first of these approaches, which may be termed a *cognitive correlates* approach, seeks to specify the elementary information processes that correlate with high and low levels of aptitude. In this approach, tests of aptitude or intelligence are used to define subgroups that are compared on laboratory tasks that have relatively well defined cognitive processing characteristics. The particular tasks chosen and their hypothesized underlying processes can be interpreted in terms of general models of human cognition. Examples of this type of research can be found in the work of Hunt and his colleagues (e.g., Hunt, 1976; Hunt, Frost, & Lunneborg, 1973; Hunt & Lansman, 1975).

The second research approach, which may be termed the *cognitive components* approach, attempts to identify directly the information-processing components of performance on tasks used to assess aptitude. In this approach, performance on psychometric test tasks becomes the object of theoretical and empirical analyses. The goal is to develop models of task performance and utilize these process models as a basis for individual-difference analysis. The models of performance are developed within the context of current theory and research on the nature of human cognition. Examples of this type of task analytic research include the discussion by Estes (1974) and the recent work of Sternberg (1977b) and Carroll (1976).

In this paper, we present an overview of research that represents an application of the cognitive components approach to the analysis of inductive reasoning skill, as frequently assessed on aptitude and intelligence tests. Before discussing this research, we briefly focus on some general operating constraints that are important in any task analytic effort aimed at understanding individual differences in aptitude processes.

A Framework for Task Analysis

Because there is an extremely large constellation of psychometric tasks, any one of which could serve as the subject of an intensive task analytic effort, the selection of tasks to be studied should be nonrandom and guided by some general principles. One basic principle for task selection is derived from the pervasiveness of a task within multiple factor analyses of aptitudes. Whether one wishes to adopt a hierarchical or nonhierarchical view of general and specific aptitude, there exists a core set of tasks that: (1) frequently occur across many widely used tests; and (2) have demonstrated consistent relationships to certain basic aptitude constructs. Thus, a particular task or set of tasks chosen for analysis should have a strong history of reliable association with an aptitude construct that is of reasonable generality, and should have consistent predictive validity with respect to a criterion performance of significant interest.

In the analysis of any particular aptitude construct—that is, some general or specific ability factor—it is important to consider simultaneously the multiple tasks or task forms that load on that factor. An adequate understanding of individual differences in a particular aptitude cannot be based upon an intensive analysis of only a single task with a high loading on that aptitude construct. Rather, it is necessary to have analyses of the various tasks that intercorrelate and thereby define more completely a substantial set of performances that comprise a particular first-order or higher-order aptitude construct. A successful process analysis of multiple tasks should provide a basis for understanding the patterns of intercorrelations among tasks giving rise to certain hierarchical ability models. More importantly, the analysis of multiple tasks should enable us to differentiate general and specific cognitive processes and thereby help direct us to a level of analysis where research can identify the extent of process trainability and transfer effects.

The analysis of a particular task must also be explicitly concerned with explicating the sources of difficulty that differentiate between test items and thereby provide the basis for individual variation in test performance. Test tasks are composed of heterogeneous item sets where the individual items vary considerably in difficulty as a function of ability or developmental level. Thus, an understanding of individual differences in task performance must include a process theory of item difficulty. For this purpose, the processes specified as the components of performance must involve a level of analysis that is sufficient to explain individual item characteristics, individual subject performance, and the interaction of the two.

The foregoing set of constraints on a task analytic effort can be expanded by including other issues of convergent and discriminant validity as discussed by Sternberg (1977b), and it should be apparent that any one research study will have difficulty meeting all the foregoing requirements. However, by systematically analyzing sets of test tasks, it should become possible to develop a process theory of aptitude that explains consistent psychometric findings and indicates the strengths and deficiencies of current testing procedures. In the course of attempting to develop such a theory, additional significant constraints arise as a result of the primary goals of the research program. In our own work, the goal is to develop a useful theory of individual differences in aptitude processes that identifies instructionally tractable components of cognitive performance. The inclusion of this goal serves to guide our analysis by providing a criterion against which to check the level and form of the theoretical effort. This is a nontrivial evaluative criterion because it is not unusual for cognitive psychologists to engage in detailed task analyses with attendant theoretical debates about very molecular levels of processing that may have little relevance to instructional issues. We propose that the empirical and theoretical results of any particular analysis of the cognitive components of a task be evaluated by asking whether such results bring us closer to an analytic scheme that is diagnostically useful and whether the sources of individual differences suggest testable instructional hypotheses. Such internal tests of the task analytic effort may be sobering indicants that we have yet to achieve a sufficiently useful level of analysis.

This general framework constitutes the schema within which we discuss research that we and others have conducted on the nature of inductive reasoning skill. The various sections of the following presentation deal with general issues surrounding the relevance of this aptitude construct and specific issues associated with the analysis of the different task forms by which it has been tested. In the final section of this chapter, we consider our current state of knowledge with respect to the various aspects of aptitude analysis already outlined.

ANALYSES OF INDUCTIVE REASONING

Psychometric and Practical Relevance of Rule Induction

One of the major classes of tasks commonly found on tests of aptitude and intelligence includes those presumed to assess a psychological capacity for rule induction. This set of intercorrelated tasks involves several task forms such as classification, series extrapolation, analogy, and matrix tasks, and these task forms simultaneously vary along a content dimension that includes letters, numbers, words, and geometric figures. Spearman (1923) considered such tasks as measures of g, which he viewed as an index of the capacity to engage in intellectual processes that he referred to as the eduction of relations and correlates. Thurstone and Thurstone (1941) treated these tasks as representative of a primary mental ability that was labeled *Induction* (I), and they suggested that rule induction as a second-order factor might be identical with Spearman's g. In more recent hierarchical aptitude models, such tasks have been treated as measures of g_f or fluid analytic ability (e.g., Cronbach, 1970). Within the literature of factor analysis, there has been debate about whether the various tasks represent one or more first-order factors. An example of this is the distinction made among: an induction factor, as measured by tasks such as letter or number series; a separate factor referred to as the cognition of figural relations, as measured by figural analogy or figural matrix tasks; and another separate factor referred to as the cognition of semantic relations, as measured by verbal analogy tasks (e.g., Horn, 1968).

Irrespective of the factor analytic debates about the appropriate higher-order construct(s) that these tasks represent, it is clear that such rule induction tasks assess basic reasoning abilities that comprise a robust aptitude construct that has relevance for a larger domain of human performance. Rule induction tasks have been characterized as examples of a major type of problem-solving task within a general problem typology (Greeno, 1978). More specifically, it has been argued that rule induction processes are similar to those demanded in concept formation, and that there is a formal basis for relating rule induction and general problem-solving processes (Simon & Lea, 1974). Egan and Greeno (1974) reinforce this point and illustrate that the main component of analogical reasoning, series completion, problem solving, and concept formation is a search for relations among elements resulting in new interconnections between the nodes of a knowledge network.

Consistent with Egan and Greeno's analysis, Norman, Gentner, and Stevens (1976) have argued that the process of instruction involves presenting students with a network of knowledge that can be assimilated into the student's existing knowledge network. The learner's role is to recognize the structural form or pattern of the facts conveyed by instruction and to detect relations between this newly communicated material and the material already existing in his or her knowledge network. This process, according to Norman et al. (1976), is really the essence of both concept formation and learning through instruction. The importance of inductive thought processes and reasoning by analogy has been emphasized in many situations, such as in science (e.g., Oppenheimer, 1956), mathematics (e.g., Polya, 1965), and in the acquisition of information in the classroom (e.g., Bruner, 1957; Forehand, 1974).

It is certainly not our intent to argue that inductive reasoning tasks of the type found on mental ability tests constitute the entire scope of inductive thought processes. Rather, we view such tasks as performance samples of the way in which an individual makes use of existing declarative and procedural knowledge to solve circumscribed problems where problem solution depends on an analysis of the underlying relations (or conceptual simialrity) among a set of problem elements. Performance on these tasks has consistently correlated with academic achievement, and individual differences in the capacity to engage in such analyses appear to have direct implications for classroom learning processes.

Series Completion Problems

Task Analysis.   Series completion items are found at several developmental levels on many standardized aptitude tests. Such items may be represented as letter series, number series, picture series, or geometric figure series problems. In all cases, the task structure is the same, such that the elements comprising the series are ordered according to some specific interitem relationships, and the individual's task is to extract the basic relationships and to generate or predict the next item(s) in the series. The acquisition of serial pattern concepts has an extensive history of psychological investigation (e.g., Greeno & Simon, 1974; Restle, 1970; Simon, 1972; Vitz & Todd, 1967). Of particular interest for our purpose is the work of Simon and Kotovsky (1963; Kotovsky & Simon, 1973) on the analysis of letter series problems of the type developed by Thurstone and Thurstone (1941) and considered as a test of the primary mental ability of induction. An example of such an item is the series npaoqapraq_____.

Simon and Kotovsky studied adult and adolescent performance in this task, and they developed a computer simulation model to represent the component processes necessary for solution.

One important aspect of the Simon and Kotovsky analysis is the distinction between the declarative knowledge and the procedural knowledge or processes necessary for the task. The declarative knowledge base for letter series problems of the Thurstone type is limited to alphabetic ordering knowledge and relational concepts of identity, next, and backwards-next (or reverse ordering). Obviously, letter series problems do not involve an extensive declarative knowledge component, and it would not be expected that individual differences would arise from declarative knowledge deficiencies. However, differences could arise from a failure to treat the alphabet as a closed loop or circular system. Such a representation is necessary for extended extrapolation of series problems—for example, axbyczda_ _ _ _.

Given that the appropriate declarative knowledge is available, the completion of any letter series problem requires a set of basic procedures that are hierarchically organized. In Simon and Kotovsky's simualtion model, there are two basic routines: a pattern generator and a sequence generator. The first of these routines can be broken down into a set of processes that involve: (1) detection of the interletter relations for the given problem elements; (2) use of the relational information to extract the period length of the pattern within the problem; and (3) generation of a pattern description or rule involving both the relations and the periodic structure of the problem. One aspect of the modeling effort involved the development of a notational system for representing the pattern description. The pattern description notation developed represents the relations, the periodic structure, and the working memory requirements associated with each problem. The notational system is sufficiently general to be applied to all problems, and it provides a basis for predicting problem difficulty.

The pattern description serves as input to the sequence generator, which applies the pattern description to the current state of the problem and then extrapolates the pattern to generate the additional elements required for problem solution. Differences in item difficulty and individual differences in problem solution may result from any or all of these specific processes.

Sources of Task Difficulty.   In the course of their analysis and modeling of task performance, Simon and Kotovsky were able to uncover a number of systematic aspects of the individual items that determined problem difficulty. Related work by Holzman, Glaser, and Pellegrino (1976) on the performance of children in this task has verified and extended the empirical data obtained. One aspect of a problem that is related to the probability of error is the type of relation involved. Identity relations are easier to detect than next relations, which in turn are easier than backwards-next relationships. The difference in difficulty between extrapolating identity and next relationships also varies as a function of the position of the relationship within a period. Most problems have a periodic structure of two to four elements, and it is possible to identify whether a particular problem blank to be extrapolated represents a beginning, middle, or end position within a period. The interaction of position and relationship is shown in Fig. 8.1. The pattern of this interaction is readily explainable if one considers the notational system developed by Kotovsky and Simon that indexes working memory requirements. Identity relationships do not place demands on working memory, whereas successive nonidentity reltionships involve accumulating placekeepers in working memory. The longer the period length, the greater the memory demands of a problem and the greater the likelihood that working memory limits may be reached with respect to placekeepers for nonidentity relationships at the end of a period. Identity relationships, however, remain invariant across positions within periods.

The overall pattern descriptions that constitute a problem also are related to problem difficulty. The length of the pattern description—which is a function of

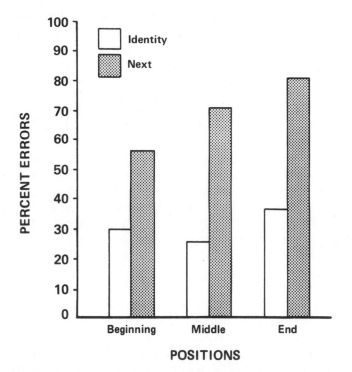

FIG. 8.1.   Performance on series extrapolation problems as a function of type of relation and position witin a period. (From "Process Training Derived from a Computer Simulation Theory" by T. G. Holzman, R. Glaser, & J. W. Pellegrino, *Memory & Cognition*, 1976, *4*, 349–356. Copyright © 1976 by The Psychonomic Society. Reprinted by permission.)

period length, the types of relationships involved, and the resulting working memory requirements—is highly correlated with problem errors. This relationship was observed in the performance of adults (Kotovsky & Simon, 1973) and of children (Holzman et al., 1976).

With respect to the foregoing sources of task difficulty, it is to be emphasized that problem difficulty is expressed in terms of objective features of the task using the formalisms of the model, but the model does not uniquely specify the solution processes that are responsible for a particular problem error. An example of this is the fact that pattern description length is related to problem difficulty, but such a relationship can arise from inadequacies in relation detection, discovery of the periodic structure, completion of a pattern description, or in the extrapolation process. It is possible, however, to develop model variants that systematically differ in execution of the various components of solution and to apply these variants to problem solution, thereby developing a set of hypotheses about potential sources of performance errors.

Sources of Individual Differences.   As already noted, the model of performance developed by Simon and Kotovsky provides a basis for analyzing problem difficulty and sources of difficulty in individual performance. Although the model has not been used to analyze individual differences in performance explicitly, there are several ways in which it could be applied. One way, and perhaps the simplest and most straightforward, would be to use it as a framework for protocol analysis of correct and incorrect solutions. Such an analysis might lead to the development of a unique model variant for a given individual where the sources of individual differences would lie in the organization of the solution process and the parameters of the individual simulations. Variations in the individual simulations could occur at a number of different levels within such programs. Kotovsky and Simon have reported that there are variants of the general model that are intended to account for individual differences.

One potential criticism of this approach to analyzing individual differences is that computer modeling, though richly detailed and meeting several sufficiency tests, is cumbersome for individual-difference analysis because such models often do not yield unique processing parameters (Sternberg, 1977b). It might, therefore, be necessary to reformulate the model into a set of increasingly more specific component processes that could be submitted to detailed analysis. One such method would be to create task forms that successively eliminate the need to engage in one or more of the processes specified by the model. For example, series problems could be shown with the periodic structure defined, thereby eliminating the necessity for that process and providing a possible method for estimating the time for its execution and for estimating whether the period detection component of the task contributes to unsuccessful performance. Whether or not such task engineering can be successfully designed and its benefits for analyzing individual differences remain to be determined.

Instructional Applicability of the Model.   Simon and Kotovsky have demonstrated that their model provides a reasonable account of adult performance in this task, and their simulation of human protocols provides a partial validation of the model. Because of our own concern with the criterion of instructional tractability, we have considered another way in which such models can be validated. If the processes embodied in a simulation model are similar to those used by humans, then those processes may be trainable for individuals whose performance represents a low or intermediate level of task competency. Such training should improve performance if the component processes specified and taught are compatible with human cognitive structures. However, if the processes are incompatible with such structures, then there will either be difficulty in training these processes, or they will not influence performance or will influence it detrimentally.

In an attempt to provide such an instructional test of the Simon and Kotovsky analysis, we conducted a study (Holzman et al., 1976) that involved direct and independent training in discovery of relations and discovery of periodicity with a sample of children from grades one through six. Both the training group and the control group were administered a 15-problem pretest, with each problem requiring series extrapolation over four blanks. The control and training groups within each grade were matched on aspects of pretest performance such as overall error rate and error distributions across problems.

The training group was given approximately 2 hours of total instruction in relations identification and periodicity training (see Holzman et al., 1976, for training details). No explicit training was given in pattern description or extrapolation because a second goal of the research was to determine whether the basic components of performance could be spontaneously assembled into these higher-order units in order to perform this task successfully. Both the training group and the control group were then given a new set of 15 problems that were identical in rule structure to the original problems but initialized at different points in the alphabet. The results showed a significant gain in performance for the training group relative to the control group, although both groups showed improvement. The training group showed a percentage reduction in errors more than twice that shown by the control group (32% versus 13%).

The quantitative difference between training and control groups was further analyzed in terms of qualitative changes in solution performance. These analyses indicated that the training group showed significantly greater gains on the problem blanks requiring the more difficult interletter relationships and on the more difficult problems overall. The latter were defined as those problems where more than 50% of the blank positions had been extrapolated incorrectly on the original test. In these more difficult problems, the training group showed a much greater tendency to shift to errorless performance, whereas the control group tended to remain the same or reduce errors on some, but not all, remaining blanks. Thus, the training appropriately functioned where it was most needed, on the more difficult relations and problems. The shift to errorless performance also suggests that the training may have provided an information management strategy that eliminated pattern description or extrapolation problems.

A second experiment examined in more detail control-group gains via extended practice rather than the explicit process training of the experimental group. In this study, third- and fifth-grade children were given four separate sessions with 15 problems matched in series structure but initialized at different alphabetic locations. The practice groups were selected such that the pretest performance was equivalent to children of the same age from the first study. The results of the study are shown in Fig. 8.2 and clearly demonstrate that only the older children showed significant performance gains as a result of practice.

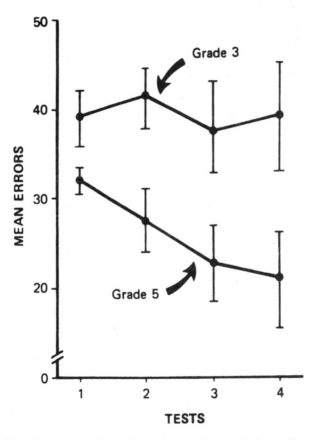

FIG. 8.2.   Perfromance of control groups on series extrapolation problems as a function of successive tests. (From "Process Training Derived from a Computer Simulation Theory" by T. G. Holzman, R. Glaser, & J. W. Pellegrino, *Memory & Cognition*, 1976, *4*, 349–356. Copyright © 1976 by The Psychonomic Society. Reprinted by permission.)

The change in performance from Test 1 to Test 4 was comparable to the performance gain of the fifth-grade training group in the first experiment.

These two studies of series completion performance serve to demonstrate the feasibility and limits of explicit training on components of task performance as derived from an extensive analysis of the task components. The interaction between training, practice, and developmental level appears to indicate that practice may be sufficient for significant gains in performance at certain levels of initial competence, whereas explicit training may be more effective than practice at earlier levels of initial competence. The source of the interaction needs to be more precisely determined by explicit analysis of the process differences that define different levels of task competency.

Matching Instruction and Performance Deficits. The training study of Holzman et al. (1976) represents a very naive form of instructional experimentation. No attempt was made to determine the particular components of performance that were responsible for the intermediate levels of task competency shown by the children of different ages. The process training that was administered was the same for all individuals, and it varied in its success. Such variability in instructional effectiveness must result when there is no real effort to match training to performance needs. However, there is no particular reason why future instructional studies cannot use the model of task performance as a basis for both the initial diagnostic assessment of individual cognitive strengths and weaknesses and the subsequent training designed to improve cognitive skills. We have at least shown that the model of series completion performance can be translated into a set of procedures for explicit process training. What remains to be shown is whether or not the model provides a useful framework for the analysis of individual differences in inductive reasoning skill. The fact that such models are capable of providing a framework for the analysis of sources of item difficulty and the fact that the components identified, when learned, influence performance suggest that they will be applicable to analyzing individual differences.

Analogical Reasoning Problems

Of the many tasks that are assumed to assess inductive reasoning, the analogy problem is the most pervasive. Analogy items have constituted a significant portion of intelligence tests over the entire course of the testing movement. Burt introduced the task in its familiar "A:B::C:D" format in a test published in 1911. Thurstone, Otis, and Thorndike all included analogy items on tests published in 1919, at which time Thorndike introduced the nonverbal geometric analogy. The extensive use of analogy items in intelligence tests was documented by Dawis and Siojo (1972), and more recently, Sternberg (1977b) has provided a detailed review and discussion of the importance of analogical reasoning within the field of differential psychology. Examples of the centrality of this type of reasoning with respect to the concept and measurement of intelligence can be found in the writings of individuals such as Spearman (1923) and Raven (1938). The Progressive Matrices Test developed by Raven (1938) was designed to test "a person's capacity to form comparisons, reason by analogy, and develop a logical method of thinking [p. 12]." Analogical reasoning tasks have also been of significance in the artificial intelligence field, as evidenced by programs such as Reitman's (1965) for solving verbal analogies and Evans' (1968) for solving geometric analogies. However, a combined theoretical and empirical analysis of the component cognitive processes involved in analogical problem solving has only recently become an active research area.

General Process Theories. A useful organization scheme for studying analogies can be found in the "process theory" postulated by Spearman (1923). According to Spearman, analogical reasoning involves three processes. First one must "apprehend," or read and understand, the elements of the item. The second process involves the eduction of the relation between the first two terms. In Spearman's (1923) words, "The mentally presenting of any two or more characters (simple or complex) tends to evoke immediately a knowing of relation between them [p. 63]." The third process is the eduction of correlates, which Spearman (1923) described as follows: "The presenting of any character together with any relation tends to evoke immediately a knowing of the correlative character [p. 91]." In other words, one must read and understand the analogy terms, find a relationship between the first two terms, and then use that relationship together with the third term to find the solution to the item. This is a component process theory that fits well into a modern information-processing framework. One obvious difficulty with Spearman's process theory is that the processes themselves are not well specified, and their description implies an automaticity of function that appears too simplistic.

The process theory of Spearman has been expanded and refined in the more precise, experimentally founded theory presented by Sternberg (1977b). He has proposed a componential theory of analogical reasoning that specifies several processes that are intended to apply across all analogical reasoning tasks. The component processes include: (1) *encoding* the individual terms of the analogy; (2) *inferring* the relationship between the first two terms; (3) *mapping* the relationship between the first and third terms; (4) *applying* the results of the inference and mapping processes to the third term to generate an ideal fourth term, which is then used to evaluate the several alternative answers presented; (5) an optional *justification* process, which is used to select among alternative answers, none of which precisely matches the ideal answer; and (6) a *response* process, which indicates the choice of an answer.

Sternberg distinguishes between theories and models that include all or some of these processes. In order to test a variety of possible models, Sternberg estimated parameters associated with each of the hypothesized component processes and then tested the models in several experiments dealing with verbal, pictorial, and geometric materials. His analyses support a model that includes all of the component processes. Of particular interest is Sternberg's attempt to relate latency measures for the various component processes to general reasoning scores derived from a standardized test battery. He obtained multiple correlations between .68 and .87 for these latency estimates and general reasoning scores. However, processing latency for the separate components was not uniformly related to general reasoning ability, and in some cases, individuals with high general reasoning scores were slower on certain component processes.

Processes, Content, and Accuracy.   The componential analysis of analogical reasoning and the individual-difference data provided by Sternberg (1977a, 1977b) represent a major contribution to a complete analysis of analogy solution and inductive reasoning skill. However, many issues remain to be addressed. One such issue deals with the nature of the processes postulated for the task and their instantiation across different content domains. In Sternberg's analyses, emphasis is placed on developing general models of analogy solution and specifying individual differences in terms of latency parameters for the various processes. The processes themselves remain largely unspecified, and a more fine-grained analysis of the encoding, inference, mapping, application, and justification processes is required if we are to understand quantitative and/or qualitative individual differences in these processes. Sternberg (1977a) has recognized some of the limits of his analyses:

> Although the models specify in some detail the alternative ways in which attribute information can be combined to arrive at a solution for analogy problems, the models do not specify what the possible attributes are for different types of analogies, nor do they specify how subjects discover these attributes in the first place [p. 355].

The importance of a more detailed understanding of the processes associated with actual task attributes is further emphasized by a consideration of the fact that individual differences exist not only in process speed but also in process success. Individual-difference analysis solely in terms of process speed ignores the fact that differences are in large part a function of performance errors. At present, we have a poor understanding of where errors occur and how they are related to process execution. To analyze errors, effort must be expended on detailing the information or content that must be processed and how such information contributes to differences in item difficulty and thereby provides a basis for differentiating among individuals.

In the research that we now describe, we have been explicitly concerned with the task attributes that must be processed and how such attributes systematically affect performance. In the analysis of individual differences, we have attempted to determine the components of task performance that differentiate between levels of skill and how these components interact with differences in item structure or content. The two task forms studied include geometric and verbal analogies, which we consider separately.

Analysis of Geometric Analogy Solution

Task Analysis. A starting point for understanding the declarative and procedural knowledge requirements in geometric analogy solution can be found in Evans' (1968) artificial intelligence analysis of this task. He developed a computer program that solved a subset of the geometric analogies that appear on the American Council for Education examinations. Although it was not intended as a simulation of human performance, the program is useful for considering some components of task performance.

The principal operations in Evans' program are: (1) decomposing the patterns comprising the terms of the analogy into subpatterns; and (2) determining the transformations that relate the subpatterns in the *A-B* and *C-D* pairs of terms. Decomposition of the *A* and *B* terms occurs first. This is accomplished by comparing the figures and determining the elements or subpatterns common to both. Evans' program has a primitive scheme for classifying the patterns and subpatterns it encountered. Figure 8.3 (panel a) shows a geometric analogy in which decomposition of the *A* and *B* terms would yield a square and a circle. In Fig. 8.3 (panel b), on the other hand, decomposition of the *A* and *B* terms might yield quite a different set of elements, despite the fact that the *A* terms are identical in both analogies. In either case, the program examines both the *A* and *B* terms in determining the appropriate constituents.

In determining the transformations relating the terms of the analogy, Evans'

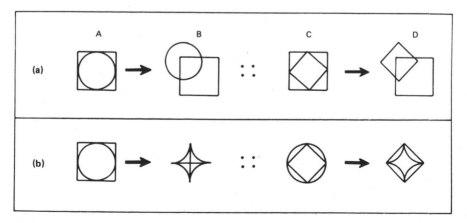

FIG. 8.3. Examples of geometric analogies illustrating a potential difference in pattern decomposition.

program matches the subpatterns in the *A* and *B* terms and generates a set of transformation rules. The class of transformations recognized by the program is not large: removing and adding constituents; and rotation, reflection, and spatial displacement of figures. Nevertheless, these transformations are sufficient to solve the problems presented to the program.

Following the identification of the constituents of the terms and the transformations relating them, Evans' program decides among the answer alternatives. The *C* term is paired with each of the *D* options; the pairs are decomposed, and transformation rules are generated in each case. A gross comparison of the *A–B* pair with each *C–D* pair, primarily in terms of the number of subpatterns present, eliminates some of the *D* terms from further consideration. For those that remain, the elements of the *A–B* terms are mapped onto the elements of each *C–D* pair, and the transformation rules corresponding to the elements are compared. The *D* term for which there is the greatest overlap in transformational rules is selected.

The processes represented in Evans' program are compatible with those specified in Sternberg's (1977b) general theory of analogy solution. In all cases, the individual must encode the analogy terms and infer, match, and test the relationships among sets of terms. These processes are influenced by the amount and type of information that must be processed to solve any given item. In the case of geometric analogies, the amount of information to be processed is a function of the number of individual elements used to construct the separate analogy terms and the number and type of transformations applied to each element. Because the elements that comprise the terms are easily perceived, plane geometric figures such as lines, circles, triangles, and quadrilaterals, item difficulty does not seem to depend on constituent recognizability. The basic transformations that are employed include: removing or adding elements; rotating, reflecting, and displacing elements; size changes; and variations in element shading.

Our analysis of items used on aptitude tests indicates that item difficulty is related to increases in both the number of elements and the number of transformations contained in an item. Evans' analysis of solution together with our own analysis of item features suggest that solution accuracy and latency depend on the total set of processes required: (1) to decompose complex figures into constituent elements; and (2) to identify and order the transformations applied to each element.

Previous experimental research on the processing of complex multielement or multidimensional stimuli suggests that individuals determine the relationships between geometric patterns by serially isolating and comparing the individual elements or dimensions (e.g., Bamber, 1969; Egeth, 1966). The time to decompose and compare complex figures is typically a function of the total number of elements to be isolated. A number of experiments have also explored how individuals process spatial transformations of geometric stimuli (Bundesen & Larsen, 1975; Shepard, 1975). Rotation, reflection, and size-change transformations also appear to involve serial and additive processing within and across transformations. The time to identify and order a set of transformations appears to be a direct function of the total number of transformations involved. Such data suggest a simple additive model for the time to solve geometric analogies. The total time to solve any given item should be an additive function of the number of elements and transformations that comprise the item. The probability of error on an item should increase as a function of the number of cognitive operations required to identify elements and/or isolate the individual transformations applied to the elements.

We attempted to test some of these general assumptions in an experiment that involved the presentation of true and false geometric analogies in a reaction-time verification task (Mulholland, Pellegrino, & Glaser, in press). The analogies were constructed such that the number and type of elements and transformations were systematically varied across items. The processing latencies for true and false items permitted an evaluation of the hypothesized additive relations involved in element and transformation processing. The processing latencies for false items also permitted an evaluation of the nature of the overall decision process.

The analogies were generated from six types of elements and six types of transformations that occur frequently in items found on aptitude tests. The elements were of the type described previously. The transformations included: rotation, reflection, size increase and decrease, doubling and halving elements, and identity or no transformation. In the case of the true items, there were 11 item classes representing the partial crossing of one to three elements with zero to three transformations. Figure 8.4 gives examples of the types of true and false items that were used. The false items were generated by a series of rules that varied the number of incorrect elements or transformations in the C-D pair. The resulting item classes (52) also permitted the testing of assumptions about exhaustive versus self-terminating processing of the individual elements and transformations.

Each of 28 undergraduates was administered a 25-item geometric analogy subtest of the Cognitive Abilities Test (Thorndike & Hagen, 1971) prior to being tested on the experimental items. The range of performance on the CAT items was from 40% to 96% correct. Average performance was 75% correct. Performance on the experimental items was highly correlated with the CAT performance ($r = .69$), and we attempted to determine if relationships existed between specific components of performance on the experimental items and performance on the CAT items.

Performance Characteristics.   The results of this study showed that individuals' latencies for solving the analogies differed as a function of item structure in a highly systematic and reliable manner. Figure 8.5 shows the latency data for

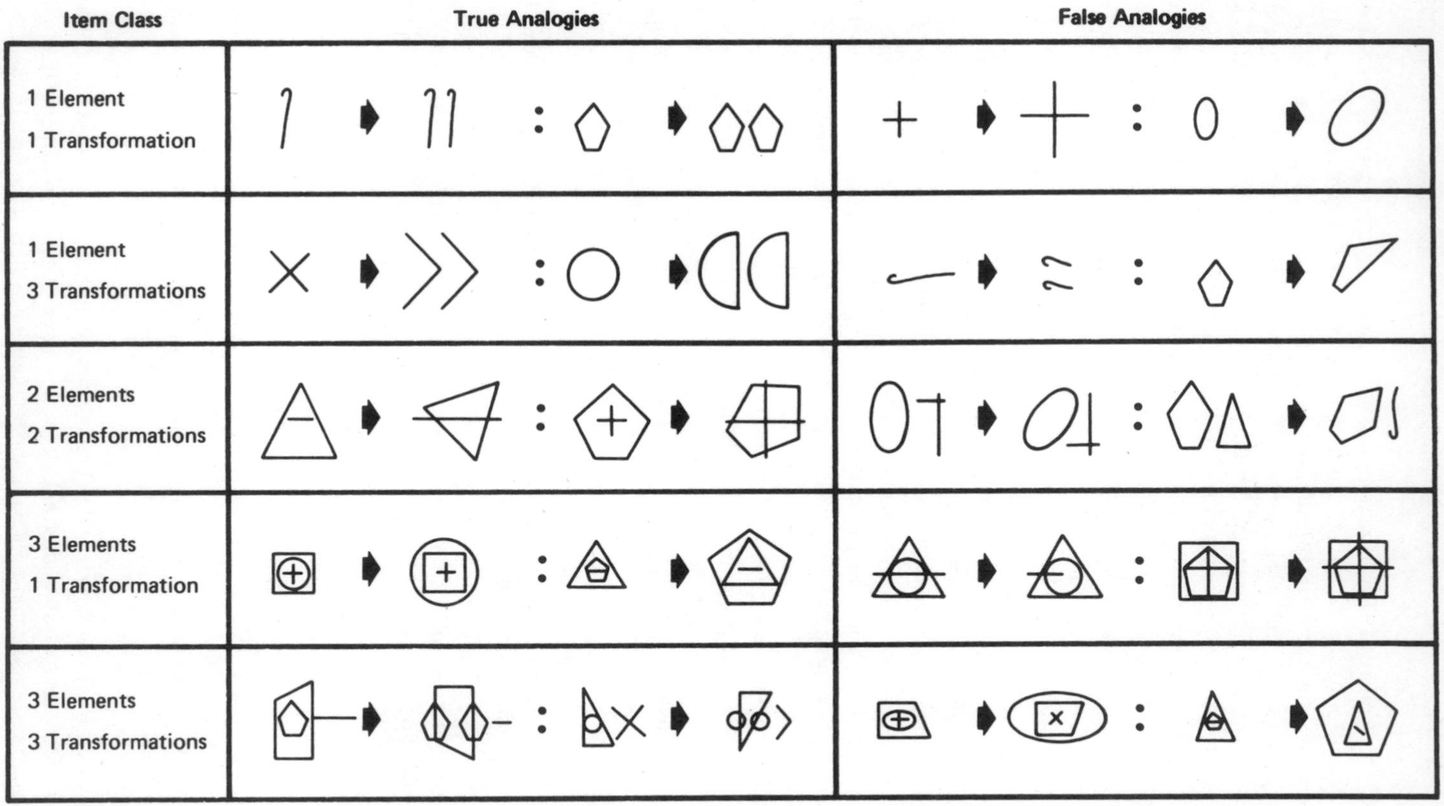

FIG. 8.4. Examples of geometric analogies used for the verification task.

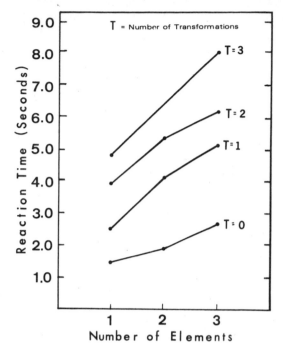

FIG. 8.5. Mean reaction time for true analogies as a function of the number of elements and transformations.

the 11 classes of true items. The data are consistent with the assumption that individuals decompose the terms of the analogies in a serial fashion; that is, they isolate the elements one by one, and with each additional element, there is an increment in time. The processing of transformations represents a similar serial and additive processing mode. Additivity held for each process when the other was held constant. The simple additivity broke down, however, in the combined effects of the element and transformation factors.

A variety of functions were fit to the data including simple and complex linear fits, and an exponential fit, with all fits based upon the total number of elements and transformations that would have to be processed in order to verify the truth of an item. The most satisfactory statistical and conceptual fits were provided by the following exponential and multiplicative functions (T = transformations; E = elements):

$$\text{RT(msec)} = 1240e^{\,(200T + 150E)} \qquad\qquad (R^2 = .93)$$

$$\text{RT(msec)} = 425T + 358E + 75(T \times E) + 797 \qquad (R^2 = .97)$$

The R^2 values are for fits to the group means shown in Fig. 8.5. When these functions were fit to individual subject data, they accounted for an average of at least 90% of the variance across item classes.

There are a variety of mechanisms that one might wish to invoke to explain either of these functions and the significant departure from simple additivity. One candidate explanation can be illustrated by extrapolating both of the foregoing functions and comparing the result to the extrapolation of a simple linear additive fit ($R^2 = .95$). If all the functions are extrapolated to determine the set of conditions that would lead to a 60-second solution latency, some dramatic differences appear. The simple linear function predicts a 60-second latency for an item comprised of approximately 23 elements and 23 separate transformations within each pair of terms. It is difficult to believe that most individuals, without extensive external aids, could solve such an item in any amount of time. (Moreover, it is difficult even to conceive of the construction of such an item.) In fact, the exponential function predicts a solution latency of over 3 months for such an item. The multiplicative function predicts a value of approximately 3 1/2 minutes for this item. With respect to a latency of 60 seconds, the multiplicative function predicts such a value for an item comprised of approximately 12 elements and 12 separate transformations within each pair of terms. The exponential function predicts a 60-second latency for an item with approximately 6 elements and 6 separate transformations within each pair of terms. Intuitively, something in between the multiplicative and exponential predictions seems most reasonable, and either prediction is more reasonable than the extrapolation of the simple linear function.

Such an intuitive evaluation is in part based upon the assumption that as item complexity increases, there begins to be a problem of mental bookkeeping. Each operation performed in decomposing the terms of an analogy and determining the individual transformations yields units of information that take up space in memory. As more partial information is accumulated and entered into memory, one may begin to approach the limits of working memory. Both processing time and processing effort may have to be partially diverted to updating and maintaining the accumulated contents of memory. The assumption of an increasing memory load in complex items further suggests that it is a potential source of performance errors. This is supported by the error data shown in Fig. 8.6. This figure shows that errors increased as a function of the number of transformations and increased most rapidly when several different transformations had to be performed on a single element. The latter result suggests that in items of this type, the special cognitive demand is retaining and operating on the intermediate products of transformation in memory. Thus, the latency and error data for the true items lead to some strong and testable hypotheses about the nature of performance difficulties and possible individual differences in this task. We return to a discussion of these issues shortly.

We would now like to turn to the latency data for the false items and what these data reveal about the nature of the decision process in this task. There were two general ways in which an item was made false, either by having incorrect elements or incorrect transformations in the $C-D$ pair. The general finding was that items were rejected more rapidly if incorrect elements were involved. Such a

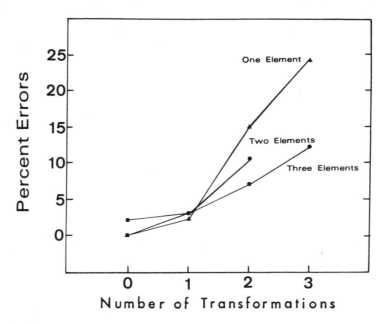

FIG 8.6.   Mean errors for true analogies as a function of the number of elements and transformations.

result would be expected given the assumption that isolation of elements is based upon a comparison of analogy terms, and that it occurs prior to specifying any transformation applied to an element. For all types of false items, it was possible to derive predictions comparing assumptions about exhaustive versus self-terminating processing of elements and transformations. Figure 8.7 shows one example of the difference in predictions and the way in which the data conformed to the predictions based upon self-terminating process execution. The figure represents a subset of items that had incorrect transformations. The upper abscissa shows the transformational structure of the A–B pair, and the lower abscissa shows the transformational changes in the C–D pair to make an item false. For example, an item could be false because the C–D pair contained an extra transformation or because a correct transformation was replaced by an incorrect one. The top panels of the figure show estimates of the average number of transformations that would have to be processed before the item could be declared false. The different estimates reflect assumptions about exhaustive versus self-terminating process execution. The middle panels contain the actual latency data, and it is obvious that they closely conform to the predictions based upon self-terminating process execution.

Given assumptions of self-terminating process execution, we attempted to fit the false-item latency data using functions of the type described earlier. Overall performance on the false items showed the same violation of simple additivity

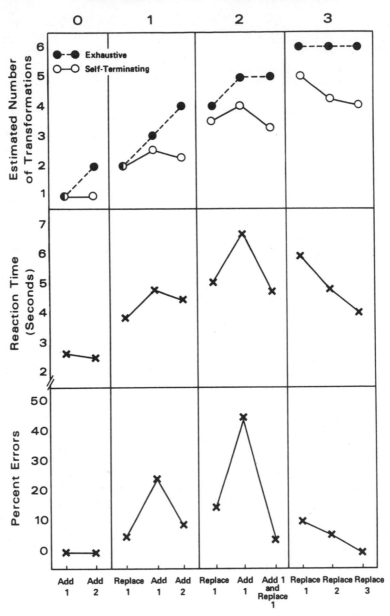

FIG. 8.7. Aspects of performance on false analogies. Top panels contain estimates of the number of transformations to be processed under serial and exhaustive-processing modes. Middle panels contain mean reaction-time results. Bottom panels contain mean error results.

that occurred for the true items. The exponential and multiplicative functions shown here are based upon fits to group means representing 52 different item classes.

$$RT(\text{msec}) = 1340e^{\,(220T+160E)} \qquad\qquad (R^2 = .79)$$

$$RT(\text{msec}) = 450T + 386E + 123(T \times E) + 873 \qquad (R^2 = .81)$$

Both of these functions were more satisfactory than a simple linear fit. Our interpretation of these results is the same as in the case of the true items. The departure from simple additivity with increases in item complexity is probably due to memory load factors associated with the need to store and maintain information about transformations applied to individual elements. This interpretation is supported by the error data for false items as shown in the bottom panels of Fig. 8.7. The probability of error increased as a function of the average number of transformations that had to be processed before an item could be declared false.

The variations in item structure and their effects upon performance suggest several hypotheses about sources of difficulty in this task and possible commonalities with series completion tasks. The essence of the geometric analogy task and the series task is to derive a transformational rule linking one major segment of an item to subsequent segments. In the series task, the segments consist of entire periods containing one or more individual elements (either letters or numbers). The major segments of the geometric analogy task (and also figural matrix problems like the Raven test) are the individual terms containing one or more individual elements. The rule that is to be derived in both problem types involves the transformations or operators (within a circumscribed system) that are applied to each element to generate the next segment of the item. The representation of the item in memory can be conceived as an element-transformation list (e.g., Kotovsky & Simon, 1973; Rumelhart, 1977). Nonidentity transformations require separate placekeepers in working memory, and as the number of transformations in a geometric analogy problem increases, the load on working memory may be substantial and give rise to errors. This is similar to the increase in errors on series problems that involve placekeepers in working memory. The same phenomenon may be involved in explaining performance differences across items on Raven's Progressive Matrices Test (e.g., Hunt's 1974 analysis of this task).

The identification of transformations applied to individual elements appears to require more processing time than identifying elements, in addition to serving as the primary source of errors. Of additional interest is the finding that multiple transformations become particularly difficult when applied to a single element. Such items may be viewed as requiring an individual to operate on a series of partial products, and the intermediate products may place additional demands on processing resources and memory capacity. With certain transformational combinations, the sequence in which the transformations are applied is particularly critical, and this may constitute a further difficulty since there is a need to maintain order information as well.

Sources of Individual Differences.   As noted earlier, error rates on the experimental items were correlated with error rates on the CAT. For the experimental items, there was evidence of a speed–accuracy trade-off across individuals, and this was also associated with sex differences. The females were faster overall than the males, and the difference increased with transformational complexity. However, females were also less accurate on the experimental items, and they performed more poorly on the CAT items.

Correlational analyses of parameters derived from the functions fit to each individual's true- and false-item data did not yield overly impressive results. The one simple correlation that achieved significance showed an inverse relationship between an intercept parameter reflecting general response latency and CAT performance ($r = -.40$). The direction and magnitude of this correlation is highly consistent with results obtained by Sternberg (1977b) indicating that a faster response process (and/or control process) is associated with high scores on tests presumed to measure g. The remaining parameters that were investigated showed an interesting pattern, even though none reached significance. The regression coefficients estimating the latency of processing individual elements and individual transformations were *positively* correlated with the CAT scores. This is indicative of possible differences in the allocation of processing effort, with skilled individuals spending more time and perhaps being more precise in deriving the complete rule that characterized an item. It must be emphasized that the limited individual-difference data obtained in this study are more suggestive than definitive. The sample was small, and the range of performance differences on the CAT was restricted.

Unfinished Business.   The study just discussed, together with the geometric analogy experiment described by Sternberg (1977b) and the artificial intelligence analysis of Evans (1968), represent virtually all of the attempts at describing performance in this task. It is obvious that this is only a beginning at understanding the sources of item difficulty and individual differences in performance. The results are encouraging, because this task is amenable to precise specifications of the information represented in a problem and the rule to be inferred. However, test items do not always have one unique rule or representation. The solution of such "ambiguous" items, as well as items of the type we have studied, depends on the representation that an individual provides for the elements of an item. The completeness of the representation, the method employed to achieve the representation and select an answer, and the role of such factors in individual differences remain large question marks.

Finally, it must be noted that performance in this task involves a considerable amount of procedural knowledge and perhaps some strategic flexibility and expertise. The strategic flexibility may be particularly important when it comes to handling complex items. As we have noted, some items place severe demands on the processing resources and working memory capacity of an individual. Expertise in this and other related tasks may include the ability to shift processing strategies in order to circumvent some of the working memory problems that arise when using a strategy that is optimal for less difficult items. For example, an exhaustive initial inference process applied to the $A-B$ pair, in which all the element-transformation relations are initially stored in working memory, may be less efficient than a process in which individual element-transformation combinations are assessed one by one across the entire problem. Whether or not such strategy shifts occur and their relationships to task proficiency remain speculations.

Analysis of Verbal Analogy Solution

Task Analysis.   For geometric, numeric, and alphabetic series or analogy problems, the declarative knowledge base necessary for solution is relatively finite and comparatively easy to identify. The rules that must be constructed are composites of simple transformations or operators that can be applied to specific elements to yield unique products. Ambiguity is associated with possibilities of more than one transformational representation, but each is a definite representation that yields a definite solution. In verbal analogy problems, the rule to be determined does not have the same transformational quality as in other content domains. Additionally, there is tremendous variability in the individual elements that may be encountered and in the representation of the elements and their relationships. Identifying a particular rule relating two terms does not mean that one can always apply that rule to generate an exact answer. These aspects of verbal analogy problems make it more difficult to specify precisely the processing components and task factors that contribute to differences in item solution and difficulty.

In attempting to analyze the semantic components of performance, it is initially useful to talk about the base or stem of the item separately from the set of alternative completion terms. Global analyses of verbal analogy items reveal that the majority of verbal analogies can be classified as representing a limited set of basic types of semantic relations (e.g., Haynes, Dawis, Monson, Lopez, & Soriano, 1974; Ingram & Pellegrino, 1977; Whitely, 1976). Included among these are: class membership, function, location, conversion, part–whole, order in time, and property. Each of these relations can be represented within the general theoretical framework developed by Rumelhart, Lindsay, and Norman (1972) and by Norman and Rumelhart (1975) for semantic networks.

Items can be classified as representative of a particular type of relationship, and undergraduates tend to sort items into subgroups that parallel such a classification scheme (e.g., Whitely & Dawis, 1974). However, this classification process does not immediately lend itself to predictions about the difficulty of solving an individual item or a group of items. One of the problems with such a classification scheme is that it only captures the most salient relational feature; it does not specify the total set of features that must be processed to define the rule for a given item. Furthermore, it does not indicate differences in the ease or likelihood of identifying the relational features. The variability in processing individual items sharing a particular type of relational feature is easily illustrated by normative data on the responses generated by undergraduates to individual items (Ingram & Pellegrino, 1977).

The normative data were collected for 150 analogy stems selected from a wide variety of tests and representative of the different types of relations mentioned earlier. The focus of our interest was the extent to which the relational features in the stem constrained the set of possible answers for the item. What we observed was that within and across relationship classes, items varied substantially in the degree of semantic constraint placed on the set of possible completion terms. We derived a variety of indices of semantic constraint, including: (1) the probability associated with the single most frequently generated response (this ranged from .10 to .99); (2) the probability that the generated responses reflected use of an appropriate semantic relationship (this ranged from .50 to .99); and (3) the number of different responses generated.

An example of these differences between items can be seen in the comparison of responses generated to the items: *Wolf:Dog::Tiger:*_____ and *City:Village::Army:*_____. In the normative data, the first of these items evoked the initial completion response *Cat* from 74% of the adults sampled. The second analogy evoked the completion response *Platoon* from 17% of the adults. In both cases, however, these were the single most dominant responses for their respective structures. The first analogy elicited 7 different initial responses, and 75% were semantically appropriate. The second analogy elicited 27 different initial responses, and 54% of these responses were semantically appropriate.

The variability across items in the type of relational features involved and the induction and application of that semantic information to solve an item constitute obvious factors in any analysis of the speed and accuracy of item solution and individual differences in performance. In this regard, it should be pointed out that the verbal analogy items studied by Sternberg (1977b) were extremely restricted with respect to the semantic constraint factor, and this probably accounts for the low error rate he obtained and the inability of any model to account for errors. The items used by Sternberg reflect one end of the continuum of item difficulty, and the processes associated with solving such items may not be representative of the processes involved in solving more difficult items, particularly items found on typical aptitude tests.

The semantic characteristics of the item as represented in the stem constitute only part of the semantic task factors contributing to performance. For any item, there is a set of possible alternatives that vary in their semantic appropriateness with respect to matching the semantic features inferred from the base or the stem. Differences between potentially acceptable responses may be considered as representing a "goodness of fit" or semantic distance factor (e.g., Rumelhart & Abrahamson, 1973; Smith, Rips, & Shoben, 1974). There are two ways in which the semantic appropriateness of an alternative can affect performance. First, the semantic features associated with the alternative, independent of other alternatives, should affect the likelihood of acceptance. Second, the difference in the features associated with a set of alternatives should affect the accuracy and speed of any choice among them. This second effect was substantiated in a study of performance on items from the Cognitive Abilities Test. One group of undergraduates was asked to rate the semantic appropriateness of each of four alternatives for a given item. A second group of undergraduates attempted solution of the same items. The semantic appropriateness ratings of the first group were used to derive a measure of discriminability (d') that related the correct choice to the set of other alternatives. The d' measure was highly correlated with the probability of choosing the correct response ($r = .87$) and the amount of time to make a choice ($r = -.79$) (Heller & Pellegrino, 1978).

The different task factors already outlined have been investigated in a series of studies conducted with undergraduates. The first of these studies was designed to evaluate the extent to which each of the different factors significantly contributed to the speed and accuracy of solving a set of verbal analogy items for which normative data were available. The second study was more concerned with individual differences in performance and the levels at which individual differences might be obtained. The third study involved a shift in both materials and procedure to pursue some hypotheses suggested by our own individual-difference data and those of Sternberg (1977b).

Study 1: Processing Characteristics.   The purpose of this first experiment (Ingram, Pellegrino, & Glaser, 1976) was to determine whether performance on a diverse set of verbal analogy items was sufficiently systematic that it could be accounted for by task factors suggested by rational analyses of item and task characteristics. The materials for this study consisted of 100 items representing eight basic relationship types with varying normative properties. For each of the 100 items, four different completion terms were constructed. Examples of the materials used in this study are shown in Table 8.1. The items were presented to undergraduates in a reaction-time verification task such that the stem and one of the completion terms were presented, and the individual was to verify if the completed analogy was acceptable or unacceptable.

For individual items, it was assumed that the semantic appropriateness of an alternative *D* term represents the degree of overlap between the set of features specifying the *A–B* rule and the feature set for the *C–D* rule. The acceptability of

TABLE 8.1
Example Analogy Items Used in Studies 1 and 2

Relationship	Base (A:B::C:)	Completion Terms			
		D_{HR}	D_{LR}	D_{HA}	D_{LA}
Location	Hat:Head::Roof:	House	Home	Top	Tin
Function	Gun:Shoots::Knife:	Cuts	Slices	Fork	Point
Part–whole	Antler:Deer::Tusk:	Elephant	Walrus	Ivory	Fossil
Property	Green:Emerald::Red:	Ruby	Garnet	White	Alive
Class member	Rose:Plant::Lion:	Animal	Mammal	Tiger	Brave
Conversion	Sail:Cloth::Oar:	Wood	Metal	Boat	Paddle

an alternative should depend on the degree to which the feature sets overlap. The speed of verifying the acceptability or unacceptability of any particular alternative should vary systematically with its semantic appropriateness, and general two stage models for semantic verification (e.g., Smith et al., 1974) should be applicable to latency differences for alternatives within an item.

The alternative D terms shown in Table 8.1 were selected to represent different possible values of semantic appropriateness. The alternative labeled D_{LA} is a low-probability free associate of the C term and is semantically inappropriate because it does not reflect the same semantic features found in the A–B pair. The verification of the inappropriateness of this type of item should require only initial gross feature-testing processes before rejection. The D_{HA} alternative is a high-probability free associate of the C term, but is also semantically inappropriate with respect to the semantic features in the A–B pair. The verification of the inappropriateness of this type of item should reflect initial feature-testing processes and may also reflect extended feature comparison processes, particularly if the initial feature test is influenced by general associative relatedness as argued by Gentile, Kessler, and Gentile (1969) and by Willner (1964). The latencies for the D_{HA} items should, therefore, be equal to or longer than those for the D_{LA} items as a function of the degree of extended feature analysis required.

The remaining two alternatives, D_{HR} and D_{LR}, represent analogically correct completion terms that vary in their semantic appropriateness as determined by differences in the normative probability that they were generated as acceptable completion terms. The D_{HR} term is the most frequently generated correct response for any given analogy, whereas the D_{LR} term is a less frequently generated correct response. In the 100 analogies that were used, the average probability associated with the D_{HR} term was .64; and for the D_{LR} term, it was .19. The range for the D_{HR} terms was .08 to .99; and for the D_{LR} terms, it was .03 to .51. With respect to the feature-testing process, both the D_{HR} and the D_{LR} completion terms should have some probability of requiring extended feature analysis. This probability should be higher for the D_{LR} alternatives, and therefore, the verification latency for those items should be longer than the latencies for the D_{HR} alternatives.

The overall results of this study are shown in Table 8.2. Both the D_{LA} and the D_{HA} alternatives were rapidly rejected, and the difference between these two types of semantically inappropriate completion terms was not significant. The lack of such a difference is important because it shows that initial feature processing and testing are not based on differences in global associative characteristics but, instead, depend on a more precisely specified semantic feature set. It is also clear that the latency to accept the D_{HR} and D_{LR} alternatives was considerably longer than the rejection time for the D_{HA} and D_{LA} alternatives. This supports the assumption that the processing of D_{HA} and D_{LA} terms involves primarily initial feature-testing processes, whereas the D_{HR} and D_{LR} alternatives involve more extended feature analysis. This pattern is consistent with the assumption of a self-terminating processing mode for falsifying both geometric and verbal analogies (see also Sternberg, 1977a). Finally, the difference between D_{HR} and D_{LR} is consistent with the assumption that D_{LR} items have a higher probability of requiring extended feature analysis.

Also shown in Table 8.2 are error rates and response latencies for errors. Errors yielded the longest latencies, and these latencies differed slightly for the correct and incorrect completion terms. The heavy concentration of errors in the D_{LR} alternatives and the uniformly slow latency for all errors imply that these items were rejected during a stage of processing involving extended feature analysis and comparison.

The data presented thus far reveal some general characteristics of processing, such as the rapid and accurate rejection of semantically inappropriate completion terms and the slower and less likely acceptance of semantically less appropriate completion terms. If errors are made, they seem to be localized in a stage of processing where additional processing of ambiguous or complex items occurs. Sternberg has referred to such a processing component as an optional justification phase, which is involved when none of the completion terms precisely fits the ideal response. Such a situation would exist for many of the D_{LR} items.

The latency pattern shown in Table 8.2 can be said to be characteristic of any individual item, and it represents systematic variance in responding to alternative

TABLE 8.2
Latency and Error Data from Study 1

Performance Measure	Completion Terms			
	D_{HR}	D_{LR}	D_{HA}	D_{LA}
Latency (correct)	3360	3680	3060	2970
% Errors	10.5	28.1	10.8	6.4
Latency (errors)		4100		4010

semantic constraints within an item. We were also interested in the extent to which there were systematic latency and error differences associated with responding to the "best" completion terms for each item. Items with high degrees of semantic constraint—that is, items where D_{HR} had a normative probability above .70—were verified 420 msec faster than items with low or intermediate levels of semantic constraint. High-semantic-constraint items also had an 8% lower error rate. Items containing certain types of relational features such as location or function were verified faster and had fewer errors than items containing relational features such as class membership. The various indices of semantic constraint together with the type of relationship accounted for over 43% of the variance in D_{HR} latency and 43% of the variance in D_{HR} errors across the 100 individual items.

The results of this study indicate that performance in verbal analogy tests is consistent with general models of semantic processing. The acceptance or rejection of any given alternative is a function of the congruence between the semantic features that define the A–B and C–D rules. Although this is generally the case, the time and likelihood of accepting the "best" alternative for an item varies considerably across items. This variability is partially accounted for by the type of relationship involved and the degree of constraint on the set of possible answers for an item. With respect to individual differences, the question that must be considered next is whether these characteristics of performance differ as a function of skill level.

Study 2: Sources of Individual Differences.   This second study (Pellegrino & Ingram, 1977) was concerned with possible sources of individual differences in analogy solution. The items were presented to undergraduates under a variety of different presentation formats that were designed to provide estimates of the time individuals spent in various stages of processing. In all cases, the final response involved verifying the acceptability or unacceptability of a particular completion term. The undergraduates were administered an analogy pretest consisting of 54 items selected from the Cognitive Abilities Test and the Lorge–Thorndike Intelligence Test. This pretest was used to balance individuals across different presentation conditions and as a basis for defining skilled and less-skilled subject groups for subsequent comparison.

The first set of results to be considered involves the latency data for correct responses when presentation conditions were identical to those used in Study 1. In this condition, there was an overall difference in verification latency, with skilled individuals ($N = 15$) responding 731 msec faster than less-skilled individuals ($N = 15$). This difference in overall latency is of interest, but it is unclear whether it is due to initial inference processes and/or to subsequent decision and response processes. The remaining presentation conditions of this study were designed to help provide an answer to this question. In all these conditions, the A, B, and C terms were sequentially or simultaneously presented, and the individual was allowed to study them for as long as he or she wished prior to seeing and responding to the D term. Across these conditions, the latency of responding to the D term again showed a skill effect, with skilled individuals ($N = 30$) responding 529 msec faster than less-skilled individuals ($N = 30$). This analysis also revealed an interaction between skill level and acceptability of the completion term. This interaction is shown in Table 8.3 and clearly indicates that there was little or no difference in the time to accept or reject items for the less-skilled group, whereas the skilled group showed the pattern more characteristic of Study 1. Regardless of truth value, the skilled individuals responded faster than the less-skilled group.

The conditions in which individuals were allowed to spend as much time as necessary in processing the $A, B,$ and C terms failed to reveal any significant difference between skill groups in the absolute amount of time spent processing these terms, although the trend was for skilled individuals to spend more time in this phase of processing. If such time is considered relative to the total time spent in processing the item, then a pattern emerges similar to that obtained by Sternberg (1977a). Skilled individuals spend proportionately more time in initial encoding and inference processes and less time in subsequent decision and response processes.

Skill differences were also related to a number of interactions involving the semantic relationship and semantic constraint factors. The skilled group showed a more consistent pattern with respect to differences in the amount of time spent processing the stem of the item and in responding to the entire item as a function of differences in semantic constraint. Items representing high levels of semantic constraint were processed more rapidly by the skilled group than items with low levels of semantic constraint. The less-skilled group showed either no effect of this factor or many reversals.

These latency data suggest skill differences in the speed of executing certain basic processing components, differences in terms of the allocation of processing effort, and possible qualitative differences in the nature of the initial problem representation. If it is assumed that the initial encoding and inference processes involve the specification of a rule based upon a set of features relating the $A, B,$ and C terms of an item, then the specificity of that rule with respect to the

TABLE 8.3
Mean Latency as a Function of Skill Level
and Type of Completion Term

	Appropriate $(D_{HR} + D_{LR})$	*Inappropriate* $(D_{HA} + D_{LA})$
Skilled	1935	1653
Less skilled	2339	2308

number and/or type of features represented must be different in the case of skilled and less-skilled individuals. A more precisely specified rule should allow one to reject false alternatives rather rapidly, and such a result only occurred in the case of skilled individuals. The amount of time required to specify a precise rule for an item should vary as a function of the number of features or complexity of the rule. This pattern of longer latencies for more complex and difficult items was observed for the skilled individuals, with inconsistent latency differences shown by the less-skilled individuals. Again, the result implies a difference in the nature of the initial processing and perhaps the quality of the rule derived for the item. These results also apear in agreement with evidence obtained by Sternberg (1977b) showing that higher scores on tests of inductive reasoning were associated with more systematic model fits to verbal analogy latency data. One possible interpretation of Sternberg's finding and our own is that skilled individuals more consistently apply the same general processing strategy over a large number of representative problems.

Differences between skill groups in the precision with which a relationship is specified, as suggested by latency data, should have parallels in error data. Error rates indeed differed significantly between the skill groups, and these differences systematically varied as a function of the type of relationship, the semantic constraint of an item, and the semantic appropriateness of the completion term. Of particular interest is an interaction involving the factors of semantic constraint and type of completion term. For high-constraint items, the difference between skill groups was greatest for false items that were associatively related to the C term (3% versus 15% errors for skilled and less-skilled individuals, respectively). Thus, less-skilled individuals were not only slower at correctly rejecting false alternatives; they also were less accurate in rejecting such alternatives, particularly those that were related in some way to part of the stem. This result again implies a difference in the quality or precision of the rule being generated for an item and being used for subsequent comparisons.

The results of this study suggest that skilled individuals specify more precisely the set of semantic features representing the interrelationships among the individual components of the item, and that this difference in the quality of encoding gives rise to different latency and error patterns. Of interest is the fact that tests of this hypothesized difference in the quality of the internal representation cannot be based solely on quantitative estimates of the speed associated with a set of component processes. We need to know not only the speed of executing a process but, more importantly, the outcome and success of that process. In the case of verbal analogies, the outcome of each component process can assume a number of possible representations that should systematically affect the speed and accuracy of responding to different response alternatives. Thus, although our initial studies have helped define some of the task characteristics and item attributes that are important for performance, we are still left with the problem of specifying how individuals achieve a particular representation and the nature of differences in the representations achieved. The third study was concerned with such issues.

Study 3: Protocol Analysis of Representational and Decison Processes.   The third study we conducted was designed to examine the processes involved in representing the relationship or rule for items of varying difficulty (Heller & Pellegrino, 1978). The study was also concerned with the decision process used for selecting from a set of alternatives. One criticism of the previous two studies was that we were dealing with an artificially constructed set of alternatives that were not completely representative of the types of multiple-choice answer alternatives typically found on aptitude tests. A related concern was that the true–false verification format—though suggesting that many difficult items involve extended semantic analysis, or feature testing—did not match the level of analysis that was often required in a choice among alternatives varying in their semantic appropriateness. These aspects of the typical analogy task could be important potential sources of performance differences across both items and individuals.

The materials selected for this study involved a subset of 25 items from the upper levels of the Cognitive Abilities Test. Each of the items was presented to undergraduates in a format that allowed us to collect extended protocol data at various points during the course of solution. An individual was initially presented the stem of the item and could study the item for as long as desired. Before being presented any of the alternative choices, the individuals were asked to describe the representation of the item that they had in mind. The alternatives then were presented sequentially; the individual studied each particular alternative and decided whether it was potentially acceptable or was to be dropped from the pool of potential answers. Each decision was probed as to the reason for acceptance or rejection, and this procedure provided information about the current state of the representation for the item. After seeing and responding to each of the four alternatives, the individual was then cycled back through the accepted choices until a final choice was made. The typical pattern under this procedure was acceptance of two alternatives on the first cycle of presentation.

The protocol data highlighted a number of performance characteristics that differentiated between items of high and low difficulty. Items that are relatively easy lend themselves to a solution process in which the relationship is readily specifiable and a potential completion term for the item is easily generated. Thus, the process of solution follows a generate and test model in which the processing of the alternatives involves a simple search for the hypothesized answer. An example of such an item is: *Seed:Sow::Rumor:_____*, which yields the predicted answer *Spread*. Difficult items are ones in which the relationship is not well specified and there is difficulty in generating a potential answer. In a separate study, we have observed that the amount of time spent processing the base of an item is significantly correlated (r's $> .69$) with both the rated ease of determining the rule for an item and the rated ease of generating a potential completion term. When difficulties arise, solution is guided by the set of alternatives, and the relationship is defined in the context of these alternatives. The protocol in Table 8.4 for the item: *Time:Age::Space:_____* is an example of such a solution process.

It was expected that the alternatives for an item would systematically influence the level of analysis or specificity required for a final choice and that this process should be associated with item difficulty. The protocol data revealed that a process of successively refining the rule consistently occurred across the alternative set, and the extent to which this process was involved was a function of the degree of precision in originally defining the rule and the potential answer. Thus, items varied on a continuum from a generate and test process, with little change in the level of feature analysis, through to a process almost totally driven by the

TABLE 8.4
Solution Protocol in Study 3

Analogy Elements Presented	*Solver's Responses*
First Cycle	
Time:Age::Space:	I don't know, I'll have to see what they're going to say.
Empty	(*Rejects alternative*) I don't know. I know that time causes a person to age. Empty describes space, but age—I'm thinking, your age gets older as time goes on, but maybe they're thinking of an age as time, like when people say era, so I don't know which age they're talking about.
Large	(*Accepts alternative*) Don't think large fits either—it could—large is an amount of space, and age could be an amount of time, I don't know. I'll put true and I can come back and look at it.
Distance	(*Accepts alternative*) This could be true too if they're talking about the other age, an age as an amount of time, and distance is a measurement of space, that sounds pretty good.
Spacious	(*Rejects alternative*) No, I don't think this one fits.
Second cycle	
Large	(*Rejects alternative*) No, I think I like that second one.
Distance	(*Accepts as final choice*) Because distance is a measurement of space and age is a measurement of time, something like that.

alternative set, with constant redefinition of the possible relevant features of the problem.

The protocol data also were analyzed to determine whether there were systematic processing differences that characterized levels of skill. The data comparing the best and worst solvers provide some bases for cautious generalization about skill differences, and the differences obtained in characteristics of performance need to be considered in terms of the level of difficulty of the items presented. For easy items of the *Seed:Sow::Rumor:_____* variety, there were no gross differences in the rule specified or in the possible completion term generated. The difference that existed was the quality of the reasoning involved in rejecting the incorrect alternatives. A high-skill individual offers a very precise explanation of the relationship between any presented alternative and the *C* term and why it violates the correct relationship. With more difficult items, there is also a difference in the relationship originally specified as the basis for solving the item, even if the individual cannot generate the exact answer. The item *Time:Age::Space:_____* provides an example of the specificity of representation generated by a high-skill individual. The description of the item prior to seeing the alternatives was:

> I could think of a few ways. I'd have to see the specific word. An age is a very large unit of time, like you can say "an age." Also, we measure the time of our life by our age. We measure the time of anything by the age it is. So you measure the space of anything by the area it is. And I think it's probably area because I can't think of any word that means [pause] like I said, age is a large amount of time and I can't think of any word that means a large amount of space in the same sense, so I guess I'll be looking for something like area because that's what you measure space by. You measure the time by its age.

This initial representation led to accurate solution, and the course of solution was again characterized by very precise explanations for why a particular alternative violated the necessary features of a correct answer and also why the "correct" answer *Distance* was not exactly correct. The foregoing protocol is to be contrasted with that shown in Table 8.4, which is a protocol of a less-skilled solver. The differences between the two protocols emphasize the initial representational processes associated with skill differences.

The protocol data that we have collected and analyzed thus far are initial attempts at providing part of a methodology for assessing individual differences in analogical reasoning performance. They are suggestive of differences in the precision with which individuals analyze and test relationships among sets of verbally presented concepts. The differences that appear are also consistent with interpretations of some of the individual-difference results obtained in Study 2—that is, interactions involving skill level and semantic constraint factors. Finally, it must be noted that certain items led to errors due to declarative knowledge deficits. Such aspects of performance must undoubtedly be included in any complete account of the variance in performance in verbal analogy tasks.

Unfinished Business.   Our analyses of the task factors that affect performance and the possible sources of skill differences in verbal analogy tasks suggest a model of performance more complex than any of the models presented by Sternberg or the general model for verification tasks discussed earlier. These models assume a process that abstracts the necessary semantic features from the base of the item and then evaluates alternatives in a generate and test mode. It is only for certain difficult items that an additional justification process is assumed. The exact nature of this justification process is unspecified. However, it would appear that for anything other than trivial items, the process of solution involves strategies of working forward and working backwards, and the relative involvement of each strategy is related to item difficulty for a given individual. The difficulty associated with the solution of any verbal analogy is a function of the fuzziness of the individual concepts, and this determines whether precise rules can be formulated to allow the "extrapolation" of the item. A working-forward strategy only is possible for relatively easy and unambiguous items, whereas for many difficult items, solution involves partially or completely working backwards from the set of choices. The variability in the path to solution and the likelihood that an individual must rely on one solution mode more than another are relevant aspects of performance in this task.

SUMMARY AND CONCLUSIONS

At the beginning of this paper, we stated two criteria that are useful for evaluating the results of an analysis of tasks representing a major aptitude construct. The first criterion is whether or not the results of the analysis move us closer to an analytic scheme that can be used to diagnose performance deficiencies, and the second is whether or not the sources of individual differences suggest testable instructional hypotheses. This paper has been primarily devoted to theoretical and empirical analyses of the properties that influence performance on aptitude test tasks. Considerably less information was presented about sources of individual differences. The latter omission is due in part to the limitations involved in studying undergraduate populations where skill differences are restricted, and there is the resultant lack of a significant amount of error data. Thus, at this point, we can only speculate about the instructional implications of individual differences in inductive reasoning skills. However, our work clearly provides a basis for individual-differences analyses, particularly with respect to the sources of task difficulty. There appear to be two major factors that contribute to task difficulty; these include: (1) the complexity of the rule to be inferred; and (2) the variability or initial ambiguity in the possible rules that may be inferred.

In all of the tasks that employ nonverbal stimuli, the *rule complexity* factor is reflected directly by the number of different operators that must be represented in working memory. The greater the number of operators (transformations) that comprise a rule to be inferred and applied, the larger the increase in both solution latency and error probability. This is due to difficulties in assembling and/or maintaining a complete description of the element–operator combinations. Such descriptions may exceed memory capacity, and only partial representations of the rule to be induced and applied may be established.

In verbal items, rule complexity is more difficult to measure because it is not directly manifested by any overt problem features. Also, verbal items seem to place somewhat different demands on working memory, particularly with respect to maintaining information about past and current hypotheses about the relevant semantic features that comprise an item's rule. The changing nature of the semantic feature set that occurs as new item terms are encountered is related to what can be called the *representational variability* factor of task difficulty. In verbal analogies, item difficulty is heavily influenced by variability resulting from the conceptual richness and/or abstractness of the individual terms and relations. Verbal concepts activate extensive semantic feature sets, and varying subsets of these features may be included as part of the problem representation. The ability to modify the semantic feature set or change it drastically during the course of solution represents a significant aspect of performance.

Representational variability as a factor in problem difficulty is not unique to verbal items. Nonverbal series, analogy, and matrix problems often have two or more possible representations for the rule governing the problem. The need to change problem representations or to entertain several different problem representations is a significant aspect of performance, although it may have much less weight in contributing to task difficulty than in verbal items.

The factors of rule complexity and representational variability provide a scheme within which to consider sources of individual differences. The limited individual-difference data that we have discussed focus primarily on the representational variability factor as manifested in verbal analogies. The data indicate that skill differences in an undergraduate sample are associated with: (1) processes of establishing a reasonably well defined problem representation; (2) the subsequent utilization of that representation as a basis for selecting among alternatives; and (3) modifying the representation as necessary. The time spent establishing an initial representation (or representations) may differ as a function of skill level, but latency differences may be less important than the particular representation(s) achieved. Indeed, there is evidence in our data and others' that high-aptitude individuals—who presumably have more elaborate semantic memory structures—may encode more item features and take more time in this aspect of processing, but with subsequent facilitation in the speed and accuracy of selecting among alternatives.

The different task analyses that we and others have carried out suggest three potential areas for instructional research. First, there is a declarative knowledge base that must be available to perform any content-based task. The declarative knowledge for rule induction tasks involves the basic elements and possible transformations for the particular content area. This is a large, relatively un-bounded set of knowledge in the case of verbal items, and thus it poses a nontrivial instructional problem. Nevertheless, it might be possible to teach the necessary declarative knowledge for a restricted content domain and thus influence performance. One way to view such instruction is in terms of defining some relevant features of a larger problem space. Such training is involved in practice booklets for tests such as Miller's analogies, where emphasis is given to possible relations that may be involved in individual analogies. However, such training may not improve those aspects of inductive reasoning that are generalizable to many domains of knowledge.

The second target for instruction would involve factors associated with the rule complexity dimension. This might involve two different types of instruc-tion—one being instruction in processes associated with storing, retrieving, and manipulating information in working memory. Whether such instruction is feasible is unclear at present. The second potential form of instruction would involve general procedures (strategies, executive processes) for organizing, con-trolling, and monitoring the analysis of problem features during the course of solution. Such procedures may substantially reduce memory load problems, and they can be viewed as forms of procedural knowledge. Examples of such proce-dures are the executive routines discussed by Simon and Lea (1974) for the General Rule Inducer and the analytic algorithm discussed by Hunt (1974) for figural matrix problems. Such procedural knowledge may be instructable; and minimal evidence for this is that partial procedures such as how to discover periodicity in series completion problems can readily be taught to children, and such knowledge affects performance within the task.

The third target for instruction involves factors associated with the repre-sentational variability dimension. In this case, the form of instruction may be linked to knowledge about general aspects of problem solving, such as defining the relevant problem space for a task and then using information within the prob-lem space to help restructure the problem. The extent to which such problem-solving skills can be operationalized and taught is also unclear at present.

The link between rule induction skill and instructional treatments that influ-ence this skill may lie in the aspects of cognition that are suggested by the rule complexity and representational variability factors. These aspects of cognition may be viewed as complex procedures that determine general and specific as-pects of problem-solving success and failure on both tests of aptitude and in the environments for learning that such tests attempt to predict.

ACKNOWLEDGMENTS

We wish to acknowledge and express our appreciation for the major contributions made by several former students—namely, Jeff Bisanz, Joan Heller, Thomas Holzman, Albert

Ingram, and Timothy Mulholland. A number of the studies cited represent master's or doctoral research done under the supervision of the authors.

The preparation of this chapter was supported by the Learning Research and Development Center, University of Pittsburgh, funded in part as a research and development center by the National Institute of Education (NIE), United States Department of Health, Education, and Welfare. The opinions expressed do not necessarily reflect the policy or position of NIE, and no official endorsement should be inferred.

James W. Pellegrino is now at the University of California at Santa Barbara on the faculty of the Graduate School of Education.

REFERENCES

Anderson, J. R. *Language, memory, and thought*. Hillsdale, N.J.: Lawrence Erlbaum Associates, 1976.

Bamber, D. Reaction times and error rates for "same-different" judgments of multidimensional stimuli. *Perception & Psychophysics*, 1969, *6*, 169–174.

Bruner, J. S. Going beyond the information given. In H. Gruber (Ed.), *Contemporary approaches to cognition*. Cambridge, Mass.: Harvard University Press, 1957.

Bundesen, C., & Larsen, A. Visual transformation of size. *Journal of Experimental Psychology: Human Perception and Performance*, 1975, *1*, 214–220.

Carroll, J. B. Psychometric tests as cognitive tasks: A new "structure of intellect." In L. B. Resnick (Ed.), *The nature of intelligence*. Hillsdale, N.J.: Lawrence Erlbaum Associates, 1976.

Cronbach, L. J. *Essentials of psychological testing* (3rd ed.). New York: Harper & Row, 1970.

Cronbach, L. J., & Snow, R. E. *Aptitudes and instructional methods: A handbook for research on interactions*. New York: Irvington Publishers, 1977.

Dawis, R. V., & Siojo, L. T. *Analogical reasoning: A review of the literature. Effects of social class differences on analogical reasoning* (Tech. Rep. No. 1). Minneapolis: University of Minnesota, Department of Psychology, 1972.

Egan, D. E., & Greeno, J. G. Theory of rule induction: Knowledge acquired in concept learning, serial pattern learning, and problem solving. In L. W. Gregg (Ed.), *Knowledge and cognition*. Hillsdale, N.J.: Lawrence Erlbaum Associates, 1974.

Egeth, H. W. Parallel versus serial processes in multidimensional stimulus discrimination. *Perception & Psychophysics*, 1966, *1*, 245–252.

Estes, W. K. Learning theory and intelligence. *American Psychologist*, 1974, *29*, 740–749.

Evans, T. G. Program for the solution of a class of geometric-analogy intelligence test questions. In M. Minsky (Ed.), *Semantic information processing*. Cambridge, Mass.: MIT Press, 1968.

Forehand, G. A. Knowledge and the educational process. In L. W. Gregg (Ed.), *Knowledge and cognition*. Hillsdale, N.J.: Lawrence Erlbaum Associates, 1974.

Gentile, J. R., Kessler, D. K., & Gentile, P. K. Process of solving analogy problems. *Journal of Educational Psychology*, 1969, *60*, 494–502.

Glaser, R. Individuals and learning: The new aptitudes. *Educational Researcher*, 1972, *1*, 5–13.

Glaser, R. Educational psychology and education. *American Psychologist*, 1973, *28*, 557–566.

Glaser, R. *Adaptive education: Individual diversity and learning*. New York: Holt, Rinehart & Winston, 1977.

Glaser, R., Pellegrino, J. W., & Lesgold, A. M. Some directions for a cognitive psychology of instruction. In A. M. Lesgold, J. W. Pellegrino, S. D. Fokkema, and R. Glaser (Eds.), *Cognitive psychology and instruction*. New York: Plenum, 1978.

Greeno, J. G. Natures of problem-solving abilities. In W. K. Estes (Ed.), *Handbook of learning and cognitive processes* (Vol. 5). Hillsdale, N.J.: Lawrence Erlbaum Associates, 1978.

Greeno, J. G., & Simon, H. A. Processes for sequence production. *Psychological Review,* 1974, *81,* 187–198.

Haynes, J. L., Dawis, R. V., Monson, E. Q., Lopez, F. G., & Soriano, L. V. *Relation eduction norms for 500 picture pairs and 10 relations: High school sample* (Tech. Rep. No. 6). Minneapolis: University of Minnesota, Department of Psychology, 1974.

Heller, J. I., & Pellegrino, J. W. *Cognitive processes and source of item difficulty in the solution of verbal analogies.* Paper presented at the meeting of the American Educational Research Association, Toronto, March 1978.

Holzman, T. G., Glaser, R., & Pellegrino, J. W. Process training derived from a computer simulation theory. *Memory & Cognition,* 1976, *4,* 349–356.

Horn, J. L. Organization of abilities and the development of intelligence. *Psychological Review,* 1968, *75,* 242–259.

Hunt, E. Quote the Raven? Nevermore! In L. W. Gregg (Ed.), *Knowledge and cognition.* Hillsdale, N.J.: Lawrence Erlbaum Associates, 1974.

Hunt, E. Varieties of cognitive power. In L. B. Resnick (Ed.), *The nature of intelligence.* Hillsdale, N.J.: Lawrence Erlbaum Associates, 1976.

Hunt, E., Frost, N., & Lunneborg, C. Individuals differences in cognition: A new approach to intelligence. In G. H. Bower (Ed.), *The psychology of learning and motivation* (Vol. 7). New York: Academic Press, 1973.

Hunt, E., & Lansman, M. Cognitive theory applied to individual differences. In W. K. Estes (Ed.), *Handbook of learning and cognitive processes: Introduction to concepts and issues* (Vol. 1). Hillsdale, N.J.: Lawrence Erlbaum Associates, 1975.

Ingram, A. L., & Pellegrino, J. W. *Response generation norms for verbal analogies.* Pittsburgh: University of Pittsburgh, Learning Research and Development Center, 1977.

Ingram, A. L., Pellegrino, J. W., & Glaser, R. *Semantic processing in verbal analogies.* Paper presented at the meeting of the Psychonomic Society, St. Louis, November 1976.

Kotovsky, K., & Simon, H. A. Empirical tests of a theory of human acquisition of concepts for sequential patterns. *Cognitive Psychology,* 1973, *4,* 399–424.

McNemar, Q. Lost: Our intelligence? Why? *American Psychologist,* 1964, *19,* 871–882.

Mulholland, T., Pellegrino, J. W., & Glaser, R. *Components of geometric analogy solution. Cognitive Psychology,* in press.

Neisser, U. *Cognition and reality.* San Francisco: Freeman, 1976.

Norman, D. A., Gentner, D. R., & Stevens, A. L. Comments on learning schemata and memory. In D. Klahr (Ed.), *Cognition and instruction.* Hillsdale, N.J.: Lawrence Erlbaum Associates, 1976.

Norman, D. A., & Rumelhart, D. E. *Explorations in cognition.* San Francisco: Freeman, 1975.

Oppenheimer, J. R. Analogy in science. *American Psychologist,* 1956, *11,* 127–135.

Pellegrino, J. W., & Ingram, A. L. *Components of verbal analogy solution.* Paper presented at the meeting of the Midwestern Psychological Association, Chicago, May 1977.

Polya, G. *Mathematics and plausible reasoning: Induction and analogy in mathematics* (Vol. 1). Princeton, N.J.: Princeton University Press, 1965.

Raven, J. C. *Progressive matrices: A perceptual test of intelligence, 1938, individual form.* London: Lewis, 1938.

Reitman, W. R. *Cognition and thought: An information-processing approach.* New York: Wiley, 1965.

Restle, F. Theory of serial pattern learning: Structural trees. *Psychological Review,* 1970, *77,* 481–495.

Rumelhart, D. E. *Introduction to human information processing.* New York: Wiley, 1977.

Rumelhart, D. E., & Abrahamson, A. A. A model for analogical reasoning. *Cognitive Psychology,* 1973, *5,* 1–28.

Rumelhart, D. E., Lindsay, P. H., & Norman, D. A. A process model for long-term memory. In E. Tulving & W. Donaldson (Eds.), *Organization of memory.* New York: Academic Press, 1972.

Shepard, R. N. Form, formation, and transformation of internal representations. In R. L. Solso (Ed.), *Information processing and cognition: The Loyola symposium*. Hillsdale, N.J.: Lawrence Erlbaum Associates, 1975.

Simon, H. A. Complexity and the representation of patterned sequences of symbols. *Psychological Review*, 1972, *79*, 369–382.

Simon, H. A., & Kotovsky, K. Human acquisition of concepts for sequential patterns. *Psychological Review*, 1963, *70*, 534–546.

Simon, H. A., & Lea, G. Problem solving and rule induction: A unified view. In L. W. Gregg (Ed.), *Knowledge and cognition*. Hillsdale, N.J.: Lawrence Erlbaum Associates, 1974.

Smith, E. E., Rips, L. J., & Shoben, E. J. Semantic memory and psychological semantics. In G. H. Bower (Ed.), *The psychology of learning and motivation* (Vol. 8). New York: Academic Press, 1974.

Snow, R. E. *Theory and method for research on aptitude processes: A prospectus* (Tech. Rep. No. 2). Stanford, Calif.: Stanford University, School of Education, 1976.

Spearman, C. *The nature of intelligence and the principles of cognition*. London: Macmillan, 1923.

Sternberg, R. J. Component processes in analogical reasoning. *Psychological Review*, 1977, *84*, 353–378. (a)

Sternberg, R. J. *Intelligence, information processing, and analogical reasoning: The componential analysis of human abilities*. Hillsdale, N.J.: Lawrence Erlbaum Associates, 1977. (b)

Thorndike, R. L., & Hagen, E. *Cognitive Abilities Test*. Boston: Houghton Mifflin, 1971.

Thurstone, L. L., & Thurstone, T. C. *Factoral studies of intelligence*. Chicago: University of Chicago Press, 1941.

Tyler, L. E. The intelligence we test—An evolving concept. In L. B. Resnick (Ed.), *The nature of intelligence*. Hillsdale, N.J.: Lawrence Erlbaum Associates, 1976.

Underwood, B. J. Individual differences as a crucible in theory construction. *American Psychologist*, 1975, *30*, 128–134.

Vitz, P. C., & Todd, T. C. A model of learning for simple repeating binary patterns. *Journal of Experimental Psychology*, 1967, *75*, 108–117.

Whitely, S. E. Solving verbal analogies: Some cognitive components of intelligence test items. *Journal of Educational Psychology*, 1976, *68*, 234–242.

Whitely, S. E., & Dawis, R. V. Effects of cognition intervention on latent ability measured from analogy items. *Journal of Educational Psychology*, 1974, *66*, 710–717.

Willner, A. An experimental analysis of analogical reasoning. *Psychological Reports*, 1964, *15*, 479–494.

9 Deductive Reasoning

Robert J. Sternberg
Martin J. Guyote
Margaret E. Turner
Yale University

During the past several years, the senior investigator has been attempting to develop a unified theory of human reasoning. This research has proceeded along two major fronts—one involving the formulation of a subtheory of inductive reasoning, the other involving the formulation of a subtheory of deductive reasoning. We discuss here work we have done on deduction.

The theory of deductive reasoning is not yet completely formulated or tested, but work on the theory is far enough along to merit a progress report. So far, we have formulated and tested models of deduction for the three main kinds of syllogisms that have been investigated by students of human reasoning: categorical, conditional, and linear syllogisms. We summarize the theory and data for each of the three kinds of syllogisms next. Then we draw some conclusions and mention the directions in which our current research is going.

CATEGORICAL SYLLOGISMS[1]

The Nature of Categorical Syllogisms

A categorical syllogism comprises three declarative statements, each of which describes a relation between two sets of items. The first two statements, called the major premise and minor premise, respectively, are givens. The third statement, called the conclusion, follows with logical necessity from the premises.

---

[1]The research summarized here is presented in detail in Guyote and Sternberg (1978) and in Sternberg and Turner (1978).

Categorical syllogisms are of two basic types. In the first type, both the major and minor premises express relations between two sets of objects, one of which overlaps between premises. The conclusion expresses a relation between the nonoverlapping sets of objects. An example of such a syllogism is: "All B are C. All A are B. Therefore, all A are C." In the second type of syllogism, the major premise expresses a relation between two sets of objects, and the minor premise expresses a relation between a particular item and one of the two sets of objects. The conclusion expresses a relation between that member and the other set. An example of such a syllogism is: "All A are B. X is an A. Therefore, X is a B." We consider in this part of the article only the first, more widely studied type of syllogism.

The Transitive-Chain Theory of Categorical Syllogistic Reasoning

Representation of Information.   Figure 9.1 names the five possible set relations and shows how these relations are represented in both conventional Euler-diagram format and in the symbolic format we propose. Each symbolic representation consists of two distinct components—one (at the left) indicating how many members of set A are also members of set B, the other (at the right) indicating how many members of set B are also members of set A. In this notation, lowercase letters stand for disjoint, exhaustive partitions of a set. Thus, for example, lowercase a_1 and a_2 are mutually exclusive and exhaustive with respect to set A. Uppercase letters refer to whole sets, and the arrow relation indicates that the partition to the left of the arrow is a proper subset of the set to the right. Components can be referred to by the order of the terms within them. Thus, all left-hand components in the figure are AB components, and all right-hand components are BA components.

Let's consider a couple of examples to see how the notation works. Consider, first, set equivalence (identity). Note that both partitions of A, a_1, and a_2 are proper subsets of B, and both partitions of B, b_1, and b_2, are proper subsets of A. Thus, all a's are B's, and all b's are A's, as is the case for set equivalence. Consider now the second set relation, subset–set. Notice at the right that although all a's are B's, only some b's are A's: In the component at the right, b_2 is a proper subset of not A, rather than of A. This relation, then, indicates that B is a superset of A. To summarize, the basic idea is that each set relation can be represented by a notation indicating the relative number of a's that are B's and b's that are A's.

Combination of Representations.[2]   Figure 9.2 shows how two simple inferential rules can be applied to the symbolic representations of set relations to

---

[2]The combination process is actually somewhat more complex than can be described here. See Guyote and Sternberg (1978) for details.

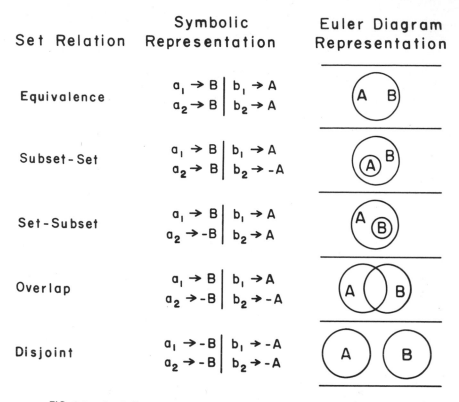

FIG. 9.1. Symbolic representation of information in transitive-chain theory of syllogistic reasoning.

effect the combination of any two representations. The proposed representation has the advantage of permitting combination to occur via the two rules. None of the alternative theories of syllogistic reasoning that have been proposed specify comparable rules by which Euler diagrams or other forms of representation can be combined.

The first rule states that if a partition x_i is a proper subset of Y and a partition y_j (where j may but need not equal i) is a proper subset of Z, then x_i is a proper subset of Z. This rule applies when the two middle terms match in polarity—that is, are both affirmative. It is from this rule that the transitive-chain theory derives its name, because elements are combined by forming simple transitive chains.

The second rule states that if a partition x_i is a proper subset of not Y and a partition y_j (where j may but need not equal i) is a proper subset of Z, then x_i may be a proper subset of either Z or not Z; one can't tell for sure. This rule applies when the two middle terms do not match in polarity—that is, when the first is negative and the second affirmative. In this case, one cannot form a transitive chain.

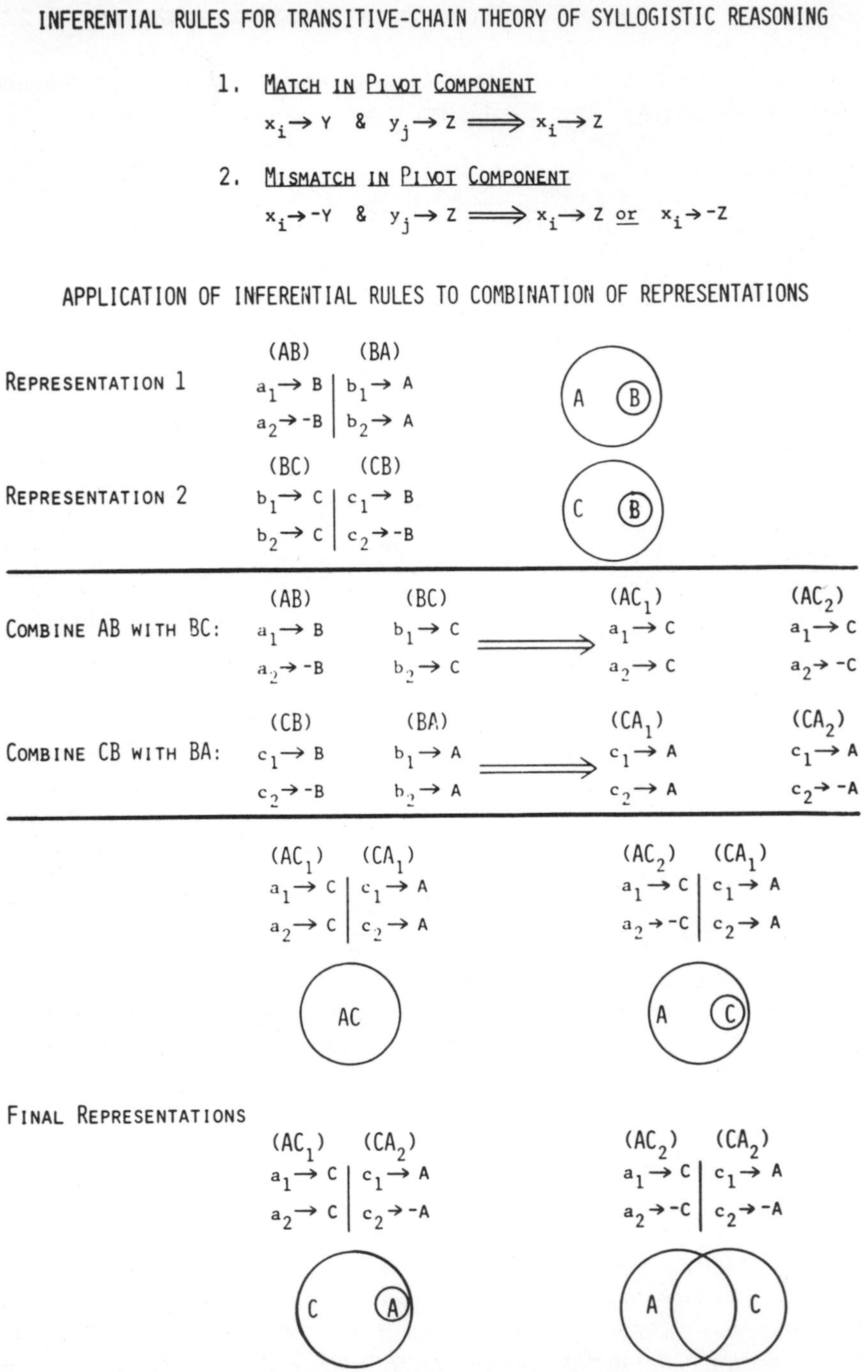

INFERENTIAL RULES FOR TRANSITIVE-CHAIN THEORY OF SYLLOGISTIC REASONING

1. MATCH IN PIVOT COMPONENT

$$x_i \rightarrow Y \quad \& \quad y_j \rightarrow Z \implies x_i \rightarrow Z$$

2. MISMATCH IN PIVOT COMPONENT

$$x_i \rightarrow -Y \quad \& \quad y_j \rightarrow Z \implies x_i \rightarrow Z \text{ or } x_i \rightarrow -Z$$

APPLICATION OF INFERENTIAL RULES TO COMBINATION OF REPRESENTATIONS

REPRESENTATION 1

(AB)   (BA)

$a_1 \rightarrow B \mid b_1 \rightarrow A$

$a_2 \rightarrow -B \mid b_2 \rightarrow A$

REPRESENTATION 2

(BC)   (CB)

$b_1 \rightarrow C \mid c_1 \rightarrow B$

$b_2 \rightarrow C \mid c_2 \rightarrow -B$

COMBINE AB WITH BC:

(AB)	(BC)		(AC_1)	(AC_2)
$a_1 \rightarrow B$	$b_1 \rightarrow C$	$\implies$	$a_1 \rightarrow C$	$a_1 \rightarrow C$
$a_2 \rightarrow -B$	$b_2 \rightarrow C$		$a_2 \rightarrow C$	$a_2 \rightarrow -C$

COMBINE CB WITH BA:

(CB)	(BA)		(CA_1)	(CA_2)
$c_1 \rightarrow B$	$b_1 \rightarrow A$	$\implies$	$c_1 \rightarrow A$	$c_1 \rightarrow A$
$c_2 \rightarrow -B$	$b_2 \rightarrow A$		$c_2 \rightarrow A$	$c_2 \rightarrow -A$

(AC_1) (CA_1)

$a_1 \rightarrow C \mid c_1 \rightarrow A$

$a_2 \rightarrow C \mid c_2 \rightarrow A$

(AC_2) (CA_1)

$a_1 \rightarrow C \mid c_1 \rightarrow A$

$a_2 \rightarrow -C \mid c_2 \rightarrow A$

FINAL REPRESENTATIONS

(AC_1) (CA_2)

$a_1 \rightarrow C \mid c_1 \rightarrow A$

$a_2 \rightarrow C \mid c_2 \rightarrow -A$

(AC_2) (CA_2)

$a_1 \rightarrow C \mid c_1 \rightarrow A$

$a_2 \rightarrow -C \mid c_2 \rightarrow -A$

FIG. 9.2. Inferential rules for transitive-chain theory of syllogistic reasoning, with application to an example of combination of representations.

Consider an example in which these two rules are applied to combining two representations, one in which B is a subset of A and the other in which C is a superset of B. There are two ways in which transitive chains might be formed from the two sets of components: first by combining AB with BC (since the middle terms match), and second by combining CB with BA (again since the middle terms match).

First, let's combine the AB component with the BC component. Rule 1 can be applied twice: We can form a first transitive chain by linking a_1 to B with b_1 to C, yielding a_1 to C; we can form a second transitive chain by linking a_1 to B with b_2 to C, again yielding a_1 to C. We write the two a-to-C relations in the first row to the right of the double arrow. Rule 2 can also be applied twice, because we are unable to form a transitive chain from a_2 to C via either b_1 or b_2. Rather than writing two redundant rows to the right of the double arrow, we simply write the result once: a_2 can be linked to either C or not C.

Next, let's combine CB with BA. Through Rule 1, the c_1 partition can be linked to A through either b_1 or b_2; the two c_1-to-A relations are indicated at the right of the double arrow. Through Rule 2, we find that c_2 can be linked to either A or not A, also as indicated at the right of the double arrow. We have now completed the combination process, ending up with two AC and two CA representations.

There's just one more step left. You'll remember that each original representation consisted of an AB component and a BA component. Similarly, each final representation must consist of an AC component and a CA component. But our representations as they now stand consist of either two AC or two CA components. Our final step, therefore, is to rearrange the components into canonical form. There are four ways in which this rearrangement can be realized: by combining AC_1 with CA_1, AC_1 with CA_2, AC_2 with CA_1, or AC_2 with CA_2. In this particular example, each of these rearrangements yields a unique final representation, although this need not be true in general. Note that by using the two simple rules of inference, we have discovered four possible final representations that can result from combination of the two original ones: C and A equivalent, C superset of A, C subset of A, and C and A overlapping.

Information-Processing Model.   The description of the transitive-chain theory up to now has been for the ideal subject—one who can process information without making errors. Subjects do make errors, of course, and the transitive-chain theory specifies the processes that give rise to these errors.

In the transitive-chain theory, as in other theories of syllogistic reasoning, there are four basic stages of processing: encoding, during which the premises are read and interpreted; combination, during which information from the premises is integrated; comparison, during which the combined representation is compared to possible labels for the representation (such as "All A are C" and "Some A are C"); and response, during which the subject communicates a response. According to the transitive-chain theory, encoding and response are error free. Erroneous responses result from errors made in combination and comparison.

Errors during the combination stage arise from limitations in the ability of working memory to hold all possible combinations. A standard classical syllogism can require as few as 1 or as many as 16 pairs of set relations to be combined. For example, in the syllogism: "No *B* are *C*. No *A* are *B*," each premise can be represented by only 1 set relation, meaning that only one combination need be performed. In the syllogism: "Some *B* are *C*. Some *A* are *B*," however, each premise can be represented by 4 set relations, meaning that 16 (4 times 4) combinations need to be performed.

According to the theory, subjects combine a maximum of four set relations. Moreover, there is a three-tier preference hierarchy that places some constraints on the order in which set relations are combined. In particular, equivalence relations are combined before nonequivalent symmetrical ones (overlap and disjoint sets), which in turn are combined before asymmetrical ones (set–superset and set–subset). This ordering reflects the ease with which relations of each kind are stored and manipulated in working memory. Symmetrical relations are those for which the polarities of the elements of the left-hand side of each component match the polarities of the elements of the right-hand side of each component. A quick glance back at Fig. 9.1 will reveal symmetry of polarities only for equivalence, overlap, and disjoint relations. Four parameters of information processing arise from the combination stage—p_1, p_2, p_3, and p_4—representing the respective probabilities that exactly 1, 2, 3, or 4 pairs of set relations are combined.

Errors during the comparison stage arise from simplifying heuristics subjects use to facilitate selection of a label for combined pairs of representations. If no label is consistent with all of the combined set relations generated during combination, the subject labels the relationship between *A* and *C* indeterminate, choosing "None of the above" as an answer. If only one label is correct, then the subject chooses that one. But sometimes two labels are consistent with the representation generated during the combination stage. For example, the final set relation *A* subset of *C* can be represented either as "All *A* are *C*" or as "Some *A* are *C*." In this case, some basis is needed for choosing between labels.

Whenever two labels are consistent with all set relations generated during the combination stage, one of these labels will be stronger than the other, and one of the labels (but not the other) will match the atmosphere of the premises. The stronger of two labels is the label with fewer possible set relations in its representation. For example, "All *A* are *C*" is stronger than "Some *A* are *C*," because the universal statement can be represented by only two set relations (equivalence and subset–set), whereas the particular statement can be represented by four set relations (equivalence, subset–set, set–subset, set overlap). The atmosphere of two premises is determined by the standard rules: It is particular (leading to the choice of a particular conclusion) if at least one premise is particular, and negative (leading to the choice of a negative conclusion) if at least one premise is negative.

The bases for choosing a label when two labels are possible take into account strength and atmosphere of the premises. It may be that each of the two possible labels meets one of the two criteria or that one of the two labels meets both. Suppose the former is true: Each label meets one criterion. When one label is weaker than the other label, but matches the atmosphere of the premises, it is chosen with probability β_1, and the stronger label is chosen with probability $(1 - \beta_1)$. Suppose the latter is true: One of the two labels meets both criteria. When one label is both the stronger label and matches the atmosphere of the premises, it is chosen with probability β_2, and the other label is chosen with probability $(1 - \beta_2)$.

There is one more source of error in the comparison stage. This arises when the final set relations generated during the combination stage have different initial components. In the example described in Fig. 9.2, for example, two of the pairs of components have a_1 and a_2 both linked to C, and two have a_1 linked to C but a_2 linked to not C. In such cases, subjects are hypothesized occasionally to mistake this discrepancy as indicating the indeterminacy of the conclusion. When this happens, the subject mistakenly labels the relationship between A and C as indeterminate with probability c.

Alternative Theories of Categorical Syllogistic Reasoning

The constraints of space unfortunately permit only the briefest description of the alternative information-processing models to which we compared the transitive-chain information-processing model. Details can be found in the original papers and in two of our own papers (Guyote & Sternberg, 1978; Sternberg & Turner, 1978).

In the transitive-chain model, errors occur during combination and comparison but not during encoding. In the complete-combination model of Erickson (1974), errors occur during encoding and comparison but not during combination. In the random combination model of Erickson (1974), errors occur during encoding, combination, and comparison. The atmosphere model of Woodworth and Sells (1935) is essentially one of alogical information processing. Subjects encode, combine, and compare only the quantification (universal or particular) and polarity (affirmative or negative) of the premises. And in the conversion model of Chapman and Chapman (1959), errors in syllogistic reasoning, due to conversion of premises, occur during the encoding and comparison stages of processing.

The numbers of parameters estimated differed widely across models, an inevitable consequence of the different information-processing assumptions the models make. Thus, the transitive-chain model involved estimation of 7 free parameters; the complete- and random-combination models involved estimation of 13 free parameters apiece; and the atmosphere and conversion models each involved estimation of 1 free parameter. We were not particularly concerned with the differing numbers of parameters, however, for three reasons. First, our major concern was with comparing the historically important models in a way that did full justice to the initial conceptualizations, and these conceptualizations differ widely in their complexity and completeness. Second, we always estimated large numbers of data points (at least 100) in comparing models, thus minimizing the opportunity for capitalization upon chance variation in the data. Third, the fits of the models showed little correspondence to numbers of parameters in the models, suggesting that number of parameters was not an important determinant of fit.

Empirical Tests of the Models

Method.   Three experiments that are relevant to distinguishing the theories already noted were conducted with Yale undergraduates.

In a first experiment, subjects received pairs of premises with abstract content and had to choose one of five possible conclusions; for example: "All B are C. All A are B. (a) All A are C. (b) No A are C. (c) Some A are C. (d) Some A are not C. (e) None of the above." Half of 38 syllogisms had at least one valid conclusion from among options (a) through (d); the other half did not. Each of 49 subjects received all of the syllogisms.

In a second experiment, subjects received pairs of premises with concrete content and again had to choose one of five possible conclusions. Content could be either factual—for example, "No cottages are skyscrapers. All skyscrapers are buildings"; counterfactual—for example, "No milk cartons are containers. All containers are trash cans"; or anomalous—for example, "No headphones are planets. All planets are frying pans." Note that anomalous premises could be either factually correct (as was the major premise of the example) or incorrect (as was the minor premise of the example): In either case, though, the subject and predicate of the premise were semantically unrelated (or close to it). Each of 20 syllogism types was presented to each of 50 subjects once with each type of content. Items were not blocked by content type. Subjects in this experiment were given the verbal reasoning, spatial visualization, and abstract reasoning tests of the Differential Aptitude Test. The tests were subjected to a principal components analysis, yielding two orthogonal components, a verbal one, and a spatial-abstract one.

In a third experiment, premises were again presented with abstract content. This experiment differed from the first experiment, however, in that: (1) the subject's task was to indicate whether a single presented conclusion was definitely, possibly, or never true; and (2) subjects might receive either a single premise or a pair of premises. Sixteen subjects received each of 4 premises, such as "All A are B," with each of 4 possible conclusions, such as "Some A are not B," and had to determine the truth value of each conclusion; 16 other subjects received 15 pairs of premises, such as "All B are C. All A are B," and had to determine the truth value of the conclusion.[3] Eleven premise pairs had at least one valid conclusion; 4 did not. This decomposition of the task permitted us to test assumptions of the models regarding encoding of single premises separately from assumptions of the models regarding combination of pairs of premises.

Results.   Three sets of results are of primary interest: fits of the models to the data, parameter estimates for the preferred model, and relationships of parameter estimates to ability test scores.

Fits of the alternative models of categorical syllogistic reasoning to the response-choice data are shown in Table 9.1. Model fits are expressed in terms of proportion of variance in the data accounted for by each model (R^2) and of root-mean-square deviation of observed from predicted values (RMSD).

The results of the experiments, considered either singly or as a whole, are unequivocal: The transitive-chain model gave a better account of the response-choice data than did any competing model. And the results of the third experiment show that the assumptions of the transitive-chain model are plausible both for encoding considered alone and for encoding and combination considered jointly. Viewed by itself without regard to the other models, the transitive-chain model also did very well: R^2 was greater than .9 for all but one data set (in which it was .89).

Although the fits of the transitive-chain model to the data are most respectable, it is important to note that the model could be rejected at the .05 level or better in every case. Thus, although the transitive-chain model is the best of the competing models, and shows respectable fits when considered just on its own, it is not the true model. The most likely source of inadequacy seemed to us to be the assumption that encoding is always complete and correct. We therefore tried relaxing this assumption, estimating parameters for errors in encoding. Generally, this bought us about .02 or .03 points of R^2, and in about half of the data sets resulted in nonrejection of the model. But the small increases in R^2 did not seem to justify the increase by over 50% in the number of parameters, and so we did not modify the theory.

Table 9.2 shows values of parameter estimates in each of the various experiments. Parameters p_2, p_3, and p_4 were highly correlated and were therefore combined. In general, the parameter estimates make good sense.

Consider first the p parameters. The value of p_1 is particularly low for syllogisms with factual content, suggesting that the working memory or other processing limitations that restrict the number of set relations a subject can combine are lessened when the subject is dealing with concrete, factual content. The value of β_1 is always considerably greater than .5, indicating that given a choice be-

---

[3]In this experiment, 32 other subjects received a slightly different task. See Sternberg and Turner (1978) for details.

TABLE 9.1

Performance of Models in Predicting Response-Choice Data
for Categorical Syllogisms of the First Type

	Model									
	Transitive Chain		Complete Combination		Random Combination		Atmosphere		Conversion	
Experiment	R^2	RMSD	R^2	RMSD	R^2	RMSD	R^2	RMSD	R^2	RMSD
1	.97	.05	.76	.14	.59	.18	.57	.18	.78	.13
2F	.91	.08	.67	.16	.34	.21	.29	.23	.46	.20
2C	.92	.08	.69	.15	.54	.18	.52	.18	.69	.15
2A	.89	.09	.66	.15	.53	.16	.46	.18	.61	.16
6E[a]	.96	.19	.86	.37	.86	.37	.73	.41	.96	.19
6C[a]	.96	.16	.89	.26	.84	.32	.53	.51	.92	.26

Note: In Experiment 2, the suffixes F, C, and A refer to factual, counterfactual, and anomalous syllogism contents respectively. In Experiment 6, the suffixes E and C refer to encoding and combination tasks respectively. Experiments 1 and 2 are from Guyote and Sternberg (1978). Experiment 6 is from Sternberg and Turner (1978).
[a] Model fits were computed using parameter estimates from Experiment 1 of Guyote and Sternberg (1978).

TABLE 9.2
Parameter Estimates for Transitive-Chain Model in Predicting
Response-Choice Data for Categorical Syllogisms of the First Type

Experiment	Parameter				
	p_1	$p_2 + p_3 + p_4$	β_1	β_2	c
1	.54	.46	.81	.92	.37
2F	.29	.71	.67	.95	.37
2C	.49	.51	.73	.94	.48
2A	.47	.53	.70	.92	.48

Note: In Experiment 2, the suffixes F, C, and A refer to factual, counterfactual, and anomalous syllogism contents respectively. Parameter estimates for Experiment 1 were used for Experiment 3, and hence estimates for Experiment 3 are not shown.

tween a stronger label and a label that matches the atmosphere of the premises, subjects prefer the label that matches the atmosphere of the premises. One would expect β_2 to be quite close to 1, because it represents subjects' preferences for conclusions that both are stronger and match the atmosphere of the premises. In fact, β_2 is quite close to 1 in each data set. Finally, we can see that when the representation for combined premises contained nonidentical first components, subjects did show pronounced tendencies (indicated by nontrivial values of the c parameter) to label the final representation as indeterminate.

We next consider the relationship between the parameters of the transitive-chain model and scores on the orthogonal verbal and spatial-abstract principal components. Means of parameter estimates in Experiment 2 were calculated for subjects high (that is, above the median) and low (that is, below the median) on the two components. The results are shown in Table 9.3 and can be summarized briefly. High- and low-verbal subjects did not differ significantly on any of the

TABLE 9.3
Parameter Estimates for Subjects High and Low in
Verbal and Spatial-Abstract Abilities:
Categorical Syllogisms of the First Type

Parameter	Verbal		Spatial-Abstract	
	High	Low	High	Low
p_1	.38	.43	.28	.53
$p_2 + p_3 + p_4$	.62	.57	.72	.47
β_1	.74	.73	.72	.75
β_2	.96	.97	.98	.95
c	.46	.45	.45	.46

Note: Parameter estimates are from Experiment 2.

parameters. High- and low-spatial-abstract subjects, however, did differ significantly on the p_1 (and hence $p_2 + p_3 + p_4 = 1 - p_1$) parameter. Thus, subjects higher in spatial-abstract ability were better able to combine more set relations, presumably because of their ability to visualize more representations or the same representations more clearly than did the lower-spatial-abstract subjects. There was no reason to expect any differences in the parameters of the comparison stage, and none occurred.

It is obviously not possible to describe here all the data analyses we performed and presented in the original reports of our results. Worth noting, however, is the fact that we formulated a response latency model from the assumptions of the transitive-chain theory and tested it in Experiment 1, the only one of the three experiments in which latency data were collected. The model accounted for 80% of the variance in the latency data, indicating that even with response latencies as long ($\bar{X} = 43.59$ sec) and as variable ($S = 5.34$ sec) as those obtained for syllogism data, it is possible to obtain a good fit of observed to predicted times.

Summary.   To summarize, we have presented a new theory of categorical syllogistic reasoning—the transitive-chain theory—which we have tested on a variety of syllogism contents and response formats. The theory accounted very well for the response-choice (and latency) data. The parameter estimates were sensible and informative, and an analysis of individual differences in parameter estimates sheds some light on the kind of ability that may distinguish good from poor deductive reasoners.

CONDITIONAL SYLLOGISMS[4]

The Nature of Conditional Syllogisms

A conditional syllogism comprises three declarative statements. The first statement, called the major premise, expresses a relation between two events—for example, "If *A*, then *B*." The second statement, called the minor premise, asserts the truth or falsity of either the antecedent (first term) or consequent (second term) of the major premise—for example, "Not *B*." The third statement, or conclusion, is either the affirmation or negation of the term not appearing in the minor premise—for example, "Not *A*."

An interesting parallel exists between conditional syllogisms and categorical syllogisms of the second type, which were mentioned earlier but not further discussed. Consider the syllogism: "All *A* are *B*. *X* is not a *B*. [Therefore] *X* is not an *A*." If *A* is taken to be the set of states of the world in which Event A is true, *B* is taken to be the set of states of the world in which Event B is true, and *X*

---

[4]The research summarized here is presented in detail in Guyote and Sternberg (1978).

is taken to be a particular state of the world, then the conditional and categorical syllogisms become structurally isomorphic. Indeed, the transitive-chain theory assumes that categorical syllogisms of the second type are represented and processed in the same way as conditional syllogisms.

The Transitive-Chain Theory of Conditional Syllogistic Reasoning

The transitive-chain theory applied to conditional syllogisms (and categorical syllogisms of the second type) is very similar to the theory applied to standard categorical syllogisms. First, the subject encodes both premises completely, using the same format for storing information as was described earlier. Then the subject attempts to construct a transitive chain involving the representations of the second premise and one of the components in the first premise. Because all major premises are universal in problems of these types, there is a maximum of two possible representations of the first premise (see Fig. 9.1) and, hence, two sets of components. If the first rule for constructing transitive chains that was described earlier permits formation of a transitive chain, then the subject forms it and completes solution. If the first rule does not apply, the subject has two choices. He or she can apply the second rule, reason that no definite conclusion exists, and respond that the given conclusion is logically invalid. Or the subject can use indirect proof, trying to form a transitive chain integrating the negation of the conclusion with one of the components in the representation of the major premise. If such a transitive chain can be formed, and if the result contradicts the representation of the second premise, the subject can respond that the conclusion is valid. Otherwise, the conclusion is deemed invalid. The probability of a subject's using indirect proof and thus being able to form a second transitive chain (given that the first rule does not apply in the subject's initial attempt to combine the two premises) depends on the number of negations in the first premise. Parameter t_0 applies when there are no negations in the first premise, t_1 when there is one negation, and t_2 when there are two negations.

Empirical Tests of the Model

Method.   An experiment was conducted with 50 adults from the New Haven area. The stimuli were 64 syllogisms—half of which presented conditional relations, and half of which presented categorical relations isomorphic to the conditional relations. The 32 syllogisms of each type were constructed according to a 2^5 design that was exhaustive with respect to the possible item types. In these syllogisms: (1) the first term of the major premise, (2) the second term of the major premise, (3) the single term of the minor premise, and (4) the conclusion were each either affirmative or negative; and (5) the single term of the minor premise was the same (disregarding polarity) as either the first or second term of the major premise. The subject's task was to label each syllogism as having either a valid or an invalid conclusion. The content in each syllogism was abstract (with the letters A and B used as terms). All subjects received all syllogisms blocked by syllogism type and also the verbal reasoning, spatial visualization, and abstract reasoning sections of the Differential Aptitude Test.

Results.   Three sets of results are again of primary interest: fits of the model to the data, parameter estimates for the model, and relationships of parameter estimates to ability test scores. It is also of interest to note that the correlation across the 32 item types for the two kinds of syllogisms was .97, suggesting that the processes used to solve syllogisms of the two types probably were quite similar, if not practically identical.

The transitive-chain model provided an excellent fit to the response-choice data for both conditional and categorical syllogisms. For the conditional problems, R^2 was .95 and RMSD was .10; for the categorical problems, R^2 was .97 and RMSD was .07. As in the earlier experiments, however, the fit of the model to each set of data could be rejected at the .05 level, indicating that the transitive-chain model, although a close approximation to the true model, is not identical to the true model.

Parameter estimates for the conditional syllogisms were .36 for p_1, .64 for p_2, .52 for t_0, .48 for t_1, and .15 for t_2. (Parameters p_3 and p_4 are irrelevant in this type of syllogism, because there are never more than two possible set relations to combine; parameters β_1, β_2, and c are irrelevant, because the presentation of only a single conclusion in this experiment obviates the need for a comparison stage.) Parameter estimates for the structurally isomorphic categorical syllogisms were .43 for p_1, .57 for p_2, .60 for t_0, .61 for t_1, and .16 for t_2.

Comparison of the value of p_1 in this experiment with that of p_1 in the first experiment with categorical syllogisms of the first kind reveals that with content type held constant, subjects combine more representations for problems of the types used in this experiment than for problems of the type used in that experiment. This result is a most sensible one, because the representation of the minor premise in problems of the present type is simpler than the representation of the minor premise in problems of the previous type. In the present problems, the minor premise consists merely of a single term (conditionals) or indication of set membership (categoricals), whereas in the previous problems the minor premise consisted of a quantified relation between two sets.

We assume that subjects have a fixed amount of processing capacity that they can devote to each problem, and that increased consumption of processing capacity for one kind of operation results in decreased processing capacity left over for other kinds of operations. Using this reasoning, we had expected the values of t_0, t_1, and t_2 to be successively smaller: The increased processing capacity allocated to comprehension of negations in the major premise was expected to leave decreased processing capacity to allocate to forming a second transitive chain from the negation of the conclusion. Instead, the values of t_0 and t_1 were approximately equal, whereas the value of t_2 was indeed considerably lower. Apparently, double negations cause considerably more difficulty for subjects relative to single negations than do single negations relative to straightforward affirmations.

Next we turn to comparison of the orthogonal verbal and spatial-abstract principal component scores for high- and low-verbal subjects and for high- and low-spatial-abstract subjects. Our general expectation was that parameters reflecting processing capacity (those relevant to the combination stage) would differ in value across ability groups, whereas those parameters merely reflecting biases in response choice (those relevant to the comparison stage) would not differ in value across ability groups. Because the representation of information combined is assumed to be symbolic, our particular expectation was that larger differences would be obtained between the two spatial-abstract groupings than between the two verbal groupings. The results of the previous experiment confirmed both the general and specific expectations, and the results of the present experiment do as well. As in the previously described experiment, the values of p_1 for high- and low-verbal subjects—.38 and .43—did not differ significantly; the values of p_1 for high- and low-spatial-abstract subjects—.35 and .52—did differ significantly. Similarly, the values of the t parameters (which are combination-stage parameters) did not differ significantly across high- and low-verbal subjects—.54 and .55 for t_0, .50 and .55 for t_1, and .16 and .17 for t_2; they did differ significantly across high- and low-spatial-abstract subjects—.66 and .43 for t_0, .63 and .42 for t_1, and .22 and .11 for t_2. The results of both experiments thus confirm that: (1) parameters measuring processing capacity vary with spatial-abstract ability, whereas parameters not measuring processing capacity do not vary with this ability; and (2) no parameters vary with verbal ability. These results provide further support for the kind of symbolic representation and for the identification of processes proposed by the transitive-chain theory.

As in Experiment 1 for categorical syllogisms of the first type, a response latency model was formulated on the basis of the transitive-chain theory. The values of R^2 for this model were .91 for conditional syllogisms and .84 for categorical syllogisms of the second type. The model thus provides a good fit to the latency data.

Summary.   To summarize, we have presented an extension of the transitive-chain theory to conditional syllogisms and to categorical syllogisms of the second type. The two problems were proposed to be structurally isomorphic, and the high correlation between response-choice data supports a claim of psychological as well as structural isomorphism. The transitive-chain theory accounted well for response-choice (and latency) data. The parameter estimates again shed light on the ways in which subjects process information, and the analysis of individual differences in parameter estimates provided indirect support for representational and processing assumptions of the transitive-chain theory.

LINEAR SYLLOGISMS[5]

The Nature of Linear Syllogisms

A linear syllogism comprises two premises and a question. Each of the premises describes a relation between two items, with one of the items overlapping between the two premises. The subject's task is to use this overlap to determine the relation between the two items not occurring in the same premise. Determination of this relation enables the subject to answer the question. In the linear syllogism: "*C* is not as tall as *B*. *A* is not as short as *B*. Who is shortest?" the subject must determine that *B* is the overlapping term, and that since *B* is shorter than *A* and *B* is taller than *C*, *C* is shorter than *A*. Hence, *C* is shortest.

Whereas subjects show a rather wide range of responses in their solutions to particular categorical and conditional syllogisms, they show little variation in their response choices for linear syllogisms. In four experiments where subjects were told to emphasize accuracy of response (Sternberg, 1980–b), 99% of the responses to the questions were correct. Hence, the priorities in modeling linear-syllogism data are reversed from those of categorical and conditional syllogisms. The primary goal is to model response latency and the secondary goal, to model errors.

A Mixture Theory of Linear-Syllogistic Reasoning

Representation of Information.   According to the proposed theory, two types of representations are used in the solution of linear syllogisms (hence, the name *mixture theory*). First, subjects are hypothesized to decode the premises of the syllogism into a linguistically based, deep-structural proposition of the type originally proposed by Chomsky (1965). A premise such as "John is taller than Mary," for example, would be represented as (John is tall+; Mary is tall) (see Clark, 1969). Next, subjects are hypothesized to recode the deep-structural representation into a spatial array that functions as an internal analogue to a physically realizable array. In such an array, John would be placed above Mary, $\frac{John}{Mary}$.

According to the mixture theory (as proposed by Sternberg, 1980–b, and modified by Sternberg, 1980–a), as many as 10 component processes may be required to solve linear syllogisms of various kinds. These processes are illustrated with reference to the sample problem already cited (*C* is not as tall as *B*. *A* is not as short as *B*. Who is shortest?):

[5]The research summarized here is presented in detail in Sternberg, (1980–a,b).

1. *Premise reading* (mandatory). The subject reads each of the two premises, "*C* is not as tall as *B*" and "*A* is not as short as *B*," comprehending their surface structure.

2. *Linguistic decoding of comparative relation* (mandatory). The subject decodes the surface-structural form into a deep-structure proposition relating the two terms of the premise. Decoding of a premise with a marked adjective (such as *short*) is assumed to take longer than decoding of a premise with an unmarked adjective (such as *tall*). In the example, the first premise is decoded into the form (*C* is tall+; *B* is tall); the second premise is decoded into the form (*A* is short+; *B* is short). Note that at this point, only the comparative and not the negative has been processed, so that the deep-structural propositions do not accurately represent the content of the premises.

3. *Decoding of negation* (optional). If a premise is a negative equative— that is, one with the relation "not as _____ as"—it is necessary to reformulate the deep-structural decoding of the premise to take the negation into account. The roles of the terms in the propositions are reversed, so that the first proposition becomes (*B* is tall+; *C* is tall), and the second one becomes (*B* is short+; *A* is short).

4. *Spatial seriation of comparative relation* (mandatory). Having decoded the premises into deep-structural propositions, the subject is now able to seriate the terms of each premise spatially. A propositional encoding is assumed to be prerequisite for spatial seriation. The subject may seriate the two terms of each premise in either a preferred (usually top-down) or nonpreferred (usually bottom-up) direction. It is assumed that the subject's choice of direction depends on whether the adjective in the original premise was marked or not. The preferred direction is used for unmarked adjectives, the nonpreferred direction for marked adjectives. In the example, *B* and *C* are seriated top-down into one spatial array, $\frac{B}{C}$. *B* and *A* are seriated bottom-up into a second spatial array, $\frac{A}{B}$.

5. *Pivot search* (optional). Once the subject has seriated the terms in each of the two premises into two spatial arrays, the subject must locate the middle (pivot) term that will enable him or her to combine the two arrays into a single array. The pivot is assumed to be immediately available if either: (1) it appears in two affirmative premises; or (2) it was the last term to be seriated in a negative equative. (The principles behind this availability are described in Sternberg, in press-b.) In the example, the last term to have been seriated was *A* (the tallest term). The subject inquires whether *A* is the pivot. As it is not, the subject must use additional time locating the pivot, *B*, which is the only term that appears in both premises.

6. *Seriation of the two arrays into a single array* (mandatory). Having found the pivot, the subject is prepared to combine the two separate arrays into a single, integrated spatial array. The subject combines the two single arrays according to the order of the original premises. Combination of these arrays is assumed to be less susceptible to error (although not less time-consuming) if the first term

to be combined (which is always the first term in the final deep-structural proposition describing the first premise) is the term that is most current in working memory—namely, the pivot (from the immediately preceding Operation 5).[6] In the example, the subject starts seriation with the B term as encoded from the bottom half of the array, ^B_C, and ends up in the top half of the array, ^A_B. Thus, the subject links the second pair of terms, A and B, to the first pair, C and B, forming the spatial array, $^A_{^B_C}$.

7. *Question reading* (mandatory). Next the subject must read the question that he or she will be required to answer. If the question contains a marked adjective, as does the question in the example, it is assumed to take longer to decode, and the subject is assumed to have to search for the response to the question in the nonpreferred end of the array. A marked adjective in the question, therefore, increases response latency. The question in the example—"Who is shortest?"— contains such an adjective.

8. *Response search* (optional). After seriation was completed (Operation 6), the "mind's eye" of the subject ended up either in the top or bottom half of the spatial array. If the question has as its answer the term that is in the half of the array in which the subject's mind's eye ended up, then the response is immediately available. If the answer term is in the other half of the array, however, then the response is not available and must be sought. This search requires additional time. In the example, the subject ended up in the top half of the array, completing seriation with the A and B terms. The question, however, asks who is shortest. The subject must, therefore, search for the response, finding it in the bottom half of the array.

9. *Establishment of congruence* (optional). The processes already described are sufficient to establish a correct answer, and under some circumstances, a response is immediately forthcoming. If, however, subjects wish to check the accuracy of the response obtained by interrogation of their spatial array, they have available to them their propositional representation by which they can verify their response.[7] If the linguistic encoding of the proposed response is congruent with the linguistic encoding of the corresponding term of the proposition, then the response immediately passes the congruence check. If the two are incongruent, however, congruence of the response term to the propositional term is established, taking additional time. In the example, C, the shortest term, was described as tall (relative to B, which was tall+). The question, however, asks who is shortest. Congruence must therefore be established by formulating the question in terms of who is least tall.

10. *Response* (mandatory). The final operation is response, whereby the

[6]The differential difficulty of problems in which the pivot is or is not the term current in working memory was previously referred to as *linguistic pivot search* (Sternberg, 1980-a,b).

[7]The precise circumstances under which the optional operation for establishing congruence is used are described in Sternberg (1980-b).

subject communicates his or her choice of an answer. In the example, the subject responds with *C*.

Alternative Theories of Linear-Syllogistic Reasoning

The mixture theory was compared to two other theories of linear-syllogistic reasoning—a spatial theory based upon the theories of DeSoto, London, and Handel (1965) and Huttenlocher (Huttenlocher, 1968; Huttenlocher & Higgins, 1971), and a linguistic theory based upon the theory of Clark (1969). Although the alternative theories as formulated here were based upon previous theories, they were not identical to them. The alternative theories were not specified in a form sufficiently rigorous to permit quantification, and in order to permit precise comparison of theories, additional assumptions had to be made that did enable quantification. Although the alternative theories as presently formulated are not identical to the previous theories, they do seem to capture many of the major intuitions of these previous theories.

The theories to be compared all agree that there are certain encoding, negation, marking, and response operations that contribute to the latency with which a subject solves a linear syllogism. All linear syllogisms contain certain terms and relations to be encoded, and they all require a response. Only some linear syllogisms contain premises with negations and marked adjectives. Although the theories agree on the presence of these operations, they disagree as to which of the operations are spatial and which are linguistic. The theories also disagree as to what further operations are required. This divergence is particularly important, because it provides the basis for distinguishing among theories. Because the theories are partially nonoverlapping in the operations alleged to be used in solving linear syllogisms, the theories make different latency predictions across item types.

Under certain circumstances (described in Sternberg, in press–b), the mixture theory has one more parameter (seven) than do the spatial and linguistic theories (six).[8] As will be shown, however, the presence of the additional parameter (the optional parameter representing the time to establish congruence) never changes the rank order of the model fits to the latency data.

Empirical Tests of the Theories

Method.   Five experiments were conducted with college undergraduates that were designed to distinguish among the mixture, spatial, and linguistic theories. All of the experiments involved presentation of 32 basic types of linear syllogisms with three different adjective pairs (usually *taller–shorter, better–worse,*

---

[8]The number of parameters is fewer than the number of component processes because of experimental confoundings of some of the operations.

and *faster–slower*). The length of the experiments ranged from one to three sessions, and all experiments included administration to each subject of tests of verbal reasoning, spatial visualization, and abstract reasoning abilities.

In the first experiment, 16 Stanford undergraduates received linear syllogisms such as: "Sam is taller than Joe. Joe is taller than Bob. Who is tallest? Joe Bob Sam." Items were presented to all subjects in both of two cuing conditions. In the first condition, subjects received a blank field in the first part of a trial. Subjects indicated readiness to see the item by pressing a foot pedal, and following this indication of readiness, the entire item appeared on a tachistoscope screen. In the second condition, subjects received the first two premises of the syllogism in the first part of the trial. Subjects processed the premises as fully as they could and then pressed the foot pedal, resulting in the appearance of the entire item on the screen.

In the second experiment, the linear syllogisms were presented to 18 Yale undergraduates with the question first: "Who is tallest? Sam is taller than Joe. Joe is taller than Bob. Joe Sam Bob." In this experiment, there were three rather than two precuing conditions. Subjects received either a blank field, just the question, or the question and the two premises in the first part of the trial. They always received the whole item in the second part of the trial.

In the third experiment, the linear syllogisms (with question last) were presented to 18 Yale undergraduates without precuing. However, subjects also received eight basic types of two-term series problems—for example: "Jim is taller than Bob. Who is tallest? Jim Bob."

The fourth experiment was similar to the third experiment except that each of the 54 Yale undergraduates participating received two-term series problems and linear syllogisms (which are also known as three-term series problems) with just one of the three adjective pairs, rather than with all three as in the previous experiments.

The fifth experiment was also similar to the third experiment except that the 18 Yale summer-session students were encouraged to solve items rapidly, and a bonus was paid to encourage more rapid (and hence less accurate) performance. The speed–accuracy trade-off manipulation proved to be successful: Mean solution latencies decreased by about a second (from approximately 7 to approximately 6 seconds), and mean error rates increased from 1% in the previous experiments to 7% in this experiment.

Results.   As in the previous analyses, we are concerned with fits of the quantified models to the data, parameter estimates, and relations between parameter estimates and ability test scores. Because of space limitations, we present only model fits for the zero-cue condition (blank field in the first part of the trial).

Table 9.4 presents model fits (in terms of R^2) for the latency data from each of the five experiments. In each experiment, the mixture theory is clearly superior to either the linguistic or spatial theory: The differences in R^2 between the

TABLE 9.4
Performance of Models in Predicting Latency Data for Linear Syllogisms:
Proportion of Variance Accounted for

| | Model | | |
Experiment	Mixture	Linguistic	Spatial
1	.81	.60	.57
2	.74	.59	.59
3	.84	.69	.58
4	.88	.64	.58
5	.84	.59	.61

mixture theory and the second-best theory (the linguistic theory in four of the five experiments) were .213, .148, .155, .240, and .237 in Experiments 1, 2, 3, 4, and 5, respectively. Thus, regardless of whether the question came before or after the premises, whether or not precuing was part of the experimental design, whether different adjectives were presented within or between subjects, and whether subjects emphasized speed or accuracy, the mixture theory best accounted for the data. The optional parameter for establishment of congruence was relevant to performance in Experiments 3, 4, and 5. With this parameter deleted, the values of R^2 for the mixture theory were .765, .832, and .761 in Experiments 3, 4, and 5, respectively. Thus, even without the optional parameter, the mixture theory was clearly superior to its competitors. Moreover, this superiority held up in every comparison for every adjective and session and with precuing conditions included in the analysis. It should be noted, though, that the mixture theory could be rejected relative to the true theory in all but the first experiment: The unexplained variance was statistically significant in four of the five experiments. Thus, the mixture theory, although the best available approximation to the true theory, is not identical to it.

Table 9.5 presents parameter estimates for the various operations that could be separated in each of the five experiments. The ENC+ (encoding plus) parameter includes a combination of times for between-premise seriation, incremental seriation of marked adjectives in the nonpreferred direction, premise reading, and encoding of unmarked adjectives. The first two processes are hypothesized to be spatial and to account for most of the estimated time. The second two processes are hypothesized to be linguistic. $ENC+_1$ differed significantly from 0 in both experiments in which it was estimated (1 and 2) and was estimated at about 4650 msec. $ENC+_2$, comprising slightly fewer operations, was estimated at about 3050 msec in the experiments with standard speed–accuracy trade-off. It seems unlikely that the small difference in the composition of $ENC+_1$ and $ENC+_2$ (see Sternberg, 1980-b) could account for the large difference in estimated values. Rather, it seems more likely that encoding operations were performed more

TABLE 9.5

Parameter Estimates for Mixture Theory in Predicting Latency Data for Linear Syllogisms

Experiment	ENC+$_1$	ENC+$_2$	NEG	MARK	PSM	RS	NCON	QR+	RES+
1	4648	—	351	337	1136	380	—	—	—
2	4666	—	366	412	1045	695	—	393	836
3	—	2986	184	307	1154	522	538	—	—
4	—	3124	244	380	1008	656	396	—	—
5	—	1354	143	327	788	485	305	—	—

Note: Parameter estimates are expressed in milliseconds. All estimates are for both cued and uncued data combined.

rapidly in Experiments 3 and 4—where ENC+$_2$ was estimated (under standard speed–accuracy trade-off)—than in Experiments 1 and 2—where ENC+$_1$ was estimated (also under standard speed-accuracy trade-off). The obtained difference is exactly as predicted by the mixture theory, according to which encoding should be more rapid and less careful in experimental paradigms leading to the use of the optional operation for the establishment of congruence. In Experiments 1 and 2, the use of precuing presumably encouraged subjects to encode the premises fully before indicating readiness to see the question and solve the problem. In Experiments 3 and 4, there was no precuing in which subjects could take as long as they needed to get a sharp spatial encoding. Hence, subjects are likely to have encoded the items more quickly and less sharply, at the expense of needing the extra check for congruence at the end.

It was possible to estimate unconfounded durations of negation, marking, pivot search, and response search times in all five experiments. Estimates (for standard speed–accuracy trade-off) of negation time center around 350 msec, of marking time around 400 msec, of pivot search time around 1100 msec, and of response search time around 500 msec. Question-reading time (plus confounded operations) could be estimated only in the second experiment and appears to be about 400 msec. Response time is about 800 msec.

For the most part, the group parameter estimates are reasonable and in close agreement across data sets. The two exceptions (for standard speed–accuracy trade-off) are that negation time was inexplicably low in Experiment 3, and response search time was inexplicably low in Experiment 1.

Correlations between parameter estimates and composite ability test scores for the first four experiments are shown in Table 9.6. Data from the fifth experiment

TABLE 9.6
Correlations Between Parameter Estimates for Linear Syllogisms
and Composite Ability Scores

| Parameter | Composite Ability Score | | |
	Verbal	Spatial	Abstract
ENC+	−.25**	−.51***	−.58***
NEG	−.14	−.34**	−.41***
MARK	−.20*	−.36***	−.38***
PSM	−.16	−.25**	−.35***
RS	−.26**	−.35***	−.34***
NCON	−.31*	−.24	−.22
RES+	−.30**	−.09	−.15

Note: Correlations are for data from Experiments 1 to 4 combined. Not all parameters could be estimated for all subjects.
    *$p < .05$
    **$p < .01$
    ***$p < .001$

were excluded because the unique speed–accuracy trade-off in this experiment rendered parameter estimates noncomparable to parameter estimates in the previous experiments.

The encoding parameter (ENC+) was significantly correlated with scores on all three types of ability tests. This pattern is consistent with the mixture theory, according to which the ENC+ parameter includes both linguistic and spatial-abstract processes. A strictly linguistic or spatial theory would have difficulty accounting for this pattern. Although ENC+ contains a mixture of operations, the predominant operation—according to the mixture theory—is spatial seriation between premises. This mixture theory therefore predicted that the spatial-abstract correlations would be higher than the verbal correlations, and this was in fact the case.

The negation parameter (NEG) showed significant correlations with the spatial and abstract composite scores but not with the verbal composite. This pattern of correlations was inconsistent with the prediction of the mixture theory, according to which negation was supposed to be a linguistic operation. It now appears that negation is accomplished spatially by reversing the positions of the two relevant terms in a within-premise spatial array.

The marking parameter (MARK) showed some relationship to all three composite ability scores, as predicted by the mixture theory but not by the spatial or linguistic theories. It thus appears that marked adjectives are both linguistically more difficult to encode and spatially more difficult to seriate in an array.

Pivot search (PSM) was significantly correlated with the spatial and abstract composites but not with the verbal composite. This pattern of correlations was consistent with the mixture theory, according to which pivot search is a spatial-abstract operation.

Response search (RS) was significantly correlated with all three composite scores. The significant correlation with verbal ability came as a surprise, because response search is postulated by the mixture theory to be a spatial operation. A possible explanation of the correlation with the verbal composite is that subjects may differ in the rates at which they read off names from a spatial array, resulting in individual differences along a verbal dimension.

Search for congruence (NCON) was significantly correlated with the verbal composite but with neither the spatial nor the abstract composites. This correlational pattern is as predicted by the mixture theory, which—like the linguistic theory—postulates that the search for congruence is a linguistic operation.

Finally, response (RES+) was significantly correlated with the verbal composite but not with either the spatial or abstract composites. Response was a confounded parameter containing mostly linguistic operations (see Sternberg, 1980-b), and hence this pattern of correlations was consistent with the theory.

Generally speaking, the results of the individual-difference analysis were consistent with the predictions of the mixture theory, according to which particular operations should show patterns of individual differences along either verbal, spatial-abstract, or both lines. The two exceptions to the predictions suggest a need for slight reconceptualization, which in the present analysis was of necessity ad hoc.

Error rates in the first four experiments were too low to permit analysis. A detailed analysis of error rates in the fifth experiment is presented elsewhere (Sternberg, in press–a), but is not discussed here.

Summary.   The results of five experiments provide strong support for the mixture theory, considered either by itself or in comparison to alternative theories of linear-syllogistic reasoning. Parameter estimates for the mixture theory were sensible and generally consistent across experiments, and patterns of individual differences generally supported predictions as to which operations were spatial and which linguistic.

CONCLUSIONS AND CURRENT DIRECTIONS

The transitive-chain and mixture theories provide plausible and empirically sound accounts of reasoning with three kinds of syllogisms. Although neither theory is "true" in the sense of accounting for all reliable variance in the data, each theory is superior to any of the currently available competitors. Thus, each theory has an interesting story to tell, but neither story is the final one. These theories will presumably go the way most theories have in the past and eventually will be replaced by better theories.

Our present research is following three principal directions: The first is an attempt to show that the transitive-chain and mixture theories are both special cases of a more general theory of deductive reasoning; the second is an attempt to extend the theories to prose processing; and the third is an analysis of the development of deductive reasoning.

We propose that the transitive-chain and mixture theories are both special cases of a general theory of deduction. We are currently studying two tasks that we believe integrate information processes from the two theories. In both tasks, subjects receive two premises such as: "All gleebs are taller than some fricks. Some fricks are taller than all quirps." Note that these premises resemble categorical syllogisms in the use of the quantifiers *all* and *some,* but resemble linear syllogisms in the use of linear relational orderings. As in both categorical and linear syllogisms, some of the items involve negations, and others do not. Subjects participating in two experiments have to perform either of two tasks. In one task, subjects must answer a question such as: "Which are tallest? All gleebs. Some gleebs. All fricks. Some fricks. All quirps. Some quirps. Can't tell." This task is similar to the one subjects confront in solving linear syllogisms. The other task presents four conclusions and the possibility of an indeterminacy: "All gleebs are taller than all quirps. All gleebs are taller than some quirps. Some gleebs are taller than all quirps. Some gleebs are taller than some quirps. Can't tell.'' Subjects choose the best conclusion. This task is similar to the one subjects confront in solving categorical syllogisms. We expect that an account of the data from the two tasks will require a generalization including components of both the transitive-chain and mixture theories.

Subjects may reason quite differently when presented with syllogisms in the format of reasoning problems from the way they do when presented with implicit syllogisms embedded in their everyday reading. For this reason, we are investigating subjects' strategies for solving syllogisms when the syllogisms are presented implicitly in the context of articles such as would be found in newspapers or magazines, and when the questions requiring solution of the syllogisms are embedded in the midst of other, more straightforward reading comprehension questions.

Finally, three experiments are underway that investigate the development of categorical, conditional, and linear-syllogistic reasoning. Our goal in these experiments is to determine what it is that develops with time. The studies investigate cognitive development within the componential framework outlined in previous work (Sternberg, 1977a, 1977b, 1978; Sternberg & Rifkin, 1979).

Neither the experiments we have done to date nor those currently planned exhaust the problem domain of deductive reasoning. We believe, however, that we have made a good, if modest, start toward an understanding of the representations and processes subjects use in solving a variety of deduction problems.

ACKNOWLEDGMENTS

Preparation of this article was supported by Contract N0001478C0025 from the Office of Naval Research to Robert Sternberg. The research described in the article was supported by Grant BNS76-05311 from the National Science Foundation.

REFERENCES

Chapman, L. J., & Chapman, J. P. Atmosphere effect re-examined. *Journal of Experimental Psychology*, 1959, *58*, 220–226.

Chomsky, N. *Aspects of the theory of syntax.* Cambridge, Mass.: MIT Press, 1965.

Clark, H. H. Linguistic processes in deductive reasoning. *Psychological Review*, 1969, *76*, 387–404.

DeSoto, C. B., London, M., & Handel, S. Social reasoning and spatial paralogic. *Journal of Personality and Social Psychology*, 1965, *2*, 513–521.

Erickson, J. R. A set analysis theory of behavior in formal syllogistic reasoning tasks. In R. Solso (Ed.), *Loyola symposium on cognition* (Vol. 2). Hillsdale, N.J.: Lawrence Erlbaum Associates, 1974.

Guyote, M. J., & Sternberg, R. J. *A transitive-chain theory of syllogistic reasoning* (NR 150-412 ONR Tech. Rep. No. 5). New Haven: Dept. of Psychology, Yale University, 1978.

Huttenlocher, J. Constructing spatial images: A strategy in reasoning. *Psychological Review*, 1968, *75*, 550–560.

Huttenlocher, J., & Higgins, E. T. Adjectives, comparatives, and syllogisms. *Psychological Review*, 1971, *78*, 487–504.

Sternberg, R. J. Component processes in analogical reasoning. *Psychological Review*, 1977, *84*, 353–378. (a)

Sternberg, R. J. *Intelligence, information processing, and analogical reasoning: The componential analysis of human abilities.* Hillsdale, N.J.: Lawrence Erlbaum Associates, 1977. (b)

Sternberg, R. J. Componential investigations of human intelligence. In A. Lesgold, J. Pellegrino, S. Fokkema, & R. Glaser (Eds.), *Cognitive psychology and instruction.* New York: Plenum, 1978.

Sternberg, R. J. A proposed resolution of curious conflicts in the literature on linear syllogisms. In R. Nickerson (Ed.), *Attention and performance VIII.* Hillsdale, N.J.: Lawrence Erlbaum Associates, 1980. (a)

Sternberg, R. J. Representation and process in linear syllogistic reasoning. *Journal of Experimental Psychology: General,* 1980, *109,* 119–159.

Sternberg, R. J., & Rifkin, B. The development of analogical reasoning processes. *Journal of Experimental Child Psychology,* 1979, *27,* 195–232.

Sternberg, R. J., & Turner, M. E. *Components of syllogistic reasoning* (NR 150-412 ONR Tech. Rep. No. 6). New Haven: Dept of Psychology, Yale University, 1978.

Woodworth, R. S., & Sells, S. B. An atmosphere effect in formal syllogistic reasoning. *Journal of Experimental Psychology,* 1935, *18,* 451–460.

10 A Cognitive-Style Approach to Metaphoric Thinking

Nathan Kogan
New School for Social Research

INTRODUCTION

The present chapter offers a conceptualization of metaphoric thinking within a cognitive-style framework. Further, the chapter describes the construction and application of a task to assess the disposition toward a metaphoric style. A brief review of cognitive-style research is first provided, so that the reader may appreciate why the construct under consideration here has been essentially ignored by that tradition of research, despite the potential importance of metaphoric thinking as a stylistic dimension. A program of research is then described, with the general aim of demonstrating the conceptual and practical utility of a stylistic construct of metaphoric thinking.[1]

In the course of the past 30 years, at least nine different cognitive styles have been operationalized (Kogan, 1971; Messick, 1970). Though some of these have ceased to generate research within recent years, other styles continue to engage psychologists in active research programs. Most prominent are field independence–dependence, reflection–impulsivity, cognitive complexity–simplicity, and styles of categorization and conceptualization. Detailed reviews of research generated by the foregoing styles have been published by Goldstein and Blackman (1977), Kagan and Kogan (1970), Kogan (1976), Messer (1976), Saarni and Kogan (1978), and Witkin and Goodenough (1977a).

Considered as a whole, the reviews treat such issues as the reliability and

---

[1]The designation *thinking* is intended loosely to cover such terms as metaphoric comprehension, understanding, and sensitivity.

long-term stability of assessments, developmental antecedents, cognitive and personality-social correlates, and modifiability. Many of these are examined in connection with the metaphor construct. Given the perspective of the present volume, it must be noted that there is a considerable literature relating cognitive styles to learning and instruction (for reviews, see Goodenough, 1976; Kogan, 1971; Sigel & Coop, 1974; Witkin, Moore, Goodenough, & Cox, 1977). Some of this research has been carried out within an ATI framework (see Cronbach & Snow, 1977; Hunt, 1975; Messick, 1976). Later, I discuss possible implications of metaphoric thinking for learning and instruction, though it should be noted that systematic research on these issues has barely begun.

A first question that can be asked in respect to cognitive styles is why such a construct is needed at all. Two forces appear to have been at work that made the emergence of cognitive-style constructs virtually inevitable. First, abilities and aptitudes as traditionally conceived are concerned almost exclusively with accuracy and efficiency, and hence new constructs were needed to account for the range of cognitive performances where the form and manner, rather than the sheer skill of performance, are at issue. Second, researchers of aptitude and ability, on the whole, have not been overly concerned with the relation of cognition to aspects of the individual that have traditionally been subsumed under the category of personality. Cognitive-style researchers, for the most part, have focused on the interface between intelligence and personality, an area they believed to be relatively neglected by researchers identified with both of those camps.

With the proliferation of research on cognitive styles, it has become apparent that the domain includes constructs that are quite different from one another. Styles have emerged from very different theoretical traditions: Some derive from research on adults, others from research on children; at one extreme, some seem very close to the ability domain, whereas at the opposite extreme, we seem to be dealing with distinctive cognitive strategies or preferences, and the link with abilities appears remote on the surface. Indeed, the closeness versus remoteness of the style to the ability domain provided the impetus for a threefold classification of cognitive styles (Kogan, 1973).

In the first category are those styles emphasizing accuracy. Performance on the operational index of the style can be described as more or less veridical. Thus, those individuals described as field independent are more adept than their field-dependent peers at locating a simple figure embedded in a complex geometric design. Not surprisingly, skill at such disembedding relates to other kinds of spatial abilities, and hence we have the ironic situation that the dominant group within the cognitive-style domain—Witkin and his associates—has concentrated on a dimension that has most of the properties of an ability. No doubt, the Witkin group would object to this characterization, and quite recently, they issued a report (Witkin & Goodenough, 1977b) maintaining that the dimension is value free and bipolar for the reason that individuals at the field-dependent end have diverse social skills and sensitivities. This may well be so, but it is nevertheless conceptually confusing to have a social skill indexed by a deficit in spatial disembedding (see also Hoffman & Kagan, 1977).

The second type of cognitive style is characterized by an explicit or implicit evaluative dimension (e.g., cognitive complexity vs. simplicity). Although accuracy of performance is not relevant to the procedures developed to assess such styles, relative superiority is attributed to certain levels or types of performance. This value judgment is sometimes made on theoretical grounds—some stylistic modes may be considered developmentally more advanced than other modes. Alternatively, the value may derive from empirical findings; the style that correlates most highly with ability indexes is deemed most valuable.

Finally, there is a third type of cognitive style, for which neither accuracy of performance nor value judgments are implicated. Initial research on categorization styles, for example, was essentially neutral in regard to the advantage of broad versus narrow categorizing (Pettigrew, 1958).

It is important to note that the designation of a particular style as Type I, II, or III is not immutable. A style of the third type may become a style of the second type if it should prove to be empirically associated with either an ability dimension or with increasing developmental maturity. Similarly, a Type I style such as reflection-impulsivity (degree of success in perceptual matching under conditions of response uncertainty) is transformed into a Type III style by those who claim that reflectives are better at detail processing whereas impulsives are better at global processing (Zelniker & Jeffrey, 1976). The transformation is less than pure, however, for the relative advantage of impulsives in global processing is considerably smaller than the relative advantage of reflectives in detail processing.

One of the favored methods of investigators studying Type II cognitive styles is the pairing or grouping of stimuli on the basis of similarity (Kogan, 1976). Sometimes stimuli are offered in large arrays and sometimes, in the form of triads. In either case, subjects have been asked to cite the reason for particular similarity pairings or groupings, and these have been classified in diverse ways. A gross distinction can be made between those groupings that employ a similarity criterion and those that involve complementary relations. Complementarity implies the attribution of a functional or thematic relation between stimuli, and implies a rejection of similarity as a basis for grouping. Within the rubric of similarity, grouping may occur on the basis of common perceptible elements, common function, or common category membership. There is evidence for developmental change at the preschool level in the differential preference for various grouping strategies (Denney, 1975; Denney & Moulton, 1976); but in later childhood, adolescence, and adulthood, all of the bases for grouping are in the individual's repertoire, and the choice of grouping becomes more dependent on the particular stimulus materials employed than on the person engaged in the sorting (Davis, 1971). All of this leads to the observation that there has been an abundance of research on conceptualizing styles in children and adults, but none of it has had anything to say about metaphoric thinking.

One possible reason for this neglect may derive from a developmental model in which the apprehension of similarity is linked to the growth of analytic and abstract thought (Bruner, Olver, & Greenfield, 1966; Gardner & Moriarty, 1968; Inhelder & Piaget, 1964; Kagan, Moss, & Sigel, 1963; Vygotsky, 1962). It hardly matters within such a theoretical context whether one employs geometric forms or real objects. Indeed, the hierarchical aspects of class inclusion can best be demonstrated with forms varying in such geometric attributes as shape, size, and color. These hardly constitute the kind of materials that lend themselves to metaphorical thinking.[2] Where schematic pictures of real objects and persons comprise the stimuli for sorting, emphasis again has been directed toward either the child's use of superordinate, logically based categories or the child's recognition of arbitrarily introduced, common physical elements (e.g., a rabbit and a boy each portrayed with one eye). In short, it appears that the guiding theoretical orientation of most of the developmentally based research led to a focus on the symmetric similarities of formal abstraction, rather than the asymmetric similarities that frequently underlie metaphor (Tversky, 1977).[3]

In the most fundamental sense, metaphor refers to similarity in the midst of difference. This definition is obviously too broad, however, for it can also characterize the standard concept-attainment paradigm wherein exemplars of a concept share a criterial attribute but differ among each other along noncriterial dimensions. One must obviously distinguish between the foregoing type of within-category similarity and the cross-category similarity relevant to metaphor. The latter implies that objects or events belonging to one category are described in terms of the objects or events belonging to a decidedly different category. As a cross-category phenomenon, metaphor implies that objects and events typically unrelated are brought together by virtue of some shared feature. We are essentially talking about the production and appreciation of subtle similarities and equivalencies.

The foregoing description of metaphor has much in common with the intent of creativity assessment by means of divergent-thinking tasks. In process terms, a divergent-thinking task taps the breadth of a subject's similarity class; fluency is enhanced when there is greater tolerance for marginally appropriate instances (Wallach, 1970). Though it is entirely feasible that subjects employ metaphorical thinking in generating ideas, the fact remains that the preoccupation with sheer fluency (an easily scorable objective index) has been at the expense of idea-quality assessments. If metaphoric sensitivity bears any relation at all to divergent thinking, the common link would clearly have to be the metaphoric charac-

---

[2]When such visual attributes are to be matched with attributes from another sensory modality (e.g., audition), then we are in a realm quite relevant to metaphor. Indeed, Gardner (1974) has described such matches as *synesthetic metaphors*.

[3]Though the issue is beyond the scope of the present chapter, it is worthy of note that a symmetric model of similarity may not be adequate even outside the realm of metaphor (see Rosch, 1975; Tversky, 1977).

ter of the ideas generated in divergent-thinking tasks. The recent development of scoring systems for idea quality (Caudle & Kogan, 1975; Ward, Kogan, & Pankove, 1972) will permit an examination of possible empirical links between metaphoric sensitivity and divergent-thinking performance. It must be noted, however, that divergent-thinking tasks require the *production* of ideas, whereas the present research is concerned with metaphoric sensitivity or comprehension. On this basis alone, one would not anticipate that correlations would be especially high.

Metaphor is typically expressed through the medium of words and possibly achieves its ultimate expression in the figurative language of poetry. There is good reason to believe, however, that metaphor is a cognitive rather than a strictly linguistic phenomenon, for examples of nonverbal metaphor can readily be found. Such examples have often been subsumed under other constructs, but the link between such constructs and metaphoric operations would appear to be close. For example, synesthesia (Osgood, 1953) concerns cross-modality matching—that is, sensitivity to the similarities between visual, auditory, tactile, and other types of sensory stimuli. Another construct that overlaps with metaphor is physiognomic perception (Werner & Kaplan, 1963). This refers to the fusion of postural-affective states and objectively neutral stimuli (e.g., the attribution of emotional properties to line patterns). It is then apparent that both synesthesia and physiognomic perception rest on the capacity to define an event or object from one category in terms of the attributes of objects or events that belong to a different category. Evidence presented later in the chapter indicates whether or not these theoretically relevant constructs actually relate empirically to metaphoric sensitivity.

One can extend the argument for nonverbal metaphor further by demonstrating the ease with which verbal metaphors can be converted into nonverbal forms. Consider the statement, ''The river lazily snakes its way to the sea.'' The comprehension of such a metaphor can readily be examined in the visual realm by appropriate pictorial representations of a winding river and a coiled snake. An obvious reason for the ease of such a verbal–visual conversion is suggested by Verbrugge (1977). That author argues that figurative language is simply a vehicle to express the ''novel perception of resemblances.'' In other words, figurative language evokes images, and it is the cognitive operations in this nonverbal realm that represent the mediating process in metaphor interpretation (see also Paivio, 1979). This, then, further implies that one can study metaphor in direct perception without the use of language. Indeed, Langer (1948) has described metaphor as ''abstractive seeing.'' Note further in this regard that psychologists in the Gestalt tradition (e.g., Arnheim, 1949; Asch, 1952; Köhler, 1937) have long emphasized the role of endogenous perceptual factors as mediators of metaphoric similarity. It is acknowledged, of course, that verbal responses from subjects will generally be necessary to study the comprehension of visually expressed metaphor.

In my opinion, there has not yet been any thoroughly systematic attempt to assess *individual* variation in metaphoric sensitivity or comprehension.[4] Research on styles of conceptualization (see Kogan, 1976) has been concerned with individual variation in the bases for judging similarity, but the cross-category type of similarity relevant to metaphor has been neglected. Divergent-thinking tasks may engage metaphoric operations for some individuals, but these entail production rather than comprehension. The intelligence domain offers analogical thinking processes, but the evidence is not yet available to decide whether or not metaphoric understanding is little more than the capacity to reason analogically. All of the foregoing clearly points to the possibility that the thorough mapping of cognitive dimensions by psychologists over a period of many years has not been exhaustive; metaphoric thinking may represent a significant gap. It can be argued, of course, that the neglect of metaphoric operations within the broad outline of psychological research is merely a reflection of the esoteric nature of the topic. Such an argument, however, would be difficult to uphold in the face of the almost universal applicability of the metaphor concept. Conceptual analyses of metaphor can be found in the writings of art critics (e.g., Gombrich, 1963), literary critics (e.g., Wheelwright, 1968), philosophers of science (e.g., Turbayne, 1971), anthropologists (e.g., Sapir & Crocker, 1977), linguists (e.g., Jakobson & Halle, 1956), and psychoanalysts (e.g., Rubinstein, 1972). Of course, psychologists have contributed conceptual analyses as well (e.g., Asch, 1958; Brown, 1958; Bruner, 1962; Piaget, 1962). This multidisciplinary focus of the metaphor concept testifies to its central role in human endeavor. Yet the empirical study of metaphoric understanding in children and adults (particularly, why some individuals are more skilled at it than are others) is exceedingly limited in relation to the magnitude of the conceptual effort. The research described here has tried to narrow this gap somewhat.[5] As a summary of a large research project extending over several years, this chapter omits numerous details. A full-scale monographic account of the present research is available elsewhere (Kogan, Connor, Gross, & Fava, 1980).

TASK DESCRIPTION

It sometimes happens that progress in a particular domain is impeded due to the lack of an appropriate technique for studying the phenomenon of interest. Con-

---

[4]A number of years ago, Klein (1951) offered some speculations about a cognitive control principle of physiognomic perception. The Physiognomic Cue Test (Stein, 1975) represents an outgrowth of these speculations. Similes tests have been devised by Schaefer (1971) and by Pearson and Maddi (1966). None of these instruments appears to have had much impact on metaphor research.

[5]Particularly noteworthy is the resurgence of interest in the topic of metaphor within the last several years. Three books (Honeck & Hoffman, 1980; Ortony, 1979; Pollio, Barlow, Fine, & Pollio, 1977) and three review articles (Billow, 1977; Gardner, Winner, Bechhofer, & Wolf, 1978; Ortony, Reynolds, & Arter, 1978) have recently been published.

ceivably, the exploration of metaphorical capacities has been inhibited by the difficulty of constructing a task that taps specifically metaphorical, as opposed to other kinds of, similarities. Given my background in cognitive-style research, there is probably little surprise in the choice of the method of triads. Adaptation of the triads technique for the study of metaphor is relatively straightforward. Given a set of three stimuli that can be paired in three different ways, the obvious goal is to have one of the pairs manifest a metaphoric similarity while the remaining pairings are nonmetaphorical in character. Although prior use of the triads method for the study of conceptualization styles has typically requested subjects to provide only their most preferred pairing, there is no inherent reason why subjects cannot be asked to form as many pairings as they wish. If a child or adult does not pair stimuli on a metaphoric basis under instructions to form all possible pairs, a reasonable initial presumption is that metaphoric understanding is not present.

There are other advantages to the triads method that deserve mention. With three viable pairing alternatives, the demand character of the task is minimized. When neutral instructions are employed, there is no reason for subjects to infer that the metaphoric alternative is the most highly valued.[6] Further, the presence of alternatives to the metaphoric (analytic, functional, categorical) implies that the subject who is not metaphorically inclined can nevertheless perform adequately. The task is designed to minimize an experience of failure.

There were other kinds of requirements that the task had to meet. It was important that task items vary widely in difficulty, so that developmental differences across a broad age span might be explored. A final consideration was that the task be easily and reliably scorable by judges without extensive training. The rationale here was to make the task readily accessible to other researchers.

The initial stage of item building is a largely introspective process. A large number of possible metaphoric similarities were considered. Given the focus on visual metaphor, only those possibilities that might lend themselves to pictorial representation were retained. In the case of each potential metaphoric pairing, I attempted to devise a third stimulus for the triad that was similar to each member of the metaphoric pair on some nonmetaphorical basis. This stimulus also had to be potentially convertible into pictorial form. This initial phase of item construction generated 15 triads, each offering sufficient imagery to suggest that a pictorial representation might be feasible. I then consulted an artist, who in due course produced a set of 45 colored plates. These constituted Set I of the Metaphoric Triads Task (MTT).

As research with Set I proceeded, it became apparent that a larger number of triads would eventually be necessary in order to enhance the reliability of the task, facilitate training studies, and permit a search for different dimensions of metaphoric sensitivity. Accordingly, the sequence of item-construction steps was

---

[6]Because it is implicitly assumed that metaphoric sensitivity is a positive attribute, classification as a Type II cognitive style is warranted. Given the presence of acceptable alternative pairings, classification as a Type I style cannot be justified.

repeated, yielding a new set of 14 triads, hereafter labeled Set II. All 29 items are reproduced elsewhere (Kogan, Connor, Gross, & Fava, 1980). A sampling of six of these items (in achromatic form) is shown in the Appendix to this chapter, and brief descriptions follow here (metaphoric pair asterisked):

Set I

1. violin*, singing canary*, tree
2. fish, winding river*, snake*
3. angry man*, thunderstorm*, man in the rain
4. wilted plant*, hot tired runner*, glass of water
5. spinning top*, girl playing, dancing ballerina*
6. a grandfather*, rocking chair, ancient tree*
7. rat, moldy Swiss cheese*, broken-down house*
8. rifle, marching men*, flock of birds*
9. house with shades pulled down*, bed, woman with closed eyes*
10. worn-out woman*, grazing goat, barren landscape*
11. snorting bull*, boxer*, leather gloves
12. ocean, plane on fire*, fish on hook*
13. old man*, candle nearly burnt down*, smoking pipe
14. city lighted up at night*, city street, woman with jewels*
15. watering can, baby*, rosebud*

Set II

16. drowsy person*, "droopy" house*, living room
17. foggy street corner*, veiled woman*, moving car
18. weeping willow*, park bench, sad woman*
19. car, car wheel*, traffic circle*
20. rooster crowing*, barnyard, farmer showing muscles*
21. waves running into sand castle*, melting snowman*, girl
22. vase on table, old woman sick in bed*, wilted flowers*
23. compass showing directions, thirsty man finds oasis in desert*, ship in storm guided by lighthouse beam*
24. hanging plant*, woman with long hair*, watering can
25. cracks in ice near skating boy*, boy with beehive overhead*, fishing rod
26. fly in spider's web*, fishing boat, fish caught in net*
27. ambulance, explosion*, man in a rage*
28. sunflower*, greenhouse, tall thin woman*
29. blind man at the top of stairs*, German shepherd dog, ship navigating through rocks at night*

There are numerous sources of variation in the foregoing items. For some, the metaphoric connection is strictly conceptual in the sense that there is no physical resemblance between the members of the critical pair. Thus, in the impending death metaphor represented in Item 13, there is no actual physical similarity between an old man and a candle on the verge of extinction. For other items, however, the basis of the metaphoric link is configurational. The snake and the winding river (Item 2) are a particularly good example of the latter type of metaphor.

Another way of viewing these two types of items is along a dimension of figurativity versus operativity (see Piaget, 1970). In the present context this distinction refers to the extent of transformation that must be performed upon the stimuli in order to apprehend the metaphoric connection. Items that are more figurative in character offer similarities that are intrinsic within the surface properties of the pictures themselves. Little transformational activity is required beyond recognition of a perceptual similarity. On the other hand, the more conceptual items require that the subject transform the critical pictures into their symbolic referents in order to appreciate the similarity between them.

There is still a further distinction among the items that is worthy of note. Metaphors as figures of speech are generally asymmetrical in the sense that one of the elements—designated the *topic*—is described in terms of the other element—designated the *vehicle*. The common property underlying the comparison is usually called the *ground*. In the case of most of the MTT items, it is possible to envision a verbal translation in which one of the stimuli would function as topic and the other as vehicle. In the case of Item 22, for example, it is possible that the "old woman sick in bed" might qualify as the topic, with the "wilted flowers" serving as the vehicle. Many of the triads have this asymmetric property, particularly those that entail comparisons between human beings, on one hand, and plants, animals, or physical events on the other. It would seem that we are more likely to seek enlightenment about men and women through the metaphoric vehicle of physical events, for example, than to enhance our understanding of physical events through the metaphoric vehicle of human characteristics. A similar generalization would seem to hold for human–animal and human–plant comparisons, though here exceptions are more likely to be found. Anthropomorphism is, after all, a rather common phenomenon. Darwin in the *Origin of Species* compared surviving plants to people who have triumphed in an athletic struggle.[7] Conceivably, evolutionary theory has contributed to the greater symmetry of metaphors in scientific work in the life sciences. Literary products, on the other hand, are more likely to cast men and women as the topic rather than the vehicle of metaphor. It is essential to note, of course, that the topic–vehicle relation characteristic of verbal metaphor may or may not be relevant to the examination of visually mediated metaphor.

Whereas the metaphoric pair in most of the MTT items can be cast in the prototypical topic–vehicle format, some do not lend themselves to this type of translation. This is especially true for those few items where the members of the

[7] I am grateful to Howard Gardner for this reference.

critical pair are at the same level (e.g., both involve human beings, both contain animal life). Thus in Item 25, both stimuli present a human being in a situation of imminent danger. In the case of such items, each member of the critical pair within the triad can be viewed as alternative visual metaphorical representations of an underlying concept (e.g., decay in Item 7, imminent dissolution in Item 26). One must bear in mind that the asymmetrical–symmetrical distinction is a logical one having to do with item structure. Whether or not different metaphoric operations are engaged by the two kinds of items is a matter for empirical examination (see Connor & Kogan, 1980).

Though initial work with children and adults employed individual administration, it quickly became apparent that large-scale data collection with the MTT could be facilitated with a group-administered procedure for adolescents and adults. Slides of the stimuli were prepared, and these were projected on a screen to groups of subjects in a classroom context. The sequence in which the three members of each triad were projected is indicated in the listing of the specific items presented earlier. A response form was prepared that enabled subjects to list most preferred as well as other pairings and to state the basis for each pairing. Each triad was exposed for 90 seconds, a time period that proved ample for complete responding in preliminary testing. Instructions were given orally prior to exposure of the first slide, and an initial practice item was used to make certain that all subjects understood the requirements of the task.

A 3-point scale was employed for scoring the extent of understanding of the metaphorical similarity within each triad. A score of 2 was given for recognition and satisfactory explanation of the metaphorical linkage; a score of 1 was assigned for recognition accompanied by less than a completely satisfactory explanation; a score of 0 implied that the subject failed to join the critical pair or paired them on a nonmetaphorical basis. A total score for metaphoric understanding was obtained by summing across items (triads).

Interjudge agreement in scoring the MTT has proven to be quite high, ranging between 94% and 97%. It should be noted that almost all discrepancies between judges equaled 1 point in magnitude. In other words, judges occasionally disagreed over total versus partial credit or partial versus no credit; they virtually never disagreed to the extent of attributing total as opposed to no credit to an item.

DESCRIPTIVE STATISTICS FOR
THE METAPHORIC TRIADS TASK

Subjects

The MTT has been administered to several samples of male and female subjects whose approximate mean ages ranged from 7½ to 28. Table 10.1 provides the

TABLE 10.1
Descriptive Statistics for the Metaphoric Triads Task

Sample	N	Sex	Age	Form[a]	Adm.[b]	No. of items	Per Item $\bar{X}$	Avg. S.D.[c]	Coeff. Alpha[c]			r
									Tot.	Set 1	Set 2	Set 1–Set 2
A_1	18	M	7.6	M	I	7	0.54					
	22	F	7.4	M	I	7	0.58					
A_2	23	M	8.7	O	I	7	0.35					
	20	F	8.7	O	I	7	0.38					
A_3	24	M	9.8	O	I	29	0.41	0.62		.74	.73	.40
	20	F	9.9	O	I	29	0.43	0.69		.74	.89	.62
B_1	31	M	9.3	O	I	15	0.55	0.70		.42		
B_2	28	M	12.5	O	I	15	0.73	0.80		.78		
C_1	30	F	9.8	O	I	15	0.66	0.77		.75		
C_2	38	F	12.9	O	I	15	0.90	0.81		.85		
D	52	M	9.6	M	I	14	0.74					
	48	F	9.7	M	I	14	0.69					
E	24	M	10.2	O	I	29	0.56	0.74	.90	.84	.84	.70
	26	F	10.3	O	I	29	0.55	0.67	.87	.76	.76	.80
F	36	M	19.2	O	G	29	1.19	0.80	.80	.58	.73	.73
	91	F	18.8	O	G	29	1.22	0.77	.80	.68	.72	.55
G	63	M	24.6	O	G	21	0.77	0.83	.86			
	84	F	23.7	O	G	21	0.78	0.82	.83			
H	20	M	27.8	O	I	15	1.26	0.81		.82		
	20	F	28.6	O	I	15	1.40	0.75		.77		

[a] Form O is the standard horizontal arrangement, and Form M is the modified arrangement shown in Fig. 10.1.
[b] I and G represent individual and group administration, respectively.
[c] These were not computed for samples A_1, A_2, and D, given the item counterbalancing required for training schedules.

basic descriptive statistics for performance on the MTT for the various samples employed. Sample-letter designations indicate schools, colleges, and universities. In the case of Schools A, B, and C, the number of subjects represent different grades within each school. Note that all the children who served as subjects (Samples A, B, C, D, and E) were drawn from private schools in Manhattan and, hence, were predominantly Caucasian and middle- to upper middle-class. Schools A, D, and E were coeducational; Schools B and C were all-boys' and all-girls' schools, respectively. Sample F consisted of freshman undergraduates enrolled in a school of design and applied arts in Manhattan. Sample G was composed of psychology majors at one of the college campuses of the State University of New York. Finally, social science graduate students at a Manhattan university comprised Sample H.

The various samples participated at different phases of the overall research program. Initial studies exploring the properties and correlates of the MTT were carried out on children enrolled in Schools B and C and graduate students from University H. The latter sample was used to provide a baseline of adult metaphoric competence. Consistency of MTT performance across Sets I and II was explored in Samples A_3 and E. Cognitive and behavioral correlates of MTT performance were explored in those samples as well as in Sample G. Training studies aimed at experimental enhancement of MTT performance were carried out in Samples A_1, A_2, and D. Samples F and G were used to try out the group-administered version of the MTT.[8]

Reliability

Coefficient alpha (Cronbach, 1951) was used to assess the internal consistency of the MTT. This statistic was not computed for the three samples that participated in the training studies, given the counterbalancing of items required for experimental purposes. With the exception of the boys in Sample B_1, where alpha fell to .42, the coefficients for Set I of the MTT ranged from the mid-70s to the mid-80s. The internal consistency of the Set II items was of the same order of magnitude as observed for Set I. On the whole, it would appear safe to assert that the MTT is sufficiently reliable to warrant validational research. This conclusion was reinforced by the evidence of very substantial and significant r's in School E between Set I and Set II MTT scores (.70 and .80, $p < .001$, for males and females, respectively) when the two sets were administered without a time interval between them. Group administration of the 29 MTT items in Sample F also yielded high levels of consistency in performance across Set I and Set II subtotals (r's $= .73$ and .55, $p < .001$, for males and females respectively). With a 6-month interval separating the administration of Sets I and II in Sample A_3, the

---

[8]Much of the information reported for Samples F and G is based upon the dissertation research of Fava (1978).

correlations—though dropping in magnitude—remained statistically significant ($r = .40$, $p < .05$, in males; $r = .62$, $p < .01$, in females). In sum, it is apparent that Sets I and II of the MTT, on the whole, attained quite respectable levels of internal-consistency reliability. The correlations between the two sets justify their combination into a single instrument with a highly satisfactory level of reliability. At the same time, it must be noted that consistency over a 6-month period was modest. Further longitudinal research with the MTT is clearly required to establish the long-term stability of the instrument.

Age and Sex Differences

No consistent sex differences in MTT performance have been observed. Examination of the means in Table 10.1 suggests a slight superiority for females, but it must be stressed that none of the mean differences achieved statistical significance.

Age differences, in contrast, were substantial. Mean levels in Table 10.1 show a progressive increase in MTT performance with age for samples exposed to the task in its standard form (the triad arranged horizontally). When the modified form of the MTT was used (see Fig. 10.1) in Sample A_1 and D, it can be seen that an enhanced level of performance was observed for those subjects relative to the samples receiving the standard form. Note that the 7½-year-olds in

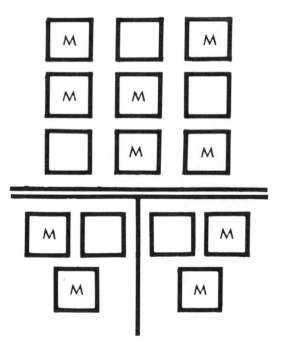

FIG. 10.1.   Alternate arrangements of triad in standard format (upper portion) and modified format (lower portion).

sample A_1 generated mean performance levels comparable to those of 9- to 10-year olds in Samples B_1, C_1, and E. When 9½-year-olds were given the modified form of the MTT (Sample D), their mean performance exceeded that of their age peers in other samples (A_3, B_1, C_1, E), although the difference for females in Samples D and C_1 was slight. Note that the males in Sample D performed as well as a sample 3 years older (B_2) that was given the standard form of the MTT.

The results obtained with the modified form of the MTT clearly indicate that the modified spatial arrangement of the triad with its accompanying elimination of one of the possible nonmetaphoric pairings can produce levels of performance in 7- to 10-year-olds that approximate those of children 1 to 3 years older who have been given the standard form of the MTT. There can be no question that the modified MTT reduces the attentional burden on children and, in addition, forces the children to consider the metaphoric pairing. Where younger children are concerned, the disposition toward thematic responding was very much reduced by the modified spatial arrangement. It is clearly the method of choice for these children. If the MTT were given to all samples in the modified form, there is little reason to expect that the developmental trends would change. Rather, we would be adding a constant to everyone's performance. As a consequence, however, we might find that the modified form could be given to children younger than those employed in our research thus far. For late adolescents and adults, on the other hand, the modified form might well produce ceiling effects. Hence, the standard form of the MTT would clearly be preferable for those age groups, particularly where the focus is on determinants of individual variation.

In the case of the young adults (Samples F, G. and H), it can be seen that the graduate students earned the highest MTT scores, but the visual-arts freshmen (Sample F) were not far behind. The lowest scores were produced by Sample G—psychology undergraduates in a state college. Note that their means are not that different from those of 9½-year-olds on the modified form, and from those of 12½-year-olds on the original form of the MTT. It is thus apparent that wide variations in adult metaphoric competence can be expected with the present instrument. Further, the indication that a ceiling is not attained in a sample of graduate students implies that the MTT can effectively be administered from the first or second grade of school through the life span.

Item-Level Differences

Item difficulties varied widely and ranged from zero successes on a specific item for the youngest subjects to complete success on another item for female graduate students. Relative difficulties of items for the diverse age groups showed only slight variations, however. Shifts in the rank ordering of mean difficulty levels were minor in scope. Kendall's coefficient of concordance applied to these ranked item-difficulty levels yielded highly significant W's for six male and six female samples (W's of .78 in each case, $p < .005$).

A further question of interest concerns the kind of item content that contributes to the relative ease or difficulty of understanding the metaphoric linkage. Where the difficult items are concerned, all appear to require sensitivity to subtle configurational cues. The relevant similarities may be physiognomic in character. The subject is required, for example, to appreciate the similarity between facial features and subtle physiognomic equivalents in the man-made and natural worlds (Items 9 and 10, respectively). In the case of the snake–river (Item 2) and woman–cityscape (Item 14) comparisons, the subtle visual similarity will be noticed only if obvious complementary pairings are suppressed (e.g., the woman lives in the city; the snake is found near the river). Perceptual similarity as such does not seem to be responsible for the difficulty, for the easiest item (5) offers highly salient visual cues of motion for the dancing ballerina and spinning top.

EXTERNAL CORRELATES OF MTT PERFORMANCE

Intellective Abilities and Achievements

For the school-age samples, scores on standardized tests of intellective aptitude and achievement were generally available in school records. The identical tests were not always used by different schools, however; hence, only gross comparisons across samples were possible. For Samples B_1, B_2, C_1, and C_2, the battery median from the Iowa Achievement Tests and the Otis–Lennon IQ index were available. Sample A_3 subjects had taken the Metropolitan Achievement Test battery, and their scores were provided to us. In addition, the Achenbach (1969) analogies items were administered. Half of these items are of the standard type, but the other half are deceptive in the sense of offering a high-probability word association that is incorrect. The two kinds of items are designated as *nonfoil* and *foil,* respectively. In the case of Sample E subjects, scores on the Stanford Achievement Tests (intermediate) were available in the records. Finally, the WAIS similarities subtest was administered to the college students of Sample G. In the case of Samples B_1, B_2, and E, teacher ratings of intelligence were obtained. All the relevant correlations are shown in Table 10.2.

The pattern of outcomes in Table 10.2 is clearly one of gross inconsistency. Sex differences in the magnitude of the correlation between metaphoric comprehension and the various intellective indices were highly salient, but these differences in turn did not assume the same direction across samples. Only in the case of foil analogies in Sample A_3 was reasonable consistency across the male and female samples obtained. These were the more difficult analogies in the sense that the subject had to suppress a strong, but incorrect, associative re-

TABLE 10.2
Correlations Between MTT and Intellective Indices

	B_1	B_2	C_1	C_2
Battery Median	− .20	.23	.23	.45*
IQ index	− .08	.22	.27	.50*
Rating—Attention span	− .16	.31	—	—
Rating—interest in school	.00	.28	—	—

	E Males			E Females		
	Set I	Set II	Tot.	Set I	Set II	Tot.
Word meaning	.67**	.24	.49*	.38	.28	.35
Paragraph meaning	.74**	.27	.54**	.29	.20	.26
Language	.60**	.31	.49*	.38	.18	.30
Intellective aptitude rating	.50*	.20	.37	.15	.10	.13

	A_3 Males			A_3 Females		
	Set I	Set II	Tot.	Set I	Set II	Tot.
Reading achievement	.37	.29	.43	.52*	.70**	.70**
Word knowledge	.27	.19	.30	.60**	.61**	.68**
Analogies (nonfoil)	.14	.22	.21	.45*	.30	.41
Analogies (foil)	.34	.41	.45*	.56**	.41	.53*

	G Males	G Females
WAIS Simil.	.30*	.01

*$p < .05$
**$p < .01$

sponse. There is reason to believe, then, that analogical reasoning enters into metaphoric thinking, but the correlations were not so high (relative to the reliabilities of the measures) as to suggest that they are tapping identical processes. A reasonable conclusion to derive from Table 10.2 is that we still have much to learn about the relationship of intelligence to the type of metaphoric skill under discussion here.

Divergent Thinking

Two of the Wallach–Kogan (1965) tasks—alternate uses and pattern meanings—were administered to one of the child and one of the adult samples (A_3 and G, respectively). The former also filled out the children's version of the Remote Associates Test (Mednick & Mednick, 1962). Correlations with the total metaphor score were nonsignificant in both males and females. For the Wallach–Kogan tasks, it can be seen in Table 10.3 that fluency scores were not consistently related to the metaphor total. More recently, we have developed a 7-point rating scale for assessing idea quality, which has yielded interjudge reliability coefficients in the 90s for quality scoring (Caudle & Kogan, 1975).

As Table 10.3 indicates, there is a fairly consistent and significant relationship between the metaphor score and the quality of divergent-thinking responses. For children, the effects are evident for both the visual and figural task. In the case of the young adults, the effect is confined to the figural task. The overall outcome is consistent with expectations, for judges are likely to assign high quality scores to appropriate and imaginative metaphorical responses to divergent-thinking items.

In the case of the young adults in Sample G, style of categorization and physiognomic sensitivity were also assessed, and the relationships of these to the total metaphor score are shown in Table 10.3 and discussed next.

Style of Categorization

As a measure of breadth of categorization, the Pettigrew (1958) category-width task was administered. Broad categorizors on that task prefer to risk errors of overinclusion in classifying stimuli, narrow categorizors prefer to risk errors of

TABLE 10.3
Correlations of MTT Scores with Divergent-Thinking,
Category Breadth, and Physiognomic Measures

	A_3 Males			A_3 Females		
	Set I	Set II	Tot.	Set I	Set II	Tot.
RAT	.31	.08	.27	.42	.17	.31
Alt. uses fluency	.28	.15	.26	.56*	.26	.44
Alt. uses quality	.51**	.33	.51**	.54*	.22	.40
Patterns fluency	− .14	− .17	− .18	.41	.12	.27
Patterns quality	.40*	.39	.48*	.49*	.53*	.57**

	G Males	G Females
Alt. uses fluency	.10	.29*
Alt. uses quality	.11	.19
Patterns fluency	− .04	.14
Patterns quality	.26*	.26**
Category breadth	.40*	.27*
Physiognomic grouping	.56**	.57**

*p < .05
**p < .01

overexclusion. The data yielded significant correlations between category breadth and metaphoric sensitivity in both males ($r = .40$, $p < .05$) and females ($r = .27$, $p < .05$). It appears that a cognitive style emphasizing similarities and willingness to include discrepant or deviant events in one's categories is characteristic of those individuals with the highest levels of metaphoric understanding.

Physiognomic Sensitivity

An open-ended sorting measure was constructed that permitted subjects to form concepts using expressive and affective dimensions as opposed to more conventional and literal dimensions. There were 25 stimuli divided into 5 categories, each of which had 5 exemplars: adjectives of emotion (e.g., *tranquil*); nouns with affective connotations (e.g., *fire*); and stick figures expressing emotional states, line patterns, and color patches. Subjects could confine their groupings to the foregoing logical categories, or they could group across categories (e.g., grouping the words *tranquil* and *meadow* with a relaxed stick figure). Each such cross-category grouping was credited. The total physiognomic sensitivity score was substantially and significantly correlated with MTT performance in both males and females; (r's of .56 and .57, $p < .001$, respectively). These results clearly confirm our earlier theoretical speculations regarding the similar cognitive processes underlying physiognomic and metaphoric sensitivity.

Correlations with Teachers' Ratings

For several of the samples studied, it was possible to obtain the cooperation of teachers for the purpose of rating the children on a number of possibly relevant socioemotional and intellective dimensions. In the initial work, I used the nine behavior-rating scales employed in the Wallach–Kogan research. Not a single one of those scales yielded a significant relation with the child's total metaphor score—a reasonable outcome of what was clearly a fishing expedition. Fortunately, I included two additional scales in the list provided the teacher—one inquiring about the child's originality, the other concerned with the child's aesthetic sensitivity. In both of the samples employed (B_1 and B_2), the aesthetic sensitivity rating was significantly related to the total metaphor score (r's of .33 and .46, respectively).

In subsequent research (Samples A_3 and E), the Wallach–Kogan scales were abandoned, and I devised new teacher's ratings scales concerned with such qualities as daydreaming, resourcefulness, originality, sense of humor, emotional expressiveness, empathy, and preference for working alone. A scale inquiring about the child's use of and sensitivity to figurative language was also included. Although correlations between these scales and the MTT score yielded various inconsistencies across samples and between sexes within samples, the overall trend of the results was sufficiently encouraging to warrant discussion. In

Sample A_3, for example, ratings of aesthetic sensitivity by the art teacher corre-lated significantly with total metaphor score in the case of females ($r = .42$), but not in the case of males ($r = .26$). All of the other ratings were provided by the classroom teacher, and because one of the two was unwilling or unable to provide ratings, resultant N's were too small for separate analyses by sex. For males and females combined ($N = 20$), the scale for figurative language usage yielded the highest r with MTT total of any of the scales employed ($r = .53$, $p < .02$). In the children of Sample E, figurative language usage represented the *only* scale that was significantly correlated with the MTT total in males ($r = .48$, $p < .02$). For females, however, correlations with all the teacher's rating scales hovered around 0.

Teachers' ratings were also obtained in another sample of 9-year-olds (Sample A_2). These children were used in one of the training experiments, and hence the metaphor score is based on only half the items (those used to obtain a baseline pretest measure). Unfortunately, because counterbalancing of items by difficulty level was not too successful, the distribution of metaphor scores in one of the two pretest groups was severely skewed. For the group where the distribution was more normal, the correlations between the metaphor score, on one hand, and the teacher's ratings of aesthetic sensitivity and figurative language usage, on the other, were statistically significant in both cases for males and females combined (r's of .43 for aesthetic sensitivity and .53 for figurative language).

In sum, there is a strong indication that the child's performance on the Metaphoric Triads Task bears at least a modest relation to activities in the school context that, on conceptual grounds, would be expected to require some metaphoric sensitivity.

TRAINING METAPHORIC THINKING

Three experimental studies have been conducted. The first was based upon a sample of 9-year-olds (Sample A_2). Using difficulty norms obtained from 10-year-olds, the Metaphoric Triads Task (Set I) was divided into two equally difficult seven-item sets (the most difficult item was dropped). In the pretest baseline phase, half of the children received one of the seven-item sets; the remaining half received the other. Following this administration, half of the children were randomly assigned to the experimental group and the remaining half to the control group. For the experimental group, the experimenter reviewed all of the items in the pretest, pointing out the three alternatives for each item. No indication whatever was given that the metaphoric alternative was better than the other two. In the case of the control group, the experimenter engaged the child in a 20-question game following the pretest. For both experimental and control groups, the posttest administration of the second set of items followed im-mediately. Midway through the experiment, it became apparent that the experimental children were not only receiving feedback about bases for pairing but were also learning that each item offered three alternatives. Hence, an additional control was essential, one in which the children were specifically requested to find three alternatives for each item. Accordingly, the children remaining in the original control group were diverted to an exhaustive-pairing condition.

An analysis of covariance (pretest scores as covariate) applied to the data of Fig. 10.2 yielded a significant between-group F ratio of 4.18 ($df = 2/40$, $p < .05$). It is strikingly clear from the figure, however, that the exhaustive-pairing control condition was almost as effective as the experimental metaphor-explanation condition in enhancing metaphoric sensitivity. It almost appears as if 9-year-olds' performance did not adequately reflect their competence in the metaphoric domain. A simple request for exhaustive pairing was sufficient to elicit a latent metaphoric capacity.

A second experimental study was based on a sample averaging 7½ years of age (Sample A_1). With this young group, the modified format (shown in the lower portion of Fig. 10.1) was used. The present experiment was identical to the previous one in its general design except that an exhaustive-pairing condition was no longer necessary. Again, the experimental group received feedback on pretest items, and the control group played a 20-question game with the experimenter.

An analysis of covariance (pretest scores as the covariate) applied to the data of Fig. 10.3 yielded a significant F value of 5.08 ($df = 1/37$, $p < .05$). The results were unequivocal. Information feedback on the pretest items enhanced posttest metaphoric performance by approximately 50%.

Various reasons can be advanced for the improvements in metaphoric thinking produced by the experimental manipulations employed in the preceding two

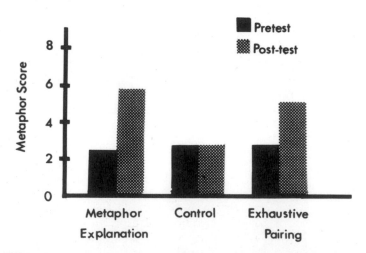

FIG. 10.2.   Pre- to posttest change in MTT score in Sample A_2 under conditions of metaphor explanation, standard control, and exhaustive-pairing control.

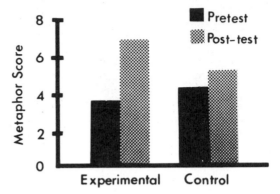

FIG. 10.3. Pre- to posttest change in MTT score in Sample A₁ under experimental (metaphor-explanation) and standard control conditions.

studies. One conjecture is that the more literal categorical and functional pairings are deemed more desirable by the child. Formal schooling in the early primary grades very likely encourages this tendency. When, as in the first experiment described earlier, the child is forced to deal with all three pairs, the expressive properties linking the metaphoric pairings are detected. Conceivably, these are less preferred and, hence, are not reported under conditions where all three pairings are not required. For the children in the experimental training conditions, the metaphoric pairings must be deemed highly acceptable by virtue of their endorsement by the examiner in the "feedback" training period. All this suggests that there might be some inhibition in reporting metaphoric pairings because of their unconventionality (relative to the more conventional categorical and functional pairs). Alternatively, the metaphoric pairings may simply be more difficult to detect, with the consequence that the added effort of exhaustive pairing or the examiner's demonstration of metaphoric possibilities serves to render the metaphoric linkage more accessible.

The third study (Sample D) continued the tradition of experimental enhancement of performance and focused on a process that might conceivably interfere with metaphoric thinking on the MTT. For children to apprehend the metaphorical basis of the relationship between the critical pair of pictures for each item, it is essential that they attend to the relevant features of the respective pictures. Whereas adults can be expected to encode a set of pictures in a fairly consistent way, children can be expected to show more variation in attentional selectivity; to the degree that the child's encoding of a picture contains irrelevant attributes (from the standpoint of forming a metaphoric connection), performance on the MTT should suffer as a consequence. This is not to imply that appropriate encoding of each member of the critical pair will insure sensitivity to the underlying metaphor. We are dealing here with a necessary, though not a sufficient, condition for metaphoric competence.

If the foregoing conjecture has any validity, it should be possible to improve children's metaphoric skill by insuring appropriate encoding of each of the pictures in the triad. This was accomplished in the present study through the use of verbal labels provided by the experimenter for all the pictures. Two control groups were necessary—a standard control in which no labels were provided, and a label control. In the latter, the child generated his or her own labels for each of the pictures in a triad prior to searching for pairwise similarities. As there was no guarantee that such child-generated labels would be universally adequate for subsequent metaphoric pairing, we might expect that the foregoing condition would produce a lower level of performance relative to the condition offering experimenter-provided labels. Indeed, there was little reason to expect any difference between the two control conditions, for the children's labeling group merely made overt whatever covert labeling process distinguished the standard control. Nevertheless, the mere introduction of verbal labeling (whether experimentally provided or child produced) might have unforeseen effects; hence, two control groups were deemed necessary.

A female examiner administered the MTT (Sets I and II) to all children individually. Half of the items were used for a pretest, with items counterbalanced within each condition. Again, the most difficult item was not used. After an interval of 1 month, children responded to the other half of the items under control, own-labeling, or experimenter's labeling conditions.

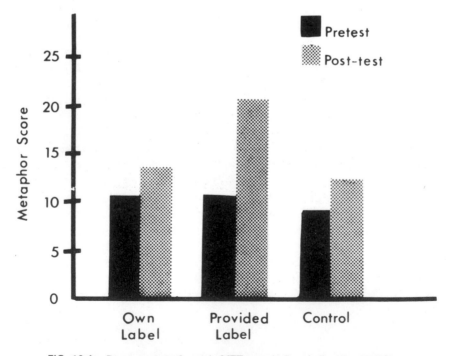

FIG. 10.4.   Pre- to posttest change in MTT score in Sample D under conditions of experimenter-provided labels, own-label control, and standard control.

An analysis of covariance (pretest scores as the covariate) yielded a highly significant effect for experimental conditions ($F = 30.7$, $df = 2/96$, $p < .001$). Inspection of the means indicated similar improvements in the own-labeling and control groups from pretest to posttest (3.1 and 3.5, respectively). By contrast, an increase of 11.1 points was obtained in the experimenter's labeling group (see Fig. 10.4).

The foregoing results strongly suggest that mislabeling (or inappropriate encoding) of particular stimuli can interfere with the recognition of metaphoric similarities between them. The provision of appropriate labels makes clear that the metaphoric competence of children in the 9-to-10 age range is underestimated in the customary condition of administration (use of unlabeled pictures). These results strongly suggest that metaphoric competence on a visual task such as the MTT involves more than the ability to make a particular kind of connection; it may also depend on selecting and attending to relevant stimulus dimensions. It may be necessary to consider both of these aspects if we are to understand developmental shifts in visual metaphoric competence. The three studies, considered as a whole, point clearly to the possibility of enhancing metaphoric thinking by means of short-term training procedures.[9]

EDUCATIONAL IMPLICATIONS AND FUTURE DIRECTIONS

It is important to note that the child-based research reported in the present chapter was carried out in nonsectarian private schools in New York City. Though these schools accept scholarship students, it is nevertheless fair to characterize the samples employed as advantaged. I simply do not know how less advantaged children would respond to the MTT, but I would be surprised if the range of individual differences were any narrower. Given the colorful visual stimuli employed, there is no a priori reason to think that more representative samples of children would be unresponsive to the task. Nevertheless, the necessary empirical comparisons clearly should be carried out.

The choice of private schools as a source of subjects for the initial studies offered the advantage of cooperative and highly sophisticated teachers who felt comfortable rating the children on such scales as aesthetic sensitivity and figurative language usage. Regrettably, we do not know what cues these teachers employed in the course of forming their judgments. The evidence reported earlier suggests that the teachers might well be sensitive to metaphoric expression in the classroom context. Indeed, it is possible that appreciation for metaphor was explicitly taught.[10]

[9]It should be noted that none of the training studies yielded a significant mean sex difference or a sex-by-condition interaction.

[10]In a visit to School B, I noted that a recent assignment (pasted on the classroom walls) required that the pupils transform a poem into a pictorial representation.

Such a state of affairs would contrast sharply with the conditions that prevail in public education as described by Pollio, Barlow, Fine, and Pollio (1977). Those authors have surveyed popular language-arts textbooks (child and teacher editions) used in elementary schools and observed, on the whole, that less than 5% of such texts are devoted to discussion of figurative language. A similar underemphasis of this topic is noted in language-arts textbooks for prospective teachers. Yet according to Pollio et al. (1977), children's readers contain figurative language in abundance, with the consequence that—due to lack of explicit instruction—children fail to appreciate much of what they read. The explanation offered for the general neglect of metaphor in relevant texts is that many educators view metaphor as little more than aesthetic ornament and, hence, deserving of being slighted in favor of more basic language and reading skills.

The general stance taken in the present chapter is that metaphoric operations constitute a basic *cognitive* process. In other words, metaphor is considered fundamental to thinking and learning in the most general sense, though it is recognized that the aesthetic domain offers a fertile ground for metaphoric expression. It is for the latter reason that teacher evaluations of aesthetic sensitivity and figurative language use and appreciation were considered as possible "real-world criteria" in relation to MTT performance. Further, it must be granted that the Metaphoric Triads Task, in form and content, is biased in the direction of expressive similarities more typical of the arts and humanities than of the sciences. The choice was largely a practical one, for the construction of a task oriented to scientific and technological metaphors is not easily accomplished. Bruner (1962) offers a colorful example of the use of metaphors by an industrial consultant group attempting to solve a technical design problem. This type of "brainstorming" has generated a large published literature (see Lamm & Trommsdorff, 1973), but its contribution to our understanding of metaphor has been negligible.

An incisive analysis of the role of metaphor in science learning and teaching has recently been offered by Petrie (1979). That author also rejects the ornamental view of metaphor and advances the idea that metaphor can assist one in moving from an old conceptual scheme to a new one in the course of scientific learning. It is Petrie's belief that scientific principles are first understood in a metaphoric, nonlinguistic mode, and that explicit definitional understanding occurs only after the basic idea is grasped. To quote Petrie (1979), "Understanding the process involved in construing metaphor is what makes intelligible the ability to learn something new while admitting we must always start with what and how we already know [p. 461]."

Unfortunately, Petrie has little to say about faulty or inadequate metaphors that might stand in the way of acquiring an accurate conceptual scheme of some natural phenomenon (see Chapter 20, by Stevens & Collins, Volume 2). Hence, metaphors are not inevitably adaptive, and it becomes the task of the instructor to teach or make the students aware of the appropriate metaphor to avoid confusion.

This is likely to be a more critical problem in the sciences than in the arts, where the issue concerns the aesthetic quality or power of metaphors rather than their accuracy or theoretical utility.

The teaching of metaphor is in a bad way, however, if the survey reported by Pollio et al. (1977) represents an accurate reflection of the facts. It is possible, of course, that much teaching of metaphor takes place at an implicit rather than explicit level. It is even possible that the acquisition of metaphoric thinking follows a developmental timetable (see Gardner, Winner, Bechhofer, & Wolf, 1978) and that formal instruction has little to do with it. The fact remains, however, that there is substantial individual variation for both children and adults in the kind of metaphoric thinking examined in the present chapter. These differences may eventually lend themselves to research within an ATI paradigm, but much more conceptual analysis will be required before we can expect to delineate promising instructional and outcome variables. In this regard, Cronbach and Snow (1977) have noted that the preponderant subject matter in ATI studies has consisted of mathematics, science, foreign language, reading, and formal English usage. With the possible exception of that aspect of science involving the learning of new paradigms, it would be fair to say that none of the foregoing subject matter has much bearing on metaphor. Cronbach and Snow (1977) go on to discuss the dearth of ATI studies concerned with "generalizations about human affairs" and with "productive kinds of thought (written expression as distinct from grammar, planning of scientific inquiry, etc.) [p. 509]." Yet these clearly constitute the domains in which metaphoric thinking is likely to play a role.

A limited start in the direction of developing instructional treatments and outcome measures appropriate to metaphor is outlined in the recent book by Pollio and his associates (1977). Those authors have used the workbook exercises developed by the Synectics Company (*Making It Strange,* 1968) to foster creative writing and thinking in Grades 3 through 6. According to Pollio et al. (1977), the series of exercises are intended to "prepare the child for the use of metaphor as an heuristic in thinking [p. 199]." An example item requests that the child specify: "What animal is like a parachute? Why?" Another item calls for the completion of the following statement: "An example of pleasing pain is _____ because _____." Teachers employed these exercises over a 6-month period, and their effect on figurative language use in written compositions was examined. In addition to a standard control, Pollio et al. also included a condition in which teachers were trained to use a variety of "motivational devices, reinforcement techniques, and discussion-sharing follow-ups" in the service of enhancing novel usage of figurative language. It was expected that the Synectics materials would enhance actual metaphoric competence and hence be superior to the teacher-intervention techniques described, which were merely intended to loosen inhibitory constraints about using figurative language.

The expected difference was, in fact, obtained in respect to novel figurative usage in written compositions, but defects in the design of the research (admitted by the authors) raise serious doubts about the meaningfulness of the findings. The research is described here only because some of the ingredients for a well-designed ATI study are present in the work of Pollio and his associates. Two instructional methods have been described, and a reasonable outcome index—novel figurative-language use in written compositions—has been developed. An individual-differences variable is lacking, and I should like to propose that the Metaphoric Triads Task deserves a trial in such an ATI context. A conceivable hypothesis is that subjects with high MTT scores would profit more from Synectics-type training, whereas low-MTT subjects would derive more from directive teacher reinforcement.

The foregoing description is obviously intended to be illustrative rather than definitive of what might be possible in respect to ATI exploration of metaphoric thinking. Other kinds of instructional techniques should be considered, and written composition hardly exhausts the range of school-relevant outcome measures. Indeed, because the MTT is a pictorial instrument, consideration must be given to the development of a verbal metaphoric task as a possible complementary measure if our hypothetical ATI study is to achieve a reasonable degree of comprehensiveness. There is little doubt that the examination of relations between metaphoric thinking in the visual domain and in the verbal domain represents one of the principal goals for the future.

It is unlikely that truly sophisticated ATI research relevant to metaphor can take place before we have additional information about the cognitive processing aspects of metaphoric operations. This may well be the most important task that lies ahead of us. The approach taken in the doctoral dissertation research of Fava (1978) is a factor analytic one. The extraction of independent factors comprising different MTT items could well prove informative in regard to the diverse cognitive-processing requirements in the visual metaphoric domain. Separate factor analyses were carried out on Samples F and G, but the former was based on all 29 items and the latter on a sample of 21 items. Less time was allotted to task administration in Sample G than in Sample F. Hence, direct comparison of factors was not feasible. Application of the scree test generated four factors accounting for 33.3% of total variance in Sample F and three factors accounting for 37.5% of total variance in Sample G. A varimax rotation to orthogonal simple structure was employed in each case. In the case of the first factor (57.2% of common variance) in Sample F (the applied-arts students), the three highest-loading items required close attention to configurational details for the metaphoric connection to be apprehended.[11] In Item 7, for example, the subjects could relate the decaying house to the Swiss cheese only if they noticed that the latter was moldy. The other items (9 and 10) required close attention to physiognomic detail. At the same time, all three items offered somber affect. The

[11]In the large majority of cases, interpretations were based on item loadings exceeding .40.

rejection of the latter interpretation in favor of processing of configurational detail rested on the character of items loading less strongly on the first factor. Nevertheless, subjectivity enters into this type of inference and is inevitably a source of concern.

The second factor (16.4% of total variance) offered greater clarity. The most highly loading items (24, 26, 28) required a global configurational comparison. Item 28, for example, required that subjects recognize the linkage between a tall, thin woman and a sunflower. Thus, separate detail and global configurational factors were distinguishable in the applied-arts sample.

The third factor (15.1% of common variance) appeared to be conceptual in character, with the highest-loading items (8, 22, 18) offering human being– nature comparisons—an army formation and a flock of geese; a sick, old woman and wilted flowers; a woman bent over with hands covering her face and a weeping willow tree. Finally, the fourth factor (11.3% of common variance) loaded items (1, 3, 5, 6) suggestive of expressive movement (e.g., a violin and a singing canary, a man gesturing angrily and a bolt of lightning, a ballerina and a spinning top). The remaining item—an old man and an ancient tree—fitted the factor less well.

In the case of the psychology undergraduates (Sample G), items loading the first factor (3, 7, 13, 16, 19, 24, 26) appeared to cut across conceptual and configurational categories. We may be dealing here with an approximation to a general metaphoric processing factor. It accounted for 77.5% of common variance. Items loaded most highly on the second factor (8, 15, 24, 28) were strongly suggestive of a human being versus nature factor (11.7% of common variance). Finally, the items loading the third factor most strongly (9, 10, 14, 27) required attention to physiognomic (facial) detail (10.7% of common variance).

An informal comparison across the two samples points to the presence of a conceptual factor involving metaphoric similarities between: (1) human beings, on one hand; and (2) lower animals and plant life on the other. Though both samples generated a configurational detail factor, it is of interest that the factor was confined to facial comparisons in the psychology students and was more highly generalized in the applied-arts students. Finally, the manifestation of two configurational factors and an additional "expressive movement" factor in the applied-arts students (in conjunction with the presence of a strong general factor in the psychology students) suggests that the visual metaphoric domain may be more differentiated in the former sample (arts) relative to the latter. This latter inference is advanced in the most tentative fashion, however, given the fact that the psychology students responded to fewer items than did the applied-arts students.

There is little doubt that the foregoing factor analytic outcomes make a substantial contribution to our knowledge about the cognitive processing requirements of MTT items. On the basis of our current knowledge about metaphoric thinking, however, it is safe to assume that the contribution is more theoretical than practical. It would be exceedingly premature to derive individual-difference dimensions based on the factor components just described, and to use these within an ATI framework. Even if the stability of the foregoing factors should be established, their conceptual importance could only be confirmed through extensive construct-validational research.

For many cognitive psychologists, the factor analytic method is too gross and indirect to shed light on the cognitive processing requirements of a task. In the case of the MTT, the raw data for the application of factor analysis consists of an item score (a scale from 0 to 2, reflecting minimal to maximal metaphoric comprehension). It is quite legitimate to claim that psychometric manipulation of these item scores is not the most efficient means to clarify the cognitive mechanisms that constitute metaphoric thinking. An alternative, of course, is a more molecular approach—one that reaches inside the metaphor, so to speak, to examine its intrinsic properties.

Empirical efforts in this latter direction have already begun. Verbrugge (1977), Verbrugge and McCarrell (1977), and Honeck, Riechmann, and Hoffman (1975) examined the encoding of metaphoric sentences through recall-prompt procedures. The evidence that transformed metaphoric "grounds" served as effective prompts to recall suggests that we encode the meaning of metaphors in a form more abstract and inclusive than is indicated by the specific lexical elements or deep structure of the original sentence. In contrast to the foregoing position, Johnson (1970) has argued that metaphoric interpretation reflects a combination of the features underlying the elements in the sentence. A weighted-feature model is proposed, wherein features shared by the two objects compared are raised in salience, whereas unshared features receive less weight in a final metaphoric interpretation. More recently, Malgady and Johnson (1976) observed a strong relationship between metaphor goodness and interpretability, with both in turn related to the number of shared constituents.

Although the foregoing studies have advanced our knowledge about metaphor, it would be fair to say that their primary objective is to use the domain of metaphor as a testing ground for the development of a more comprehensive theory of the nature of meaning. The research has emphasized the importance of similarity in the comprehension of metaphor but has not gone far in clarifying the nature of this similarity. To accomplish this last objective requires closer study of the functional relationship between the topic and the vehicle of a metaphor.

The Metaphoric Triads Task lends itself quite directly to the study of the topic–vehicle relation in metaphoric thinking.[12] Indeed, the pictorial format necessarily insures that the potential topic and vehicle terms are separated rather than part of an already formed linguistic unit. As a consequence, it is possible to ask subjects to specify the topic and vehicle of a particular similarity relationship. After the nature of a metaphor is explained to them, the critical metaphoric pairs

---

[12] Most of the future directions discussed in this section of the chapter are currently under investigation in the doctoral dissertation research of Kathleen Connor.

from the MTT can be presented with instructions to write a metaphoric statement of the general form: "_____is like_____because.... "The null hypothesis in the present context would predict that for each item, one member of the metaphoric pair should occur as topic for about half the subjects in the sample. Comparison with the binomial distribution should indicate which metaphors have "natural" topics and vehicles and should permit a separation of the MTT into symmetrical and asymmetrical metaphors. A detailed description of this research can be found in Connor and Kogan (1980).

An alternative to the foregoing research strategy is the use of direct similarity scaling in which potential topics and vehicles are used either as "focal" or "comparison" stimuli. Rosch (1975) and Tversky (1977) have shown that in comparisons of the form "_____ is like _____", the less salient object is placed in the first blank and the more salient object in the second (the referent). The bridge to metaphor is provided by Verbrugge and McCarrell (1977), who found that the ground of a metaphor bore a closer relation to its vehicle than to its topic. Hence, in the context of Tversky's model, the vehicle should be the more salient of the two terms. It should then follow that the distance between the vehicle as "focal" stimulus (referent) and the topic as "comparison" should be smaller than the distance between the topic as "focal" and the vehicle as the "comparison" stimulus.

Additional consequences for cognitive processing flow from the model already outlined. If the vehicle is in fact more salient, the metaphoric similarity should be recognized faster and more frequently when the vehicle is presented first and the topic second (in comparison with the reversed sequence). Naturally, these predictions should hold only for asymmetrical metaphors, because topic and vehicle designations are essentially arbitrary in the case of a symmetrical metaphor.

A final direction for future research on the cognitive processing of metaphors is to explore the contextual influence of topic and vehicle upon each other. There is a considerable likelihood that the presence of the vehicle leads to a different view of the topic than would be the case for the topic in isolation. In other words, qualities inherent in the vehicle may be transferred to the topic. The use of appropriate adjective-rating scales for topic and vehicle, for the topic and the nonmetaphoric member of the triad, and for the vehicle and the nonmetaphoric member of the triad should permit fairly accurate specification of the contextual effects in the topic–vehicle relation.

As indicated earlier, the use of the pictorial items of the MTT limits generalization. It is essential that a verbal MTT be developed so that we can achieve a better appreciation of the similarities and differences between visual and verbal metaphors in respect to cognitive processing. It should be noted in this connection that all of the projected research described earlier will be carried out with both the pictorial MTT items and a newly constructed verbal MTT.

It is obviously too much to expect that the proposed future research will tell us all that we shall ever want to know about the cognitive processes underlying metaphoric thinking. It would be most surprising, however, if we failed to gain some additional insights into what a metaphor is and how it works. Armed with such information, the study of metaphor from the standpoint of individual differences, learning, and instruction could proceed with renewed vigor.

SUMMARY

In few fields of psychological endeavor can one find so large a gap between conceptual analysis and empirical research as in the case of metaphor. This gap has narrowed in recent years, as the scope of the research effort has increased. Most of the recent work, however, has concerned developmental changes in metaphoric comprehension and experimental tests of the linguistic processing of metaphors. The amount of research devoted to metaphor from a stylistic individual-differences perspective has been extremely limited. This chapter has considered metaphoric thinking as a possible cognitive style and has offered a new measuring instrument for its assessment. The Metaphoric Triads Task (MTT) consists of a set of pictorial triads, each of which offers three possible pairings; one of these is of a metaphorical character. Under instructions to form all possible pairs, a subject's score reflects the number of metaphoric pairings formed and the adequacy of the explanation offered for each such pairing.

The MTT has been administered to 12 samples of subjects with a mean age range from approximately 7½ to 28 years. Interjudge and internal-consistency reliability has proven to be highly satisfactory. A progressive improvement in MTT performance with age was noted, though a change in the task format succeeded in raising performance levels of children beyond those of peers 1 to 2 years older who were given the standard form of the MTT. Construct validation of the MTT was undertaken, and a number of hypotheses were confirmed. Thus, higher MTT scores were associated with high quality responses on divergent-thinking tasks, broad categorizing, and physiognomic sensitivity. Relationships with a diversity of intelligence and achievement tests were highly inconsistent. A pattern of associations between MTT scores and teacher's ratings of aesthetic sensitivity and figurative language usage suggested that the cognitive processes tapped by the MTT were relevant to certain kinds of classroom activities. Three experimental studies conducted with children 7½ to 9½ years of age indicated that metaphoric thinking could be enhanced (relative to control groups) by means of brief training procedures.

Educational implications of metaphor research were considered, with particular emphasis on the requirements for ATI studies. Cognitive processing aspects of the MTT were discussed in the context of a factor analysis of MTT items. The chapter concluded with a discussion of projected research on the topic–vehicle relation. It is expected that this new work will offer a sharp advance in our knowledge about the cognitive processes that underlie metaphoric thinking.

APPENDIX: SAMPLE METAPHORIC TRIADS
TASK (MTT) ITEMS

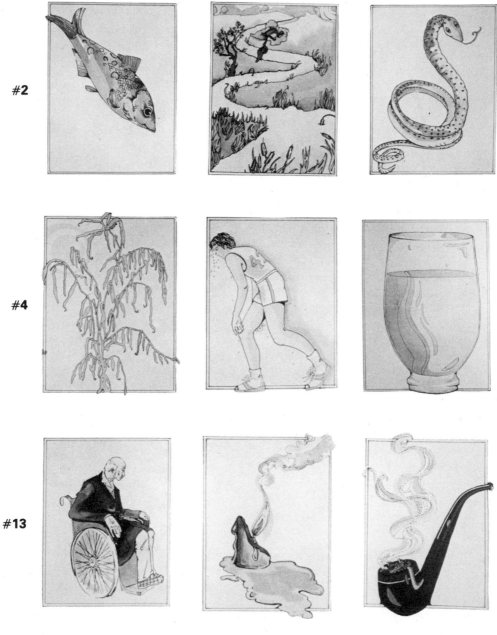

#15

#16

#27

ACKNOWLEDGMENTS

I should like to express my gratitude to Kathleen Connor, Augusta Gross, and Donald Fava for their invaluable assistance in carrying out much of the research described in this chapter.

REFERENCES

Achenbach, T. M. Cue learning, associative responding, and school performance in children. *Developmental Psychology,* 1969, *1,* 717–725.

Arnheim, R. The Gestalt theory of expression. *Psychological Review,* 1949, *56,* 156–171.

Asch, S. E. *Social psychology.* Englewood Cliffs, N. J.: Prentice-Hall, 1952.

Asch, S. E. The metaphor: A psychological inquiry. In R. Tagiuri & L. Petrullo (Eds.), *Person perception and interpresonal behavior.* Stanford, Calif.: Stanford University Press, 1958.

Billow, R. M. Metaphor: A review of the psychological literature. *Psychological Bulletin,* 1977, *84,* 81–92.

Brown, R. *Words and things.* New York: Free Press, 1958.

Bruner, J. S. The conditions of creativity. In H. E. Gruber, G. Terrell, & M. Wertheimer (Eds.), *Contemporary approaches to creative thinking.* New York: Atherton, 1962.

Bruner, J. S., Olver, R. R., & Greenfield, P. M. *Studies in cognitive growth.* New York: Wiley, 1966.

Caudle, F. M., & Kogan, N. *Instructional effects on divergent thinking: Attention deployment or experimenter demand?* Paper presented at the 83rd annual convention of the American Psychological Association, Chicago, September 1975.

Connor, K., & Kogan, N. Topic–vehicle relations in metaphor: The issue of asymmetry. In R. P. Honeck & R. R. Hoffman (Eds.), *Cognition and figurative language.* Hillsdale, N.J.: Lawrence Erlbaum Associates, 1980.

Cronbach, L. J. Coefficient alpha and the internal structure of tests. *Psychometrika,* 1951, *16,* 297–334.

Cronbach, L. J., & Snow, R. E. *Aptitudes and instructional methods.* New York: Irvington Publishers, 1977.

Davis, A. J. Cognitive styles: Methodological and developmental considerations. *Child Development,* 1971, *42,* 1447–1459.

Denney, D. R. Developmental changes in concept utilization among normal and retarded children. *Developmental Psychology,* 1975, *11,* 359–368.

Denney, D. R., & Moulton, P. A. Conceptual preferences among preschool children. *Developmental Psychology,* 1976, *12,* 509–513.

Fava, D. *Sensitivity to metaphor: Dimensions of individual variation.* Unpublished doctoral dissertation, Graduate Faculty, New School for Social Research, 1978.

Gardner, H. Metaphors and modalities: How children project polar adjectives onto diverse domains. *Child Development,* 1974, *45,* 84–91.

Gardner, H., Winner, E., Bechhofer, R., & Wolf, D. The development of figurative language. In K. Nelson (Ed.), *Children's language.* (Vol. 1). New York: Gardner Press, 1978.

Gardner, R. W., & Moriarty, A. E. *Personality development at preadolescence.* Seattle: University of Washington Press, 1968.

Goldstein, K. M., & Blackman, S. Assessment of cognitive style. In P. McReynolds (Ed.), *Advances in psychological assessment.* San Francisco: Jossey-Bass, 1977.

Gombrich, E. H. *Meditations on a hobby horse.* London: Phaidon Press, 1963.

Goodenough, D. R. The role of individual differences in field dependence as a factor in learning and memory. *Psychological Bulletin,* 1976, *83,* 675–694.

Hoffman, C., & Kagan, S. *Field-dependence–independence: Some methodological and conceptual criticisms.* Paper presented at the 85th annual convention of the American Psychological Association, San Francisco, August 1977.

Honeck, R. P., & Hoffman, R. R. (Eds.). *Cognition and figurative language.* Hillsdale, N.J.: Lawrence Erlbaum Associates, 1980.

Honeck, R. P., Riechmann, P., & Hoffman, R. R. Semantic memory for metaphor: The conceptual base hypothesis. *Memory & Cognition,* 1975, *3,* 409–415.

Hunt, D. E. Person–environment interaction: A challenge found wanting before it was tried. *Review of Educational Research*, 1975, *45*, 209–230.

Inhelder, B., & Piaget, J. *The early growth of logic in the child*. New York: Harper & Row, 1964.

Jakobson, R., & Halle, M. *Fundamentals of language*. The Hague: Mouton, 1956.

Johnson, M. G. A cognitive-feature model of compound free associations. *Psychological Review*, 1970, *77*, 282–293.

Kagan, J., & Kogan, N. Individual variation in cognitive processes. In P. Mussen (Ed.), *Carmichael's manual of child psychology* (Vol. 1). New York: Wiley, 1970.

Kagan, J., Moss, H. A., & Sigel, I. E. Psychological significance of styles of conceptualization. In J. C. Wright & J. Kagan (Eds.), Basic cognitive processes in children. *Monographs of the Society for Research in Child Development*, 1963, *28*(2, Serial No. 86), 73–112.

Klein, G. S. The personal world through perception. In R. R. Blake & G. V. Ramsey (Eds.), *Perception: An approach to personality*. New York: Ronald Press, 1951.

Kogan, N. Educational implications of cognitive styles. In G. S. Lesser (Ed.), *Psychology and educational practice*. Glenview, Ill.: Scott, Foresman, 1971.

Kogan, N.   Creativity and cognitive style: A life span perspective. In P. Baltes & K. W. Schaie (Eds.), *Life span developmental psychology: Personality and socialization*. New York: Academic Press, 1973.

Kogan, N. *Cognitive styles in infancy and early childhood*. Hillsdale, N.J.: Lawrence Erlbaum Associates, 1976.

Kogan, N., Connor, K., Gross, A., & Fava, D. Understanding visual metaphor: Developmental and individual differences. *Monographs of the Society for Research in Child Development*, 1980, in press.

Köhler, W. Psychological remarks on some questions of anthropology. *American Journal of Psychology*, 1937, *50*, 271–288.

Lamm, H., & Trommsdorff, G. Group versus individual performance on tasks requiring ideational proficiency (brainstorming): A review. *European Journal of Social Psychology*, 1973, *3*, 361–388.

Langer, S. K. *Philosophy in a new key*. New York: Mentor Books, 1948.

Malgady, R. G., & Johnson, M. G. Modifiers in metaphors: Effects of constituent similarity on the interpretation of figurative sentences. *Journal of Psycholinguistic Research*, 1976, *5*, 43–52.

Mednick, S. A., & Mednick, M. T. *Remote associates test: Elementary grades level*. Unpublished manuscript, 1962.

Messer, S. Reflection-impulsivity: A review. *Psychological Bulletin*, 1976, *83*, 1026–1053.

Messick, S. The criterion problem in the evaluation of instruction: Assessing possible, not just intended, outcomes. In M. C. Wittrock & D. Wiley (Eds.), *The evaluation of instruction: Issues and problems*. New York: Holt, Rinehart & Winston, 1970.

Messick, S. (Ed.). *Individuality in learning*. San Francisco: Jossey-Bass, 1976.

Ortony, A. (Ed.). *Metaphor and thought*. Cambridge, England: Cambridge University Press, 1979.

Ortony, A., Reynolds, R. E., & Arter, J. A. Metaphor: Theoretical and empirical research. *Psychological Bulletin*, 1978, *85*, 919–943.

Osgood, C. E. *Method and theory in experimental psychology*. New York: Oxford University Press, 1953.

Paivio, A. Psychological processes in the comprehension of metaphor. In A. Ortony (Ed.), *Metaphor and thought*. Cambridge, England: Cambridge University Press, 1979.

Pearson, P. H., & Maddi, S. R. The similes preference inventory: Development of a structured measure of the tendency toward variety. *Journal of Consulting Psychology*, 1966, *30*, 301–308.

Petrie, H. G. Metaphor and learning. In A. Ortony (Ed.), *Metaphor and thought*. Cambridge, England: Cambridge University Press, 1979.

Pettigrew, T. F. The measurement and correlates of category width as a cognitive variable. *Journal of Personality*, 1958, *26*, 532–544.

Piaget, J. *Play, dreams, and imitation in childhood.* New York: Norton, 1962.

Piaget, J. Piaget's theory. In P. H. Mussen (Ed.), *Carmichael's manual of child psychology* (Vol. 1). New York: Wiley, 1970.

Pollio, H. R., Barlow, J. M., Fine, H. J., & Pollio, M. R. *Psychology and the poetics of growth.* Hillsdale, N.J.: Lawrence Erlbaum Associates, 1977.

Rosch, E. Cognitive reference points. *Cognitive Psychology,* 1975, *7,* 532–547.

Rubinstein, B. B. On metaphor and related phenomena. In R. R. Holt & E. Peterfreund (Eds.), *Psychoanalysis and contemporary science* (Vol. 1). New York: Macmillan, 1972.

Saarni, C., & Kogan, N. Cognitive styles. In G. Steiner (Ed.), *The psychology of the twentieth century* (Vol. 7). Zurich and Munich: Kindler, 1978.

Sapir, J. D., & Crocker, J. C. (Eds.). *The social use of metaphor: Essays on the anthropology of rhetoric.* Philadelphia: University of Pennsylvania Press, 1977.

Schaefer, C. E. *Similes test manual.* Goshen, N.Y.: Research Psychologists Press, 1971.

Sigel, I. E., & Coop, R. H. Cognitive style and classroom practice. In R. H. Coop & K. White (Eds.), *Psychological concepts in the classroom.* New York: Harper and Row, 1974.

Stein, M. I. *The physiognomic cue test.* New York: Behavioral Publications, 1975.

Synectics, Inc. *Making it strange.* New York: Harper & Row, 1968.

Turbayne, C. M. *The myth of metaphor.* Columbia, S.C.: University of South Carolina Press, 1971.

Tversky, A. Features of similarity. *Psychological Review,* 1977, *84,* 327–352.

Verbrugge, R. Resemblances in language and perception. In R. Shaw & J. Bransford (Eds.), *Perceiving, acting, and knowing.* Hillsdale, N.J.: Lawrence Erlbaum Associates, 1977.

Verbrugge, R., & McCarrell, N. S. Metaphoric comprehension: Studies in reminding and resembling. *Cognitive Psychology,* 1977, *9,* 494–533.

Vygotsky, L. *Thought and language.* Cambridge, Mass.: MIT Press, 1962.

Wallach, M. A. Creativity. In P. Mussen (Ed.), *Carmichael's manual of child psychology* (Vol. 1) New York: Wiley, 1970.

Wallach, M. A., & Kogan, N. *Modes of thinking in young children.* New York: Holt, Rinehart & Winston, 1965.

Ward, W. C., Kogan, N., & Pankove, E. Incentive effects in children's creativity. *Child Development,* 1972, *43,* 669–676.

Werner, H., & Kaplan, B. *Symbol formation.* New York: Wiley, 1963.

Wheelwright, P. *The burning fountain.* Bloomington, Ind.: Indiana University Press, 1968.

Witkin, H. A., & Goodenough, D. R. Field dependence and interpersonal behavior. *Psychological Bulletin,* 1977, *84,* 661–689. (a)

Witkin, H. A., & Goodenough, D. R. *Field dependence revisited* (ETS RB-77-16). Princeton, N.J.: Educational Testing Service, 1977. (b)

Witkin, H. A., Moore, C. A., Goodenough, D. R., & Cox, P. W. Field-dependent and field-independent cognitive styles and their educational implications. *Review of Educational Research,* 1977, *47,* 1–64.

Zelniker, T., & Jeffrey, W. E. Reflective and impulsive children: Strategies of information processing underlying differences in problem solving. *Monographs of the Society for Research in Child Development,* 1976, *41*(5, Serial No. 168).

11 Discussion: Maps, Models, Methods, and Metaphors

Richard E. Snow
Stanford University

The four preceding chapters are insightful, provocative contributions. They take us from spatial reasoning through various forms of inductive and deductive reasoning to metaphoric comprehension. I cannot give a detailed critique, point by point; frankly there is little to be critical about. Instead, here are some general, hopefully integrative remarks. First, in keeping with my compulsion to map the correlational terrain, an attempt is made to fit the kinds of tasks described in all the chapters up to this point into the multidimensional space for cognitive reference tests shown previously (see Chapter 2, this volume). This mapping will, of course, be speculative—based as it is only on what correlations can be gleaned from the present chapters plus a few other sources. Following this, some common themes are identified, with discussion along the way of those details from each that seem especially noteworthy.

Figure 11.1 retains the dots and factor identifications of the earlier figure, though dropping the test names. Traced onto this are regions presumably close to where each researcher's tasks would fall had they been included in the correlation matrix and the subsequent multidimensional scaling.

Rose and Hunt have used mainly simple digital tasks with reaction time as the base measure. These seem closest to the kinds of tasks found in the perceptual speed (PS) and memory span (MS) clusters. Such tasks have shown some correlation with some verbal and quantitative ability tests, so their region cuts in closer here. Hunt (1974), of course, has also investigated the Raven Progressive Matrices Test, so his contour should have been drawn even closer. Frederiksen started from the same region, with tasks that seem similar to those tests requiring simple letter and word segmentations and transformations, but ended up showing substantial relation to the more complex language processing represented in

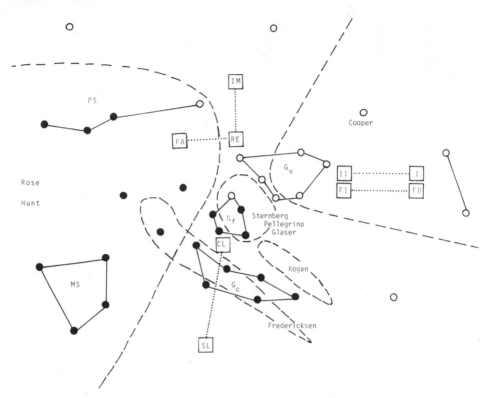

FIG. 11.1.   Multidimensional scaling of between-test correlations revisited (see Fig. 2.2) to suggest the regional reference of tasks used by authors of previous chapters and various cognitive-style theorists. (See text for symbol identification.)

reading and other crystallized ability (G_c) tests. Sternberg and Pellegrino and Glaser have chosen tasks straight from the center—series completion, analogies, and various other verbal and figural reasoning tasks. And their data yielded consistent relation to such tests and also to spatial reasoning tests. Kogan's metaphoric thinking measure showed some correlation with analogical reasoning and also with Wechsler similarities, so it is placed closest to those points.

Cooper has been working in the northeast region with various spatial and visual memory tasks. She distinguished two types of processing strategies (and individuals), labeled Type I and Type II. It may be convenient to distinguish such categories at this stage, but hopefully the typological idea can be replaced by a continuum as the work progresses. Her Type I appears to be a form of holistic parallel processing, whereas Type II is a dual analytic process. Thus, in my figure her distinction has been stretched between the more complex spatial tests in G_v, which are thought to represent more analytic processing, and those called "closure speed" (CS), which are thought to represent more holistic visual processing. She asked the question: ''What kinds of tasks might force a Type I strategy?'' My candidates would be tasks built on the closure speed model. These are object identification problems in which the subject sees only partially erased silhouettes or photographs of the objects. A word of caution is in order, however. A check of the history of such tasks should show that Thurstone had a clear, holistic process hypothesis in mind, and he designed the original task such that responses were judged correct only if they occurred within 3 seconds of stimulus onset; this ruled out attempts at longer, more analytic processing by the subject. But the group-administered, paper–pencil versions now available as ''Gestalt'' tests are total-timed, not item-timed; so time is available at the item level for analytic processing. This is an example of how good psychological hypotheses can be blurred inadvertently by moves to ''more efficient'' testing technology. An incidental footnote is that closure speed measures have correlated with hypnotizability (Lohman, 1978). Another is that hypnosis experiments have been used to demonstrate the existence of control processes in the cognitive system (Hilgard, 1977).

Another suggestion for Cooper is that Witkin's cognitive-style construct—called ''field independence–dependence'' and labeled FI–FD in the figure—should span the same region in almost the same way. Witkin (1973) has acknowledged that field independence is essentially identical to what seems to be measured by the Wechsler block design, object assembly, and picture completion subtests, and these typically fall into the G_v or G_f clusters. Kogan also implied that field independence was essentially analytical ability. But some of Witkin's data also suggest that individuals scoring low on his measures—who are thus field dependent—are often adept in social sensitivities and, notably, in memory for faces. This then is another candidate task to help bring out the kind of sensitivity to structure in visual patterns that may be represented by Cooper's holistic Type I processing. An added note here is that Dr. Ralph Kiernan, a neuropsychologist at Stanford, has gathered data suggesting that analytic and holistic strategies can be detected on Wechsler block design. Analytic approaches generally serve the individual better, but some items with simple designs are more readily solved by a kind of Gestaltic matching. In turn, there are potentially important connections between these block design performances and certain kinds of brain disorders.

Kogan (see also 1976) has categorized cognitive-style constructs as a function of their proximity to ability constructs. Two other notes about cognitive styles—at least those in Kogan's first and second categories—can be added in here, because these categories seem closest to the ability domain. Kagan's construct of reflection–impulsivity is shown in the figure as a two-pronged dimension, to pinpoint a confusion often ignored in work on this construct. The bivariate distribution of error and latency on Kagan's task often shows a triangular or rectangular form. Reflectives (RE) are subjects who are slow and accurate. Impulsives (IM) are fast and inaccurate. But there are also many subjects who are fast and accurate (FA) and some who are slow and inaccurate. The task is essentially a perceptual-speed matching test; so fast–accurate subjects are showing high perceptual-speed (PS) ability, whereas impulsives and slow–inaccurate subjects are showing low PS ability. Reflective subjects are probably using a slower, more analytic approach and hence are placed nearer to G_v and G_f in the figure. Finally, conceptual level or complexity—which is David Hunt's style construct (see, e.g., Hunt & Sullivan, 1974)—is measured in such a way that verbal abstractness is considered to indicate a complex level of processing (CL), whereas a simple level (SL) is indicated by concrete responses. Conceptually, this dimension has to span the G_c region, and it is noteworthy that Hunt's data show that low-conceptual-level individuals do better with more structured instructional situations, whereas high-conceptual-level individuals do better with less structured instructional treatments. These findings are essentially replications, I think, of the $G_c \times$ IPI interaction discussed earlier (see Chapter 2, this volume).

One could locate still other constructs and tasks on the map and read off their hypothesized correlations with various neighbors. But the suggestions already given should be sufficient to make the point that one never studies an ability or style construct in isolation. In earlier days, and even today in some circles, investigators have been too quick to proclaim a new kind of individual difference, different in substance from all others. But we need to recognize that all these tasks are but models thrust as a sword into an underlying cognitive fundament that is undoubtedly more intricately structured than our crude measurements show. Some cognitive-style theorists and some cognitive processing theorists, as well as some factor theorists, have been particularly strongly fixated on proliferating new constructs and studying them in relative isolation. Fortunately, Kogan has given us a good positive example of how one goes about carefully designing, testing, and elaborating measures of newly hypothesized constructs.

Cooper, Pellegrino and Glaser, and Sternberg all take a multitask approach, with tasks chosen directly out of the kinds of test tasks that lie close to Spearman's g. These researchers are also sensitive to the importance of strategy choice and strategy shifts in a flexible conception of information processing. In my view, the Pellegrino–Glaser work is nicely complementary to that of Sternberg. Both take a componential approach. Pellegrino and Glaser recognize explicitly that processing success must be examined, not just processing speed. Latency on simple items does not by itself capture all, and perhaps not even most, of the psychologically important individual differences in processing. Sternberg also now shows that his models fit error data as well as latency data and seem to account for increasing complexity of processing. Both papers show that task models must become more complicated to account for the data. Additivity breaks down in some experiments, and the best-fitting equations turn out to include multiplicative and exponential functions. Additivity breaks down particularly as item complexity increases.

There is also evidence here and there in all of the papers that some kind of control or higher executive processes operate in many of these tasks. Pellegrino and Glaser talk about placekeepers and information management strategies provided by training. They also share a finding with Sternberg concerning the correlation between test and intercept parameters. Sternberg's interpretation (in his original work of 1977) of why his residual "preparation-response" component correlated so highly with reasoning ability tests suggests attentional, bookkeeping, and other possible control activities that may be involved. Cooper shows important strategy shifts as a function of rather special task characteristics, again implying some kind of control or monitoring.

Methodologically, there are a few other points to be made. The unique power of the componential approach initiated by Sternberg has been hailed elsewhere; I need not echo that. But some important extras have been added here. Pellegrino and Glaser add the importance of training studies to explicate the nature of the processing involved. Kogan also used training to suggest that deficiencies in metaphoric comprehension can be rather easily removed. This suggests perhaps that such deficiencies are "production deficiencies" of the sort shown by Flavell (1970) and also by Jensen and Rohwer (1965) in different tasks with children, rather than inabilities that are somehow permanent. Cooper shows the value of task variations focused on process differences, and it is certainly encouraging to see experimentalists plotting individual curves in such studies. This should become routine. Advances can also be expected from developmental analyses of individual differences in information processing. Sternberg has been doing developmental studies of reasoning. And Kogan also includes developmental data.

The eye-movement tracking methodology demonstrated earlier (see Chapter 2, this volume) may also be useful in further research to expose the kinds of process differences discussed in this book. Eye tracks may help distinguish among theoretical models that fit the error or latency data equally well. As a brief example, Fig. 11.2 shows eye tracks collected in our work with multiple-choice verbal analogy items. We used some model distinctions from Sternberg's (1977) earlier work, but it should be noted that the data were not collected to test Sternberg's theory in any direct sense. Recall that Sternberg posited a five-stage process for verbal analogies: encoding, inference, mapping, application, and response. In his Model I, each processing step is executed exhaustively on all features of the terms in an analogy before the next step is applied. Model II assumes that the application step is self-terminating rather than exhaustive; Model III considers both mapping and application steps self-terminating; and in Model IV all steps are self-terminating. We sorted our obtained eye tracks into categories representing the kinds of eye movements we might expect each model to produce. There were 144 tracks, representing 24 subjects' performance on each of 6 items. Figure 11.2 shows one archetypical eye track for each model and the percent of the 144 tracks that seemed similar to it. One track that seemed to indicate a mixture of two models and another that suggested a variation on Model I are also shown. Sternberg suggested in discussion that the mixed track might indicate inclusion of an optional justification step in the model. The distinction between Models III and IV was most difficult to make. When in doubt, the

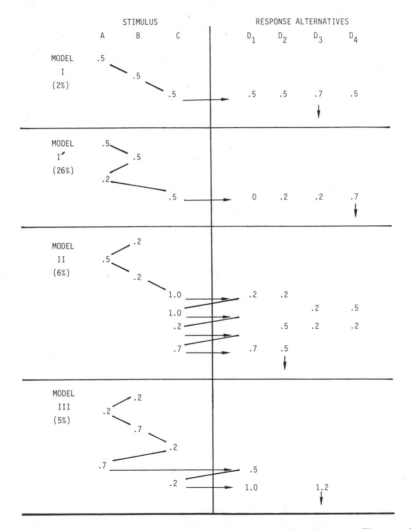

FIG. 11.2.   Eye movement tracks for six subjects on selected verbal analogy items. Time runs from top down in each track. Numbers indicate pauses in seconds. Movements among response alternatives are not shown. These tracks were selected to exemplify Sternberg's (1977) four models and some possible mixtures and alternatives. Percentages indicate how many of 144 tracks could be classified into each model category.

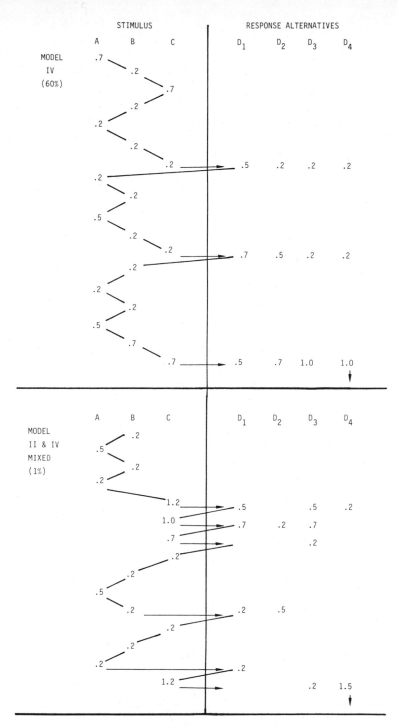

FIG. 11.2.   *continued*

sorting assumed Model IV was depicted. This probably inflated the percentage obtained for that model. Nonetheless, Model IV did appear to be the most frequently appearing eye track. Alternative Model I represents the next most popular pattern. This kind of track could indicate an inference-checking step, or perhaps it suggests that exhaustive encoding can be imperfect. Although these preliminary data cannot support particular conclusions, they do suggest that the methodology deserves further development.

There is a further and particularly important new suggestion from Pellegrino and Glaser that has both methodological and theoretical implications. If it is the case—as one might well suspect—that *no* truly basic processes can ever be identified, then the search for such a level is a reductionistic regress to infinity. Pellegrino and Glaser suggest that an important criterion for choosing an appropriate level of analysis is whether that level identifies *instructionally tractable* process components. Carroll (p. 144), in his discussion of algorithms, seemed also to be suggesting that that might be a more useful level for thinking about training and instruction. Related here, too, is the concern that tasks designed to isolate more and more "elementary" processes retain virtually no ecological validity as a base for generalization. I think a lot more attention needs to be given to this kind of criterion if cognitive process analyses are to end up serving instructional purposes, as of course the sponsors of this conference hope they will.

A final point in this discussion concerns visual-spatial imagery; some such phenomenon was referred to in all four of the preceding papers. Research on imagery has been of great interest in the last decade because demonstrations of its relevance to learning, memory, and problem solving have important implications for cognitive process theories—particularly, I would say, for theories about individual differences in processing (see e.g., Paivio, 1971). Visual imagery has been regarded as an ability akin to spatial ability, and spatial tests have been used to distinguish high and low imagers. It has also been interpreted as a cognitive style; there are self-report questionnaires dealing with vividness and control of imagery. It is not yet clear what relation holds between questionnaire measures and the spatial or other performance tasks discussed in preceding chapters. But the questionnaire measures have been related to learning from instruction, and a good example was identified recently for me by Marshall Farr. Johnson (1978) reported an Air Force study of procedural learning on an electronic control panel. The instructional treatments contrasted were: conventional practice on the panel; reproduction practice, in which photographs of the panel were used by the learner to practice drawing the sequence of control moves with a pencil; and blind practice, in which learners practiced reproducing the sequence of control moves without any record being left by drawing on the photographs.

To quote from the conclusions (Johnson, 1978):

These results indicate that the conventional [training] strategy is sufficient (or possibly superior) for the less vivid imager but that it is handicapping to the more vivid imager. Performance of low imagers was comparable to the performance of high imagers when the reproduction strategy was used. Furthermore, the mean performance of the reproduction strategy group was superior to the mean for the conventional strategy group. The resulting interaction, however, resulted in the relative performance being in the favor of the conventional strategy for the low imagers, but in the opposite direction for the high imagers. This also supports the contention that performance can be enhanced by matching the training strategy with the trainee's cognitive style [pp. 71–74, passim].

I have always thought that spatial imagery and visual metaphor, coupled with subsequent analytic reasoning processes, were at the heart of scientific and technical creativity. Certainly there is evidence for this in the introspections of Einstein and other notable theorists, and also of people such as Seymour Cray (described in the "News and Comment" section of *Science,* January 27, 1978), who reports that he visualizes the insides of a new and faster computer entirely mentally, then sits down and designs it. Certainly the writings of McKim (1972) on visual thinking in engineering design and of Arnheim (1969) on visual thinking in general also support the view that Kogan's work, particularly, is striking out toward a new and rich level of complex thought, and of cognitive theory.

But direct study of metaphoric thinking may also be dangerous to one's mental health. It forces us to face squarely the fact that all our theories and models and measurements are but metaphors at base—metaphors that we pursue, hoping dearly that they are apt. It thus seems fitting to close with a sobering thought, in the form of an old shaggy-dog story.

A youth sought guidance from an old hermit sage concerning the meaning of life. After pondering for some time, the wise man said to the boy: "Life is like a waterfall." The boy held this great thought through all his life's toils. Guided thereby, he achieved many worldly successes. Many years later, he returned to the sage to learn at last the true meaning of this phrase, which—despite his success—had always seemed just beyond his grasp. Faced with his question, the old sage thought for a moment, then said: "OK, so life isn't like a waterfall!"

Human beings are more complex than information-processing machines. Our theories about human beings must be more complex than information-processing models.

REFERENCES

Arnheim, R. *Visual thinking.* London: Faber & Faber, 1969.

Flavell, J. H. Developmental studies of mediated memory. In H. W. Reese & L. P. Lipsitt (Eds.), *Advances in child development and behavior* (Vol. 5). New York: Academic Press, 1970.

Hilgard, E. R. *Divided consciousness: Multiple controls in human thought and action.* New York: Wiley, 1977.

Hunt, D. E., & Sullivan E. V. *Between psychology and Education.* Hinsdale, Ill.: Dryden, 1974.

Hunt, E. B. Quoth the Raven? Nevermore! In L. W. Gregg (Ed.), *Knowledge and cognition.* Hillsdale, N.J.: Lawrence Erlbaum Associates, 1974.

Jensen, A. R., & Rohwer, W. D., Jr. Syntactical mediation of serial and paired-associate learning as a function of age. *Child Development,* 1965, *36,* 601–608.

Johnson, S. L. *Retention and transfer of training on a procedural task. Interaction of training strategy and cognitive style* (Rep. No. DJ-6032-M-1). Buffalo, N.Y.: Calspan Corp., January 1978.

Kogan, N. *Cognitive styles in infancy and early childhood.* Hillsdale, N.J.: Lawrence Erlbaum Associates, 1976.

Lohman, D. F. *Spatial abilities: Individual differences and information processing* (Tech. Rep. No. 8). Stanford University, School of Education, Aptitude Research Project, September 1978.

McKim, R. H. *Experiences in visual thinking.* Monterey, Calif.: Brooks/Cole, 1972.

News and Comment. *Science,* January 1978, *199,* 27, 404–407.

Paivio, A. *Imagery and verbal process.* New York: Holt, Rinehart & Winston, 1971.

Sternberg, R. J. *Intelligence, information processing, and analogical reasoning: The componential analysis of human abilities.* Hillsdale, N.J.: Lawrence Erlbaum Associates, 1977.

Witkin, H. A. *The role of cognitive style in academic performance in teacher–student relations.* Princeton, N.J.: Educational Testing Service, 1973.

12

Independent Process Analyses of Aptitude–Treatment Interactions

Robert C. Calfee

Larry V. Hedges
Stanford University

People differ in what they know, in how they learn, and in how they think; and hence they should differ in the types of instructional programs that provide them the greatest benefit and meet their needs most comfortably. This proposition, for all its reasonableness, does not find general support in the current literature (Cronbach & Snow, 1977; Labouvie-Vief, Levin, Hurlbut, & Urberg, 1977). These findings rest on an empirical base and on commonsense analyses of "aptitudes" and "treatments." Despite repeated calls for development of a more systematic theoretical base for research on instruction (Atkinson, 1976; Glaser, 1976), progress has been slow, and there has been some skepticism about the feasibility of general theoretical treatments of the problem (Snow, 1977).

We think that a theoretical analysis can be proposed that yields insight into aptitude–treatment-interaction (ATI) mechanisms, which provides guidance in the design and analysis of ATI studies, and which points to the application of ATI concepts in practice. The purpose of our paper is to sketch an outline of one version of such a theoretical approach.

LEARNING MODELS

One can distinguish models of learning and cognition on the basis of their assumptions about the learning process, and of their specification of the factors that affect learning. The simplest class of models—"minimum-assumption" models—assume that learning occurs as a function of the amount of time spent in study and practice. Little else may be stated as to the nature of the learning process or the factors affecting learning. For an idea of how far one can go with no more than this assumption, see the work of Smallwood (1962).

Input-Factor Models

Another class of models concentrates on the input factors that influence learning—the independent variables. Learning has been found to vary considerably as a function of the nature of the task, the teaching method, the instructional materials, the context of learning, and the character of the learner. The theoretical ideas that guide such research tend to be more or less heuristic. The methods of analysis—the analysis of variance, multiple regression techniques, and the general linear model—lead to a systematic and structured decomposition of the variance in student performance on a learning task. As Suppes (1974) has pointed out, these methods of analysis provide a largely unfulfilled opportunity for theory development in educational research. Research using input models has remained largely atheoretical.

In general, this line of research has led to mixed findings, with the result that serious questions have been raised about the potential for generalization. As just one instance, we can appreciate the disenchantment with the copious literature on discovery learning (Shulman & Keislar, 1966). We think this literature also illustrates why findings have been inconsistent; in the absence of theory, there is neither adequate definition nor clear guidance. The "factor" under investigation seems on the surface to be simple: Should students be taught in a rule-based expository fashion, or should they be provided the basic essentials and then be allowed to discover what they need to learn on their own? The effectiveness of the programs, despite the crude distinction being drawn, does seem to depend on the character of the students (Greeno, 1972). Low-ability students need to have principles made very clear, whereas higher-ability children are able to induce them on their own. As Cronbach and Snow discovered (1977; also cf. Snow's chapter in this volume), general verbal ability is a potent aptitude and not infrequently interacts with program factors.

Up until a few years ago, research in instructional factors was subject to a number of unrecognized shortcomings. Following what was conceived as the "natural science" model, it tended to rely heavily on the "Method A/Method B approach" (Cronbach, 1963/1964; Walker & Schaffarzick, 1974). An experimental treatment was applied to one group of students, and a control treatment to another group. Then measurements were taken, and a statistical test administered to see whether the two groups differed. Complex treatments cannot be adequately described by such a simple design. Crude and insensitive univariate measures provide poor indices of effects. And finally, the approach totally ignores individual differences and the possibility of interactions between treatments and individual differences.

The aptitude–treatment-interaction concept provided a way to incorporate individual differences into the input-factor research at a straightforward, empirical level of design. As noted earlier, this line of research, though an improvement over previous efforts, has not fulfilled its promise. Descriptions of treatments continue to be rather simplistic, and though we see greater sophistication in the analysis of aptitudes and match of aptitudes and treatments, common sense and heuristic wisdom remain the chief guideposts. Theoretical progress has been limited.

Process Models

We refer to the third major class of models as "process models." In the 1950s there was great activity in the development of stimulus-sampling-theory models of the learning process. The first models, the linear-difference equation models of Estes (1959) and Bush and Mosteller (1955), attempted relatively modest statements about the nature of the learning process. By the 1960s, Markov models were being developed that rested upon rather complex assumptions about the underlying process of learning (Luce, Bush, & Galanter, 1963). Though this category of models is capable of rich and varied characterization of human learning, and of demonstrated effectiveness in guiding the improvement of learning effectiveness (Atkinson, 1976), actual application of the principles remains quite limited (Calfee & Drum, 1978).

Recent years have seen the development of information-processing models. These models—which arose partly as a reaction against the "simple associative learning models" that preceded them—attempt to explain thought and learning by postulating a series of stages, each stage carrying out a particular cognitive function. The digital computer serves as an analogy; in the computer, the stages comprise such elements as a card reader for accepting information, a computer register for calculating, a memory core for storage, and a line printer for recording output information. Computer systems and the programs that perform computational operations are frequently described by flowcharts, and information-processing theorists turn to this format to express their ideas. These models have the capability to represent performance in a variety of skilled tasks, in our opinion, and they can provide a comprehensive theoretical framework for research on aptitude–treatment research—for the study of individual response to instruction. In the remainder of this paper, we attempt to support this proposition.

INDEPENDENT PROCESSES

In 1963, S. Sternberg pointed out the central importance of the concept of the *independence of stages* for the validation of information-processing models (Sternberg, 1969). Prior to Sternberg's paper, information-processing theorists felt relatively free to draw boxes and arrows to whatever degree of complexity and interrelations they felt necessary to describe a process. The models were heuristically interesting but were not really amenable to rigorous test.

These models would comprise testable statements, Sternberg argued, if for each stage or "box," the theorist had to specify a unique and well-defined set of factors that influenced the stage and a unique and well-defined set of response measures that represented the output of the stage. Sternberg was interested in a particular set of problems, memory and visual search, for which the measurement of latency was quite appropriate. Accordingly, he developed what was known as an additive-factor approach. If several sets of factors—each selected to influence a unique underlying independent process—were simultaneously varied, the prediction of the model would be additivity in the latencies; there should be no interaction among factors affecting different processes. The "no-interaction" restriction, coupled with the statistical power of the analysis of variance, put rigor into the evaluation of information-processing models. Theorists were still free to propose complicated models. Sternberg's point was that if every stage in the model was complexly related to every other stage, little understanding was likely to be gained from the model. Stage independence put limits on the extent of permissible complexity. The additive-factor analysis of stage independence has served as the basis for a large amount of laboratory research on perception, cognition, and problem solving, and we think it may represent one of the major breakthroughs in the last two decades for the understanding of human thinking.

In the 1970s, other investigators began to develop theoretical extensions of the independent process concept. Among other things, the extensions emphasized individual differences in information processing and the role of instruction in the growth of information-processing skills. One example is R. Sternberg's (1977) theoretical work on componential analysis. His work builds upon the "subtractive" approach to analysis of independent stages. He begins by designating the components or elemental information-processing operations for a particular task. The verification of the model proceeds by means of an intensive task analysis— the total task is partitioned into a number of subtasks, each of which involves a successively smaller set of components. The student then performs the entire series of interrelated subtasks. For instance, if two subtasks, A and B, require the same components except that subtask B involves one less component, then subtask B should be no more difficult than subtask A and, in general, should be easier. Using a combination of regression, factor analysis, and analysis of variance techniques, Sternberg examines the data for certain properties to be expected if performance is based on a simple combination of the underlying components.

Another approach to the problem has been taken by Calfee and his associates (Calfee, 1976; Calfee & Drum, 1979; Calfee & Elman, 1977) through an extension of S. Sternberg's original concept of independent processes. The basic concept is presented in Fig. 12.1. To determine whether or not two processes are independent, the theorist must specify the factors that uniquely influence each process and the performance outcomes that measure the operation of each pro-

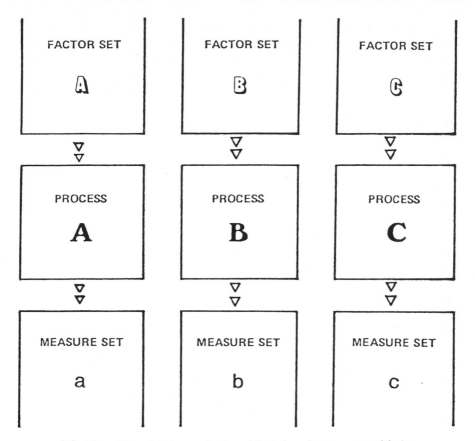

FIG. 12.1.   The original generalization of the independent process model. Associated with each component process is a set of factors and a set of measures, each assumed to be uniquely linked to the process. (After Calfee, 1976.)

cess. Figure 12.1 represents the simplest case of such a model; later in this chapter, a somewhat more complicated extension is considered. For now, we simply point out that this approach leads to multifactor/multimeasure designs as a way of identifying the independent processes that operate jointly to determine performance on a task. The approach relies very strongly on the analysis of variance technique.

The several independent process approaches share a number of features in common. First, they direct the researcher to relatively complex within-subject designs, where the potential complexity of the data is strongly constrained by the model. Where independence fails in a data set, the results generally point toward a testable reformulation of the model. There is a strong emphasis on detailed analysis of various sources of individual differences. As R. Sternberg has pointed out, such differences may occur because students use different processes to think, because different structural relations link the same basic set of processes, or because the parameters of operation of the models are different. The approach provides a structured framework for test design. The within-subject layout may be thought of as a "test." This way of thinking about the design leads naturally to an analysis of the reliability of patterns of performance, and to a novel method for establishing test validity. The researcher is led to include contextual and aptitudinal factors in the design of an assessment system, and to the analysis of aptitudes in terms of underlying processes. The investigator is provided guidance about proper scales of measurements [for example, what relations in the data should be expected from latencies (response time), from rating scales, from percentages or proportions, and so on?]. Finally, we believe that the approach provides a theoretical framework for a more useful analysis of instructional treatments. Examination of patterns of performance leads naturally to the design of "patterned treatments." Rather than define a treatment *in vacuo,* the curriculum developer can design treatment combinations that are modeled after the underlying processes. In some instances, instructional components provide a proper basis for specifying the cognitive processes: What the student is taught as separable chunks operate as independent processes in thought. For instance, reading instruction often is separated into decoding, vocabulary, and various aspects of comprehension. In these cases, it is reasonable to propose that these instructional activities produce independent processes in thought.

In the present chapter we elaborate and extend these general ideas. The chapter is conceptual—we present no data. We stress our own approach, but we could have easily built upon one of the other independent process approaches. Finally, we should make a point that is repeated: The independent process analysis of a task provides a baseline description of one way in which a person may think while carrying out the task. Other, generally more complex ways of performing the task can be imagined. Departures from a pure independent process model may be one of the more significant forms of individual differences. It is not clear to us at present how best to characterize such departures; for now, all we can say is that they are complex and hard to understand.

In Fig. 12.2 is our most recent version of a generalized independent process model. The model builds around a particular task of interest to the researcher (reading a paragraph, solving an anagram problem, deciding on a career, writing a computer program, and so on) and the set of underlying processes presumed to be the basis for performance of the task. It can be seen that in addition to independent processes (A through M), we propose the existence of general processes (N through S), which may influence the operation of other processes. We also propose that some performance outcomes may be composites (e.g., measure set $a \cdot b$), which reflect the joint operation of several processes.

What is required for a test of the model is that for each process identified in the model, a minimum set of factors and measures be specified for the design of a series of variations in the basic task. Each subject then performs the task several

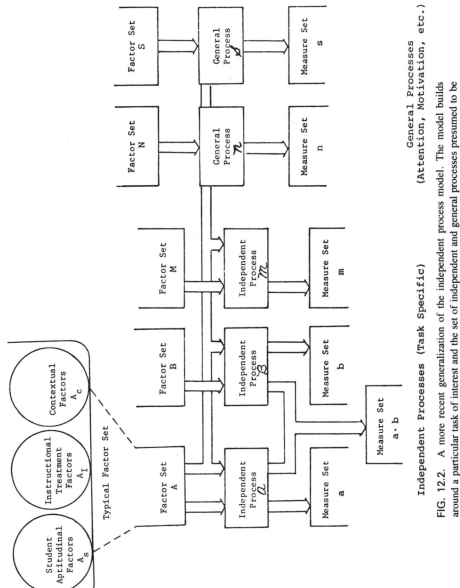

Independent Processes (Task Specific)

General Processes
(Attention, Motivation, etc.)

FIG. 12.2. A more recent generalization of the independent process model. The model builds around a particular task of interest and the set of independent and general processes presumed to be the basis for performance of the task.

times while the relevant factors are varied systematically. We have indicated the important categories of the factors to be considered in a typical factor set. These may include student aptitudinal factors, instructional treatment factors, and contextual factors. In much previous research, the unfortunate tendency has been to emphasize one or another of these classes of factors to the exclusion of others.

The principal prediction for validation of the model is that variation in the factors associated with a particular process should influence only the measures for that process. The occurrence of more complex patterns in the data is a sign either that the researcher has been imprecise or off the mark in describing the processes, or the factors, or the measures; or that the model is wrong.

The theoretical approach just described has a number of implications for ATI research. First, it provides a theoretical base for a broader conceptualization of ATI. Second, it leads the investigator to conceive of treatments and aptitudes in relation to common, underlying cognitive processes. We believe that the analysis will provide the framework for a richer and more enlightening examination of both treatments and aptitudes. We have previously criticized the single-treatment/single-aptitude design as too sparse to encompass the complexities of performance on any task (Calfee, 1974). Finally, the approach emphasizes the place of outcomes in the system. What the researcher discovers about the structure of performance on a given task depends on the choice of the treatment variations, the choice of the aptitudinal dimensions, *and* the choice of outcome measures. Aside from the ubiquitous influence of general verbal ability on learning and performance, the trend in previous ATI findings seems to be that ATI is most commonly observed only when there is a close link between treatment, aptitude, and measure—the essence of the independent process hypothesis.

An Independent Process Model for Reading

As a concrete example, we now show how the independent process approach can be applied to the assessment of a student's ability to decode and understand a word presented in isolation. The task we have in mind is a common one at the primary-school level. The student is shown a list of words selected to represent a particular "level of difficulty," generally based on frequency of occurrence in print. He or she is asked first to pronounce each word and then to demonstrate an understanding of the common meaning of the word. What mental processes must the student bring to bear on the task in order to perform successfully? How can a "test" be properly designed to measure these processes?

We begin with a description of the underlying processes. In Fig. 12.3 we propose an independent process model for test design that incorporates three processes—*attention, decoding,* and *lexical interpretation.*

First we consider the process by which the student attends to the task. This is a complex entity in its own right—which includes the overall level of activity, the extent to which the student selects relevant cues and rejects irrelevant informa-

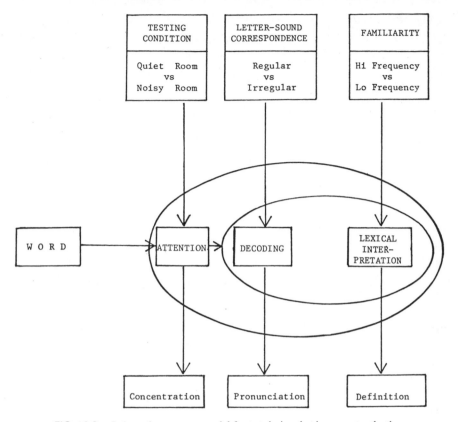

FIG. 12.3.   Independent process model for test design that incorporates the three processes. (After Calfee & Juel, 1978.)

tion, and the degree to which the student can concentrate the maximum available mental capacity on the task (Piontkowski & Calfee, 1979). For present purposes, we lump these into a single "box." We include this component in the model because it seems likely to influence the operation of the other two processes. For instance, learning disability specialists consistently identify attentional dysfunction as an important reason for reading failure (Ross, 1976). Incorporating this element in the design of the assessment system allows us to examine the pattern of attentional functioning for each individual student.

The second process, decoding, handles the translation of print into some equivalent of spoken language. Undoubtedly, there are subprocesses that handle specific aspects of the translation task, but for our purposes we consider these as an aggregate. We leave open the question of precisely how the translation is handled. It should be noted that students might have been taught to decode in different ways or might not have learned to decode at all.

The third process, lexical interpretation, allows the student to demonstrate that he or she can recall one or more common meanings of a word. Although this is a central process in reading and other language activities, it is not very well understood. Does the task we have described tap the same process that operates in normal reading? One may argue, and rightly so, that the student thinks in quite a different manner during the silent reading of connected prose than when he or she is shown a word in isolation and asked what it means. The point is well taken but not altogether relevant. Students perform both tasks while learning to read, and the high correlation between performance on the two tasks points to the importance of vocabulary in comprehension. Whatever the process of lexical interpretation in "normal" reading, it seems likely to have much in common with the "definition" task.

Once the processes have been specified, the next step in test design is to designate one or more factors—variations in testing conditions—that are likely to influence the operation of each process. An example of a potentially relevant factor is shown above each of the processes in Fig. 12.3. For instance, it seems to us that the operation of the attentional process should lead to better overall performance when the student is individually tested in a quiet room than when he or she is tested with a group in a noisy room. We also propose that regularity of the letter–sound correspondences of the stimulus words should affect the decoding process, and the familiarity of the words should influence the lexical interpretation process.

The design of the test calls for each student to be tested under all combinations of factors. Thus, in one set of situations, the student is taken into a quiet room and asked to pronounce and to define words from combinations of letter–sound regularity and frequency. The testing is then repeated with different words from the same design in a regular, noisy, crowded classroom.

Having specified variations that influence each process, we next need to find a way to measure the operation of each process. We recommend selecting the most direct measures possible. Thus, in this situation the tester might record the correctness of the *pronunciation* and *definition,* as well as the teacher's rating of the student's *concentration* on the task.

The purpose of the design variations is to measure the student's *relative* strengths and weaknesses under different conditions. This principle is akin to the clinical tester who, besides noting a person's *overall* intelligence test score, also considers the *difference* between the verbal and performance subtests (e.g., Searls, 1975).

The adequacy of an independent process model for a task is evaluated as follows. If a student's thinking fits the model, then variation in a factor will affect only the performance for the process associated with that factor. For instance, variation in decodability should influence only pronunciation; this factor should not affect either definition or concentration. There should be no crosstalk between factors and measures.

With this approach, one can readily see where a particular model is *not* fitting the data. For example, Mason (1977) found that the relative familiarity of words had an effect on pronunciation, contrary to the prediction of the model in Fig. 12.3. Such a failure in prediction could mean either that the familiarity factor was not precisely defined, that the decoding measures were not "clean," or that the model was wrong for some or all of the students. In fact, Mason found that variation in familiarity was partly confounded with letter–sound characteristics of the words, which may have been responsible for some of the cross talk. Juel's (1977) study of the same task suggests that the independent process model in Fig. 12.3 was more appropriate for higher-ability students. In her study, students whose reading was rated above average by the teacher read words and sentences in the analytic fashion described by the model. Children with below-average ratings read in a more complex interactive manner, with considerable crosstalk between factors and measures.

There is no reason why a single model should fit all children. The independent process approach provides a tool for detecting variations in the reading process from one student to another, a tool that should be useful in determining how the student's predispositions and the instructional program work together in the development of reading skill. The model in Fig. 12.3 is based on our analysis of how a child should read, given that he or she has received instruction stressing certain principles. Not all children are taught to read in this fashion, and not all who are taught acquire the principles.

A model may be wrong for a particular student or class of students because of the way they have been instructed or because of the way they choose to think in a particular context. We agree with R. Sternberg (1977) (and S. Sternberg, 1969, as well) that an important task in the analysis of individual differences is to discover methods that account for individual differences in the structure of how people think, a task that is quite different from the usual methods for measuring quantitative differences in the speed and accuracy of operations within a particular structure.

Incidentally, this illustration, which is based upon some of our early work, does not deal adequately with a number of matters that we now know require further work. For instance, we provide only a single model, and we do not describe any way of sorting out students on the basis of whether they fit one model or another. It provides no clear role for the operation of differential aptitudes; nor is the analysis of instructional components very sophisticated. The analysis of the processes is fairly gross, and more insight can be gained by a more detailed decomposition of the processes.

Though much work remains to be done, we think that the approach exemplified by the model in Fig. 12.3 has provided useful insight about the nature of the thought processes of beginning readers. Although this work opens the way to a clearer theoretical representation of these processes, it also has shown practical value for the design of assessment systems (Calfee & Calfee, 1977) and potential benefits for the development of instructional programs.

AN INDEPENDENT PROCESS PERSPECTIVE
ON APTITUDES AND TREATMENTS

An aptitude is an individual propensity in ability, preference, or style that gives rise to consistent differences in performance on a larger set of tasks. Included under the heading of aptitudes are the student's typical or preferential responses to different instructional treatments.

How can aptitudes be incorporated into the independent process approach? Our basic answer, as suggested earlier, is to analyze aptitudes in relation to the processes that underlie a task. There are at least three distinctive sources of individual differences in process models (also cf. R. Sternberg, 1977). First, individual students may use different component processes to perform a task; the nature of the component processes or the number of processes may vary from individual to individual. Second, the structure of information flow through the component processes of the model may vary; for instance, processes that operate independently for students with one level of an aptitude may operate interdependently for students at a different level. Third, the process parameters (such features as speed, accuracy, or quality of response) of each component process may vary from student to student.

Aptitudes, from this perspective, can be defined as consistencies in the information-processing models that most adequately describe how the student performs a set of tasks, or a consistent set of structural relations among processes, or a consistent set of processing parameters and correlations among parameters for a model. Such consistencies are frequently attributed to "the individual," and the debate has focused on heredity versus environment and on the interaction (or common variance) between these two. Without meaning to beg either the substantive or political questions in this contrast, we would like to emphasize the role of previous experience as a determinant of aptitudes. The way a student is formally introduced to reading, the degree of independence permitted and fostered in primary classrooms, the emphasis on collegiality in the first year of graduate school—all of these experiences may have a substantial and lasting impact on the individual's predisposition toward new opportunities to learn and perform.

An Illustration of the Independent
Process Approach to ATI

We now want to illustrate how an analysis of aptitudes might be carried out for a particular situation. Suppose the task is to read a passage, spot the important ideas, and remember them for a subsequent comprehension test. The emphasis, to begin with, is on a comparison between two instructional treatments—either the student is taught to "slow down" or to "slow down and look for ideas." In addition, the student is tested on the aptitude of impulsivity–reflectivity. Impulsive students tend to carry out tasks quickly and without sufficient thought, whereas reflective students are slower and more often successful in handling tasks. There is also evidence that impulsive students can be trained to slow down and to think about what they are doing. If such training is of extended duration, and if the student is provided guidance about how to use the time when he or she slows down, the training transfers to new situations—the student behaves more like a reflective individual (Egeland, 1974). We refer to instructions to "slow down," to "think," and so on as abbreviations for these more extended and comprehensive training programs; we have in mind more than the brief imperatives presented in quotes.

The results of a "made-up" experiment are shown in Fig. 12.4. There is an apparent aptitude-treatment interaction—within the range shown, the effects ordinally favor the more complex instruction; but the impulsive students benefit greatly from the more complex instructions, whereas the reflective students improve only slightly.

There are a number of ways in which we might proceed to develop an independent process model for this task. We propose the model in Fig. 12.5 as a first approximation. The model builds upon two independent processes that are directly linked to the jobs of finding ideas in the test and memorizing ideas. We also propose a general speed/accuracy process, which we think probably influences both the other processes.

The independent process approach now directs us to think about the instructional treatments as factors influencing the processes, and to think about the treatments in a more systematic manner than did the original "experimenter." In particular, we are led to consider the effect of the instructions on each of the

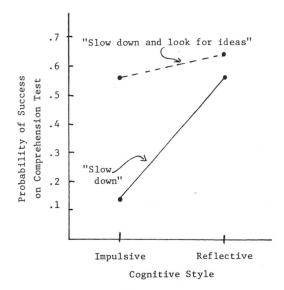

FIG. 12.4. Results of a fictitious experiment indicating benefits to impulsive and reflective students.

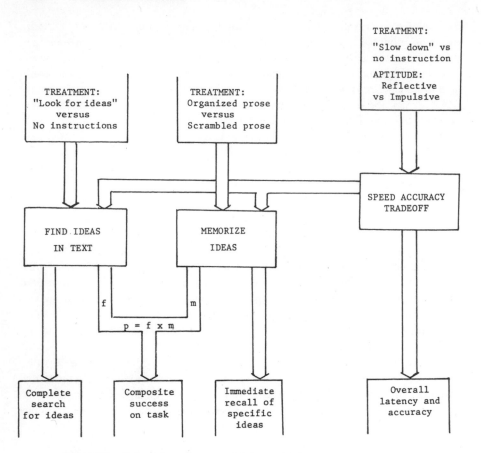

FIG. 12.5.   Independent process model that builds upon two independent processes linked for the tasks of finding and memorizing ideas. The speed/accuracy
process would influence both of these processes.

processes. Thus, the instruction to slow down should have primary impact on the
speed/accuracy process, and the instruction to look for ideas should influence
the find-ideas process. If we consider the complementary instructions in each
instance (no instructions to speed up or to find ideas), it becomes apparent that
the full design comprises the four combinations of two factors: A student can be
instructed to slow down or be given no such instruction; he or she can be directed
to look for ideas versus no such instructions. Thus the design in Fig. 12.5
provides information about only two cells out of the four possible. The other cells
would comprise: (1) a control condition with no instructions in either category;
and (2) instructions to look for ideas without instructions about speed. Without
these two additional cells, it is not possible to distinguish the effects of the
treatments according to their impact on the various processes. We are also led by

the independent process approach to consider variation in some factor that would affect the memory process; we have listed the use of organized prose versus scrambled prose as one such factor.

Figure 12.5 shows that the impulsivity–reflectivity aptitude should be placed in the factor set for the speed/accuracy process. The data on this aptitude are not as robust as one might wish, but it appears that there is a trend for certain people to be slower in approaching a task and other people to be faster. We have not attempted to consider student aptitude factors for the other two processes; our example will soon be complex enough. However, a fully adequate design would probably include factors of this sort.

You will notice in Fig. 12.5 that we have introduced measures for each of the processes and suggested that the overall probability of success in the comprehension task is a composite measure reflecting the joint operation of the two independent processes. We would propose to experimenters that for each task, they measure overall latency (the speed of response to each of the tasks performed by the student) and overall accuracy; these might be best calculated as averages over the several variations. We would also recommend some measure of the completeness of the student's search for ideas during the original study period, and a measure of his or her recall of specific ideas immediately after these had been searched for and found.

Figure 12.5 shows one proposal for how the composite measure derives from the two underlying independent processes. We assume that there are two underlying measures of success for the component processes; f is the likelihood that a particular idea is found in the text, and m is the probability that the idea is satisfactorily memorized. If the two processes are *statistically* independent on this combined measure, then the probability of success on the comprehension task, p, is the product of f and m.

We should emphasize the distinctions among statistical independence, process independence, and noninteraction. Statistical independence is obtained when a data set is compared to a statistical model. For instance, when proportions are the dependent variables, the natural assumption that the proportions are estimating probabilities leads to the conclusion that independence is multiplicative: If A and B are two multiplicatively independent events, then $P(AB) = P(A) \times P(B)$. The analysis of variance assumes that measures are additive, so that independence in this case is reflected in the extent to which measures are noninteractive: If A and B are two additively independent events, then $M(AB) = M(A) + M(B)$. When analysis of variance or regression techniques are applied to data without regard to the underlying statistical model, statistically significant interactions (or "noninteractions") may be observed that have little bearing on the degree of process independence for a given model. More generally, such findings may be of neither theoretical nor practical use, but reflect only a misconstruing of scales of measurement (Loftus, 1978).

In Fig. 12.6, we have shown data that might be generated by the complete

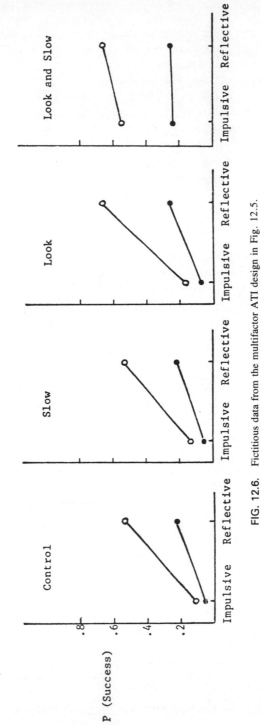

FIG. 12.6. Fictitious data from the multifactor ATI design in Fig. 12.5.

design. The dependent measure in this figure is the composite, p, the probability of success on the comprehension task. There are now eight treatments—the four instructional treatments and the two variations in prose. One could analyze this as a multifactor ATI design. The fact that several of the lines are nonparallel would appear to reveal a number of interactions, some of a fairly complex sort.

From our point of view, the more interesting questions have to do with the relation of the underlying parameters, f and m, to the treatment and aptitude factors. In Fig. 12.7, we show the set of parameters that were actually used to generate the data in Fig. 12.6. The only substantial source of individual differences represented in Fig. 12.7 is on the reflective/impulsive dimension. What we have represented in Fig. 12.7 is the finding that reflective students are only modestly affected by instructions either to slow down or to look; they already tend to be relatively slower than impulsive children and to use the time reasonably well. Impulsive children, on the other hand, find a few more ideas when they are told to slow down or to look but are most likely to find ideas only when they are told both to slow down and to look. The find-ideas process, in short, is influenced by the "speed/accuracy" and "find ideas" instructions in a complex way, depending on the student's aptitude. This complexity is permitted within the model, given the general nature of the speed/accuracy process.

The memory process is influenced in this example only by the factor that is directly related to the memory process and not by the speed/accuracy variation. These data are only illustrative, but our example reflects what is known presently about memory; impulsivity–reflectivity doesn't seem to have a very large affect on memory, given that students are equated in their ability to seek structure and organization in a collection of ideas. In summary, there are large individual

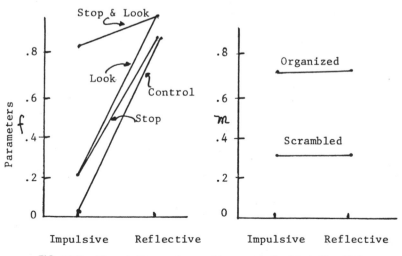

FIG. 12.7.   The set of parameters used to generate the data in Fig. 12.6.

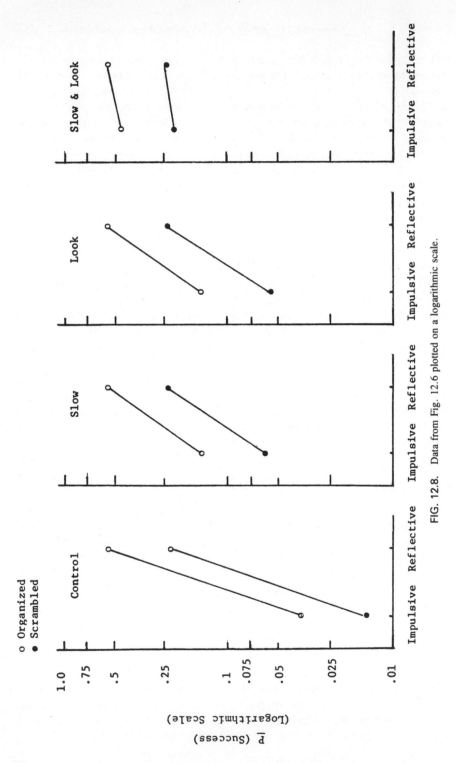

FIG. 12.8. Data from Fig. 12.6 plotted on a logarithmic scale.

310

differences in the f parameters as a function both of the instructional treatments and of the student aptitudes, but the m parameters are influenced only by the materials.

The underlying structure of the data becomes apparent when the probability of success is plotted on a logarithmic scale (Fig. 12.8). It can be seen, then, that the effects of the prose organization factor are constant over all combinations of the treatment and aptitude factors. Analysis of variance of the log $[P(\text{Success})]$ scores for individual students permits an evaluation of the independent process model in Fig. 12.5 for the composite measure of comprehension. (Recovery of the actual parameters in Fig. 12.7 is a more difficult matter, to be sure.) The other measures (latency, accuracy, search for ideas, and immediate recall of specific ideas) also enter into the evaluation. For instance, one would expect to find strong correlations between f and complete search for ideas, and between m and immediate recall of specific ideas if the task is performed as described by the model.

What might appear in the data that would lead to modification or rejection of the model? For one thing, the find-ideas factor could influence the m parameter, or the prose organization factor could influence the f parameter. Either of these findings would cast serious doubt upon the independence of the underlying processes and lead us to reexamine the basic formulation of the model. Complex interactions of this sort might also lead to a reexamination of the treatments. If the ''look for ideas'' training stressed the need to search for organization in prose, one might expect an interaction with the prose organization factor. Such a result is not undesirable per se, but an independent process analysis would lead the investigator to separate instruction on looking for ideas from instruction on the use of organizational structure in text.

We might mention, in passing, that alternative models are generated depending on the assumptions about the character of the processes and changes due to learning. The implicit assumption in the preceding discussion is that f and m are continuous ''strength'' measures. We might have developed the model around the notion that finding ideas and memorizing them are all-or-none events, as is the retrieval process. These assumptions lead naturally to characterization of comprehension as a Markov chain and to the independent process prediction that the parameters of the chain are influenced by specific factors in the design. Learning could be characterized in a variety of ways within this general framework.

CONCLUSION

Theoretical work in the absence of data has a beguiling fascination. The mind has a freer rein to consider ideas when it is not constrained by ''hard'' and uncertain facts. The data in our example are made to order for the model. One could argue with the assumptions underlying the model, as well as with the methods of analysis.

Nonetheless, we believe that the illustration points up a number of interesting possibilities for the examination of ATI effects, and shows the danger of the traditional "two treatment/one aptitude/one measure design." Such designs leave too many factors uncontrolled and provide little insight into the scale properties of the performance measures. We think that analysis of aptitude–treatment interactions in terms of the underlying component processes yields a deeper understanding of these phenomena, as well as providing potentially greater practical benefits.

REFERENCES

Atkinson, R. C. Adaptive instructional systems: Some attempts to optimize the learning process. In D. Klahr (Ed.), *Cognition and instruction*. Hillsdale, N.J.: Lawrence Erlbaum Associates, 1976.

Bush, R. R., & Mosteller, F. *Stochastic models for learning*. New York: Wiley, 1955.

Calfee, R. C. *Hunting the elusive ATI*. Paper presented to Convention of American Educational Research Association, Chicago, 1974.

Calfee, R. C. Sources of dependency in cognitive processes. In D. Klahr (Ed.), *Cognition and instruction*. Hillsdale, N.J.: Lawrence Erlbaum Associates, 1976.

Calfee, R. C., & Calfee, K. H. *Interactive reading assessment system (IRAS)*. Unpublished manuscript, Stanford University, 1977.

Calfee, R. C., & Drum, P. A. Learning to read: Theory, research, and practice. *Curriculum Inquiry*, 1978, *8*(3), 183–249.

Calfee, R. C., & Drum, P. A. How the researcher can help the reading teacher with classroom assessment. In L. B. Resnick & P. A. Weaver (Eds.), *Theory and practice of early reading* (Vol. 2). Hillsdale, N.J.: Lawrence Erlbaum Associates, 1979.

Calfee, R. C., & Elman, A. The application of mathematical learning theories in educational settings: Possibilities and limitations. In H. Spada & W. Kempf (Eds.), *Structural models of thinking and learning*. Bern, Switzerland: Hans Huber, 1977.

Calfee, R. C., & Juel, C. L. How theory and research on reading assessment can serve decision-making. In R. Beach & P. D. Pearson (Eds.), *Perspectives on literacy: Proceedings of the 1977 Perspectives on Literacy Conference*. Urbana, Ill.: National Council of Teachers of English, 1978.

Cronbach, L. J. Evaluation for course improvement. *Teachers College Record*, 1963, *64*. Also in R. W. Heath (Ed.), *New curricula*. New York: Harper & Row, 1964.

Cronbach, L. J., & Snow, R. E. *Aptitudes and instructional methods*. New York: Irvington Publishers, 1977.

Egeland, B. Training impulsive children in the use of more efficient scanning techniques. *Child Development*, 1974, *45*, 165–171.

Estes, W. K. The statistical approach to learning theory. In S. Koch (Ed.), *Psychology: A study of a science* (Vol. 2). New York: McGraw-Hill, 1959.

Glaser, R. Components of a psychology of instruction: Toward a science of design. *Review of Educational Research*, 1976, *46*, 1–24.

Greeno, J. G. On the acquisition of a simple cognitive structure. In E. Tulving & W. Donaldson (Eds.), *Organization of memory*. New York: Academic Press, 1972.

Juel, C. L. *An independent-process model of reading for beginning readers*. Unpublished doctoral dissertation, Stanford University, 1977.

Labouvie-Vief, G., Levin, J. R., Hurlbut, N. L., & Urberg, K. A. In pursuit of the elusive relationship between selected cognitive abilities and learning. In A. J. Edwards (Ed.), *Contemporary educational psychology*. New York: Academic Press, 1977.

Loftus, G. R. On interpretation of interactions. *Memory & Cognition,* 1978, *6,* 312–319.

Luce, R. D., Bush, R. R., & Galanter E. *Handbook of mathematical psychology.* New York: Wiley, 1963.

Mason, J. M. Questioning the notion of independent processing stages in reading. *Journal of Educational Psychology,* 1977, *69*(3), 288–297.

Piontkowski, D., & Calfee, R. C. Attention in the classroom. In G. Hale & M. Lewis (Eds.), *Attention and the development of cognitive skills.* New York: Plenum, 1979.

Ross, A. O. *Psychological aspects of learning disabilities and reading disorders.* New York: McGraw-Hill, 1976.

Searls, E. F. How to use WISC scores in reading diagnosis. *IRA reading aid series.* Newark, Del.: International Reading Association, 1975.

Shulman, L. S., & Keislar, E. R. *Learning by discovery: A critical appraisal.* Chicago: Rand McNally, 1966.

Smallwood, R. D. *A decision structure for teaching machines.* Cambridge, Mass.: MIT Press, 1962.

Snow, R. E. *Individual differences, instructional theory, and instructional design* (Tech. Rep. No. 4). Aptitude Research Project, School of Education, Stanford University, June 1977.

Sternberg, R. J. *Intelligence, information processing, and analogical reasoning: The componential analysis of human abilities.* Hillsdale, N.J.: Lawrence Erlbaum Associates, 1977.

Sternberg, S. The discovery of processing stages: Extensions of Donder's method. In W. G. Koster (Ed.), *Attention and performance II.* Amsterdam: North-Holland, 1969.

Suppes, P. The place of theory in educational research. *Educational Research,* 1974, *3,* 3–10.

Walker, D. F., & Schaffarzick, J. Comparing curricula. *Review of Educational Research,* 1974, *74,* 83–111.

13 Cognitive Learning Strategies and Dualities in Information Processing

Joseph W. Rigney
University of Southern California

INTRODUCTION

In this paper, I propose to review some general conceptual geography for the study of cognitive learning strategies, to describe several kinds of dualities of structure and/or function of the human information-processing system, and then to discuss some implications of one of these dualities for understanding and using cognitive learning strategies. This particular duality deals with the organization and control of processing operations. This is an old problem for psychology. If you take something apart to understand how it works, you should be able to put it back together again and make it work. My time as a graduate student happened to coincide with the golden age of factor analysis. I was taught that mental abilities soon would be identified and neatly classified in rectangular bins, and that combinations of factor-pure tests soon would be available for predicting real-world performances. Being rather slow-witted, I accepted this doctrine of the times, and I actually tried to use batteries of these tests on several occasions before I discovered that one good job sample test had more predictive power than a half dozen or so factorially derived aptitude tests.

The problem of putting the pieces together again is still with us. Although there still is widespread reluctance to face it, it is being addressed by some information-processing theorists, who recognize that the elements of the new mental chemistry—which we now call cognitive primitives or basic processing operations or schemata—must somehow be organized and controlled (e.g., Frederickson, 1978; Hunt, 1978; Schneider, 1978; Sternberg, 1978).

Because my interest here is in the implications of this problem for cognitive learning strategies, I present what seems to me a reasonable view of cognitive control of cognitive processes, suggested by evidence in the current literature of cognition, as well as by some data from my laboratory. Nevertheless, what I have to say about this is speculative and is intended to provoke further thought and discussion. Before presenting my view of control processes, I want to summarize a way of thinking about the nature of cognitive learning strategies and how they might be taught.

SOME CONCEPTUAL GEOGRAPHY

It is misleading to treat cognitive learning strategies as distinct from the cognitive processing strategies that function while we are just fuzzing around, going about our daily lives. We can identify special tricks—such as the method of Loci—or the keyword list, or bizarre mental imagery that can be used to improve memory temporarily. However, the events of daily experience stimulate us to develop coping mechanisms that are also rich sources of cognitive learning strategies. The requirement that one learns to speak one's native language is an example. I prefer not to make a sharp distinction between cognitive learning strategies and cognitive processing strategies in general. Rather, I acknowledge that some processing strategies can be more effective than others for facilitating acquisition, retention, and retrieval for particular subjects and particular subject matter, given particular objectives in particular situations. According to this view, cognitive learning strategies are a fuzzy subset of the universe of cognitive processing strategies. Both govern mental processing operations that the individual performs. Both sometimes are accompanied by overt motor operations, such as verbalizing, drawing, note taking, and the like.

A cognitive learning strategy can be thought of as a form of orienting task that implicitly or explicitly prescribes certain uses of processing resources, together with a statement of the learning objective or objectives to be attained by this processing. Its general form might be thought of as: "Process this information in this way to attain this learning objective more effectively." It is useful to think of these orienting tasks as being communicated in three ways: by instructions, by questions, or by content structures. In Bower's (1972) studies of verbal learning and mental imagery, one may find examples of instructions to students to form bizarre mental images in which to embed paired associates, so that they may be remembered better. In Collins' (1976) version of the Socratic method, one may find an extensive catechism of questions designed to drive the subject's information processing in certain directions. In the subject matter of training and education, one may find numerous examples of content structured to force the student to perform certain processing operations. (Most drill and practice materials are so organized.) There are varying degrees of explicitness in instructions, questions, and content structures with regard to processing operations and goals. Content structures tend to be the least explicit, often assuming

Explicitness of Cognitive Strategy	Control Over Cognitive Strategy	
	Self-Assigned	Externally Assigned
Detached	A	B
Embedded	C	D

FIG. 13.1.   Four conditions for using cognitive learning strategies.

that the student understands the processing implications of the structures. However, even the most explicit orienting task does not describe all the cognitive processing that it triggers off.

Cognitive learning strategies can be self-assigned by the student, or they can be assigned to the student by an external agency such as an instructor, an instructional system, or content structures. The student may ignore or modify externally assigned cognitive strategies, so that the processing that actually goes on may be some mixture initiated from both sources.

These two variables—relative explicitness and source of assignment—define four situations, illustrated schematically in Fig. 13.1. In A, the student decides to use a particular strategy, which he can describe to himself, on some subject matter. For example, a Naval aviator may decide to rehearse mentally some emergency procedure—say, a sequence of actions to counter the effects of wind shear during final approach.

In B, the strategy is externally assigned by being explicitly described. For example, an investigator studying the effects of mental imagery on recall of verbal material may instruct her experimental group to think of mental images to represent sentences. In C, the student uses a strategy that is already well learned and that may be intimately bound up with the nature of the task. The student probably is not aware either of the nature of the strategy or of the fact that he has assigned it to himself. This is discussed in more detail later. Finally, the combination represented by D very commonly occurs in training and education as a consequence of the special arrangements of content structures. Again, the student is not necessarily aware of the processing strategies involved. Different combinations of A, B, C, and D might be used during instruction; for example, in a course to teach problem-solving strategies, B might be followed by A.

Cognitive learning strategies vary in generality of application. Mental imagery can be used widely, for tasks as diverse as enhancing the recall of paired associates and facilitating the recall of complex performances. Or strategies may apply only to one class of problems, as illustrated by this example from Becker's (1977) description of the Direct Instructional Model used in Project Follow Through:

Problem-solving rules consist of sequences of operations that can be used to solve problems of a particular type. After having been taught some element of the problem set, students should be able to do any element. Assuming, for example, that the concepts equal and plus have been taught, as well as symbol identification and making lines for numbers, addition problems of the kind shown below can be taught using Rules 1–4.

$$2 + 4 = \square$$
$$\text{II} \quad \text{IIII}$$

Rule 1. Find the side to start on. (That side cannot have an unknown).
Rule 2. Make lines for each number on that side.
Rule 3. Count the lines.
Rule 4. Make the sides equal by placing the number counted in the box on the other side.

By teaching one additional skill, counting from-a-number-to-a-number, the students can also do problems of the form shown in the equation below.

$$2 + \square = 6$$
$$\text{IIII}$$

Rule 1. Find the side to start on.
Rule 2. End up with the same number on the other side by saying the first number "two" and counting to 6, making a line under the box for each count.
Rule 3. Count the lines under the box and write the number in the box [p. 532].

Cognitive learning strategies may vary in the scope of content affected. Advance organizers derived from skimming a block of text could conceivably facilitate recall of the gist of several pages. On the other extreme, some mnemonic tricks may be specific to one item of information, such as the height of Mount Fujiyama, or a person's name.

Finally, cognitive learning strategies may vary in the complexity of goals and orienting tasks. In my laboratory, we are investigating both simple elaborative strategies and complex self-directing strategies entailing many interrelated goals and tasks. We find it useful to use schema theory to represent knowledge structures in long-term memory (LTM) that we want to result from teaching these complex strategies. The following is a schema-theory description (Munro, Rigney, & Crook, 1978) of such a knowledge structure, which we hope exists in students' LTMs as a consequence of a course of training in becoming more self-directed in acquiring the information needed to fulfill job performance requirements:

In schema-theory terms, the knowledge that subjects acquire as a result of the training described elsewhere in this report is best represented in terms of a *prescriptive schema*. A prescriptive schema is a conceptual structure, which, when activated, gives people the impression that they are giving themselves instructions. Prescriptive schemata are responsible for the effects that we attribute to "self-direction strategies." The set of schemata that students acquire from our training program is an abstract conceptual structure with considerable scope. (The uses of the terms "abstractness" and "scope" with respect to schemata are discussed in Munro & Rigney, 1977). Here are the hypothesized schemata that we believe students acquire as a result of their training.

(1) SELF-DIRECTED-LEARNING (TASK)
　　　 is when
　　BUILD-GOAL-STRUCTURE (TASK)
　　TASK-PURSUE (TASK)
　　　 end.

(2) BUILD-GOAL-STRUCTURE (TASK)
　　　 is when
　　ANALYZE (TASK, for OBJECTIVES (TASK))[1]
　　PREREQUISITE-SEARCH (for EACH (OBJECTIVE), in OBJECTIVES)
　　PREREQUISITE-SEARCH (for EACH (OBJECTIVE), in CONTENTS)
　　　 end.

(3) TASK-PURSUE (TASK)
　　　 is when
　　EXAMINE (GOAL-STRUCTURE)
　　UNTIL (CHECKED (EVERY (OBJECTIVE)), PURSUE (OBJECTIVE))
　　TASK-ATTEMPT (TASK)
　　　 end.

(4) TASK-ATTEMPT (TASK)
　　　 is when
　　IF (DO (TASK), then QUIT, else SELF-DIRECTED-LEARNING (TASK)
　　　 end.

(5) PREREQUISITE-SEARCH (for GOALS, in SUBGOAL-SET)
　　　 is when
　　FOR-EACH (MEMBER, of SUBGOAL-SET,
　　　　 IF (PREREQUISITE (MEMBER, for GOAL),
　　　　 then (SPECIFY-DEPENDENCY (MEMBER, to OBJECTIVES-
　　LIST))))
　　　 end.

(6) PURSUE (GOAL)[2]
　　　 is when
　　FOR-EACH (SUBGOAL (NECESSARY (SUBGOAL, to GOAL)), in
　　GOAL-STRUCTURE,
　　　　 WHILE (ANY (UNSATISFIED (SUBGOAL' (NECESSARY (SUB-

---

[1]The ANALYZE sub-schema has not yet been represented. How people are able to discover the prerequisites or component actions of a task is not well understood.

[2]This structure is a variant of Rumelhart & Ortony's (1977) schema for TRYing, a subschema of their PROBLEM-SOLVING schema.

```
    GOAL', to
        SUBGOAL)))),
            PURSUE (SUBGOAL'))
        TRIAL (SUBGOAL))
        end.
(7) UNSATISFIED (GOAL)
        is when
    NOT (CHECKED (GOAL))
    NOT (ELIMINATED (GOAL))
        end.
(8) TRIAL (GOAL)
        is when
    ATTEMPT (GOAL) to ATTEMPT (ACTION, of GOAL)
    EVAULATE (GOAL)
        end.
(9) EVAULATE (GOAL)
        is when
    IF (NECESSARY (GOAL, to HIGHER-GOAL),
        then IF (SATISFIED (GOAL), then CHECK (GOAL),
            else TASK-PURSUE (TASK)),
        else ELIMINATE (GOAL, from GOAL-STRUCTURE))
        end.
(10) ATTEMPT (GOAL)
        is when
    IF (BELIEVE (CAUSE (ACTION, SATISFIED (GOAL))),
        then DO (ACTION),
        else when SUCCEED (PREREQUISITE-SEARCH (for GOAL)),
            ATTEMPT (PREREQUISITE (GOAL)))
        end.
```

According to the first of these schemata, the student believes that the way to achieve a task through self-directed learning is first to build a goal structure and second to pursue the task, using that goal structure. The second schema listed above describes what is involved in building a goal structure. One analyzes a task for objectives (subgoals necessary for the performance of the task), then one searches for prerequisite relationships among these objectives, between the available information resources. However, the schema does not contain explicit reference to the process of adding these relationships to the goal structure, because the goal structure is constructed for the student by the program that aids him or her in self-directed learning. The fifth schema listed above is an essential part of the goal-structure-building schema, since it specifies how the search for prerequisites is conducted.

The second major part of self-directed learning, after building a goal structure, according to the above schemata, is to pursue the task. The third schema above gives the top-level structure for task pursuit. One examines the newly constructed goal structure first; then one pursues the objectives included in that goal structure until every one of them has been checked. (Checking is the process by which a student marks the attainment of a subgoal, using the aids program on PLATO). When all the necessary objectives have been checked, the student attempts the task. If the attempt fails (see schema #4), then he begins the self-directed learning process again, reconstructing or modifying the goal structure.

The pursuit of objectives is governed by the sixth schema given above. This is a recursive procedure that traces down dependency relationships in the goal structure. When a goal is found that has no prerequisites, that goal is subjected to a trial. This means (see #8, 9, & 10) that the student does an action to bring about the goal and then evaluates the results of that action. If the goal is satisfied, he checks the goal and then pops back to the appropriate point in the procedure that is pursuing an objective. If it is not satisfied, he looks for a new way to pursue his overall task. If the attempt reveals that the goal was unnecessary to the attainment of its higher goal, then it is dropped from the goal structure.

The above schemata constitute working hypotheses about the nature of the conceptual changes brought about by training in the self-directed learning aids program discussed above.

The prose explanations of these schemata, above, emphasize the way in which these schemata call each other in a top-down, conceptually-driven processing mode. Naturally, there is also a bottom-up, data-driven aspect to the activation of these schemata in normal circumstances. For example, when a student finds that he has satisfied a goal (say, as a result of reading one of the relevant information resources), this activates the sub-schemata in the fourth line of the ninth schema presented above. The activation of these subschemata (IF (SATISFIED (GOAL), then CHECK (GOAL, . . .) activates, in a data-driven fashion, its "parent" schema, EVALUATE. The activation of EVALUATE, in turn, can activate the schema that calls *it*, and so on, so that activation spreads in an upward as well as a downward direction [pp. 27–32].

In summary, Fig. 13.2 lists general categories of variables in the conceptual map. Obviously, different combinations of these variables are possible and would lead to different forms of implementation and different outcomes. I might say that I feel least comfortable with the classification of information types I have presented. I know these kinds of information exist, but other kinds may also exist; and other structural features may be more important from the standpoint of the cognitive processes that transform information into knowledge. Several laboratories, including mine (Gordon, Munro, & Rigney, in preparation), are studying informational structures for different kinds of texts, including story grammars (such as those studied by Mandler & Johnson, 1977; Rumelhart, 1975; Thorndyke, 1977). The general idea is that something like these metasentential structures may exist as acquired knowledge in long-term memory and may contribute to conceptually driven processing when different types of textual information are encountered, thereby facilitating comprehension and recall.

Processing Resources	Orienting Tasks	Subject Matter

Representational:
    Perceptual
    Imaginal
    Verbal
	Communication:
	    Instructions
	    Questions
	    Content Structures
		Information:
		    Narrative
		    Explanation
		    Representation
		    Prescription

Procedural:
    Processing
    Meta-Processing:
        Selectional:
            Attention
            Intention
    Self-directional:
        Self-programming
        Self-monitoring
	Location:
	    Preceding
	    Embedded
	    Following
	
	Generality
	Scope
	Complexity
		Performance:
		    High or low
		    Semantic/
		    High or Low
		        Motor

Technology:
    High
    Intermediate
    Low
	Implementation
	Populations:
	    Children
	    Adults
	    Special
		Environment:
		    Schools
		        Conventional
		        CMI
		        CBI
		    OJT

FIG. 13.2.   Some conceptual geography for cognitive strategies.

DUALITY IN THE HUMAN INFORMATION-PROCESSING SYSTEM

I would like to turn now to another province of this conceptual map. This involves some aspects of the functional organization of the human information-processing system suggested by recent research, which should influence our understanding and teaching of cognitive learning strategies.

Evidence exists for (at least) four kinds of duality in this system. One kind is the lateralization of cerebral functions, chiefly the concentration of language functions in the left hemisphere and the localization of nonlanguage functions in the right. Bogen (1975), Gazzaniga (1967), Hellige and Cox (1976), and Nebes (1974) have described some tantalizing functional differences and interrelationships between the two cerebral hemispheres.[3]

---

[3]We are just at the beginning of the lateralization story. It is likely to be long and complex. Broadbent (1974) has argued against simple hemispheric specialization models. He has claimed that for complex decisions and for input–output stages, man functions as a single-channel organism. He pointed out that simultaneous performance of two tasks with known hemisphere differences should be better than indicated by current experimental evidence. Hardyck, Tzeng, and Wang (1978) argued that:

Cerebral lateralization experiments are detecting only a memory process occurring after subjects

Lateralization may be responsible for a second kind of duality, the dual encoding system—imaginal and linguistic—proposed by Paivio (1974) and others. The extent to which imagery and language are separate systems or simply aspects of the same system is debatable. Jerison (1973) concluded, in his account of the evolution of the human brain, that language evolved primarily to evoke cognitive imagery:

> The quality of language that makes it special is less its role in social communication than its role in evoking cognitive imagery, and I suggest that it was this kind of capacity that was evolving in the early hominids. . . . It was for this kind of capacity that central neural structures that involved visual, auditory, tactile, and motor units (including motor systems of the tongue and larynx) had to become more elaborate, and it was appropriate that the structures, the ''speech'' areas, evolved at an anatomical position near the confluence of the primary or secondary areas associated with the central neural representation of these modalities in other anthropoids [p. 427].

A third kind of duality is the duality of the self. There are two selves—one a ''doer'' and the other a ''watcher'' of the first. The watcher gives orders, monitors performances, and rewards or punishes the doer. It appears that the watcher also can berate, deprecate, devaluate, or otherwise punish the doer, causing the doer great misery. There is an interesting clinical literature about the resulting mental health problems and techniques for treating them (Kanfer & Goldstein, 1975; Spielberger, 1977).

In my laboratory, we are attempting—through the duality of the self—to teach students to be more self-directed in their learning in the context of acquiring just the knowledge they need to meet some job performance requirement. As this study is described in detail elsewhere (Munro, Rigney, & Crook, 1978), I do not discuss it here. However, the duality of the self obviously is important in the organization and control of processing.

Finally, there is a fourth kind of duality of the human information-processing system that seems to me also to have fundamental implications for understanding or for teaching cognitive learning strategies. I have tried a number of ways to

---

have learned all the stimuli to be presented. When new stimuli are presented on each trial, no cerebral lateralization effects are found, suggesting that active ongoing cognitive processing is independent of lateralization [p. 56].

Molfese (1978) recorded auditory evoked potentials from the left and right hemispheres of 16 adults during a phoneme identification task. He concluded that:

> Although there is a great deal of ambiguity as to the actual functions of the brain processes identified in the present study, one point appears remarkably clear: prior notions of hemispheric differences which insist that only the LH is involved in the processing of language related materials must be seriously questioned, if not rejected. Both hemispheres actively responded to speech materials. In some cases, both were involved in similar operations—while in others—the two hemispheres processed the material in quite distinct ways [p. 33].

characterize this duality, none of them altogether satisfactory, so I use one that is used in the current literature and refer to it as the duality of conscious and unconscious processing. Posner and Snyder (1975), La Berge (1975), and Mandler (1975) have discussed this duality in some detail. Mandler (1975) described five adaptive functions for consciousness:

1. The first, and most widely addressed function of consciousness considers it as a scratch pad for the choice and selection of actions systems. Decisions are made often on the basis of possible outcomes, desirable outcomes, and appropriateness of various actions to environmental demands. Such a description comes close to what is often called "covert trial and error" behavior in the neobehaviorist literature. This function permits the organism more complex considerations of action-outcome contingencies than does the simple feedback concept of reinforcement, which alters the probability of one or another set of actions. It also permits the consideration of possible actions that the organism has never before performed, thus eliminating the overt testing of possible harmful alternatives. In this sense the process is similar to the TOTE system of Miller, Galanter, and Pribram (1960).

2. Within the same general framework as the first function, consciousness is used to modify and interrogate long-range plans, rather than immediate-action alternatives. In the hierarchy of actions and plans in which the organism engages, this slightly different function makes it possible to organize disparate action systems in the service of a higher plan. For example, in planning a drive to some new destination one might consider subsets of the route, or, in devising a new recipe, the creative chef considers the interactions of several known culinary achievements. Within the same realm, consciousness is used to retrieve and consider modifications in long-range planning activities. These, in turn, might be modified in light of other evidence, either from the immediate environment or from long-term storage.

3. In considering actions and plans consciousness participates in retrieval programs from long-term memory, even though these retrieval programs and strategies themselves are usually not conscious. Thus, frequently, though not always, the retrieval of information from long-term storage is initiated by relatively simple commands—in program language, rather than machine language. These may be simple instructions such as, "What is his name?" or, "Where did I read about that?" or more complex instructions, such as, "What is the relation between this situation and previous ones I have encountered?" This process has the adaptive function of permitting simple addresses to complex structures.

4. Comments on the organism's current activities occur in consciousness and use available cognitive structures to construct some storable representation of current activity. Many investigators have suggested that these new codings and representations always take place in consciousness. Such processes as mnemonic devices and storage strategies apparently require the intervention of conscious structures. Certainly many of them, such as categorization and mental images, do. Once this new organization of information is stored, it may be retrieved for a variety of important purposes.

First, in the social process consciousness provides access to the memory bank which, together with an adequate system of communication, such as human language, has tremendous benefit to cooperative social efforts. Other members of the species may receive solutions to problems, thus saving time if nothing else; they may be [apprised] of unsuccessful alternatives, or, more generally, participate in the cultural inheritance of the group. This process requires selection and comparison among alternatives retrieved from long-term storage, all of which apparently takes place in consciousness.

Second, both general information, as well as specific sensory inputs, may be stored in either propositional or analogue form. The rerepresentation at some future time makes possible decision processes that depend on comparisons between current and past events, and the retrieval of relevant or irrelevant information for current problem solving.

5. Another aspect that consciousness apparently permits is a "troubleshooting" function for structures normally not represented in consciousness. There are many systems that cannot be brought into consciousness, and probably most systems that analyze the environment in the first place have that characteristic. In most of these cases only the product of cognitive and mental activities are available to consciousness; among these are sensory analyzers, innate action patterns, language-production systems, and many more. In contrast, many systems are generated and built with the cooperation of conscious processes, but later become nonconscious or automatic. These latter systems may apparently be brought into consciousness, particularly when they are defective in their particular function (see also Vygotsky, 1962). We all have had experiences of automatically driving a car, typing a letter, or even handling cocktail party conversation, and being suddenly brought up short by some failure such as a defective brake, a stuck key or a "You aren't listening to me." At that time, the particular representations of actions and memories involved are brought into play in consciousness, and repair work gets under way. Thus, structures that are not species specific and general but are the result of experience can be inspected and reorganized more or less easily [pp. 243–245].

Another way to think of this duality is in relation to routine and nonroutine events. Unconscious processing creates representations of the world and runs the machinery of the visceral and the skeletomuscular systems. So long as the parameters of events do not exceed familiar ranges, conscious processing is minimally involved. But when these boundaries are exceeded, more conscious processing becomes necessary. It is useful to think of the human information-processing system as continually asking these questions with respect to changes in its representational model of itself and of the world:

1. What is it?
2. What should I do about it?
3. How do I do it?
4. Can I do it?
5. How am I doing?
6. Am I through?

For routine events, it knows how to answer all of these questions and therefore need not devote conscious processing resources, other than some monitoring of progress, to coping with these events. For nonroutine events, the answers to none of these questions may be immediately apparent, requiring the commitment of substantial conscious processing resources to derive semantic interpretations, to organize, to execute, and to monitor a plan of action to cope with the perceived implications of the nonroutine event.

The particular aspects of this duality that I want to discuss are what might be called linkages between concurrent conscious and unconscious processes that are driven by the same stimulus material. These linkages are a source of continuity and discontinuity in human information processing and of transitions of processing from conscious to unconscious levels. They are important in accounting for differences between novice and expert.

The general idea is that conscious processing—which is relatively slow, serial, and of limited capacity—is supported by a vast substrate of unconscious processes that are relatively fast, generally thought to be parallel, and that probably constitute the bulk of processing resources.

At this stage in our knowledge, it would be premature to make too sharp a distinction between conscious and unconscious processes and processing, or to claim that organization and control of processing are always conscious. This is a gray area. It is not all black or all white. The duration of the processing episode is an extremely important consideration. Laboratory studies of the problem tend to use short-duration processing, ranging from a few milliseconds to a few seconds. In this range, cognitive control and cognitive processing are likely to be mostly unconscious, and subjects are not required to maintain continuity of processing through self-monitoring and self-programming operations. In the world of work, information processing and the performance it controls often go on for much longer periods of time. Here, there is the requirement to maintain continuity, and there is the opportunity for the processor to use self-talk and other slow control processes that are well known to all of us. It also would be premature, and inappropriate here, to become concerned with detailed processing models. Human information processing obviously is both data driven and conceptually driven, but the details of how this occurs currently are specified differently by different investigators (e.g., Anderson, 1977; Norman, Rumelhart, & LNR Group, 1975). Instead of getting into this, I would like to describe three aspects of the conscious–unconscious processing duality: continuity, discontinuities, and transitions; and a fourth, which I call the novice–expert distinction, that involves the first three.

Continuity

Continuity in human information processing desirable. We want to be able to read and to understand text, to solve problems smoothly, to speak another language fluently, to recall information from memory on demand, to ski or play tennis gracefully, to operate a vehicle proficiently, and so on. This continuity is a consequence of experiences that develop appropriate conscious and unconscious processing resources and of the appropriate linkages between them. If the linkages between these categories of processing resources fail the information processing, then any performance based on it will be interrupted or degraded. Norman and Bobrow (1975) have discussed some of these considerations in terms of data-limited and resource-limited processing.

Discontinuities

Breakdown in the linkages between conscious and unconcious processing could result from deficiencies in one or the other, from competing unconscious processes, from short-term memory limitation, from distractions, or from failures of retrieval from long-term memory. Although some linkages between conscious and unconscious processes might be wired in, it is likely that many of them are established by learning and that they are not inherently reliable. I would like to illustrate two kinds of discontinuities with data from two studies in my laboratory.

The first data come from a study in which we sought electrophysiological correlates of cognitive processing (Williams, in preparation). Slow cortical potentials between the vertex and the right mastoid were recorded while subjects solved five-letter anagrams, simply recognized five-letter words, or saw a blank in the stimulus box. Sixty anagrams were used, based on 60 words selected from two lists—concrete–abstract and high–low frequency. In Table 13.1, the data show that all subjects quickly recognized the word on the word trial and that the variance was relatively low. On the other hand, solution times for the anagrams were much longer and much more variable. (The shapes and durations of the positive deflections in the slow potentials at solution time and at word recognition time are very similar.)

I interpret these results as follows. I assume the stimulus, the word or anagram, served two functions: It initiated an unconscious search for the target

TABLE 13.1
Response Latencies for Solving Five-Letter Anagrams Derived
from Four Categories of Five-Letter Words,
and for Recognizing a Five-Letter Word[a]

	Concrete/ Familiar	Concrete/ Unfamiliar	Abstract/ Familiar	Abstract/ Unfamiliar	Control Word
$\bar{X}$	8.925	9.812	9.800	13.093	1.275
SD	3.648	3.800	3.163	3.886	.529

[a]$N = 16$. Times in seconds and milliseconds.

information in memory, and it initiated conscious stimulus processing. According to Norman and Bobrow (1977), long-term memory search processes utilize a description for retrieval of information, which has the property of discriminability, which is the ability of the description to discriminate among all possible records within memory. Thus, in the word condition (e.g., *tango*), the word was known to the subject, discriminability was high, and a match for the word could immediately be retrieved from memory. However, when the stimulus was an anagram, the discriminability power of the retrieval description was much poorer, extending only to "it must be a record of a word with these five letters."

I propose that the presentation of an anagram initiated operations on the stimulus that resulted in the generation of new descriptions. These new descriptions had more power to discriminate among targets in memory as they initiated unconscious retrieval of a set of possible targets to be discriminated. Thus, retrieval specifications were modified, as a consequence of reordering the letters, until the correct word "popped" into consciousness. I believe this interpretation is supported by the differences among mean response latencies for the four different categories of word sources of the anagrams. Mean latency for the solution of anagrams derived from abstract, unfamiliar words was highest; mean latency for solution of anagrams derived from concrete, familiar words was lowest. Because order of anagrams, control words, and blank trials was randomized, and because order of letters in anagrams was randomized, conscious processing had no clues as to the category of words from which these anagrams came, and should not have been influenced by concreteness or familiarity. Yet these differences in mean latencies would have been predicted for the source words from what is known about the effects of familarity and concreteness on recall. Unconscious retrieval processes were selecting target words, not anagrams. (Anagram "freaks" report that correct solutions often "pop" into their consciousness before they have consciously rearranged the letters in that exact order.)

According to this interpretation, anagrams cause a discontinuity between the conscious and unconscious processes for word recognition that is manifested as a temporary failure of retrieval from long-term memory. This may be similar to other temporary LTM retrieval failures we all experience, such as temporarily forgetting people's names.

Another kind of discontinuity is illustrated by data from the second study. In this study the discontinuity has more complex causes. Its sources seem to be in short-term memory limitations, in failure to retrieve additional information from prior knowledge about the given information, and in the failure of conscious processing to develop an effective sequence of processing operations.

The data come from a study of linear syllogisms (Bond, MacGregor, Schmidt, Lattimore, & Rigney, 1978). A simple linear syllogism is shown in Fig. 13.3. This is one of the simpler problems, but even in this one, it is apparent that short-term memory can be overloaded by a holistic approach to its solution. In

```
Mr. Scott, his sister, and his son and daughter
        were tennis players.

The best player's twin and the worst player
        were opposite sexes.

The best player and the worst player
        were the same age.

Who was the best player?
```

FIG. 13.3.   An example of a simple linear syllogism.

this illustration, I claim that just reading the sentences involves processing operations that have become highly automized in adults and therefore are mostly unconscious processing. All subjects could read the sentences relatively quickly. On the other hand, answering the question "Who was the best player?" requires conscious organization of processing operations. Not all subjects could accomplish this, and those who could required a great deal more time than they did just to read the sentences (see Table 13.2).

Another kind of discontinuity, due to competition among unconscious processes, was demonstrated by Posner and Snyder (1975), using the Stroop effect. At more complex levels of processing, this competition is well known as negative transfer. An example is doing octal or hexadecimal arithmetic—say, addition or multiplication—and experiencing interference from highly automatized decimal arithmetic processes. A fascinating example of discontinuity due to competing processes was given by Day (1978). She found that her language-bound (LB) subjects could not easily learn to speak "secret" languages—for example, languages created by interchanging all *L*'s and *R*'s in words. Her language-optional (LO) subjects easily learned to do this.

Discontinuities caused by inadequate or inappropriate unconscious processing resources are of growing concern to the military. Many recruits have been found lacking in basic reading skills. Without these, conscious processing for comprehension is not supported. Some of the oil countries have funded programs in

TABLE 13.2
Means and Standard Deviations for
Just Reading Versus Solving
a Linear Syllogism[a]

	Reading	Solving
$\bar{X}$	41.88	92.57
SD	18.90	98.76

[a]$N = 51$. Time in seconds.

the United States to have their citizens taught technolgical subject matter so that they may become technicians instead of camel drivers. Their prior knowledge base is inappropriate to support comprehension of technical material, and their sole learning strategy is memorization of the material.

We are just beginning to understand the implications of prior knowledge structures for learning from textual material. Anderson, Reynolds, Schallert, and Goetz (1977) reported a study of "frameworks for comprehending discourse," which they summarized as follows:

> Thirty physical education students and 30 music education students read a passage that could be given either a prison break or a wrestling interpretation, and another passage that could be understood in terms of an evening of card playing or a rehearsal session of a woodwind ensemble.
>
> Scores on disambiguating multiple choice tests and theme-revealing disambiguations and intrusions in free recall showed striking relationships to the subject's background. These results indicate that high-level schemata provide the interpretative framework for comprehending discourse. The fact that most subjects give each passage one distinct interpretation or another and reported being unaware of other perspectives while reading suggest that schemata can cause a person to see a message in a certain way, without even considering alternative interpretations [p. 367].

Because their discussion of the implications of the study is so relevant here, I quote them (Anderson *et al.,* 1977) at some length (see also Rigney & Munro, 1977):

> We turn now to several interesting implications of schema theory for education. Consider first speculative implications for reading instruction. It may turn out that many problems in reading comprehension are traceable to deficits in knowledge rather than deficits in linguistic skill narrowly conceived; that is, that young readers sometimes may not possess the schemata needed to comprehend passages. Or, they may possess relevant schemata but not know how to bring them to bear. Or, they may not be facile at changing schemata when the first one tried proves inadequate; they may, in other words get stuck in assimilating text to inappropriate, incomplete, or inconsistent schemata. Worst of all, it is not unreasonable to suppose that the frequent demand for veridical reproduction in oral and written exercises may bias children against bringing high-level schemata into play at all. For if the child seriously brings his/her own knowledge to bear s/he will, from an adult point of view, often make mistakes. It is the teacher's responsibility to purge errors. Thus, children may sometimes learn from the very lessons intended to upgrade comprehension skills that it's best to play it safe, to read word-by-word and line-by-line.
>
> From the perspective of schema theory, the principal determinant of the knowledge a person can acquire from reading is the knowledge s/he already possesses. The schemata by which people attempt to assimilate text will surely vary according

to age, subculture, experience, education, interests, and belief systems. Merely laying on a new set of propositions will not necessarily change high-level schemata. Wyer (1977) has summarized social psychological evidence in support of this premise, indicating that it is "likely that the implications of new information will be resisted if its acceptance would require a major cognitive reorganization, that is, if it would require a change in a large number of other logically related beliefs in order to maintain consistency among them." Apparent inconsistencies and counterexamples often are easily assimilated into the schemata a person holds dear. Or, it may be possible for a student to maintain the particular identity of lesson material, keeping it segregated from logically imcompatible beliefs.

Experience in helping to revise an introductory college economics course has suggested that the typical freshman or sophomore comes to class with a point of view more akin to Adam Smith than John Maynard Kenyes. Our conjecture is that many students can complete an economics course, acquiring a large amount of information and a number of concepts and principles in a piece-meal fashion, without integrating the new learnings into existing knowledge structures, and without understanding the *Weltanschauung* of contemporary economics [p. 378].

Transitions

What starts as conscious processing may, through long practice, become automatized to the extent that it becomes mostly unconscious (La Berge, 1975). I would like to illustrate this kind of transition with data that come from two studies in which we used simulator-trainers to give technical personnel in the Navy intensive practice in learning complex performances. In the first of these, we gave 60 Radar Intercept Observers (RIOS) an average of 10 hours of practicing air-to-air intercepts (Rigney, Morrison, Williams, & Towne, 1974). The data of interest here describe the changes in means and standard deviations for time to solve for a set of six values in the intercept triangle (Fig. 13.4), using simple algorithms for doing mental arithmetic. Figure 13.5 illustrates impressive reductions in mean solution times and in variabilities of solution times.

In the second study, we used a simulator-trainer to give 25 electronic technicians practice in troubleshooting a communications system at the systems level (Rigney, Towne, King, & Moran, in preparation). The data of interest here also describe the reductions in means and variances in time to solve a problem (malfunction) over an average of 10 hours of practice.

The RIO and the systems troubleshooting data illustrate at least the direction that automatization might take. Among 60 students, mean times to solve the six mental arithmetic problems dropped from 68 seconds to 30 seconds (2.30x), and standard deviations from 49 seconds to 15 seconds (3.27x). Similar changes are apparent in the troubleshooting data.

Hatano, Miyake, and Binks' (1977) study of the performance of expert abacus operators reveals information about intermediate stages of automatization:

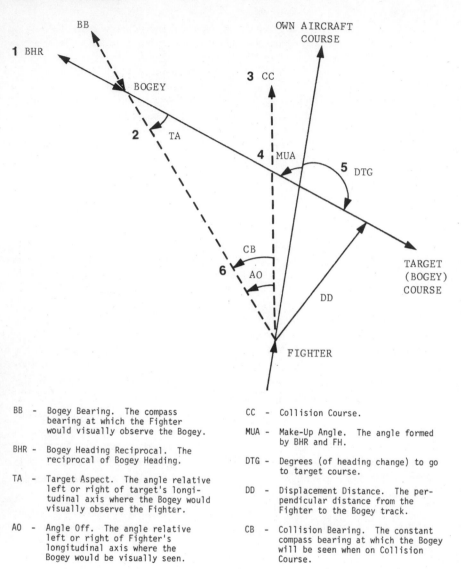

BB - Bogey Bearing. The compass
      bearing at which the Fighter
      would visually observe the Bogey.

BHR - Bogey Heading Reciprocal. The
      reciprocal of Bogey Heading.

TA - Target Aspect. The angle relative
      left or right of target's longi-
      tudinal axis where the Bogey would
      visually observe the Fighter.

AO - Angle Off. The angle relative
      left or right of Fighter's
      longitudinal axis where the
      Bogey would be visually seen.

CC - Collision Course.

MUA - Make-Up Angle. The angle formed
      by BHR and FH.

DTG - Degrees (of heading change) to go
      to target course.

DD - Displacement Distance. The per-
      pendicular distance from the
      Fighter to the Bogey track.

CB - Collision Bearing. The constant
      compass bearing at which the Bogey
      will be seen when on Collision
      Course.

FIG. 13.4.   The Intercept Triangle. Values of numbered variables were computed
mentally by RIOS.

Ten expert abacus operators were given various restrictions and distractions during
addition of ten numbers of 3–5 figures. All subjects except one could calculate very
rapidly without an abacus, probably relying upon its mental representation. Some
of those at an intermediate level of mastery moved their fingers as if they had been
manipulating a real abacus, and prohibition of this movement or interfering with
finger-tapping reduced their performance. All the subjects could answer simple

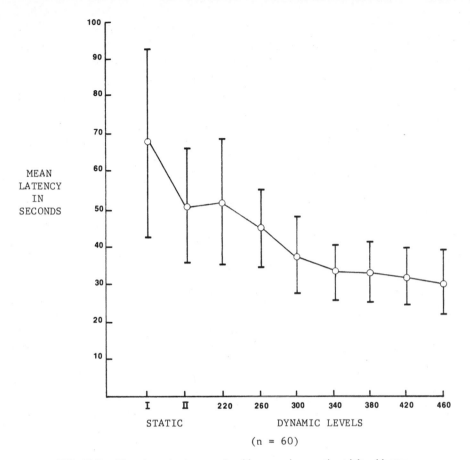

FIG. 13.5. Mean latencies in seconds with successive practice trials with standard deviations around means for each condition.

non-mathematical questions during abacus calculation without increasing time or errors, but answering extraneous mathematical questions was very hard [p. 47].

The Novice–Expert Distinctions

Transitions of processing from conscious to unconscious levels during the course of automatization are, I believe, the major hallmark of human learning. But other changes also occur that represent differences between novice and expert. These differences have been discussed by de Groot (1966) and Simon (1976) for chess players and by Rumelhart and Norman (1976) in terms of their concepts of restructuring and tuning. Simon's (1976) discussion of differences between novice and expert chess players summarizes a number of common points:

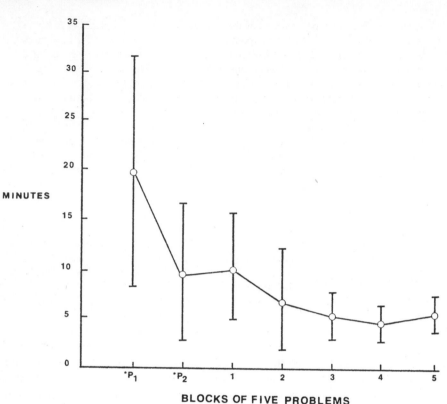

FIG. 13.6.　Average solution times per problem within blocks. Means and standard deviations are computed between problems. $N = 25$. (*Help function available.)

1.　A chess master or grandmaster, on seeing a chess position from a game for five seconds (with about 25 pieces on the board), can reconstruct the position from memory with 80 or 90% accuracy. A weaker player will be able to remember the positions of only some half dozen pieces.

2.　If the same pieces are placed on the board at random, chess master and duffer will perform equally badly—neither will be able to recall the positions of more than about half a dozen pieces.

3.　A strong chess player can play at a speed of ten seconds or so per move with only a moderate loss in playing strength. To put the matter in extreme form, there are probably not a hundred players in the world who could beat Bobby Fischer if they were permitted the usual time for a move (say 20 moves per hour) while Fischer was limited to 10 seconds per move.

The second of these three facts permits us to conclude that there is nothing unusual about the general capabilities of chess masters for visual imagery. The

surprising visual memory revealed by the first fact is specific to chess. The fi
is most readily explained by the hypothesis that the short-term memory of a
master has the same capacity, measured in chunks, as the short-term memor   a
duffer, but that the duffer's chunks consist of individual pieces, while the master's
chunks consist of configurations of pieces, averaging three or four pieces each, that
have become thoroughly familiar and recognizable from their frequent recurrence
in the tens of thousands of chess positions he has seen. The master's ability to
remember the positions of 25 pieces then becomes no more mysterious than a
reader's ability to recall a sequence of 25 Roman letters after a brief exposure—
provided that the letters are arranged as four or five familiar English words. Both
phenomena follow from the postulate that short-term memory has a fixed capacity
in chunks, and that any familiar, recognizable visual (or auditory) pattern constitutes a chunk (Simon, 1974).

    If we accept this explanation, then we can use it to arrive at some estimates of the
number of familiar configurations of chess pieces that are stored in the long-term
memory of a chess master. Such estimates can be made from consideration of the
variety of chess positions that occur in games, and the size of the "vocabulary" of
chunks that would be required to generate this variety. Estimates can also be made
by writing a computer program that simulates the chunking process and measuring
its recall performance as a function of the number of familiar chunks it has acquired
in long-term memory [p. 80].

Hatano et al. (1977) described what they called "internalization" during the
course of automatization of abacus operations: the shift from moving the abacus
beads with the fingers, to moving the fingers without the abacus, to—in the most
expert—entirely mental operations, which these investigators presumed to rely
upon a mental representation of the abacus.

    Greater speed and fluency of performance certainly seem to be a general
difference between the expert and the novice. The data I presented on automatization of mental arithmetic in RIOS was for students. Our simulator operator,
who scheduled and monitored students during their training, happened to have
had a number of years of practice, albeit intermittent ones, in solving for intercept triangle variables. He was able consistently to solve for the six values in 8
seconds, 3.75 times faster than the mean for the 60 students at the end of 10 to 15
hours of training. Rumelhart and Norman (1976) cited Crossman's (1959) finding that cigar makers' performance continued to improve for at least 10 years and
Siebel's (1963) finding of continual improvement in reaction-time tasks over at
least 75,000 trials. Certainly, anyone who has observed a great pianist, say
Horowitz, playing would agree that speed and fluency (continuity) are distinguishing characteristics of the expert.

    A second general distinguishing characteristic of the expert seems to be an
enormously richer store of appropriate knowledge in LTM. The chess master has
played thousands of games; the expert programmer has written hundreds or

thousands of computer programs. This great store of knowledge also evidently is better organized for retrieval, as Simon (1976) noted. It is possible that the first characteristic, speed and fluency, may actually be an artifact of the second. Having a specialized memory structure for many commonly occurring situations reduces the amount of computation necessary.

A third distinguishing characteristic of the expert is that at least some of his or her processing operations differ from the novice's. I refer to the several levels of expertise in abacus operators described by Hatano et al.

A fourth distinguishing characteristic of the expert may be the automatization of control of processing. Control operations that would require the slow, conscious processing of the novice have been transferred to unconscious levels, where they operate more quickly.

I suggest that all these differences between the novice and the expert reduce the amount of uncertainty involved in answering the six questions I listed earlier: "What is it?" "What should I do about it?" "How do I do it?" "Can I do it?" "How am I doing?" and "Am I through?"

IMPLICATIONS FOR COGNITIVE LEARNING STRATEGIES

The general objective for cognitive learning strategies is to reduce the deficiencies in processing resources that result in discontinuities, and to facilitate transitions that will make the novice into an expert through avenues that will be effective at the appropriate processing levels.

All the dualities—lateralization, the dual encoding system, the self-concept, and conscious and unconscious processing—undoubtedly have implications for cognitive learning strategies. Wittrock (1979) has discussed the implications of lateralization. Richardson (1978) discussed implications of the duality of the self. I discuss some implications of the conscious–unconscious processing duality.

The principal implication is that to be effective, cognitive learning strategies must themselves be well enough learned: (1) to support rather than interfere with learning subject matter; and (2) to displace or augment the student's own already well learned, though less effective, congnitive processing strategies.

A great deal of work must be done to identify cognitive learning strategies that are most appropriate for reducing the different known sources of processing discontinuities in the context of achieving particular learning objectives with particular kinds of subjects, subject matter, delivery systems, and environments. In view of the enormous individual differences among subjects with respect to these sources, we need more sensitive diagnostic tools than conventional mental tests to identify individual patterns of processing resources. It seems to me that progress along these lines is likely to be slow, and that we shall have to be content with less discriminating approaches in the interim.

Preserving Continuity of Processing

As I suggested earlier, many human information-processing tasks in the real world are nontrivial, calling for integration of several kinds of conscious and unconscious processes over appreciable intervals of time. Sustaining continuity of processing resources under these circumstances depends on a variety of processing skills and processing resources. When this is not possible, the individual must fall back to simpler kinds of processing that are less effective or that are totally ineffective. One way of addressing the question of how acquisition of this capability could be facilitated by cognitive learning strategies is to look at sources of discontinuity and possible methods for coping with them.

Coping With Sources of Discontinuities in Conscious Processing

Limited Short-Term Memory (STM).   Because STM is a wired-in limitation, we long ago discovered ways of working within or around its limitations. Language is printed word by word, in linear strings. The conceptual structure of prepared subject matter is serialized, and so on. I suggest that there are two categories of applicable cognitive learning strategies—strategies for working within the limitations of STM, and strategies for working around them. Strategies for living with the limitations of STM include rehearsal, and serialization of subject matter and processing operations. Strategies for getting around these limitations are hierarchical organizations of subject matter, such as chunking, and imposition of external structures on subject matter, usually by means of mnemonic devices—for example, the method of Loci. These establish linkages between the new material and structures already in LTM.

Limited Self-Programming Skills.   Conscious processes sometimes are not capable of organizing sequences of processing resources that cope effectively with nonroutine events. In the word problem studies cited earlier, some students were not able to solve some anagrams, and some students were not able to solve the linear syllogisms because they could not organize appropriate sequences of operations. Bond (1978) was able to derive an indicator of ordering skill to apply to records of processing of students working on these puzzles. He found that this indicator correlated well with puzzle solution scores ($r = .77$, $N = 34$).

Strategies for remedying this deficiency include teaching the students effective sequences of processing operations in the form of heuristics and algorithms, and teaching them to explore alternatives. to try different sequences of operations to break out of an impasse.

Limited Self-Monitoring Skills.   Keeping one's "place" in a long sequence of operations, knowing when subgoals have been attained, detecting and correcting errors, and recovering from errors by returning to the last correct operation or by making quick fixes are examples of self-monitoring skills. Persons performing tasks in situations where errors can have disastrous consequences should be especially motivated to acquire these skills. Self-monitoring in these situations also may be supported by checklists and the like. Strategies for self-monitoring would depend on the particular combination of subject matter, situations, and processing operations. Checking for errors in the use of a statistical algorithm obviously uses different processes than checking for errors in flying an aircraft. Nevertheless, the general requirement can be characterized as demanding "looking-ahead" and "looking-back" processing skills during the execution of a sequence of processing operations. Looking-ahead skills include learning the structure of this sequence; identifying parts of it where errors are most likely to occur; developing strategies for avoiding errors at these points and for recovery of continuity if errors do occur; identifying the kinds of feedback information that will be available at these points; and evaluating the usefulness of this information. There can be parts of processing sequences in which feedback is minimal or absent. This is, unfortunately, characteristic of computer programming. Writing and debugging a computer program require that extra operations (e.g., breakpoints and print statements) be included to provide the programmer with feedback about intermediate results. Without these provisions, it is impossible to tell if intermediate goals have been attained.

Looking-back skills are needed to detect errors already committed, and to maintain a history of processing up to the current place in the sequence that will serve as the basis for determining what comes next and for making judgments about the reasonableness of successive outcomes. For example, a technician making a series of voltage measurements in a circuit uses his knowledge of the circuit and the context established by all the values he observes to identify an abnormal value. The computer programmer recalls the history of the processing operations up to the place in the sequence of instructions she is looking at to judge whether outcomes at that point are reasonable. Both technician and programmer have to consider alternative explanations for observed outcomes. The technician's voltmeter may be set on the wrong scale; he may have shorted a probe or not made good contact when making a voltage measurement. The programmer's knowledge of what the program is doing may be inaccurate. It may, in fact, be doing something else at some point. It seems to me that there probably are large individual differences with respect to the patterns of these skills.

Distractibility of Attention.   The distractibility of attention certainly must be one of the best known facts of conscious processing. Perhaps it is a survival function of attention to be distractible by changes in the representations of the world constructed by our sensory-perceptual systems, and to be time-shared by different information-processing requirements. We are not capable of prolonged concentration on any one processing task. So maintaining continuity of processing really means returning again and again to the task after attention has been captured by more powerful demons, often the agreeable or disagreeable demons of emotionality. Spielberger (1977) has done a great deal of work in the effects of anxiety on academic performance. Kanfer and Goldstein (1975), Thoresen and Mahoney (1974), and Richardson (1978) have described techniques for reducing the distracting effects of anxiety and other disagreeable demons on cognitive information processing. (In this literature, there is less concern with the distractions caused by agreeable demons, although their influence may be as great or greater!) This literature should be mined for strategies for managing attention during learning.

Coping With Sources of Discontinuities in Unconscious Processing

The principle avenue to modifying unconscious processes is through drill and practice over extended periods of time sufficient to bring about automatization of the processing operations originally described to the student through conscious channels.

Inadequate Basic Processing Skills.   Many human performances obviously depend on a substrate of specific processing strategies: Reading, playing a musical instrument, speaking a language, playing tennis, and skiing are examples. Each requires the support of a fairly well defined set of unconscious processing skills. Cognitive learning strategies that would facilitate the acquisition of these skills would be concerned with specification of effective processing strategies and with making practicing them more efficient.

Inadequate Knowledge Bases.   The problems of functional illiteracy in the military services, now receiving attention in the press, are symptomatic of functional illiteracy in society. Although remedial reading courses may be necessary, it is unlikely—as discussed earlier—that they can result in knowledge bases comparable to those of good readers who have been accumulating knowledge for many years. There may be no quick way of completely reducing this difference. However, cognitive learning strategies could be concerned with how to acquire knowledge through the use of analogy, paraphrase, mental imagery, and similar techniques.

Processing Interference.   Negative transfer is a well-known problem in training. Previously automatized processes are triggered and cannot be shut off. Several examples were given earlier. Techniques of behavioral modification may help cope with negative transfer by shortening the amount of practice needed to overcome it. The basic strategy seems to be to strengthen the desired processes and to weaken the undesired ones.

LTM Retrieval Failures.   Strategies for searching LTM are not well understood. Under some circumstances, searching back through temporally ordered records of events in episodic memory may be a successful strategy for recall. Theoretical controversies over relationships between acquisition (encoding) and recall, and over the nature of retrieval (reacquisition involving reconstruction or not), have not yet resulted in any clear prescriptions—other than that frequency of use improves recall—beyond the techniques of the mnemonists (Bower, 1972).

SUMMARY

In this chapter, I outlined some of the major features of a conceptual geography for cognitive learning strategies. Then I explored implications of the conscious–unconscious duality of the human information-processing system for understanding and for teaching cognitive learning strategies. We need to learn more about the linkages, continuities, discontinuities, and transitions in this duality, so that we can deal with them effectively in our instructional paradigms. The methods for augmenting or improving the utilization of unconscious processing resources are likely to be different from those required for augmenting or improving the utilization of conscious processing resources. Automatization brought about primarily by practice over extended periods of time seems to be the principal avenue to influencing unconscious processing. Instructions, questions, and structured content seem to be the principal tools to use in influencing conscious processing. Neither side of this duality can be dealt with in isolation. Both are involved, to varying degrees, in all human information processing. However, the view I advance here is that conscious processing—being slow and serial and limited by short-term memory capacity—must be supported by a substrate of a large number of probably parallel, unconscious processes for continuity of processing during the performance of complex tasks. The principal implication of this is that to be effective, cognitive learning strategies must themselves be well enough learned: (1) to facilitate rather than interfere with learning subject matter; and (2) to displace or augment the student's own already well learned, if less effective, cognitive processing strategies.

ACKNOWLEDGMENTS

The author acknowledges the support of the Personnel and Training Research Programs, Office of Naval Research, Contract No. N00014-75-C-0838. The suggestions of Allen

Munro and Kathy Lutz for improving the paper are acknowledged. The author accepts full responsibility for the views, conclusions, and errors in the paper.

REFERENCES

Anderson, R. C. The notion of schemata and the educational enterprise: General discussion of the conference. In R. C. Anderson, R. J. Spiro, & W. E. Montague (Eds.), *Schooling and the acquisition of knowledge*. Hillsdale, N.J.: Lawrence Erlbaum Associates, 1977.

Anderson, R. C., Reynolds, R. E., Schallert, D. L., & Goetz, E. T. Frameworks for comprehending discourse. *American Educational Research Journal, 1977, 14,* 367–381.

Becker, W. C. Teaching reading and language to the disadvantaged. *Harvard Educational Review,* 1977, *47,* 518–543.

Bogen, J. E. Educational aspects of hemispheric specialization. *UCLA Educator,* 1975, *17,* 24–32.

Bond, N. A. Personal communication, 1978.

Bond, N. A., MacGregor, D., Schmidt, K., Lattimore, M., & Rigney, J. W. *Studies of verbal problem solving. II: Prediction of performance from sentence-processing scores* (Tech. Rep. No. 87). Los Angeles: Behavioral Technology Laboratories, University of Southern California, 1978.

Bower, G. H. Mental imagery and associative learning. In L. Gregg (Ed.), *Cognition of learning and memory*. New York: Wiley, 1972.

Broadbent, D. Division of function and integration of behavior. In F. O. Schmidt and F. G. Worden (Eds.), *The neurosciences: Third study program*. Cambridge, Mass.: MIT Press, 1974.

Collins, A. *Processes in acquiring knowledge* (Tech. Rep. No. 3231). Cambridge, Mass.: Bolt Beranek and Newman, January 1976.

Crossman, E. R. F. W. A theory of the acquisition of speed-skill. *Ergonomics,* 1959, *2,* 153–166.

Day, R. *Language bound and language optional differences*. Paper presented at the Office of Naval Research Contractor's Meeting, Individual Differences in Cognitive Performance, Stanford University, Palo Alto, Calif., January 1978.

de Groot, A. D. Perception and memory versus thought: Some old ideas and recent findings. In B. Kleinmutz (Ed.), *Problem solving: Research, method, and theory*. New York: Wiley, 1966.

Frederickson, J. R. *Cognitive skills in reading*. Paper read at ONR Contractor's Meeting, Individual Differences in Cognitive Performance, Stanford University, Palo Alto, California, January 1978.

Gazzaniga, M. A. The split brain in man. *Scientific American,* 1967, *217,* 24–29.

Hardyck, C., Tzeng, O. J. L., & Wang, W. S. T. Cerebral lateralization of function and bilingual decision processes: Is thinking lateralized? *Brain and Language,* 1978, *5,* 56–71.

Hatano, G., Miyake, Y., & Binks, M. G. Performance of expert abacus experts. *Cognition,* 1977, *5*(1), 47–55.

Hellige, J. B., & Cox, P. J. Effects of concurrent verbal memory on recognition of stimuli from the left and right visual fields. *Journal of Experimental Psychology: Human Perception and Performance,* 1976, *2,* 210–221.

Hunt, E. *Time-sharing attention*. Paper presented at the Office of Naval Research Contractor's Meeting, Individual Differences in Cognitive Performance, Stanford University, Palo Alto, Calif., January 1978.

Jerison, H. J. *Evolution of the brain and intelligence*. New York: Academic Press, 1973.

Kanfer, F. H., & Goldstein, A. P. (Eds.). *Helping people change*. New York: Pergamon Press, 1975.

La Berge, D. Acquisition of automatic processing in perceptual and associative learning. In P. M. A. Rabbitt & S. Dornic (Eds.), *Attention and performance V*. London: Academic Press, 1975.

Mandler, G. Consciousness: Respectable, useful, and probably necessary. In R. L. Solso (Ed.), *Information processing and cognition: The Loyola symposium*. Hillsdale, N.J.: Lawrence Erlbaum Associates, 1975.

Mandler, J. M., & Johnson, N. S. Remembrances of things parsed: Story structure and recall. *Cognitive Psychology,* 1977, *9,* 111–151.

Miller, G. A., Galanter, E. H., & Pribram, K. *Plans and the structure of behavior.* New York: Holt, 1960.

Molfese, D. L. Neuroelectrical correlates of categorical speech perception in adults. *Brain and Language,* 1978, *5,* 25–35.

Munro, A., & Rigney, J. W. *A schema theory account of some cognitive processes in complex learning* (Tech. Rep. No. 81). Los Angeles: University of Southern California, Behavioral Technology Laboratories, July 1977.

Munro, A., Rigney, J. W., & Crook, D. E. *A formative evaluation of a computer-based instructional system for teaching job-oriented reading strategies* (Tech. Rep. No. 84). Los Angeles: University of Southern California, Behavioral Technology Laboratories, January 1978.

Nebes, R. D. Hemispheric specialization in commissuratomized man. *Psychological Bulletin,* 1974, *81,* 1–14.

Norman, D. A., & Bobrow, D. G. On data-limited and resource-limited processes. *Cognitive Psychology,* 1975, *7,* 44–64.

Norman, D. A., & Bobrow, D. G. *A basis for memory acquisition and retrieval* (Rep. No. 7703). La Jolla: University of California at San Diego, Center for Human Information Processing, November 1977.

Norman, D. A., Rumelhart, D. E., & the LNR Group. *Explorations in cognition.* San Francisco: Freeman, 1975.

Paivio, A. Language and knowledge of the world. *Educational Researcher,* 1974, *3,* 5–12.

Posner, M. I., & Snyder, C. R. R. Attention and cognitive control. In R. L. Solso (Ed.), *Information processing and cognition: The Loyola symposium.* Hillsdale, N.J.: Lawrence Erlbaum Associates, 1975.

Richardson, F. Behavior modification and learning strategies. In H. F. O'Neil, Jr. (Ed.), *Learning strategies.* New York: Academic Press, 1978.

Rigney, J. W., Morrison, D. K., Williams, L. A., & Towne, D. M. *Field evaluation of Model II of the computer-based, individual trainer for the radar intercept officer* (Tech. Rep. No. 73–C–0065-2). Los Angeles: University of Southern California, Behavioral Technology Laboratories, July 1974.

Rigney, J. W., & Munroe, A. *On Cognitive strategies for processing text* (Tech. Rep. No. 80). Los Angeles: University of Southern California, Behavioral Technology Laboratories, March 1977.

Rigney, J. W., Towne, D. M., King, C., & Moran, P. *Field evaluation of the generalized maintenance trainer-simulator: Fleet communications system.* Manuscript in preparation.

Rumelhart, D. E. Notes on a schema for stories. In D. G. Bobrow & A. Collins (Eds.), *Representation and understanding: Studies in cognitive science.* New York: Academic Press, 1975.

Rumelhart, D. E., & Norman, D. A. *Accretion tuning and restructuring* (Rep. No. 7601). La Jolla: University of California at San Diego, Center for Human Information Processing, August 1976.

Rumelhart, D. E., & Ortony, A. The representation of knowledge in memory. In R. C. Anderson, R. J. Spiro, & W. E. Montague (Eds.), *Schooling and the acquisition of knowledge.* Hillsdale, N.J.: Lawrence Erlbaum Associates, 1977.

Schneider, W. *Automatic and controlled processing.* Paper presented at the Office of Naval Research Contractor's Meeting, Individual Differences in Cognitive Performance, Stanford University, Palo Alto, Calif., January 1978.

Siebel, R. Discrimination reaction time for a 1,023-alternative task. *Journal of Experimental Psychology,* 1963, *66,* 215–226.

Simon, H. A. How big is a chunk? *Science,* 1974, *183,* 482–488.

Simon, H. A. Identifying basic abilities underlying intelligent performance of complex tasks. In L. B. Resnick (Ed.), *The nature of intelligence.* Hillsdale, N.J.: Lawrence Erlbaum Associates, 1976.

Spielberger, C. D. *The measurement and treatment of test anxiety.* Paper presented at Learning Strategies: Measures and Modules Seminar, Carmel, California, December 1977.

Sternberg, R. *Toward a unified componential theory of human reasoning.* Paper read at ONR Contractor's Meeting, Individual Differences in Cognitive Performance, Stanford University, Palo Alto, Calif. January 1978.

Thoresen, C. E., & Mahoney, M. J. *Behavioral self-control.* New York: Holt. Rinehart & Winston, 1974.

Thorndyke, P. W. Cognitive structures in comprehension and memory of narrative discourse. *Cognitive Psychology,* 1977, *9,* 77–110.

Vygotsky, L. S. *Thought and language.* Cambridge, Mass.: M.I.T. Press, 1962.

Williams, L. *Electrophysiological correlates of cognitive processes in solving anagrams.* Doctoral dissertation, University of Southern California, Los Angeles, in preparation.

Wittrock, N. C. Applications of cognitive psychology to education and training. In H. F. O'Neil & C. D. Spielberger (Eds.), *Cognitive and affective learning strategies.* New York: Academic Press, 1979.

Wyer, R. S. Attitudes, beliefs and information acquisition. In R. C. Anderson, R. J. Spiro, W. E. Montague (Eds.), *Schooling and the acquisition of knowledge.* Hillsdale, N.J.: Lawrence Erlbaum Associates, 1977.

Author Index

Subject Index